ROCK 'N' ROLL
IS HERE TO PAY

The History and Politics of the Music Industry

Steve Chapple & Reebee Garofalo

 **Nelson-Hall**/Chicago

Library of Congress Cataloging in Publication Data

Chapple, Steve.
    Rock 'n' roll is here to pay.

    Bibliography: p. 331
    Includes index.
    1. Music trade—United States. 2. Rock music—
United States—History and criticism. I. Garofalo,
Reebee, joint author. II. Title.
ML3790.C44   338.4'7'784   77-10488
ISBN 0-88229-395-8 (hardbound)
ISBN 0-88229-437-7 (paperback)

Manufactured in the United States of America

*This book is dedicated to Phil Ochs
who talked to us a lot when we were
producing concerts. We wish we could
have talked with him more.*

CONTENTS

ACKNOWLEDGMENTS

After the initial draft, *Rock'n'Roll Is Here to Pay* is the result of long arguments, in the end productive ones, between both of us.

Fortunately, we had the help of many others along the way. Major credit must go to our principal researchers, Joel Rogers and David Beal. We would like to thank those who read and criticized our first draft: Ellen Shaffer, Ellin Hirst, Dorothy K. Dean, the New Haven Women's Liberation Rock Band, and the staff of the Saints Bar in Boston who gave special attention to "Women in Rock"; Wesley Profit who read "Black Roots"; and Kathy Borgenicht, Charlie Gillett, David Helvarg, Andrew Kopkind, Jim Miller, Larry Minch, Jonah Raskin, and Mark Zanger — who critiqued it all. Careful readings by Charlie, Jonah, and Larry allowed us to avoid a number of factual errors. Larry contributed to the thinking that went into the concluding chapter, although the outcome may not be what he had in mind. Allen MacDougal, Beberly Mier, and Norm Winter helped to plot out the Marketing Trends and Styles Chart.

Radical analytical books are not as popular with publishers in the seventies as they were in the sixties. More than one division chief turned thumbs down against the recommendations of his editors. But in the beginning Mary Jo Von Mach, and later Melissa Frumin, Buck Bagot, and, again, Jonah Raskin provided concrete support. Ira Goldenberg smoothed our way, and Nelson-Hall, the publisher, made this book possible.

Numbers of agents, managers, concert promoters, broadcasters, rock critics, record executives, and performers sat still for our cassette machines. They provided the real meat of our book. Russ Sanjek and Ahmet Ertegun especially helped us with our understanding of how the industry first reacted to rock'n'roll in the fifties. Joe Smith did his best to make our trips to Warner-Reprise as productive as possible. The troops at the Tower and Banana record stores in San Francisco submitted to more than a few last minute fact-checks. Lee Zhito and Is Horowitz at *Billboard* explained their charting and have allowed us to reprint certain of their graphs.

And not least we thank our editor Elizabeth Hansen. Elizabeth smoothed the wrinkles, some of them at least, from a long book.

PREFACE

"It's Not the Meat, It's the Motion": There's More to Rock'n'Roll Than Music

We found out, and it wasn't years till we did, that all the bread we made for Decca was going into making little black boxes that go into American Air Force bombers to bomb fucking North Vietnam. They took the bread we made for them and put it into the radar section of their business. When we found that out, it blew our minds. That was it. Goddamn, you find out you've helped to kill God knows how many thousands of people without even knowing it. I'd rather the Mafia than Decca.
—Keith Richard of the Rolling Stones

I don't make culture. I sell it.—Dick Clark

Rock music is the most important cultural expression in the United States today. For this generation it serves the function TV did for the last as the primary source of entertainment and values. Rock music, which accounts for more than 80 percent of all records and tapes sold, is also the core of a $2 billion business that dwarfs other entertainment industries. It is bigger business than the $600 million made in 1974 in professional sports, or the $1.6 billion in movie revenues.

The music industry is interwoven into the fabric of American business. Through their directorates and primary stockholders, record companies are linked into other corporations. Many record companies are directly owned by outside firms, or they are subsidiaries of large corporate conglomerates. The Allman Brothers, for example, are million-selling artists on the Capricorn label, distributed by Warner Brothers, which is part of the record division of Warner Communications. John Denver records for RCA Records, one division of a multinational corporation that markets more than 60,000 products and is tied into the United States military establishment, with more than several hundred million dollars in defense contracts annually.

Most other books on rock'n'roll deal only with rock music as music, as if its development were a closed aesthetic process. We believe that rock'n'roll in the United States must also be understood as part of an ever-growing and highly profitable cultural industry. The hard-nosed scrabbling of the small entrepreneurs of the fifties and the careful strategies of the monopoly corporations of the sixties have greatly influenced the development of rock'n'roll.

Likewise the development of the music cannot be separated from the politics of the industry. Power in the music industry is as elsewhere political power. This power has determined who got recorded and who got paid. In the past the groups in the rock'n'roll pantheon who were short changed were blacks and women. This book tries to explain how power was concentrated in the hands of a few industry moguls. It tries to give credit where credit is due. In the end, we think, a different view of rock'n'roll and pop culture emerges from our analysis: a view that links the music to the lives of the musicians and the history of the musicians to the economics and politics of the music industry. And it is an industry.

Rock'n'Roll Is Here to Pay touches on the corporate background to the music industry before World War II, but it really begins by locating the music and the industry in the social and political environment of the post-war period, when Joe McCarthy and Eddie Fisher were high on the charts and Chuck Berry and Elvis Presley were still in the wings.

With Europe and Asia devastated, the United States was in a fortunate position economically. American corporations, increasingly multinational in nature, scampered to fill the marketing vacuums left by the British, the French, the Dutch—and the Germans and Japanese. To protect this new private investment the U.S. government mustered out the troops in no less than twenty foreign interventions. The period began with the Korean War and ended with involvement in another "police action," Vietnam.

At home in the early fifties, as the productive power of U.S. industry continued to increase, a "consumer economy" was encouraged as one strategy for absorbing the surplus of goods from domestic business. The consumption of nonessential goods ranging from hula hoops and annually restyled cars to Florida vacations and phonograph records increased enormously. Television, a spectacular consumer business, became a potent cultural force in its own right, bankrupting the local newspaper as a source of information by making possible a homogeneous flow of news and images to the mass American audience. The consumer and consciousness industries and their promise of uniform "beautiful living" were directly dependent on U.S. world power, but distracted attention from the realities of that power and how it was exercised. The popular prevailing political analysis of the U.S. world role was as defender of democracy in the Cold War against monolithic communism. From the political hysteria of McCarthyism through the business-as-usual conservatism of the Eisenhower era. Americans were lulled with the dream that they had almost achieved paradise if only they could protect it from the enemy.

Into this placid world of domestic consumption in the middle fifties came rhythm and blues, a raucous, rip-it-up music that preferred city sounds and simple lyrics to Patti Page pretensions. It held out an illusive promise of sexual revolt. Rhythm and blues for the first time "crossed over" into a white teenager market from its black base. Black-inspired rock'n'roll popularized by white performers like Elvis Presley and Jerry Lee Lewis, and black artists like Chuck Berry and Little Richard, entered the pop mainstream. The major record companies at first tried to ignore the new music, which was marketed largely on independent labels. When it remained popular they tried to coopt it through "cover records" by middle-of-the-road performers like Pat Boone. In 1959-60 came the fraudulent government investigations of broadcasting payola, directed largely at the rock'n'roll menace.

But the music survived the decade and was boosted again by the Beatles' and Rolling Stones' revival of r&b in the early 1960s. In America countless blues bands, folk rock artists, and progressive rock bands grew up during the second flowering of rock that continues to this day.

The record industry grew right along with the popularity of the music. From the mid-fifties to the present it has expanded at an annual rate far surpassing the average American business. It followed the familiar pattern of growth, consolidation, and monopoly, but compressed the dynamic into a very short period of time. The major problem of the industry has been learning how to harness artistic creativity to corporate production and marketing structures without killing it. The hits have to keep coming, but few executives are going to strap on a Fender bass. Finally, the record industry has spawned an elaborate support structure of radio and personal appearances that help sell its creations. The different music businesses are now interdependent.

We have divided the book into two broad areas.

The first area treats the history and economics of the music industry in five chronological chapters. The first three of these chapters outline the growth of the record companies and radio. The fourth chapter discusses some of the additional support industries that expanded in the late 1960s. The fifth describes the current structure and functioning of the record business, with special profiles on Warner-Reprise and RCA.

The second main area of the book is a discussion of the political character of the music industry. It begins with a chapter on the corporate interlocks and shared ownership patterns that align the industry with other powers in American business. A second chapter discusses the industry's historical relation to black artists, who have been the main sources of rock music. A third chapter in the politics area describes the industry's relation to women, who have traditionally been the subject and not the source of rock but who are now developing their own music and breaking into the business. The last chapter deals in a general way with the economic importance of industries like the music business, and the cultural impact of rock'n'roll.

A comprehensive chart of pop music trends and styles has been included. The chart shows the historical development of various rock styles through their best-selling exponents as well as the percentage of record sales which can be attributed to each category. It can be used to chronicle the commercial growth of rock from the fifties to the present, and it is worth consulting at many other points in the book.

Rock'n'Roll Is Here to Pay tries to cover a lot of ground, perhaps too much. The book is meant to be a reasonably comprehensive history of the pop music industry in this country and at the same time a muckraking analysis of the way popular culture is manhandled in a corporate society. *Rock'n'Roll Is Here to Pay* is both a source book and a polemic. We hope the two are not irreconcilable.

Major Interviews

Paul Ackerman — Editor Emeritus, *Billboard*

Lou Adler — Independent producer (Carole King, Cheech and Chong, and others)

Frank Barsalona — President, Premier Talent

Stan Cornyn — Head of Creative Services, Warner-Reprise

Tom Donahue — General Manager, KSAN-FM (San Francisco)

Ahmet Ertegun — President, Atlantic Records

Shelly Finkel — Concert promoter (East Coast, Watkins Glen)

Sam Goody — Owner of the Sam Goody retail record chain in New York

Amos Heilicher — Heilicher Brothers — Distributors and rack-jobbers, Pickwick Records

Is Horowitz — Editor, *Billboard*

Bruce Johnson — President, RKO-General Broadcasting

Roger Karshner — Former Vice President for Sales, Capitol

Jon Landau — Music Editor, *Rolling Stone*

Don Law — Concert promoter in Boston

Mike Maitland — President, MCA Records

Ralph Mann — President, International Famous Agency (IFA)

Joe Martin — Independent distributor (Apex-Martin, New Jersey)

Beverly Mier — Music Director, WBZ (Boston)

Scott Muni — Program Director, WNEW-FM (New York)

Johnny Otis — Rhythm and blues artist and writer

Fred Parris — Founder and lead vocalist of the Five Satins

Varner Paulsen — Station Manager, WNEW-AM (New York)

Eliot Roberts — Head of G-R Management (Joni Mitchell, Crosby, Stills, Nash, and Young, and others)

Russ Sanjek — Vice President, Broadcast Music, Inc. (BMI)

Barbara Skydell — Vice President, Premier Talent

Joe Smith — Former President, Warner-Reprise

Russ Solomon — Owner of the Tower Records chain in California

Herb Spar — Head of the concert division, IFA

Dick Waterman — Manager (Bonnie Raitt, Buddy Guy and Junior Wells, Robert Pete Williams, Johnny Shines, and others)

Nat Weiss — Manager and lawyer (Mahavishnu Orchestra, John McLaughlin, Return to Forever [with Peter Asher], James Taylor, and others)

Tonight on the Sentimental Moon Dog Matinee We Would Like to Play the Next Song:

To Dog-Woman, Dorothy M., and Little Gil from the Chapper,

To Evelyn and Big Mario in New Haven, to Grant Street (Larry, Katherine, Tim, Tequila, and Jack) for withstanding three years of the music industry, to Prospect Street for the night Diane C. spilled scotch on The Chart, to Marcia Steinberg, Dinah Vaprin, Melanie, and Laura Tillem for struggle and daring in Jamaica Plains to Janet Axelrod who thinks Beatle lyrics ain't macho, to Annie and Pris, and Jimmy, Danny, and Tommy, all for encouraging occasional and much-needed drunks; to Karen Shatz (have a good baby), to Patty-O Stein with love, and last but most, to Nic with a very special love — all from Reebee,

To Pope John XXIII in Venice from Oboe in Bernal Heights,

And, never to be forgotten, those who fueled fabulous Entropy, Inc., for two oh-so-long years: Buck Bagot, Jeff Bean, Tim Bernett, Brandy Brandt, David Minard, Laurie Nicholson, Evelyn Rosenthal, Peter Wassyng, and Herb York; Patty Fountain, Andy Gould, John McLaughlin, Joel Rogers, Tony Rostain, Sarah Siskind, and Tricia Tunstall.

Where's the ice pick?

1 THE EARLY YEARS

The Corporate Background

When Thomas Edison, deaf at the time, invented the phonograph, he probably never anticipated rock'n'roll, let alone Elvis Presley and Alice Cooper. The possibilities he imagined for the recording industry began with the spoken word and ended with classical music. The first records were cylinders of wax.

The recording industry grew quickly from the start, manufacturing spoken word and classical records, and later the pop music of the day, directed at a white audience. The early years of recording in the United States were dominated by two companies, the Victor Talking Machine Company, formed in 1901, and the Columbia Graphophone Company, which amalgamated a series of early record and phonograph companies growing out of the old Charles Tainter-Chichester Bell (Alexander's brother) sound laboratories. The years after World War I until about 1922 were golden years for records. In 1921 over $106 million worth of records were sold. In the absence of commercial radio and in the early years of film, the money spent on records exceeded all other leisure time expenditures.

But success was short lived. Radio became popular by 1922 and drew attention from the phonograph. Sales fell until the depression when they were almost nonexistent.

The two big companies competed with a number of independent companies throughout the twenties. The mainstream pop music of the period consisted of "show tunes" written by the composers from Tin Pan Alley, the area near the Twenty-seventh Street vaudeville theaters, and later from the Brill Building uptown. In 1920 Mamie Smith became the first black person to record. The title was called "Crazy Blues," and to the surprise of the Okeh Recording Company executives who put it out, the record began to sell 7,500 copies a week. The black market was "discovered." Records aimed for the black community—mainly blues music—were quickly dubbed "race records" by Ralph Peer, Mamie Smith's producer. Even though the "race" market was small at the time, it bought 5 million copies yearly in the early twenties. After the stock market crash in 1929, most of the smaller companies went out of business or were bought out by the larger ones.

Victor itself was bought out by the Radio Corporation of America (RCA) in about 1929. Radio had become a giant in a few short years as it expanded from naval and industrial use into the consumer market. Until the fifties, money from radio, in the corporate form of RCA and the Columbia Broadcasting System (CBS), would finance much of the record business. Not until the sixties would records eclipse radio, and by then RCA and CBS were already placing their emphasis on a much more lucrative development—television.

David Sarnoff, the president of RCA responsible for many of the decisions that dictated the course of media industry development in the United States over the last half century, spoke in a characteristically callous manner when he explained how Victor records came to be subsumed in the radio corporation:

> I remember when the Victor Talking Machine Co.—and those who founded it did a great job in their day—could not understand how people would sit at home and listen to music that someone else selected for them to hear. They contended that music on the air would be infested with static; they rated the "radio music box" and radio broadcasting as a mere toy. Result? Not many years passed before RCA acquired Victor Talking Machine Co., the little terrier listening to His Master's Voice changed its master, and a greater phonograph industry was built.[1]

The formation of the Radio Corporation of America was an interesting process that points up the role the U.S. government has played from the beginning in helping the biggest corporations in the communications and electronics industry. Radio was developed by Guglielmo Marconi (the Italian inventor turned entrepreneur) and originally marketed by him in conjunction with a group of British investors. During World War I the importance of radio for radio communications, ship-to-ship and ship-to-shore, and in maintaining overseas territories became obvious. At the Paris Peace Conference, Woodrow Wilson made it clear that maritime communications could no longer remain a British monopoly. America was beginning to edge Britain aside as the leading imperial power. The U.S. Navy recommended that in this country radio equipment and Marconi's patents be turned over to the government.

But such a solution would have removed a highly profitable industry from private corporations and was not acceptable to U.S. firms like General Electric (GE), Westinghouse, and American Telephone and Telegraph (AT&T), which were beginning to develop communications equipment. Meeting in secret with government leaders, GE's general counsel at the time, Owen Young, worked out a compromise whereby all of the Marconi assets and operations in the United States would be turned over to a holding company—the Radio Corporation of America—in exchange for stock in the new corporation.

Bemoaning what was in essence a partial nationalization of its assets, the president of Marconi's American subsidiary told stockholders:

> We have found that there exists on the part of the officials of the Government of the United States a very strong and irremovable objection to (American Marconi) because of the stock interest held therein by the British Company.[2]

Owen Young astutely suggested that foreign ownership of the new RCA corporation be limited to 20 percent and that a representative of the United States government be given a seat on the board of the company. The government reciprocated by helping Young, RCA, and GE in removing French, German, and English corporations from their radio investments in South America. Over the next few years GE, Westinghouse, and AT&T assumed varying degrees of control over the corporation and pooled their various patents so that radio could develop as a standardized medium. The corporations split up the manufacture of radio equipment. AT&T made the transmitters, for instance, GE made radio parts, and everything was marketed by RCA.

Radio grew so rapidly, however, with $650 million worth of receiving equipment sold during 1928 alone, that these initial backroom agreements broke down and had to be renegotiated. RCA and Western Electric (part of AT&T) became competitors in the production of transmitters, while RCA was given a monopoly hold on broadcasting. AT&T promised not to manufacture home receivers, but got all of RCA's relay business for the early network broadcasting going on at the time. Also AT&T was paid $1 million for WEAF, a "toll broadcasting" station in New York at which advertisers bankrolled their own programs.*

---

*The toll broadcasting concept was an unusual one. The early days of radio had seen stations set up and programmed only to stimulate the market for home receivers. Their operating expenses were covered by the parts manufacturing company, and no advertisers were allowed on the air.

In 1926 RCA formed the National Broadcasting Company as a subsidiary, sharing stock with General Electric (20 percent) and Westinghouse (20 percent). The first NBC broadcast was four and a half hours of coast-to-coast entertainment that included the New York Symphony Orchestra, Will Rogers in Kansas, Mary Garden the opera singer in Chicago, and many others. NBC divided itself the next year into two subnetworks. the Blue originating from its WJZ studios in New Jersey, and the Red based on the old AT&T chain and WEAF.

RCA was still closely tied to GE and Westinghouse until 1930 when a government antitrust suit was prompted by other manufacturers angry at the harassment they were receiving from the combine. The suit essentially forced GE and Westinghouse out of NBC and into competition with RCA in the manufacture of radio sets.

RCA's chief negotiator in these talks was David Sarnoff, the ambitious, disciplined executive who joined the company as a telegraph operator when he was fifteen, worked his way to the presidency in 1930, and was chairman of the board from 1947 to 1969. An immigrant who got off the long boat from Russia as a boy, Sarnoff was a tough and blunt man. He angered more than a few associates. One man who felt double-crossed by Sarnoff was Arthur Judson. He then formed what was to become RCA's chief broadcasting and record rival—CBS.

Enter CBS: La Palina Hands Out Cigars

Judson was a former violinist who had turned to business. He managed a number of individual artists and symphony orchestras in New York, Philadelphia, and Cincinnati. Although Judson knew little about broadcasting, he was concerned about its impact on the concert business. In 1924 he had approached Sarnoff with a plan for booking talent on network radio. Sarnoff liked it and promised the young manager that when RCA did form its networks, Judson would be in charge of supplying talent.

By 1927, however, when it was clear that RCA would be the only corporation involved with network radio, Sarnoff told Judson his plan was no longer interesting. The manager was outraged. He retaliated by forming his own rival network of twelve radio stations. After various ownership and creditor changes, and several hundred thousand dollars in losses, the new network became the Columbia Broadcasting System. It did not come under effective management until 1928, when it was bought by one of its advertisers, a cigar manufacturer based in Philadelphia. The manufacturer had advertised his family brand of La Palina Cigars on CBS radio, and he had been pleased with the sales results. After he bought the company, he gave it to his son, William Paley.

Paley was twenty-six when he took over CBS. His background was quite different from Sarnoff's. He had been born into wealth and given power at an early age. He was educated at the University of Pennsylvania and the Wharton School of Finance. If the head of RCA was a go-getter who wielded authority with vengence and cut a broad swath of resentment before him, Paley was by comparison a smooth, almost relaxed operator. He protected himself from the messier aspects of corporate maneuvering with his sidekick henchman Edward Klauber, a former newspaperman, whose first act upon getting hired was to fire the person who had suggested him to Paley.

With Klauber handling the details of management, Paley was free to evolve corporate policy. As he dealt with various programming crises, from tasteless commercials to the demagogic Father Coughlin and broadcast religion, he was simultaneously praised in press and business circles for his "shrewd" and "statesmanlike" handling of CBS affairs. He emerged in the thirties and forties as a spokesman for the industry, always judicious, always turning a profit.

But if their style of operation was different, Paley was no less effective than his counterpart at RCA. Weeks after taking over CBS he negotiated a deal with Paramount Pictures that traded a minority stock share in the company for $5 million in much needed investment capital from the Hollywood studio. Within a year CBS was turning a profit, and by 1931 it made more money than the larger RCA networks. That year CBS supported 408 employees and made a profit of $2,346,000, while the RCA Red and Blue networks supported 1,359 employees and showed a slightly smaller profit of $2,325,000. The next year Paley bought back all the Paramount stock. Using extra money to buy up new stations, he increased the CBS network from the nineteen outlets it had in 1928 when he took over to ninety-seven in 1935.

Whereas Sarnoff's executive strengths lay in developing new technologies, Paley excelled in programming innovations and developing broadcasting policy. During this period, for instance, RCA was using a complicated billing procedure for its affiliate stations. Affiliates were paid for carrying sponsored national shows, and billed for so-called "sustaining" programs that did not have commercial sponsors. Paley simplified the whole procedure. He charged affiliates nothing for sustaining programs, provided he got an option on any part of the affiliates' schedule for sponsored network shows. The revenues from these shows were then split seventy-thirty between the network and the local affiliate. In this way CBS attracted new affiliates with little operating capital, and streamlined and homogenized national programming schedules. Advertisers were happier. Affiliates were happier. It was shrewd and statesmanlike, and profitable. RCA sales plummeted after the CBS innovation, until RCA adopted a similar advertising policy a few years later.

In 1934 the American Record Corporation, which handled the Brunswick and Vocalion labels, bought the old Columbia Graphophone company, and four years later Columbia Broadcasting System purchased the combined companies. It was not until then that CBS had a record division. The rivalry between RCA and CBS began to extend beyond radio to records. The late forties brought the RCA-CBS Battle of Record Speeds. In the fifties the rivalry expanded to television. Records were something of a sideline to the big networks in the 1930s, however. Electronically and musically radio and records were related, of course, but an equally compelling reason for their acquisition was probably the low purchase prices for companies being sold during the depression.

In the late thirties NBC, along with CBS, had acquired such a monopolistic hold over major stations that RCA was forced to divest itself of its Blue network. The Blue was bought up by candy magnate Edward Noble, who renamed it the American Broadcasting Company (ABC). ABC waited until the fifties to open its record division.

The third major record company of the prewar period was Decca. It was also formed in the middle of the depression and launched with a merchandising strategy. Sir Ted Lewis of British Decca and Jack Kapp, the company's first president, decided to slash Victor's and Columbia's prevailing price of 75 cents a record to 35 cents or three for a dollar. When the two other big companies followed suit, records became an entertainment bargain, and sales began to climb.

A second rather clever idea served to establish Decca in America. Kapp had been working for Brunswick, a precursor to Columbia's record division, when he approached Sir Ted with the idea of starting American Decca. At Brunswick he had signed a number of artists including Guy Lombardo, Louis Armstrong, and Bing Crosby, to an unusual personal services contract. In effect they were contracted to him personally, so that when he formed Decca he was able to take them along. It was a surprise for Brunswick.

By the late thirties many of the records manufactured by Decca, Victor, and Columbia were now headed for jukeboxes. By 1940 there were 350,000 jukeboxes in the bars and cafes in the United States, and 44 percent of all the records manufactured reputedly went into them.* Since it cost a nickel to play a record on the juke and only 35 cents to buy one, the new machines were very profitable.

The power of the music industry as a whole did not yet lie with the record manufacturers. It was held by the music publishers who derived

---

*Many of the records in Decca's first release reportedly were too wide to fit jukeboxes. They had to be returned, and the jukebox operators, many of whom were crime figures, were placated with refunds. Decca later became part of the Music Corporation of America (MCA).

the bulk of their income from the sale of sheet music and from royalties for live performances of their copyrighted songs. Record and jukebox exposure was helpful but not so important as live performances over network radio and in the clubs and stage musicals which had replaced the vaudeville theaters of earlier years.

By 1939 the improving prewar economy, the Decca-led price slash, the popularization of the jukebox, and the increasing exposure of record artists over radio had brought record sales up from a low of $6 million in 1933 to $44 million by the close of the decade. Power in the music industry was a combine of major publishers and the major record companies, with the publishers still holding the initiative.

A publisher would pick out a song that he thought should be the next hit tune and bring it to the record companies. The song would then be recorded by several companies, perhaps for instance by Hal Kemp for Columbia's Brunswick label, then by Bing Crosby or the Andrews Sisters for Decca. Often, as in the case of Crosby, the song would be connected to a motion picture too. The different versions would appear at about the same time, so that the song would be heard on the air and at the movies, bought in record stores, and sold as sheet music. The publisher's royalty was assured.

The Evolving Music

By the late thirties self-contained "big bands" or swing bands such as those led by Artie Shaw, Harry James, and Glenn Miller began to dominate the charts. From 1937 to 1941 band recordings made up twenty-nine of the forty-three records that sold more than a million copies each.[3]

In the background were the black big bands of Louis Armstrong and Louis Russel, Duke Ellington, Count Basie, Cab Calloway (the "Hi-de-ho Man"), and others. The black big bands were paid less in the segregated concert structure of the time than were the white bands. Armstrong and Ellington would sometimes play the white theaters but mostly they and the others would stick to the separate black circuit. Jazz and blues records, especially those directed in the United States only to the black market, were seen as something a little extra by the record companies. They continued to record these records because they were inexpensive to produce and satisfied a worldwide market interested in American jazz. Records produced for $150 would still be selling fifteen years later in Belgium, France, Germany, and England, where the three large companies had subsidiaries and reciprocal agreements with foreign companies.

Since most of the material for the big bands in the prewar years was written and arranged by band members—nobody told Duke Ellington what to play—the publishers had fewer of their Broadway-type songs recorded. In the war years 1942-46 the singers in the bands were becoming in some cities more popular than the bands themselves. This trend was helped by a strike against radio by musicians but not singers. The situation brought business back to the publishers who could now get their material sung by men like Frank Sinatra.

The war years also broadened the field of popular music. Country music, then known as "hillbilly music," and "race music," soon to be renamed "rhythm and blues" (r&b), were heard by audiences outside of the South and the black ghettos. Large numbers of blacks and poor whites moved North and West to work in defense plants and brought their music with them. At the same time many Midwesterners and Easterners were stationed in the South where they were bombarded by some 600 hillbilly stations. The new audiences liked what they heard. Detroit jukebox operators reported in 1943 that hillbilly records were the most popular, and in Europe the American Armed Forces Radio Network voted Roy Acuff, a Nashville Grand Ole Opry star with a fiddle, to be more popular than Frank Sinatra.

Black music, too, was becoming more popular, although it was still confined to the nonwhite market. The newly immigrated Southern blacks had enough money from wartime prosperity to begin to sustain a few black-oriented radio stations and the large variety of race records that were being issued by the record companies.

The major companies—Columbia, Victor, and Decca—had gained a firm control of race music during the depression with the failure of independent companies like Black Swan and Paramount. These companies had their catalogues bought out by the majors, or they simply disappeared. Similar control by the majors had existed in the hillbilly market ever since Ralph Peer had made the first country recording, of Jimmie Rogers and the Carter Family in 1927, while he was a producer for Victor. (This is the same Peer who made the first "race recording," and who first applied the terms "race" and "hillbilly" to the record industry.)

But during the Second World War there was a shortage of shellac, the principal ingredient used in making 78 rpm records. It became virtually impossible to obtain the material from India where it was secreted by a type of tree-crawling scale insect. To combat the shortage, record buyers were required in many stores to turn in a record for every new one they bought. This measure was not sufficient, however, and the major firms decided to abandon the specialty fields of hillbilly, race, and gospel records, and to stick to mainstream pop.

After the war they tried to recapture the market. In the country field this was relatively easy because many of the leading country singers had preserved their ties to the majors. Several independent companies— principally King, which had managed to sell 4 million-selling records for two of its artists (Moon Mullican and Cowboy Copas), and Imperial, which had sold a huge quantity of Slim Whitman's records—were active for a few years, but the field was soon firmly back in the hands of the majors, where it remains today. For a number of reasons the rhythm and blues field proved too difficult for the majors to recapture (this is the subject of the next chapter). Their failure hardly bothered them at the time. Rhythm and blues was still confined to the small black market.

The Larger Context: *Sarnoff's New Baby Puts FM in an Early Grave*

The development of music in this country has not been a closed aesthetic process. New technologies such as radio, TV, and the long-playing record have had a strong impact at several points on the evolution of the music, most obviously by determining the speed at which new types of music are popularized. In at least one instance, the suppression of a technology has had equal impact. The suppression of FM radio by RCA in the thirties and again in the forties to insure the stable introduction of television limited the number of radio stations in the United States and stalled the real development of FM itself until the 1960s.

RCA's Sarnoff had once said he wished "someone would come up with a little black box to eliminate radio static." Edwin Armstrong, an important inventor who had earlier sold RCA various useful circuit devices, had been thinking about the same problem for years and committed himself to finding a solution. From the early days of radio, engineers had realized that messages could probably be sent as well by modulating the frequency (or rate of propagation) of electromagnetic waves as by modulating their amplitude (or size). Armstrong discovered in fact that messages could be sent much better by frequency modulation (FM), than by the traditional amplitude modulation (AM). In 1923 he started working in a small laboratory at Columbia University, and then years later emerged with patents on four separate inventions relating to FM radio. The following year RCA allowed Armstrong to use some of its Empire State Building space for transmission. The quality and range of the broadcast were astounding. FM radio waves propagate or move in a straight line. They are not able, like AM waves, to bend slightly following the surface of the earth. But the FM wave suppresses interference (static) from other stations much better than the AM. Thus with less power and using a smaller space on the electromagnetic spectrum, FM can provide better reception than AM radio. FM also provides a greater range of sound frequency than AM, because it can include overtone harmonics in broadcast music. Combined with the lack of static, this means a more faithful reproduction of broadcast sound. FM was high fidelity radio.

RCA was not interested. In 1935 it asked Armstrong to leave his office at the top of the Empire State Building. Then within days it announced a $1 million corporate commitment to research and development of an entirely different form of broadcast, *television*. Sarnoff, who had promised Armstrong he would back the new invention, broke his word.

In 1936, after a public demonstration of the new radio device, Armstrong approached the FCC with a plan for allocating spectrum space to his invention. The FCC ruled against him. It was not a surprise judgment. At the same hearing David Sarnoff presented arguments for reserving all of the Very High Frequency (VHF) band on the electromagnetic spectrum for television. With him as counsel was C. B. Jolliffe, who only a few weeks before had been the chief engineer for the Commission. Armstrong was allowed to build an experimental FM transmitter in Alpine, New Jersey, however. That station was completed in 1939. The same year he won a small victory from the FCC. Backed by the newly formed FM Broadcasters Association he got Channel 1 removed from the television band and assigned to FM radio. It was important that FM get some space in the VHF area of the spectrum, rather than the higher Ultra High Frequency (UHF) range. The signal in the lower range carried about twice as far, and was more than twice as effective in cutting down on static.

Armstrong had contracted GE to build him twenty-five receiver sets for FM radio, to be used in popularizing the device. The corporation was soon interested in building sets commercially. Shortly after GE, Freed, Stewart-Warner, Stromberg-Carlson, Western Electric, and Zenith all were producing FM radios and radio parts. They all paid royalties to Armstrong on his various patents. RCA also got involved in some Armstrong patents, but did not pay royalties on their production. The giant corporation approached the inventor looking for unlimited reproduction rights in return for a cash settlement. The outbreak of war interrupted negotiations. RCA got involved in a lucrative series of contracts with the navy to develop radar, and Armstrong donated his FM patents and personal services for free for temporary use by the army.

Immediately after the war, again at the urging of Sarnoff and RCA, the FCC finally decided, once and for all, to move FM radio up into the UHF part of the electromagnetic spectrum. FM, which had been heralded as a major radio innovation for the postwar period, fell quickly on bad times. Investors withdrew for easier profits in TV. Only 80,000 FM radio sets were produced in the first three quarters in 1946, as compared to 6.5 million new AM radios. As an added insult, RCA used many of Armstrong's patented FM devices in its new TV models, as well as continuing pirate production of a few FM radios.

In 1948 a desperate Armstrong brought suit against RCA, but was little match for their battery of Cravath, Swaine, and Moore lawyers who, adept at corporate stalling, insisted on an entire year of pretrial investigation during which information like Armstrong's name, occupation, and street address were gone over several times. One day the inventor, who had never been afraid of climbing transmitter towers, walked out of a thirteenth story window in his apartment house above midtown Manhattan. A few months later RCA settled with his widow for an even $1 million, and unlimited reproduction rights on all outstanding patents.

When David Sarnoff blocked the rise of FM radio in 1936, and again in 1945-46, he was acting no more out of personal malice toward Edwin Armstrong than he was several years later when he instructed his law firm to stall the inventor into a cash settlement on patent royalties. Sarnoff simply had a keen, if ruthless, sense of RCA's priorities. Even in the 1930s he had realized that the future of big money in broadcasting lay in television, that TV would one day replace radio as the main media fixture in American homes. A commitment to commercial FM broadcasting during the lush postwar years, when AM radio was peaking commercially, would have brought the broadcasting world into chaos as well as drawn money away from research and development on television.

RCA had made the most progress in development of the new medium, and wanted to establish a quick, monopolistic hold on the industry. That was the main reason for urging the Federal Communications Commission to push FM out of the VHF band. The lower frequency was more crowded, and would limit the number of possible TV stations, giving a special long-term advantage to early investors. The FCC decisions in the late thirties and 1945-46 favored the major networks, particularly RCA, to the detriment of the general radio audience.

The FCC decisions in the end of the war years to limit FM radio to UHF and reserve VHF for TV came as a shock to Columbia Broadcasting. Paley had been lobbying for years for federal acceptance of a proven method of CBS, color broadcasting designed for the UHF range. CBS formally petitioned the FCC for permission to market its system in September 1946. Sarnoff took the occasion to announce that within six months RCA would have a color TV system on the market that would be compatible with the current black and white VHF transmitters. When questioned how his engineers could produce the system in so short a time, Sarnoff replied, "Because I told them to." The next spring he produced his model, right on schedule. It was crude, but compatible. In

March the FCC decided to assign all TV, black and white and color, to the VHF range.

In the later 1940s, TV sales boomed. By 1951 RCA had already recovered from its decade of technological development and the early years of programming TV stations at a loss. As in radio, however, Paley and CBS showed better programming sense. While NBC experimented with spectacular shows and multiple sponsorship ("magazine packaging") Paley was more cautious. He used the old techniques of radio broadcasting—solid programs and regularly scheduled single sponsors. By 1953 television set sales were greater than sales of radios, and CBS commanded a bigger radio and television audience than NBC. That same year, American Broadcasting Company and Paramount Theaters merged, with Paramount providing the talent necessary to make ABC a force within the new business.

By 1957, the relative positions of radio and TV that had existed ten years before were reversed. While in 1948 fewer than 172,000 families owned televisions, and those that did tended not to watch them for hours on end, by 1957 there were 39 million TV sets in the United States, each watched several hours daily, filling 80 percent of the homes. Although 85 percent of U.S. homes had radios in 1948, listenership, especially national listenership, steadily declined. Still the absolute number of radio sets in use continued to be greater than the number of TVs, with radio moving into the youth and car markets for its biggest growth.

During the transition years from network radio to network TV, government again was a help to big business. In addition to stopping the growth of FM in the late forties, the FCC was instrumental in another way. In late September 1948 it imposed a freeze on applications for new television station licenses. The freeze continued through the. middle of 1952. In other words, during television's crucial initial growth spurt, when the sales of individual sets increased by more than six times, no new firms were able to set up stations. Control was solidified in the hands of the networks. By the time the freeze ended, television was an extremely capital intensive business, which required huge amounts of money and connections to enter. The freeze, which the FCC announced "in the public interest," effectively shielded the market from any entrepreneurs outside of the huge corporations, like RCA, that already dominated it. Since the freeze was lifted in 1952, there has been no successful challenge to major network monopoly.

Records are not dependent on an elaborate transmission system, as is television, and are not affected by government decisions concerning, for example, frequency assignments. In part for this reason records have not been as easy for a small handful of giant electronics firms to monopolize. Actual musical styles and audience choices have played a much more important role in determining which firms are to dominate the record industry, although CBS and RCA have usually held a technical edge over other record companies and have usually been in the top five in terms of record sales.

The emphasis that CBS and RCA placed on the truly big money television market provided the context in which records and rock'n'roll developed. RCA's preoccupation with television, for instance, made it give much less attention to its relatively unimportant record division. And the lack of high corporate emphasis given to network radio in comparison to network TV allowed independent radio stations, mostly of secondary stature, to experiment with rock'n'roll music, new disc jockey (dj) styles, and Top 40 formats. The rock'n'roll stations eventually pushed aside the more staid network stations and in the process helped to revitalize the then smaller record industry. In the sixties the relation between radio and records was reversed, with records assuming primary importance and radio becoming *in effect* a promotional adjunct. But before we describe this long process of reversal, it is necessary to understand the structure of the fifties record industry.

In Search of Elvis

In 1950 record sales in the United States had reached $189 million. This was almost a 10 percent improvement from the year before but was still far below the 1947 peak of $224 million, and still further beneath the 1955 figure of $277 million.* Part of the reason for the middling figure was that the United States had only just recovered from a post-World War II production slump and was beginning to refuel the economy with the Korean War buildup (wars being the simplest although the bloodiest way to prime the pump and revitalize the national economy). But part of the explanation lies with the lackluster state of the recording industry. With the exception of crowd inciters Frank Sinatra and Frankie Laine, and screamer Johnny Ray ("Cry"), there were few exciting performers in the pop market. Most records were directed at an upper-middle-class audience, and sales for hits were low (again with several exceptions, like "Cry," which sold 2 million copies for Columbia). The excitement of rock'n'roll seems to have been the major factor in the take off of the record industry in 1955. (See Chart 1.1.)

In 1950 the five leading record manufacturers made only a 3.81 percent return on investment after taxes. The majors felt that the principal problem was the low ratio of hits to records released. In 1952, for instance, only about one out of thirty-six single sides made the Top 20 of

---

*Based on manufacturers' list price, which in these years was probably 10-20 percent above the actual retail price.

the leading trade magazine, *Billboard*. But a low hit-to-release ratio has been a chronic problem with the record industry. An A&R (artist and repertoire) man at Capitol admitted ten years later that they simply "threw records against the wall to see what would stick." The concern was only given significance at the time because it was a fairly new one, coinciding with the production of records mainly for a home audience rather than for jukeboxes and network radio.

Chart 1.1
Total U.S. Record and Tape Sales 1921-1973

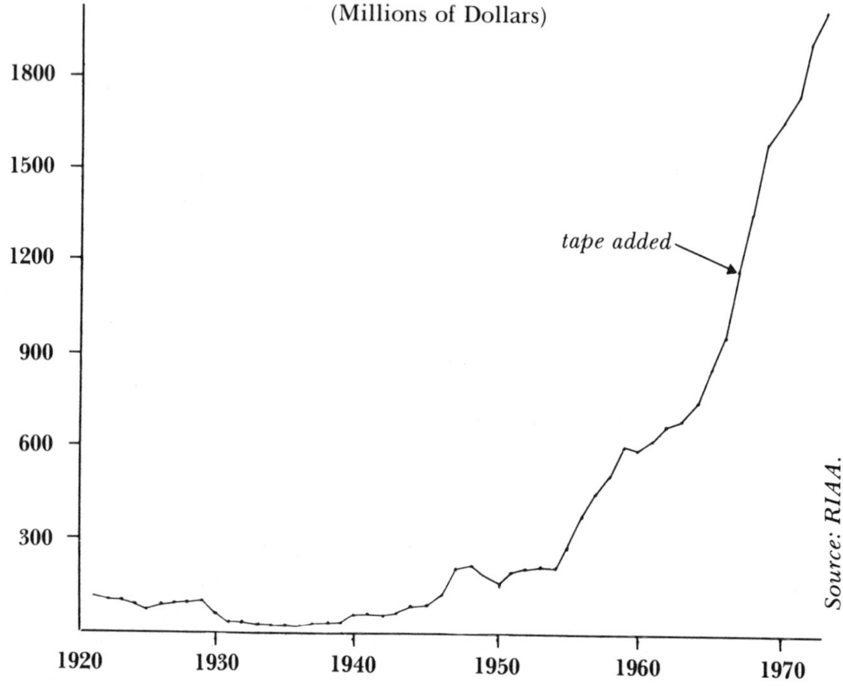

(Millions of Dollars)

1800 —

1500 —

1200 —   *tape added*

900 —

600 —

300 —

Source: RIAA.

1920   1930   1940   1950   1960   1970

A greater problem, perhaps, was the centralization of A&R control (what songs were done and by whom) in one man at each of the companies. By 1955, with the rise of the independent record companies and their new rock'n'roll music, conditions were evolving for the breakdown of this control.

For the major companies the most important developments of the period were in the technological and merchandising fields. The growth of the rhythm and blues audience was ignored by the major companies, at least until rhythm and blues hits began to penetrate the pop (white) market, and by then it was too late, anyway. These technological developments—the introduction of magnetic recording tape to America,

14

the invention of the LP, the introduction of the 45, the development of high fidelity, and the continuing spread of the phonograph—combined with the initial modernizing of the retail record business to economically prepare the industry and the public for the musical explosions which were heating up beyond the reach of the old-line companies.

The Majors

In the early fifties record companies were termed "major" when they owned their own manufacturing plants and directly controlled their distribution outlets in addition to simply producing records. By this definition there were six major companies in 1950: Columbia, RCA, Decca, Capitol, MGM, and Mercury (some would also include the smaller London Records). Columbia and RCA were the leaders with Columbia, after 1950, acting as the spokesman for the industry. Columbia and RCA were usually able to wield far more power than the other companies because they had the immense financial backing of the Columbia Broadcasting System and the Radio Corporation of America behind them. In the 1960s the definition of "major" broadened to include companies that were selling as many records as the old majors but that nevertheless did not do their own pressing and that often used independent distributors.

Columbia became the leading label in the early fifties, edging aside its long-time rival, RCA. It became the most successful company in the pop field in 1951 and stayed there until the resurgence of Warner Brothers in the sixties. The company was not as strong as RCA in the classical field, but as the record audience was becoming less elite this pop orientation of CBS was becoming a strong advantage. The main pop stars that carried them through the early fifties were Frankie Laine, a torch singer who attracted a following at least as frenzied as Sinatra's; Johnny Ray, a flash from rural Oregon who gave the company "Cry," their top selling hit for 1952; Jimmy Boyd ("I Saw Mommie Kissing Santa Claus"); Guy Mitchell; and a bland assortment of women singers including Rosemary Clooney, Doris Day, and Jo Stafford.

Even more important than its artists in moving Columbia in front of RCA was the success of its hardware. Columbia took a big chance with the introduction of the LP, since RCA had already tried and failed in the thirties with a similar although poorer quality long-playing record. The newer microgroove LP that CBS introduced proved a huge success among listeners who wanted to hear long sections of uninterrupted music. They chose the Columbia LP over the packages of five-minute 45s that RCA issued as "albums."

The company was not elaborately structured into a number of specialized divisions, as it is now. It was too early to have separate album departments for different types of music. There was the classical department (Masterworks), the pop department, the international department, the children's department, and the country department.

RCA like Columbia was willing to take chances in order to monopolize the profit on new innovations, but the company was not as successful as Columbia. In fact because the company spent so much money and energy developing and promoting the 45 rpm record in the late forties only to lose out to Columbia's LP in audience interest, sales fell from an estimated high of $80 million to $50 million in 1950. By the end of 1953, however, the company was again doing well. It had a series of pop hits and issued two extremely successful special packages by Toscanini and Glenn Miller. Like Columbia, RCA had the financial resources to enable them to bounce back from a series of wrong decisions. They could buy name artists away from smaller labels, as they did with Elvis Presley in 1955, in order to provide stable sales. Or they could use their corporate ties with RCA's NBC television network to set up long-term deals.

Some artists like Perry Como and Vaughn Monroe made twenty-five-year contracts with RCA-Victor and NBC. RCA executives usually hired a "show biz figure" or a "handler," as it was termed on the street, to handle these deals for both the television and record divisions. In addition to Monroe and Como, Victor had million sellers with Eddie Fisher, Spike Jones ("My Two Front Teeth"), and Mario Lanza, along with a few others, in the 1948-53 period. Although the record division was successful, RCA as a corporation was doing much better in television.

Decca was more loosely run under Milt Rachmil than either RCA-Victor or Columbia, but did not influence the industry as a whole during this period, as it was to do in 1954 with the recording of Bill Haley and the Comets or in 1957 with its distribution of Buddy Holly's records. In February 1952 the company merged with Universal Pictures. In December 1952 the United States government enjoined Decca along with British Decca and EMI (Electrical and Mechanical Industries, Limited) from their policy of cartelization—dividing up areas of the world for exclusive rights.

Capitol was the first new company after Decca to make an impact. The company was formed in 1943 by singer/songwriter Johnny Mercer, Glenn Wallichs, who came out of the retail record business (his brother owns the Wallichs Music City chain in California), and Buddy de Sylva of Paramount Pictures. Their original investment was reportedly $10,-000, and it was quickly recouped by two typical hits of the time: Ella Mae Morse's "Cow Cow Boogie" and Mercer's "Strip Polka." The company grossed $195,000 in the first six months with these artists and a few more like Paul Whiteman. Capitol branched out quickly and moved into the country and rhythm and blues fields. They were sensitive to the Chicano and black populations in Los Angeles long before majors in other cities took stock of their ethnic markets. At different times the company signed Frank Sinatra, Nat King Cole, Dean Martin, Stan Kenton, Ferlin Husky, and Tex Ritter.

By 1955 they were the third or fourth largest company in the country with sales the preceding year of over $17 million. Their success attracted the huge British holding company EMI (interestingly enough, the company that eventually fell heir to the European Marconi patents), which bought out surviving founders for about $8,500,000. Since net profit for that year was $736,000, EMI got a label that was showing about a 10 percent annual return on investment. EMI bought Capitol partly to get access to U.S. acts. This relationship was reversed in the sixties when Capitol became the U.S. distributor for EMI's Beatles.

MGM Records was formed in Hollywood in 1946 as a division of Metro-Goldwyn-Mayer, the film company. Although it was intended to be an outlet for movie sound tracks, it expanded to most types of music. MGM was especially strong in country music. Hank Williams ("Your Cheatin' Heart," "Hey, Good Lookin'," "Jambalaya") recorded eleven songs for MGM that sold a million or more copies between 1949 and 1953.

The Mercury Recording Corporation was started in Chicago in 1947. The company was formed by Berle Adams, a manager and booking agent, and Irving Green, the son of Al Green, a plastics maker who had started National Records to give himself a product to manufacture. Except for its size and the fact that it owned a pressing plant, Mercury was more like many of the new independents of the time. The company even limited itself to two specialty fields at first—polka and rhythm and blues, where it recorded Eddie "Cleanhead" Vinson. The early Mercury also had the flair of an independent. According to a former high executive of the company, "Mr. Green would do or say or play anything. He would cheat, steal. . . . It was a swinging company for a major." Like most independents, Mercury soon acquired a reputation for seldom paying full royalties to its nonwhite artists.

. . . And the Major-Domos

As the bulk of records began to be sold to private buyers rather than to jukeboxes, and as radio stations began to look to what the record-buying public wanted when it chose its own records, the executives at record companies began to gain power over the publishers in choosing songs. This change coincided with a decline, of about 15-20 percent in the early fifties, in sheet music sales. Publishers were angry at both developments.

At the record companies the new power was centered in the A&R chiefs. A&R stood for artist and repertoire. He (never she) decided what tunes were to be recorded, and which singers would record them. He worked out the orchestral arrangements, picked the sidemen, and did the arrangements, or at least hired the person who did them. The A&R man was the producer in the modern sense. Studio work was not nearly as involved then as it is now. Sessions were usually done in one or two sittings. Few recording techniques had been developed for improving most aspects of the sound, so little editing was necessary. The engineer was not yet important either. The A&R chief was responsible for the total output of the company. This presented no problem in the days before the LP and 45 because a company release may have consisted of only ten or twelve 78s. When the sheer number of records had increased by the middle fifties, however, and several different genres had to be recorded, it became impossible for the A&R chief to ride herd over everything. His power was diffused. Later, rock'n'roll singers and bands were self-contained and did not need an A&R chief, who usually did not like rock'n'roll anyway, to put together each and every ingredient necessary to the recording. The technical aspects of studio work fell to the new producer and to the engineer, whose equipment was always expanding and becoming more sophisticated. By the mid-sixties most rock groups were also composing and arranging their own songs.

But in the fifties the A&R chief was boss. The musical publisher would come into his office and pitch songs. He could say that he thought a particular tune was suited for Rosemary Clooney or Vaughn Monroe, for example, but the A&R man had final word in most cases. If he did not like a song, he would ask the publisher to rewrite it. A few refused—Arthur Schwartz, the songwriter, once walked out of Mitch Miller's office at Columbia—but most agreed. Payola under this structure passed from publisher to A&R man. There were so few releases that some publishers had to make sure they got some of them. There were also cases at the time where the A&R man would overpay musicians by arranging for extra sessions and then receive a kickback. This became more widespread in the sixties with independent producers, but it really began in the early fifties with staff A&R personnel.

Mitch Miller, the A&R chief at Columbia Records, was the archetypical A&R man of the period. He had absolute power, great commercial success, a chef's attitude toward mixing the ingredients of a popular song, and a gut hatred for the rock'n'roll which edged him aside in the late fifties. He had a way of producing clever songs so that the studio record sounded different from the simple reproduced live performances of a few years back; he put a harpsichord with Rosemary Clooney and French horns with Guy Mitchell, for instance. He arrived in 1948 and by 1952 had produced twenty-two hits. One of his greatest knacks was adapting country music to the pop market. He turned a country singer from Detroit named Al Cernick into pop singer Guy Mitchell. He covered a number of Hank Williams hits for MGM with sanitized versions from pop singers on the Columbia roster: Jo Stafford did "Jambalaya—On the Bayou," Rosemary Clooney sang "This Ole House," and Tony Bennett covered "Cold, Cold Heart." As Ian Whitcomb pointed out in *After the Ball*, "Maybe the songs were originally salty stories about sin, sex, and salvation, full of morality and retribution and guilt—but Miller turned them into healthy pop."

At Victor and Columbia there was a separate A&R man for classical records. The classical division had always been the elite of the two companies, but this was changing. Classical records never reached the commercial success of pop tunes. In 1950 George Marek, then head of the RCA classical division, later to become general manager of the record division, established that for every two records the classical A&R department wanted to issue on aesthetic merit, there had to be eight records of "what the public wants." In terms of classical music, what the public wanted was mood music. Marek brought in Melachrino to compete with Columbia's Kostelanetz and London's Mantovani. Columbia and RCA kept strong classical departments because they could charge more for the records, and because it was good for the company's image.

Promotion: *Harry Cook Hits the Road*

As practiced by the major companies in the forties and early fifties, promotion was neither frenzied nor sophisticated. The majors did not get involved in an aggressive way with promotion, especially radio promotion, until they were forced to by the initiatives of the independents in the early fifties. The network radio of the late forties did not really lend itself to record promotion. Martin Block, the most popular disc jockey in New York during this period, simply played fifteen minutes of, say, Bing Crosby, then fifteen minutes of Glenn Miller, then fifteen of Tommy Dorsey. The jostling Top 40 format which played different records one after the other did not evolve until much later, when radio was forced to change itself to adapt to the impact of television.

Promotion existed during the forties, of course, but it was a gentlemanly art. When a new Dinah Shore record was ready, for example, Howie Richmond, her promotion man, would fly around the country for several days talking to key jocks like Howard Miller in Chicago or Bill Randall in Cleveland, who were his friends. The big companies rarely sent promotion men even to the established stations. They just mailed out the records. Promotion was not necessary, or so they felt. They knew their name artists would be played. Newly formed

Capitol became the first major to bother to send out complimentary copies of records to disc jockeys.

When a special promotion campaign was done with a radio station, it was regarded as a new and unusual practice. Mercury sponsored radio contests, for instance, in which listeners called in their favorite Frankie Laine song to 150 djs around the country. The goal was to stimulate sales of all Laine songs. Mercury claimed that it was the first record company to sponsor a promotion tour for one of its artists—again Laine, in 1948. The tour consisted of twelve one-nighters, and Laine with Jan August and his Trio, and the Harry Cook Orchestra, traveled in a railway car with the Mercury logo on the side. Mercury distributors sold the tickets through retail record stores for $1 to $2.50. It was a long way from the Rolling Stones' Lear jet.

At this time promotion departments were nonexistent or just beginning at record companies. Promotion was often done independently by publishers or by independent distributors for those labels that used them.

Technical Development: *Hitler in High Fidelity*

Several technological developments modernized the record industry in the late 1940s. The changes created a new interest in records that coincided with the expansion of popular music in the mid-fifties.

The first of these developments was the introduction into the United States of magnetic recording tape and the modern tape recorder shortly after World War II. Both were stolen from the Nazis who had developed remarkable taping systems to increase propaganda broadcasts, especially of Hitler's speeches. Besides bringing the obvious advantages of editing and of better sound reproduction, tape recorders made it possible to record anywhere in the United States. Recording was no longer confined to elaborate studios in a few major cities. Only then was it possible for a Buddy Holly to record from Clovis, New Mexico. Independent producing and the formation of independent labels were encouraged.

The high fidelity long play record was introduced in 1948 by Columbia. It was invented, along with a myriad of necessary byproducts and processes, by Dr. Peter Goldmark, head of CBS labs for over thirty-six years. Goldmark, a player of chamber music, claims he was angered by the interuptions in a symphony recorded by Toscanini caused by the short playing time of the old 78s. In an interesting interview in 1972, he rather concisely explained the development of the LP:

> It was a system task, really—involving so many theoretical calculations. . . .
> First of all, to provide more playing time, it was necessary to change the number of grooves—which then necessitated changing the speed—which, in turn, required offsetting the resulting distortion—which then required

offsetting the limitation of frequency response which would have occurred. But of course, we wanted just the opposite: a record with *better* frequency response, *less* distortion, and *less* noise. Everything pointed in the opposite direction, so this meant calculating just the type of transducer required, which in those days was measured in ounces.

The styli available were maybe cactus, or something else reasonably sharp. So we had to miniaturize the groove in order to avoid distortion, because when you slow a record down, that means the linear speed toward the inside of the record would have created unbearable distortion. So we had to change the radius of the stylus. We went from sapphire to diamond. But in order for the tiny radii not to chew up the record, we had to reduce the pressure . . . but then the stylus wouldn't stay in the groove. So we had to introduce the old concept of compliance, which meant that the stylus had to have a certain vertical elasticity.

In other words, we had to develop a whole new science. The narrower groove was more sensitive to the various changes of speed of the motor, which wasn't designed for 33 1/3. The magnetic field of the motor created hum, and because of the lower signals it generated, we had to provide that they be united. So we had to design new motors and new drive systems, new pickup arms.

The pickup arm's resonance was well within the frequency spectrum . . . well within the new record's, well outside of the old one's. So we really had to tackle everything. Even microphones. So much was hidden in the shellac. People didn't realize why the record was noisy. I thought shellac was a very quiet material, but it made noises, you see. Shellac had to have mixed into it an abrasive so that the stylus wore off and not the shellac . . . so what we had to do was come up with a new material.

In those days vinyl was used experimentally for records, but it wasn't good enough, because the vinyl was expensive. But when we decided that you could put the whole work on a single record, then the cost of extra vinyl would be more or less offset. To use less vinyl we had to make the records thinner. But when the records were made thinner, you had trouble with warping and you had to find new ways of stabilizing the vinyl, and that means different kinds of pressures.

Then you had a wonderful sound quality, but you didn't have a microphone capable of creating wonderful sounds. We found then that the microphones were unable to reproduce what we called the buzz of the violin. So we started a whole study in microphones—using pistol shots to create sharp sound waves, and we learned that we had to discover how to develop a new kind of microphone, which turned out be the condenser microphone, which was smaller compared to the wave length. Which, after we developed it and spent an awful lot of money, we found out what [sic] the Germans already had invented.

Then we turned to the loudspeaker, and had to develop an instrument. I'm not sure it's known, but we came up with the first so-called table hi-fi equipment; it was called a 360. We had to show that you didn't need a tremendous instrument to produce outstanding quality. So we found how you can produce loud speakers and good low frequencies in a small enclosure by air venting and elastic suspension—out of which came the hi-fi industry.[4]

When Dr. Goldmark came to the United States in the thirties as a physics Ph.D from the University of Vienna, he was turned down for a job at RCA. Although he was a well-to-do man with some 160 patents, he received no royalties from the invention of the LP. Those royalties went to CBS.

The first LPs were ten inches across. They were designed to carry all of a four-record 78 package. The same amount of studio time, two sessions, went into producing the 10″ LP as had gone into the four 78s. The early pop LPs were hardly "concept" records. They served as a repository for a singer's hit singles. One or two hits that sold the album, such as "Cry" for Johnny Ray, would appear with a group of his unknown songs to fill out the album. Companies issuing LPs were a little greedy with their classical records. One symphony was divided in two and put on both sides of a record—the label was enlarged to take up the extra room. In the amount of music received for the money spent, however, LPs meant a savings to the record buyer.

By introducing the LP, Columbia got the jump on RCA in what was to be known as the Battle of the Speeds. Columbia's achievement especially irked General Sarnoff of RCA—so the story goes—because RCA had tried a 33 1/3 rpm LP in the 1930s, abandoning the concept when the public rejected it, most likely for its poor sound quality. It was not a microgroove LP. Sarnoff was determined to introduce a product line that would outcompete the Columbia LP.

His answer was the 45 rpm record. The 45 had certain advantages. Since it was lighter and less breakable than the 78, it could be shipped at lower cost and with greater speed. This suited it well for the pop singles market where it was important to get out the company version of a song before the cover version might be released. The 45 began to catch on for singles. RCA fed its growth by marketing a 45 record player that was sold at low cost. By 1953 they had sold 10 million players and overcome consumer reluctance to the speed. Radio stations were also wary of the 45s because of the expense involved in changing their equipment to accommodate them. RCA and Mercury forced the pace of the change in 1954 when they announced they would send 45s instead of 78s to radio stations. With the 78 on its way out (it lasted until 1957 in the r&b market), the Battle of the Speeds was narrowed to a fight between the 45 and the LP.

For longer selections of music, especially for symphonies and classical music, the 45, though of superior sound quality, was not much better than the 78; it was still necessary to play six or seven 45s to hear one symphony that could be compressed on a single LP. This fact was not so obvious to certain RCA executives, to their misfortune. After a shakeup at RCA in 1950, an executive said to George Marek, the new classical chief, "45s play five minutes, and the break between them is only seven seconds. Does anybody really care about *seven seconds?*" "It's like this," replied Marek in an answer that reflected the humor of the time. "You're in bed with your best friend's wife, and every five minutes the door opens. It isn't open long, only seven seconds. . . ."

Columbia's liability in the competition was, from the beginning, the lack of a player to go along with the new LP record. In fact Columbia records division executives had been told in the late forties by their superiors in the parent corporation to go ahead with the LP without waiting for a corresponding player. The Columbia parent corporation was worried that the RCA combination of player and 45 record would make too great an inroad into the market if given a leeway of several years before a corresponding combination could be marketed by Columbia. The struggle was a bitter one at the time because it involved more than the record division at both companies. There was also the battle for the television market which involved far greater sums of money.*

At any rate, Columbia came up with a partial solution, an adapter. They were helped by New York City retailer Sam Goody who "gave away" an adapter to customers who purchased $25 worth of LPs at list price. Thousands of adapters were given away through the Goody stores or the chain's mail order department.

The end result was that both the LP and the 45 were established, the 45 for singles and the LP for album compilations and classical music. Mostly because of the introduction of high fidelity (hi-fi) and the establishment of two new speeds, sales of phonographs now picked up. Two-thirds more phonographs were sold in 1954 than in 1953, twice the number sold in 1952. The number was still far below the 1947 figure which reflected the postwar consumer boom, but it was still significant. Radio sales for the same 1952-54 period, for instance, remained the same. The growing number of phonographs in American homes served as a

---

*Such competition was repeated more recently with the introduction of alternate video systems by various companies. Although these struggles are irrational or wasteful on the face of it, they are "necessary" to a corporate system. If one corporation succeeds in monopolizing the market with its model of machinery, it is then in a position to control the lucrative and long-term business in spare parts, dictate the future development and improvements to the system, and keep ultimate control of the software line that accompanies the hardware. In addition the company will be able to license its system worldwide, and receive royalties.

base for record sales and specifically for rock'n'roll and the progressive rock explosion in the 1960s.

"Shoes, Records, It's All the Same": *Sam Goody Goes to Town*

The distribution of records in the early fifties was a staid business compared to what it became in the sixties. In the fifties the major companies—Columbia, RCA-Victor, Decca, and Capitol—distributed through factory-owned branches. With RCA this meant their franchised appliance dealers. Independent distributors handled the majority of independent record labels. Each distributor carried a number of labels such as Atlantic, Dot, and Jubilee, and sometimes larger firms such as MGM and London. These distributors were given what amounted to franchised rights to one area of the country.

By this time a specialized distributor called a "one-stop" had taken hold. One-stops carried singles from most companies and sold them to jukebox operators who did not want to go to the different distributors to get their records. Distribution is a function little talked about outside of business circles, but it is extremely important in the record business. Superior distribution was often one of the things that enabled a major to outsell an independent label when both came out with competing versions of the same song. Later, however, promotion by independent distributors was one of the factors responsible for the rise of the independent label.

The major change in retailing which occurred at this time was the rise of record discounting. For some time records had been mostly sold in small mom and pop record stores at "manufacturer's suggested retail price" or "list price." At the time this meant $3.98. The owners of these stores did little advertising and generally operated in the unsophisticated manner of the small businessmen they were.

The fifties brought broad changes to mechandising in the United States. Chain stores such as Sears, Korvettes, and Montgomery Ward were expanding, supermarkets were replacing corner groceries in cities and large towns, and the modern idea of cutting prices on merchandise and then mass-advertising the reduction in order to do volume business was taking hold.

In the retail record business the most famous of these new discounters was Sam Goody of New York City. Goody was a flamboyant merchant who started out selling used jukebox records as a sideline to his "tricks, games, and magic" store on Cortland Street. Goody was surprised at how well records sold, and began to pick up more of them through basement sales. After building up a clientele, he began to apply what he called general merchandising principles. "It could have been anything we sold," he said later, "shoes, records, it's all the same." Almost immediately Goody took 30 percent off manufacturer's list price, selling a $3.98 record for $2.80. Since the record cost him about $1.86, he still made a dollar off a $2.80 sale, or about 30 percent for himself. "If you take 30 percent off list price, it don't mean you're only making 10 percent—you're still making 30 percent. The other people could never see that." Goody managed to do a volume business by widespread advertising of sales and prices in newspapers, a new idea at the time. And he set up his store in such a way that overhead was kept at only 12-15 percent. Goody prospered, and record discounting spread.

Not without opposition, however. As the marginal mom and pop dealers began to be forced out of business, those remaining banded together in the Association of Record Dealers and charged "unfair trade practices." Goody pointed out that manufacturer's list prices were not government-regulated "ceiling prices," and in any case that fair trade laws would be impossible to enforce, given the large number of retail record stores. Fair trade law was never applied to the retail record business, but it may simply have been that the forces in favor of it were not strong enough politically to get government action. In other consumer industries, fair trade law was implemented at the behest of manufacturers in order to maintain artificially high consumer prices, and prevent competition. These industries were more powerful than the record business of the time.

Price-cutting continued—in Washington, D.C., some retailers even united with Columbia to give away one album with every three sold— until 1954 when price-cutting was pretty much institutionalized, and smaller dealers were no longer around to protest.

Victor sales in 1953 were 20 percent above those of the preceding year and overall industry sales were up slightly as well. Company head Mannie Sachs attributed the increase to additional multispeed turntables and to the heightened interest in records generated by high fidelity sound. It looked like the record business was ready to climb out of its six year stagnation. In a moment of optimism Sachs then predicted that sales might be $300 million by 1959. He was only off by $211 million (70 percent). Sales in 1959 were to reach $511 million. The expansion of the industry was soon to surprise even those who ran it.

2 ROCK'N'ROLL IS HERE TO STAY

The Record Business in the Fifties

The exuberance and spontaneity of rock'n'roll broke with a crash on the Lonely Crowd younger generation of the 1950s. America was a boring place to be. With the election of Eisenhower in 1952, the country entered an unprecedented period of conservative hegemony and control. The doddering general with a weak heart and bad golf game presided over an expanding Pax-American economy, the McCarthy era of anti-communist hysteria, a number of military interventions abroad in support of U.S. investment, and the necessary "containment" Cold War foreign policy. At home millions of children were growing up in a new place, suburbia. Each day their fathers commuted to the city centers to earn their daily bread and fuel the consumer economy. The postwar babies were barely walking, but their older brothers and sisters were already treading circles, and sensed a certain desperation in the future. While workers were supposedly moving into a happy middle-class existence, their new found affluence concealed an unrewarding lifestyle. It had no spirit. But rock'n'roll did. And it was to this energy that kids were attracted.

While this new music was brewing in the South and in the city ghettos in the years following World War II, the major companies happily issued mainstream pop by crooners like Frank Sinatra and Frankie

Laine. Half a decade passed before the major companies' concept of popular music was drowned by the increasing tide of rhythm and blues and rock'n'roll. Here's what happened.

During the war years rhythm and blues music, still called "race music" in the industry, expanded its audience among blacks. With the development of black-directed radio which could be heard by young whites as well, rhythm and blues music began to spill over into the white market. Eyeing the success of the independent companies in the expanded r&b market, the majors, who had controlled this market before World War II, tried to recapture the field by recreating r&b subsidiary labels and covering r&b songs with their own pop singers. These attempts failed, except for specific songs, and rhythm and blues music controlled by the independents continued to grow. In the middle fifties a number of country-based white musicians began to fuse black r&b with country music in a form then labeled "rockabilly" and now seen as pure rock'n'roll. Sun Records in Memphis, which discovered Elvis Presley, Carl Perkins, and Jerry Lee Lewis, pioneered this new rock aided by the Chicago-based blues company Chess, which recorded Chuck Berry. This new rock'n'roll was promoted by an increasing number of radio stations who played it and through integrated concerts. The development of pure rock'n'roll exploded the pop music scene and forced the major companies to try to adapt to the new music and the growing audiences. When they tried, however, they failed, until at least 1958 when the music, although not the independents, became somewhat calmer.

In that period which extended from about 1958 to the arrival of the Beatles in 1964, there *was* a softening of the rip-it-up rock'n'roll style of the Sun and Chess artists, although some valid styles of rock'n'roll such as city-based vocal harmony groups stayed popular. A number of interwoven factors were responsible for this lull, chief among them being the arrival of the television show American Bandstand.

Although the most important dynamic in the rock'n'roll period was the competition between the majors and the independent record companies, a few other developments affected the industry. Mail order record clubs were started, and the stereo record was introduced.

The Expansion of Rhythm and Blues

World War II created most of the conditions that led to the expansion of rhythm and blues music. Large numbers of black people moved out of the South and into the big city ghettos of the North and West; more than three times as many (1,260,000) left the South in the forties as in the decade before. Since the war caused a labor shortage, blacks were allowed to work in the relatively high-paying defense jobs. Full employment provided a new affluence that enabled black people to spend more money on entertainment.

The war also created a vacuum in the recording of rhythm and blues music. During the 1920s, as mentioned earlier, quite a few independent record companies serviced the black market along with the majors, but as the smaller companies were wiped out in the depression, control of the race field passed to the majors. Then during the war the majors abandoned black music along with the other specialty field of country and western music because of a shortage of shellac. They decided to keep up only their pop lines.

Coming at a time when there was considerable demand by the black community for records, the abandonment of the r&b field provided the opportunity for a large number of independent record companies to enter the business. According to some observers such as Nat Shapiro, some four hundred new companies were started in the forties. Probably about a hundred survived until 1952. The most important were Atlantic in New York, Savoy in Newark, New Jersey, King in Cincinnati, Chess in Chicago, Peacock in Houston, and Modern, Imperial, and Specialty in Los Angeles.

Although a few of the companies were started out of an interest in jazz and blues, most were started because the owners saw that it was a good way to make money. Besides the lack of competition from large companies and the rising demand for the records, the r&b field had another important attraction to it. Unlike in the pop field it was not really necessary to pay the artists any royalties. Composers' rights were bought for a few dollars or even signed away for the "privilege" of recording. Said Saul Bihari, the founder of Modern, which included on its roster Lightnin' Hopkins, John Lee Hooker, Etta James, and B.B. King, among others:

> We used to bring 'em in, give 'em a bottle of booze and say, "Sing me a song about your girl." Or, "Sing me a song about Christmas." They'd pluck around a little on their guitars, then say "O.K." and make up a song as they went along. We'd give them a subject and off they'd go. When it came time to quit, we'd give them a wave that they had ten seconds to finish.[1]

The majors had been no more principled when they controlled black music. Even the best musicians were only paid $5 for performing on one side of a record, $10 to the leader.

Even though the r&b independents were hampered by lack of funds for promotion and expansion, and were faced with inadequate, often regional distribution, profits on hits could be substantial. Modern sold its blues singles in the late forties for $1.05 each while the majors received 78 cents for their pop singles. Blacks were willing to pay more for their music.

"Rhythm and blues" was an umbrella term that covered several styles of black music in different areas of the country. In the most simple sense rhythm and blues was just that: prewar blues styles with a dancing rhythm added, but it included vocal harmony groups as well. Early r&b has been categorized in several ways, perhaps overcategorized since audiences most often did not make the many distinctions among styles that blues historians have. To audiences there were really only three kinds of r&b: the cool West Coast sounds that usually employed smooth singers, horns, and supple rhythm sections, the electric blues of the Muddy Waters — John Lee Hooker variety. and the vocal harmony groups like the Dominos or Clyde McPhatter and the Drifters. To many independent companies there was not much difference at all. Said Don Robey, the founder of Duke-Peacock in Houston, "I don't believe there's any difference between blues and r&b; it's just that what we release, by the time it gets to New York, it's something else. Sometimes it's even called folk music." To the larger music industry and to the white audience, "rhythm and blues" was simply a euphemism for "race music," any music directed to the black audience and designed for it.

In addition to the migration of black people into the cities and the abandonment of the race field to the independent companies, the rise of radio stations beamed at the black community expanded the audience for rhythm and blues music. R&b stations sprang up in the war years because blacks en masse were earning higher wages, although as always, of course, still far less than white workers. The first advertisers on the stations were spare rib joints and hair grease manufacturers. These stations broadcast blues, jazz, gospel, and the various styles of r&b, and naturally stimulated the sales of the independent record companies.

The growth of r&b stations paralleled a rise in the number of other nonnetwork stations in the late forties and fifties. Television, which was being mass-marketed for the first time in the early fifties, forced many radio stations, especially the network ones, to become more local in character. The national audience was switching to TV.

Radio more than any other factor allowed black music to spill over into the white community. For the increasing number of white teenagers dissatisfied with a diet of Rosemary Clooney and Frankie Laine, a different world was available with a turn of the dial. It was impossible to segregate the airwaves. White teenagers began tuning in to the r&b shows of Hunter Hancock in Los Angeles, Dewey Phillips in Memphis, Poppa Stoppa in New Orleans, John Sharp Williams in Oakland, Daddy-O-Daily in Chicago, and Gene Noble in Nashville.

The exposure of r&b on the radio soon led to a phenomenon that was to change the record business drastically: white teenagers began to buy rhythm and blues records. This occurred as early as 1952 in Los Angeles and Cleveland, and slightly earlier in the South. In May of 1952 the Dolphin Record Store in Los Angeles reported that 40 percent of their business was being done with whites, whereas a few months before it had been almost exclusively done with blacks. The biggest r&b sellers among whites shopping at Dolphin were instrumental. Early records that were popular in both white and black markets included Fats Domino's "The Fat Man" for Imperial in 1950, Jackie Brenston's "Rocket 88" for Modern in 1951, Lloyd Price's "Lawdy Miss Clawdy" for Specialty in 1952, Joe Turner's "Chains of Love" (1951), "Sweet Sixteen" (1952), and "Honey Hush" (1953) and Sticks McGhee's "Drinkin' Wine Spo-dee-o-dee," all for Atlantic.

Ahmet Goes to the Mountain and Atlantic Crosses Over

Perhaps the most important independent record company active in the rhythm and blues field was Atlantic Records in New York. The company has remained extremely important in the record industry, profiting from the expansion of r&b to whites in the Freed era, and later from the recycling of blues from Britain, and the rise of progressive rock in the United States in the late sixties.

Atlantic Records was started by Ahmet Ertegun and Herb Abramson in October 1947 in New York. Unlike the founders of many other independent record companies, Ertegun was hardly a scrapping record store owner or a penniless immigrant. He was the son of a prominent Turkish diplomat who was an ambassador to the United States in the forties. He and his brother Nesuhi, who joined the company in 1955 to head the jazz division, were avid fans of jazz and blues. They hosted jazz concerts in the Turkish Embassy, and amassed some 30,000 records in their private collection. Their love for the music gave them an intuitive feel for what was good, and also for what was commercial in the r&b field. Their own taste gave them quite an advantage over the men who started other r&b labels simply to cash in on an obvious market. .

Abramson had been an A&R man at National Records, a successful early independent, while he was still attending NYU. He had signed Joe Turner and the Ravens for National. He had also founded Jubilee Records. Abramson was called into the army as a dentist in 1953—he had several talents—and Jerry Wexler was brought into Atlantic, originally to handle administrative work. Wexler had been an assistant to Abe Ollman at Robbins Music and also a member of the *Billboard* staff. Wexler soon became producer/A&R chief along with Ahmet Ertegun. Abramson sold his interest in 1958 and formed Triumph Records.

Ertegun and Abramson started the company out of the living room of

Ertegun's one-bedroom apartment in a Manhattan hotel before moving to slightly more comfortable offices in the same building as Stillman's Gym on Eighth Avenue. The company's first releases were Tiny Grimes' "Old Black Magic" and Joe Morris' "The Spider." The early records were mostly instrumental. Their first hit was "Drinkin' Wine Spo-dee-o-dee" by Sticks McGhee, and their first "star" or repeating singer was Ruth Brown, who began with "So Long."

By 1953 they had had a string of hits with artists like Ruth Brown, who in addition to "So Long" recorded "Teardrops from My Eyes" (1951) and "5-10-15 Hours" (1952); LaVerne Baker; The Drifters— "Money Honey"; Joe Turner; and the Clovers—"Don't You Know I Love You" and "One Mint Julep" (1952). Since many of their most popular r&b artists represented a middle ground between country blues and sophisticated jazz big-band blues, neither of which became popular with white audiences, they were in a strong position when r&b records began to cross over into the white market. In the years 1954-56 many of Atlantic's records began to go pop: the Chords' "Sh-Boom," LaVerne Baker's "Tweedle Dee" and "Tra La La," Ruth Brown's "Oh What a Dream" (1954) and "Lucky Lips" (1956) and Joe Turner's famous "Shake, Rattle, and Roll" (1954). In 1950 Atlantic had three records that made the Top 10 in the r&b market, but by 1956 the company had seventeen Top 10 hits, or slightly over 20 percent of the r&b market for that year.

It's not clear if Ertegun began to direct his artists toward the white pop market, but from the beginning he strove to make them commercial, and they began to cross over. He recalled in 1967:

> I said to Ruth Brown "Let's sing some blues" and she told me she didn't like blues. So I had artists like her sing one blues song for me, as a favor. They had that church feeling. As a result the blues records we made with Ruth came out like urbanized, watered-down versions of real blues. But we discovered white kids started buying these records because the real blues were too hard for them to swallow. Distributors started telling us they were selling these records pop.[2]

Atlantic's forte from the beginning has been production work. It has been able to take artists that had been recording for other companies, like Ray Charles, Ivory Joe Hunter, Chuck Willis, Joe Turner, and Aretha Franklin, and give them distinctive new styles. With Turner and Franklin the company was able to give them their first real successes. In the fifties Atlantic contracted Lieber and Stoller to do some production work, and they turned out a long series of hits with the Coasters. Tom Dowd was engineer in the fifties. In the sixties they added younger producers such as Bert Berns, although Wexler has stayed on with what seems like unbroken success. In the fifties the company was also blessed with extremely capable session musicians: King Curtis and Sam Taylor on sax, Mickey Baker on guitar, and Henry Van Wells on piano, along with a few others.

The Erteguns and Wexler enjoyed a reputation of getting along well with artists, white or black. "They love Ahmet," said Phil Spector in *Rolling Stone* years later, "because he looks like Lenin, he has his beard and he's sophisticated and he comes on and he jives all these cats and he goes to Harlem and he cooks and he smokes the shit and everybody digs him."

Ertegun's credibility gave Atlantic certain financial leverage with black musicians who had to deal mostly with blatantly dishonest managers and record executives. Spector tells another story in the same interview:

> Several years back we were all sitting around with some colored group, and one of them said, "Shit man, your contract ain't worth shit." We were in a restaurant and Ahmet looks around to make sure nobody'd hear us. The guy said, "Mercury gonna give me seven percent, you only give me five percent. That's like jive-ass." Ahmet said, "Not so loud." And he said, "Yeah man, I can't sign your contract for five percent when I can get me seven percent over at Mercury."
>
> And I was just sittin' back waitin' for what Ahmet was gonna say to this cat. The guy has the Mercury contract with him, and it does say seven percent. And he's got Atlantic's cockamamie contract for five percent. Now he's got Ahmet up a wall, he's trapped, and Ahmet knows he's trapped, and we're all sittin' around, and Ahmet hit him with a line: Ahmet said, "Man, listen man, you know what. I gonna give you 15 percent, but I ain't gonna pay you." The guy said, "What?" Ahmet said, "That's what they gonna do. They gonna give you seven percent but they not gonna pay you, and I gonna give you five percent and pay you. Now that's a big difference isn't it?" The guy said, "That's right—never thought of it that way. That makes a lot of sense. I'm gonna sign with you, Ahmet."

Ertegun also wrote a few songs in the early days of the company when he was still producing. He reversed his name to "Nugetre" on the credit line. Two of the songs were "The Mess Around" done by Ray Charles and "Chains of Love" by Joe Turner.

Although based in New York, Atlantic seems to have paid particular notice to Southern rock'n'roll and r&b and has often made use of studios and musicians in New Orleans and Atlanta as well as entered into production agreements with independent producer/managers in Memphis (Stax, which gave them Otis Redding and others) and Macon (Capricorn with the Allman Brothers and many others).

As rock'n'roll became popular Atlantic's records were often covered by the major companies. The most obvious example was Bill Haley's cover for Decca of Joe Turner's "Shake, Rattle, and Roll." Atlantic was flexible enough to contract at least one white rock'n'roller, however — Bobby Darin, who created a series of hits for them in the late fifties.

The company made good use of its network of independent distributors until 1967 when it merged with Warner Brothers and melded into the Warner branch distribution system. The independent distributors did most of the work required to promote Atlantic's records because the company had too few people to hire promotion men itself, although Wexler had a reputation of talking for hours on the phone to key disc jockeys. Independent distribution was the reason for having the subsidiary labels Atco and Cat. Explained Wexler, "Suppose you have ten records, all with good potential. It would be a lot to expect one distributor to make them all go. But divide them into two groups of five each, with each group to a different distributor, and you've got a considerably better chance." Atlantic maintained a careful billing policy in the fifties, unlike another successful independent, Dot, and offered records on consignment only when they were trying to beat a cover of one of their records by a major. This policy, along with the inducement of a steady stream of hits, prevented them from being caught short, as many independents were, by independent distributors or retailers who took too long to pay.

The Majors Respond (Sort Of)

By 1952 an estimated $15 million worth of records were being sold in the expanded rhythm and blues market, and by the end of 1954 a number of r&b records had had significant success in the white pop market as well. Southern distributors, especially, were clamoring for r&b records. The majors felt they had to react. After all, hadn't they completely dominated the "race" field before they abandoned it to the indies (independents) during the war?

Columbia switched the distribution on its Okeh subsidiary to independent distributors, thinking that independent distribution was the mainstay of the smaller record companies. Decca reactivated the Brunswick label for rhythm and blues records. RCA-Victor formed Groove, an r&b subsidiary in 1953. It had on its roster Mickey and Sylvia, Piano Red, and the Du Droppers, but never developed anyone who could compete with the singers and musicians on independent labels. Almost annually the company announced a talent search or a stepped-up release schedule or a new "close-to-the-ground" label head such as Roy Clark, formerly their Southern field man, but they were never able to recapture the position they had held in the race field. This failure was especially irking to Columbia and Victor because they had extensive catalogues of blues music from the twenties and thirties. A few of their older artists could be repackaged, like Bessie Smith, but the new black artists and the white teenagers preferred modern, urbanized rhythm and blues music.*

At the end of 1954, independent companies retained near total control of the r&b market. The independents had twenty-three of the Top 30 hits that year. (Atlantic and its Cat subsidiary had eleven, Federal-Deluxe four, Herald two, Chess two, and Imperial, Rama, and Vee Jay each had one. Columbia's Epic label managed three hits, and its Okeh label got one, while Mercury obtained two.) By 1956 the majors had virtually given up on r&b. At the end of the year Victor closed down its Groove label, not having had a hit in two years.

Although the majors were unable to recapture the r&b field, they managed to find a temporary way out of the crossover problem through the practice of "covering" r&b hits, or recording them with their own pop artists. "The thinking of both the Victor and Columbia heads," reported *Billboard* in 1955, "is that if this was what the kids wanted, this was what they were going to get." The strategy made sense since the majors had superior distribution system that could often get their version of a song to stores before the independents, and because network disc jockeys (although not the newer breed) agreed to play the major cover versions.

Several dozen songs were successfully covered by the majors in the next few years. RCA began by covering "Kokomo" by Gene and Eunice (Combo) with Perry Como. Columbia covered the same song with a version by Tony Bennett. Columbia and Victor as corporations were so reluctant to have anything to do with "rock'n'roll," which is what a white cover of a black song was at this point, that they were rarely successful even with cover versions. Mercury and Decca had the most luck of the majors, probably because they had always been run in a looser fashion that resembled the independents in certain ways.**

Most covers lacked the feeling and the sense of the audience that the originals conveyed. An important exception was Haley's treatment of "Shake, Rattle, and Roll." It combined fast country rhythms, themselves r&b influenced, with Joe Turner's lackadaisical blues, and completely changed the tone of the song. The difference was the difference between what was to become "pure rock'n'roll," or rockabilly, and older r&b.

Cover versions were sometimes aided by the owners of the independent labels that had produced the original versions. Since these owners were

---

*Black artists that did not "sound black," like Nat Cole (Capitol), the Mills Brothers, and the Ink Spots (both Decca),presented no problems for the majors that signed them, but they appealed to the mainstream pop audience, not the audience of teenagers and blacks, and therefore did not solve the real problem.

**See Chapter 7, Black Roots, White Fruits, for more on covers.

often holders of the publishing rights to the songs, they encouraged the major companies to do cover versions in order to obtain the far greater royalties from performances, record sales, and sheet music sales available in the white market. Such practices, of course, kept the black version of the song out of the pop market and denied the original singer the royalties that would have come if the original record company/publisher had pushed the first version as a potential crossover. The practice also angered the company's independent distributors, who watched as the major company's version distributed by factory branches beat out the original.

Covering rhythm and blues songs was becoming an inadequate solution for the majors by 1956, when songs by the original singers began to make the pop charts in significant numbers. At that point the majors were faced with a situation far more distasteful to them than a widened market for rhythm and blues. A new form, rock'n'roll, was emerging along with r&b, and was threatening to become *the* pop mainstream, edging out the "good music" that had long provided the majors with their dominant position in the industry. The majors were forced to make additional commercial adaptations when that occurred, but that story later.

"Rockabilly" exploded onto the pop market in the middle fifties.

Pure Rock'n'Roll: *Haley, Berry, Presley; Chess and Sun*

Bill Haley was one of the most effective popularizers of rock'n'roll. He performed the first songs that were a hybrid of rhythm and blues and country, saw them to the top of the pop charts, and then promoted them in three movies that spread rock'n'roll worldwide.

Haley came from Detroit, but played standard country and western music of the Bob Wills western swing variety, calling his bands The Four Aces of Western Swing and The Saddlemen before amalgamating elements of rhythm and blues and country into a clear, tight-sounding brand of rock'n'roll. "The style we played back in '47, '48, '49 was a combination of country and western, Dixieland, and the old style rhythm and blues," he said in 1952.[3] "I felt that if I could take a Dixieland tune and drop the first and third beats and accentuate the second and fourth, and add a beat the listeners could clap to as well as dance, this would be what we were after."[4] This was what white teenagers turned out to be "after" and Haley's "Crazy, Man, Crazy" made the national charts in 1953, as did "Shake, Rattle, and Roll" in 1954. In 1955 he put out "Dim Dim the Lights," which became the first rock'n'roll record by a white artist to penetrate the black rhythm and blues charts. The black audience preferred original r&b with a few other exceptions, like Johnny Ray's "Cry." (Black artists had already made the r&b charts with a few records that legitimately could be called rock'n'-roll, such as "Gee" by the Crows, released in 1954.)

When *Blackboard Jungle* was released in February 1955, Haley's time had finally come. The movie contained a hit "Rock Around the Clock" which had been released the year before without great success. But when the movie tied teen rebellion to rock'n'roll, the record became the Number One pop hit of the year. The movie was followed by a second film, *Rock Around the Clock,* which caused riots (good natured ones by today's standards) in New Jersey and London, and grossed five times what it cost to make in less than a year. *Rock Around the Clock* told how Haley and his band were discovered and put on national TV by Alan Freed, who played himself in the picture.

Haley recorded all but his earliest hits while at Decca. There is some doubt whether Decca consciously signed Haley for his new rock'n'roll or whether they admired his country playing instead. After Haley, however, they knew enough to tie into another rockabilly, the clear sounding Buddy Holly, and his group The Crickets, both of whom released records for Decca subsidiaries beginning in 1957. Haley was nearly middle aged before he became the first "rock star," far too old to inspire hysteria. Although his songs were somewhat contrived after the first few, it was his music that put him over. At about the same time, one of the most accomplished and outrageous of all rock'n'rollers was producing his first instant hits: Chuck Berry. Berry had only one problem: he was black. But for that he would have probably rivaled Elvis Presley as king of the fifties rock'n'rollers.

Believe What Leonard Tells You

Chess Records, where Berry recorded, was a Chicago blues company started in 1949 by two Polish immigrants named Leonard and Phil Chess. The brothers operated a series of wide-open after-hours joints, the last being the Macamba Lounge, that played jazz and bar blues. One night a Hollywood agent dropped by to hear one of the singers, Andrew Tibbs, and Leonard Chess decided that "if he was good enough for Hollywood," he could put him on record "himself." The result was a moderate although controversial hit (flip side "Bilbo's Dead" was banned in the South), and the Aristocrat label was formed. On the advice of a Southern distributor the name was changed to Chess in 1949.

Chess's first hit, their second release, was a country blues number called "Rolling Stone" by Muddy Waters. It sold well for a country blues record, about 70,000 copies, much less than a current r&b hit would have. The success of the record prompted Chess to begin his car tours of the South in search of new, mostly rural talent. Legend has it that he sold records out of the trunk of his car, and muddied his boots making recordings between the rows, but what he mostly did was make contracts, often with small town record dealers who kept an eye out for local talent. He bought the rights to Fats Washington's "I'll Be Home" from Stan "The Record Man" Lewis in Shreveport, Louisiana, for instance. He had the Flamingoes cut the song on Chess's Checker subsidiary when he got home and the song became an r&b hit which was soon covered by Pat Boone who turned it into a million-selling record in the pop market.

As Chess's influence in what was to be called the Chicago bar blues style grew, he signed Little Walter, Howlin' Wolf, and Sonny Boy Williamson in addition to Muddy Waters. In 1954 the company expanded into the more updated r&b market by releasing the Flamingoes' "I'll Be Home" and the Moonglows' "Sincerely." Both were sentimental tunes done in vocal group style, and both were covered, the first by Boone, the second by the McGuire Sisters on Decca's subsidiary Coral. The Chesses had always shown considerable savvy in the behind-the-scenes dealing of the music business ever since their Chicago club days, and they enlisted the help of Alan Freed in promoting their records. He had originally steered these two groups to Chess.

Leonard, the dominant brother, has been credited with musical "genius" by some later writers, but his abilities actually lay in more commercial areas, especially in getting songs played one way or another. The company did pioneer a number of recording techniques that gave Chess its distinctive sound. They got the first echo chamber effect by hanging a mike in a bathroom on Junior Mance's "Foolish Heart," and they produced a tenth of a second delay by hanging a sewer pipe from the ceiling. But some effects were completely accidental, as Phil Chess admitted later, and the others may have been created by staff engineers like Willie Dixon. Ahmet Ertegun has said that Chess got involved for the money, and developed some taste along the way. "You see," said Marshal Chess recently, "my father was a music lover in a very strange way. People used to talk, they'd think he was kind of a freak, because all he'd ever want to do was go to these little funky clubs that no white person would ever dream of going to, to hear new acts, to buy new talent. I don't think he ever thought of himself as a music lover. But he was in his own way."[5]

Singers like Johnny Shines and Berry credited Chess with having a special knack of bringing out the best in his singers, but Etta James, who joined the label in 1960, recording "Sunday Kind of Love" and "Tell Mama" for them, among others, is more bitter:

> The Chess brothers didn't know A from Z in a beat. Leonard Chess would get in the booth with me while I was recording, and when I would get to a part where he thought I should squawl or scream *wheeaow!* he'd punch me in the side, I mean literally *punch* me. Or he'd pinch me real hard, so I'd go

yeeaow! And whatever tune had the most "oooch" or "eeech" or whatever, that's the one he thought was going to be the hit.

Then he'd sit there and listen to the playback, and he wouldn't pat his foot until I'd see him sneaking a look at *my* foot. He'd have to look around and see if my foot was patting. And sometimes, just for evilness, I wouldn't pat my foot. And if he couldn't see it patting, he'd say, "Etta, I don't think that tune's any good." And then I'd wait till some old jive tune that wasn't anything came on, and I'd pat my foot and say, "How do you like that one?" And he'd say, "That's it! That's going to be a hit record! Believe what Leonard tells you." He knew nothing about it.[6]

Whatever his faults it seems clear that Chess could recognize talent. When Chuck Berry walked into the Chess offices on the recommendation of Muddy Waters, who had heard him play the day before, Berry's "Ida Red" (backed with a blues number, "Wee Wee Hours") had been turned down at both Capitol and Mercury. The other companies felt that "Ida Red" was too country sounding, two decades before Charlie Pride, for a black man to do. Leonard Chess told Berry to give it a "bigger beat," and they changed the title to "Maybellene," taking the name from a hair creme bottle.

"I liked it, thought it was something new," said Chess a few weeks before he died. "I was going to New York anyway, and I took a dub to Alan (Freed) and said 'Play this.' The dub didn't have Chuck's name on it or nothing. By the time I got back to Chicago, Freed had called a dozen times, saying it was his biggest record ever. History, the rest, y'know? Sure, 'Wee Wee Hours,' that was on the back side of the release, was a good tune too, but the kids wanted the big beat, cars, and young love. It was a trend and we jumped on it."[7]

Berry's best-selling hit (assuming Chess's tally was not understated) was not "Maybellene" but one of the teen-directed songs he turned out a few years later: "School Days" in 1957, "Sweet Little Sixteen" and "Johnny B. Goode" in 1958, all of which reached the weekly Top 10 in the pop charts. Berry was a city kid from St. Louis, the son of a carpenter, and was not rooted in the rural past as were the country blues artists at Chess. Like Presley he seemed able to relate to white teen culture, black r&b, and country western music with a success matched only by Haley and the Sun artists Carl Perkins and Jerry Lee Lewis. Little Richard is perhaps the only black rock'n'roller to come close. All of these singers came out of Southern backgrounds that mixed black and white cultures and music in ways not possible before the fifties.

Berry's career was cut short in 1962 when he was convicted of a violation of the Mann Act and sent to the penitentiary. He had done no more than bring a girl back with him from a tour in Mexico, but since she was underage and the court wanted to make an example of a black rock'n'roll singer, he was convicted. It took two trials. The first was vacated because of the prejudice shown by the judge, who referred to Berry as "this Negro." The underlying meaning of the conviction was shown in a headline of the time, cited by Michael Lydon. It read "Rock'n'Roll Singer Lured Me to St. Louis, Says 14 Year Old." Berry's songs continued to be recorded, and he staged a comeback in 1972 with a song as commercially successful as it was puerile: "My Ding-a-Ling." But the trial and his experience in jail seem to have left him somewhat paranoid.

Chess recorded other successful artists such as Bo Diddley, and even Ramsey Lewis, but the company's peak had come with Berry. Leonard died, and Phil sold the company in 1969 to GRT, the tape manufacturer, for around $10 million. Phil remained at the company for a while working under Leonard's son Marshal, who had been named president by GRT, then left to head WVON, the leading Chicago soul station his brother had bought in 1963 (paying cash in the forthright Chess manner—1 million dollars in $10,000 bills). Marshal Chess left GRT later to form the Rolling Stones label.

Along with Presley, Chuck Berry had the greatest influence on rock'n'roll of any fifties singer. But for the mass audience of the fifties it was Elvis that symbolized the complete arrival of rock'n'roll.

Sam Phillips Finds His White Boy

"If only I could find a white man who had the Negro sound and the Negro feel, I could make a million dollars," Sam Phillips used to say, according to his secretary.* Phillips, owner of Sun Records in Memphis, found his white boy in Elvis Presley. And before he was through he had found a few more in Carl Perkins and Jerry Lee Lewis. Phillips was an ex-radio engineer from Florence, Alabama. He set up a small studio in Memphis in 1950 and began to record musicians from Memphis and the South such as B.B. King, Walter Horton, Howlin' Wolf, Little Junior Parker, and Bobby "Blue" Bland. He sold the tapes to Modern Records in Los Angeles and later to Chess. He met Leonard Chess on one of Chess's recording trips through the South. In fact he sent masters of Howlin' Wolf to Modern's RPM label and to Chess at the same time. Both labels put out the records, and Modern angrily dropped Phillips, who then started Sun. Modern hired Ike Turner, who was not yet twenty, to replace him.

Phillips produced primarily blues records, releasing thirty by artists

---

*This account of Phillips follows the one by Peter Guralnick in his short chapter, "Boppin' the Blues: Sam Phillips and the Sun Sound," part of his excellent book of profiles on the Chicago and Memphis blues scenes, *Feel Like Going Home.*

such as Rufus Thomas and Little Junior Parker, before he recorded "That's All Right" (backed with Bill Monroe's "Blue Moon of Kentucky") with Elvis Presley. "That's All Right" was written by a black sharecropper named Arthur "Big Boy" Crudup, who penned a few more hits like "Rock Me Mama" and "Everything's All Right," none of which he received any royalties from. In discovering Presley, and later Perkins, Lewis, Melvin Yelvington, and others, Phillips tapped into the first generation of white Southern singers that had been influenced by black blues and hillbilly music. Haley, who was not from the South, had put the styles together to a certain extent but never managed the feeling that the Sun artists were able to bring to rock'n'roll.

Each of Phillips' singers had grown up in an environment that mixed black and white cultures to a degree unknown in the North, and rare before the fifties in the South. This crossover of cultures created the conditions that gave rise to rockabilly, and through it to the dominant strain of rock'n'roll itself. Presley was raised in Mississippi until his late teens when his family moved to Memphis in search of work. Later he described growing up:

> I'd play along with the radio or phonograph, and taught myself the chord positions. We were a religious family, going round together to sing at camp meetings and revivals, and I'd take my guitar with us when I could. I also dug the real low-down Mississippi singers, mostly Big Bill Broonzy and Big Boy Crudup, although they would scold me at home for listening to them. "Sinful music," the townsfolk in Memphis said it was. Which never bothered me, I guess.[8]

Perkins, who learned guitar from a champion black cotton picker, and Jerry Lee Lewis, who hung out at all-black concert clubs as a boy, were also heavily influenced by black music and culture.

Ralph Bass, an A&R man for years at Chess, told recently what the breaking down of racial barriers was like in Southern concert clubs like Haney's Big House, where Lewis used to go:

> When I used to go on the road with the black acts I was handling in the forties they didn't let whites into the clubs. Then they got "white spectator tickets" for the worst corner of the joint, no chairs and no dancing, and the tickets cost more too. But they had to keep the white kids out, and by the early fifties they'd have white nights sometimes, or they'd put a rope across the middle of the floor. The blacks on one side, whites on the other digging how the blacks were dancing and copying them. Then, hell, the rope would come down, and they'd all be dancing together.[9]

Presley had been coming to the Sun studio which was fifteen blocks from his home for a year and a half before Phillips did a session with him. Presley sang a country tune which, he said later, sounded terrible.

Then Phillips called him up one day and asked if he wanted to try again, this time with some blues songs. "I hung up and ran fifteen blocks to Mr. Phillips' office before he'd gotten off the line—or so he tells me. We talked about the Crudup records I knew—'Cool Disposition,' 'Rock Me, Mama,' 'Hey, Mama,' 'Everything's All Right,' and others, but settled for 'That's All Right,' one of my top favorites. . . ."[10] Legend has it that it was produced during a break, when Presley and the session men were feeling relaxed.

The record was a hit in the country market, but it caused a little confusion among djs and others; was the singer white or "colored"? Dewey Phillips, who broke the record in Memphis on his Red Hot and Blue Show, put Presley on the air to tell the folks he had gone to Humes High School, which was all white. "I wanted to get that out," said the dj, "because a lot of people listening had thought he was colored."

Presley produced five records for Sun, five sides of blues-influenced rock'n'roll and five straight country. The records sold well in the country market and Presley was beginning to make a name for himself— shrewdly managed by (honorary) Colonel Tom Parker, who had graduated from the carnival business, where he had once sold painted sparrows as canaries, to managing country singers. By the end of 1955 Presley had attracted enough attention that Steve Sholes, RCA-Victor's A&R man for the South, recommended that the company buy up his contract from Sun. RCA paid $35,000* for Presley and acquired rights to five unreleased Sun pressings as well. Presley got a pink Cadillac in the deal.

Why Phillips sold Presley is not completely clear, but the money was a lot for the time and Phillips needed it to provide a secure base for his operations. (To raise money for his business ventures, Phillips had once tried to sell the whole Sun roster, including Presley, to Chess Records. They refused. "We didn't consider ourselves a hillbilly label at the time," said Phil Chess later.) Probably Phillips thought he could repeat his success with Presley using other Southern white singers that were trooping to Memphis on Presley's heels.

His next rock'n'roll success came in 1956 with Carl Perkins' "Blue Suede Shoes," an incredible high-energy rock'n'roll song that was the first million seller in the rockabilly style. Phillips followed that with Johnny Cash's "I Walk the Line," a mournful country number he pepped up in the studio, and then with Jerry Lee Lewis' "Whole Lotta Shakin' Goin' On," which was a big hit in 1957. "Blue Suede Shoes" and "Whole Lotta Shakin'," along with Presley's first song for RCA, "Heartbreak Hotel," were the first songs to reach high in all three

*Different figures have been bandied about. This is the one RCA quotes.

42

musical fields at the same time—pop, r&b, and country. Presley has been able to sell well in the r&b and soul market ever since, with more consistency than any other white singer.

In the next several years the major Sun artists left for larger labels. Cash and Perkins went to Columbia, Lewis to Mercury, and Presley, of course, to RCA. Phillips, who had been one of the original investors in the Holiday Inn chain of motels, started another label in the sixties called Holiday Inn Records, but for the most part tended to his other business interests.

RCA, which swore just months before they signed Presley that the company would never touch rock'n'roll, promoted their new star in all three musical markets. Presley's first release for them, "Heartbreak Hotel," became the number one record in the country. RCA used television to break Presley nationwide. He appeared for six weeks on the Jackie Gleason show, next with Milton Berle, then with Steve Allen (who told him to appear in evening dress and not to wriggle), and finally with Ed Sullivan. Sullivan had first turned Presley down, branding him as "unfit for a family audience," but then reversed himself when it became impossible to avoid the phenomenon of Elvis' popularity. Sullivan paid him $50,000 for three short appearances, but filmed him from the waist up. He performed "Love Me Tender" on the show, and within a month RCA had orders for a million copies even though they had not yet pressed the record.

Presley's records sold so fast that RCA had to use the pressing plants of rival companies to catch up on the orders! The sale of Presley's records soon accounted for nearly 25 percent of Victor's overall sales, and carried the company through the latter part of the fifties, much as the Beatles were to carry Capitol in later years.

A Man Who Loved *April In Paris* Is Not Going to Like *Louie, Louie*

By the end of 1956 rock'n'roll records, consisting of rhythm and blues crossovers and rockabilly songs, were accounting for better than a third of the Top 10 hits, according to the *Billboard* charts. Of the nineteen records in the Top 10, ten were from independent companies, and nine from major companies. That the majors were able to do so well was almost entirely attributable to Elvis Presley on RCA and Bill Haley, who was still riding on his "Rock Around the Clock" image on Decca.

But by the end of the next year, the majors had only half as many rock'n'roll hits as the independents, fourteen compared to twenty-nine. What was even worse from the majors' point of view, was that the independent companies were beginning to dominate the entire pop singles charts. In 1957 there were already more pop singles by the independents than by the majors, and by the end of 1959 there were almost twice as many singles hits coming from the independent companies as there were hits from the majors. The extent of the inroad made by independents can be seen by comparing the situation in the years 1946-52. In those years only five of 162 million-selling records were produced by independent record companies.

The threat posed by the independents was not yet a critical one because only a part of the majors' profits came from the sales of pop singles. The market for albums, established by the major firms who had introduced the LP, was still firmly in their hands because they had the resources to produce and market them. Big albums often cost $50,000 to produce, and sometimes took years to return the capital invested in them. Albums represented over half the dollar volume of the industry in 1955. Classical records, which still accounted for significant sales and for a greater share of the market than they were to hold a decade later, were monopolized by the major companies. And foreign sales, always important, were almost completely taken care of by the majors who had long been used to dealing on the international level.

The pop market was becoming more sophisticated, however. The industry sales surge which began in 1955 was due in large part to the increased prosperity in the nation that allowed the mass of Americans to spend more on entertainment. Teenagers now had money and were becoming a separate group of consumers. Younger buyers preferred rock music. The increased number of million-selling singles was attributed by the industry to the buying power of teenagers. A best seller now sold a million copies whereas just a year or two before a top selling record had usually sold only 500,000 or so. The pop rock'n'roll market was where record industry profits would come from in the future.

So, in 1956 or thereabouts it was becoming clear that the majors would have to respond to independent record companies. However, the resistance to rock'n'roll music was so strongly felt at the older companies that they were unable to catch up with the independents in the rock field until the mid-sixties, when they simply bought them out. In the fifties the majors tried everything—"Everything," said Atlantic president Ahmet Ertegun later, "but the music."

To compete with the independents in the pop singles market, the majors streamlined distribution so that, at RCA for instance, delivery could be made ten days after cutting instead of in the two or more weeks it had taken before. The number of singles released was reduced so that supposedly more attention could be given to each record released. (This method had to be abandoned by most companies because they came to feel that they had a better chance at coming up with a success if they applied a hit or miss method, even if this was wasteful, since they had great difficulty in predicting hits beforehand.)

44

The majors restructured their pop divisions, separating the production and marketing of singles from that of albums. This made sense because at the time pop singles sold to a younger audience than did albums. Once separated, single records could be promoted in ways that duplicated the aggressive methods of the independent companies and their distributors. The majors began to send promotion men to radio stations and to sponsor radio contests. Their methods were still far more subdued than those of the independents, especially in regard to payola; but to compete they had to at least participate. The most reluctant company was RCA, which seemed to be worried about possible government or stockholder dissatisfaction over illicit promo methods.

Mercury began to adopt the concept of "spreading" hits that had been employed by some of the independents and by the country divisions of several of the majors. Instead of promoting a single simultaneously in all thirty of their designated market areas, the company began to limit initial promotion to several cities until the record became successful, at which point it would be "spread" to other markets.* Both independents and majors began to send in-store displays to retail outlets in an attempt to influence radio playlists that were based on local sales. More money was spent on all forms of advertising in these efforts, but radio became the most widely used medium starting in the early sixties.

In a taste of the future RCA initiated an independent production deal with Moe Gale in 1957. He was to produce "r&b with a pop appeal." After disbanding the unsuccessful Groove label RCA was trying a new tack in the r&b field. Harnessing outside production talent was to serve the majors well a decade later, but nothing much came of this early attempt. Columbia made some of these changes but did not worry much about pop singles in these years because they were doing so well merchandising the albums they had introduced.

In hindsight the simplest solution to the threat posed by the independents would have been for the majors to have begun to produce rock'n'roll in a big way. But with a few exceptions—Presley at RCA, Haley and Buddy Holly at Decca, the Big Bopper at Mercury, Gene Vincent at Capitol—rock'n'roll was adamantly resisted by the big companies.

There were a number of reasons why the majors opposed rock'n'roll. The first was on aesthetic grounds, inane as that might seem now. The executives at RCA and Columbia, especially, felt that Cole Porter songs

---

Billboard noted in a survey carried out with New York University in November 1958, that 25 percent of all record sales were made in New York and California, while these states accounted for only 20 percent of other business sales. Six states accounted for 51 percent of all record sales: New York, California, Illinois, Pennsylvania, Ohio, and Michigan.

or classical pieces were simply "better" than rock'n'roll. Their taste was upper class and European-directed. "You couldn't expect a man who loved 'April in Paris' or who had recorded Hudson DeLange in the thirties when he was beginning in the business to like lyrics like 'I wanna boogie your woogie,' and 'Louie, Louie,' " said Ahmet Ertegun recently. "He had always thought race music and hillbilly were corny, and so he thought rock'n'roll was for morons."

Commercially, the majors were also committed to mainstream pop music. Dozens of artists were under five year contracts; producers and A&R men were trained in middle-of-the-road music (MOR). It would have seemed risky to switch to a type of music that had only recently "surfaced" and might well prove to be a fad. This was a fairly sensible reason, of course.

Stronger objections were raised to the sexual content of some of the songs and to the fact that black people were often singing them. These objections were heard throughout the country and influenced record company executives who usually felt the same way themselves. The Catholic Church took a stand against sexuality in rock'n'roll. Boston's Very Reverend John P. Carroll declared that "the suggestive lyrics on rock'n'roll records are a matter for law enforcement agencies," and Cardinal Stritch of Chicago told a lenten congregation that rock'n'roll dancing and "tribalism" "could not be tolerated by Catholic youth." In a self-serving appearance before Congress in 1958 Frank Sinatra told congressmen that rock'n'roll was "the most brutal, ugly, desperate, vicious form of expression it has been my misfortune to hear," that it was written and sung "for the most part by cretinous goons," and that "by means of its almost imbecilic reiterations and sly—lewd—in plain fact dirty—lyrics . . . [it] manages to be the martial music of every side-burned delinquent on the face of the earth." The rebelliousness of the music which was noted by Sinatra was hardly missed by other adults of the time.

As for the contribution of blacks to the music there were various criticisms ranging from the snide prejudice of Congressman Emanuel Celler: "Rock'n'roll has its place. It's given great impetus to talent, especially among the colored people: it's a natural expression of their emotions and feeling," to the beating that Nat King Cole received by members of the White Citizens' Council at a concert in 1956 in Birmingham, Alabama. Alan Freed and *Billboard* magazine got complaints about "nigger music." Freed was asked not to play it and *Billboard* was asked not to chart it.

Rock'n'roll with its sexuality and blackness also brought out fears of miscegenation. Alan Freed's national TV show "Rock 'n' Roll Dance Party" was canceled when Frankie Lymon was filmed dancing with a white girl. The fifties in America was a time when it was necessary for *Harper's* to warn that integration did not necessarily mean miscegenation. "It was a time when many a mother ripped pictures of Fats Domino off her daughter's bedroom wall. She remembered what she felt toward her Bing Crosby pin-up, and she didn't want her daughter creaming for Fats," recalled Russ Sanjek, now vice president of Broadcast Music, Inc. (BMI).

Given their dislike for rock'n'roll in the first place, the risk its adoption threatened, and the reaction of the adult public to its sexual content and its black performers, the majors, especially those that were subsidiaries of larger, public corporations, did not need any more reason to resist it. But they had one: the organized lobby of ASCAP (American Society of Composers, Authors, and Publishers), the association of Broadway and Hollywood publishers.

ASCAP licensed most songs played on network radio until 1940, when in a play mostly for higher fees, they decided to boycott broadcasters. The broadcasters established their own licensing agency, BMI, and began to play old standards that were not copyrighted as well as the hillbilly and r&b music that ASCAP shunned. BMI beat the boycott, and from then on ASCAP had an economic stake in preventing BMI, "Bad Music Incorporated," from being played. In 1954 they succeeded in banning Johnny Ray's version of "Such a Night" from airplay in the United States, on the grounds that it was sexually suggestive. The song, written by Clyde McPhatter and licensed by BMI, had lyrics that were at most only affectionate ("Ooh, such a kiss/such a night"). ASCAP kept up such harassment against rock'n'roll songs licensed by BMI. No complaints were made about "Rock Around the Clock," which was interestingly enough an ASCAP song.

ASCAP failed in later suits against BMI (see pages 64-68) but was effective in creating publicity against rock'n'roll and such publicity influenced some of the larger companies to treat rock'n'roll with caution. At Columbia they were especially effective because Mitch Miller, the powerful A&R director who stayed through the early sixties, maintained close relations with Broadway publishers and despised rock'n'roll.*

Dot Joins the Majors

The independent companies kept a firm grip on the pop singles market well into the sixties when the majors simply bought them up or

---

*In an interview with Sammy Davis, Jr. in 1957 Miller called rock'n'roll records "the comic books of music." "If rock'n'roll is here to stay," replied Davis, "I might commit suicide." Unfortunately for rock'n'roll, he broke his promise.

merged with them, but the type of rock'n'roll music in that singles market changed significantly from 1958 onward. Before explaining that change it is necessary to talk briefly about Dot Records, an independent that played an important role commercially during the rock'n'roll period.

Dot was started in Gallatin, Tennessee, in 1950 by Randy Wood. Before starting the label, Wood ran a mail-order record business that became, in the days before record clubs, one of the largest mail-order houses in the country. Before that he had operated a small radio repair shop. Figuring that his records would sell if dealers would only stock them, he offered retailers a 100 percent return privilege; that is, all unsold records could be returned. Because Dot did have some popular artists, the policy proved successful, and it allowed the company to expand at an extremely rapid pace. Previous to Dot, a 10 percent return privilege had been common. The new return privilege was copied by most other companies, and changed the nature of merchandising. Record companies began to put more stock into record stores in order to sell more records and to be ready for possible hits. The policy was one of the factors that allowed the U.S. record industry to grow at such a high rate, but it led to a serious problem of "returns" or overstocking in the sixties. The labor and shipping costs involved in returning records has cost tens of millions of dollars to manufacturers, distributors, and retailers.

Wood initiated other merchandising techniques that were widely copied. A delayed billing technique was the most important. Delayed billing provided retailers with a credit incentive to stock Dot records.

Dot was assuming the stature of a major. They added LPs and began a national promotion network, and by the end of 1956 had reached $6 million in sales. They surpassed Atlantic, the independent with the next highest sales, by $2 million. Dot resembled the majors in the way it handled music as well as by the extent of its sales. It was an extremely predatory company, covering the r&b hits of other independents with watered down rock'n'roll versions. Some of the better known were the Charms' "Ivory Tower," covered by Dot singer Gale Storm, and Fats Domino's "Ain't That a Shame," the El Dorados' "At My Front Door," Little Richard's "Tutti Frutti," and Fats Washington's "I'll Be There" — all by Pat Boone.

In the beginning Wood had the same idea as Sam Phillips at Sun, that a wide market existed for a white singer who could sing blues music. His method, however, was to direct Boone and his other singers toward the pop market, making any stylistic compromises necessary to sell the records. The company also had a schlock mood music group, the Billy

Vaughn Orchestra, that competed nicely with major company orchestras recording in the same genre.

In 1957 Wood sold his company to Paramount pictures for $2 million in Paramount stock. He was asked to stay on as head of the record company for five years, at a salary of $100,000 a year. Dot was the first big independent to sell out to a larger company. The practice would become widespread in the sixties.

The Lull in Rock: *1958-63*

During the late fifties and early sixties the raw rock'n'roll typified by the Sun and Chess artists seemed to soften out. The original energy of rock'n'roll subsided during what Peter Guralnick has called this "treacle period." A number of related factors were responsible for the lull. Most of the major rock'n'rollers were removed from the scene, for a variety of individual reasons, although a couple more arrived to carry on the tradition. Most important was the establishment of the television show American Bandstand. Its immense promotional power eclipsed earlier forms of rock'n'roll with the watered-down "Philly sound."

Only too happy to help remove rock'n'roll from the stage, the majors supported several fads, such as calypso and clean folk music, while some of the powerful independent companies like Dot essentially joined forces musically with the majors by "going pop." With such backsliding on all fronts, what rock'n'roll that was left, such as the remaining rockabilly-influenced singers and the vocal harmony groups, barely held its own until a revitalized form of rock'n'roll crossed the Atlantic in the middle sixties.

There was a litany used in the early sixties to bemoan the loss of hardline rock'n'rollers: "Elvis in the Army, Buddy Holly dead, Little Richard in the ministry, Jerry Lee Lewis in disgrace, and Chuck Berry in jail." Even when Elvis got out of the Army his music seemed to lack the old rawness. He stayed completely isolated, making no concert tours until 1969, and churned out a series of high-grossing pablum movies such as *Blue Hawaii* and *Viva Las Vegas* in which he sounded too much like Pat Boone. Holly died in a plane crash in 1959 along with Richie Valens and J.P. "The Big Bopper" Richardson. Lewis married his thirteen-year-old cousin, and outraged public opinion destroyed him in the pop market in both the United States and Britain.

The situation was not completely bleak, however. Two fine, often overlooked rockabilly-influenced singers arrived in 1959 and produced hits into the sixties: Roy Orbison and Brenda Lee. Orbison did "Only the Lonely," which was the fifteenth best-selling single in 1960, "Running Scared" and "Crying" in 1961, and "Oh, Pretty Woman," which was Number Four at the end of the year in 1964. Brenda Lee turned out "I'm Sorry" and "I Want to Be Wanted," both in 1960, and "Dum Dum" in 1961. In addition, the Everly Brothers, while too soft for some, carried on the light rockabilly tradition of Buddy Holly in hits like "Bye Bye Love" (1957), "Bird Dog" (1958), "(Till) I Kissed You" (1959), and "Cathy's Clown" (1960).

The lull years also produced a steady stream of rhythm and blues rock'n'roll that is too often overlooked. The Platters, the Drifters, and the Coasters, who had been around in one form or another since 1955, continued to make the charts at different times in the lull years. Ray Charles and Sam Cooke began to hit the pop charts in 1957. A number of black vocal harmony groups had hits, like Little Anthony and the Imperials, the Impalas, Elegants, and later, Maurice Williams and the Zodiacs. They were joined by white vocal groups like the Teddy Bears, the Fleetwoods, the Crescendos, and Dion and the Belmonts, among others. The white vocal groups have often been discounted by later critics who seem to feel that they were only aping their black counterparts. Most of the white groups, however, did authentically reproduce the street corner culture shared by both blacks and whites in racial and ethnic ghettos in Northern (usually Eastern) cities. Criticisms of these groups usually stem from a strange sort of reverse racial snobbery.

In 1957 Columbia and RCA latched onto calypso music which they hoped might make a dent in rock'n'roll. Columbia had hits with the Tarriers, and Terry Gilkyson and the Easy Riders, while RCA was successful with Harry Belafonte, a New Yorker who had spent a few childhood years in Jamaica. Capitol chimed in with Nat Cole's "When Rock'n'Roll Comes to Trinidad." Despite the hoopla that the major companies gave calypso, it was ignored by teenagers and never spread beyond the adult night club circuit. The majors tried again with their clean version of folk music. In 1958 Capitol promoted the Kingston Trio, for instance, and several years later in 1962 the new major, Warner Brothers, got behind Peter, Paul, and Mary. Both groups were popular but appealed mostly to the well-heeled college audiences of the late fifties and early sixties who did not like rock'n'roll. Folk music, of course, represented a legitimate type of music, with its own traditions and long-standing audience. Still, in the hands of larger corporations it was seen mostly as a possible substitute for rock'n'roll. More important than the majors in muffling rock'n'roll, however, was Dick Clark's national TV show, American Bandstand.

When the big rock'n'rollers receded in the late fifties, they were not replaced by the r&b artists or those few rockabillies that hung on. Instead the vacuum was filled by "Philadelphia Schlock," a sound produced by three Philadelphia-based independents, and a few other labels elsewhere, and popularized on American Bandstand. Philadelphia Schlock mini-mized the impact of whatever good r&b/rock'n'roll that had managed to survive into the treacle period. The Bandstand show consisted of an informal dance party for local teenagers. Bandstand originated when teenagers witnessing a televised radio show jumped up and started dancing. A cameraman turned his camera on them and the spontaneous dance format was born, embellished later by contests. Between the records were the lip-synched performances by guest singers. The MC was genial Dick Clark. The show became so popular in Philadelphia that network executives looking to cash in on the new teenage market made it nationwide in 1957. The show appeared every weekday from 3-5 P.M., right after school, and attracted a huge audience of teenagers from across the nation. The immense popularity of the show gave it a promotional capability that propelled the singers who appeared on it to the top spots on record charts.

Almost immediately Clark began to take advantage of the situation by featuring the artists of several local companies that he partly owned: Cameo-Parkway, Swan, and Chancellor. These small independent companies had more to do with the weakening of rock'n'roll than did the resistance of the majors.

Cameo-Parkway put over "The Twist" by Chubby Checker, making it the number four record of the year in 1960 and number one in 1962. Checker's "Limbo Rock," another twist tune, was number one, accord-ing to *Cashbox,* in 1963 as well. Checker was black but antiseptic enough to be on the Bandstand show. The company also succeeded with Bobby Rydell ("Wild One," "Volare," and others), Charlie Gracie, and Deedee Sharp ("Mashed Potato Time"). Swan featured Freddie Canon ("Tallahassee Lassie" and "Way Down Yonder in New Orleans"). Chancellor recorded Frankie Avalon ("Venus," "Why," and many more) and Fabian ("Tiger"). The company had eight Top 10 hits with Avalon and Fabian alone.

These Philadelphia singers were joined by a number of others like Paul Anka (ABC-Paramount), Bobby Darin (Atlantic), and Johnny Tillotson (Cadence), all of whom appeared regularly on Bandstand and sounded just like each other. All sang an extremely watered-down version of rock that resembled more the style of the early fifties crooners than it did rock'n'rollers like Carl Perkins or Chuck Berry.

The degeneration of the music did not bother Clark in the slightest, of course. He was making over $500,000 a year through his Bandstand salary, ownership in music corporations, and "composer's" royalties. "I don't make culture," he said later. "I sell it."

Philadelphia Schlock was so successful commercially that it domi-nated the charts until it was finally brushed aside by the Beatles and the other English groups in 1964. The only groups of singers to rival Philadelphia Schlock were the black "girl groups," as they were called.

Even more than Brenda Lee, Roy Orbison, and the earlier, late fifties vocal groups, the girl groups like the Shirelles, the Crystals, the Shangri-Las, and the Ronnettes have been unjustly ignored. The Shangri-Las and the Ronnettes, in particular, projected a "tough" image that came close to rivaling the image of Presley or the Sun artists, but they have gone unheralded by male rock critics. The onslaught of the Beatles and the other British groups pushed most of these "girl groups" from the charts. The tradition continued a little later with the Motown girl groups, but they were even more heavily produced and had lost the tough rocker image of the girl groups just before them.

The surfing music that appeared in the early sixties should not be seen as just another fad that softened rock'n'roll. Rather it was a precursor to the psychedelic and underground progressive rock of the sixties. Several of the important people involved in surfing music—especially the Beach Boys ("Surfin' Safari," "Surfin' USA," "Surfer Girl") and Lou Adler, one of the first producers of Jan and Dean, became central figures in sixties rock. Surfing music represented an authentic West Coast rock'n' roll culture that differed in one important way from earlier rock'n'roll produced by urban blacks and Southern rockabillies: it was made by middle-class whites.

Record Clubs and Stereo

The trend toward fewer and larger retail stores continued in this period. Discounting, now established, expanded to smaller cities and towns.

The most significant retailing event in the rock'n'roll period was the introduction of record clubs. Columbia opened their Columbia Record and Tape Club in 1955, eyeing the substantial business being done by mail-order firms like those of Sam Goody in New York and Randy Wood in Tennessee. Capitol later started a club as did an independent firm called the Record Club of America.

Tremendous antagonisms were expressed toward the clubs by record retailers who charged unfair competition. A move was even made to boycott Columbia Records, but when the company came out with the extremely successful album "My Fair Lady," the dealers dropped principle in order to turn a quick profit and stocked the record. An antitrust suit was later filed against Columbia for practices that "restrained competition." Columbia actually lost the suit to the Justice Department, but succeeded in having the ruling reversed on appeal. The case took years to decide finally and had little effect on the real world. Record clubs were firmly established, cutting into retailer sales long before their methods were ruled upon in court. Record club sales amounted to $110 million in 1965, or 14 percent of all records sold in that year. Columbia was doing a $60 million annual business with 1,750,000 members.

Stereo records were introduced in 1957 by the giant British major EMI and by the American independent Audio Fidelity, whose first stereo record featured the Dukes of Dixieland on one side and "Railroad Sounds" on the other. Stereo was resisted by most majors, but was so popular with record buyers that by the early sixties the vast majority of albums were in the mode. In fact, stereo caused the same sort of excitement that the introduction of the LP had created, and overall record sales were boosted as a result. To phase mono out and make an extra profit the majors raised the price of mono records to equal the stereo price.

The crossover of rhythm and blues to the white market and the staying power of rock'n'roll created chaotic conditions in the music industry, from the point of view of the major companies who still dominated the business. The majors were never able to produce rhythm and blues with the success of Atlantic or Imperial, duplicate the rock'n'roll of Chess and Sun, or even cash in on Philadelphia Schlock to the extent that New York and Philly independents did. The larger companies were inherently conservative in their reaction to new styles.

The situation changed with the arrival of the Beatles. The Beatles and the other British groups generated such incredible financial success that new forms of music could no longer safely be ignored or even coopted (until much later). "Too much money was at stake," said Ahmet Ertegun, "for personal taste to get in the way."

After the Beatles the old forces in the industry developed a more sophisticated approach to new trends. They realized that new styles stimulated buyer interest and tapped elements of the market that they found difficult to understand and predict. The problem was to find structures that could take advantage of market instability and financially harness creativity to the old-line companies, rather than eliminate it. The solution was often found in the institution of the independent producer, who maintained enough distance from the big companies to be close to trends happening in the street, yet who turned over his material to the large companies for distribution and promotion. When musical and commercial innovation resided in successful independent companies like Atlantic or Elektra, the larger firms simply bought them up, keeping the old leadership under salary to insure creativity.

But before that story is told, the development of radio in the rock'n'roll period must be covered.

Rock'n'Roll Radio

The migration of blacks to industrial centers in the North and West following World War II, the abandonment of the race music field by the majors, the growth of local radio, and the spillover of black music styles into the white community all dovetailed to create the rock'n'roll phenomenon. A central figure in the process was the disc jockey (dj). In the early 1940s the Federal Communications Commission had noted that music comprised more than 75 percent of overall radio programming, and that nearly half the stations in the country were using music as the sole basis of programming. More important still, nearly half (40 percent) of the music was prerecorded. As one historian of the period noted:

> Those stations placing chief reliance on recordings and transcripts were non-network operations in communities under fifty-thousand population, with five hundred watts or less power, having time sales under $75,000 and a profit under $7,500. These, said FCC chairman James Fly, amounted to 60 percent of all radio stations. They depended on records to exist. [11]

As radio suffered from the threat of televison, local stations sought cheaper forms of programming. Records with top talent provided just such a resource. By the early fifties, record programming was the rule for radio, and the disc jockey had replaced live entertainment personalities that had dominated network radio in the 1930s and 40s.

The Early DJs

Of course, there had been djs before the 1950s. Reginald Fessenden, who played a recording of Handel's Messiah during a Christmas eve broadcast off the New England coast in 1906, may be the first one. Discouraged by the networks, however, who opposed "canned" music as illegitimate straight through the 1940s, the practice did not get a second chance until 1935. Then, during a break in the Lindbergh, kidnapping trial, WNEW announcer Martin Block played a number of tunes recorded by bandleader Clyde McCoy and had an imaginary conversation with the musician over the air. So began Block's fabulously successful "Make Believe Ballroom," an idea he had actually stolen from the less successful L.A. jock Al Jarvis.

Block was a master salesman, demonstrated from his first days selling "Retardo Weight Reducing Pills" ("be fair to your husband by taking the reducing pill") to the day in 1938 when he sold more than three hundred refrigerators for a Newark department store during a blizzard. All this was surprising to the established network radio powers, who thought live entertainment was needed to sell products. The networks were slow to realize that the jocks themselves had become important "personalities." Block was a crooning, serious on-the-air type, but quite a different approach was shown equally effective by down home jocks like Arthur Godfrey.

During the late thirties and early forties djs and recorded music were used over radio to popularize swing bands and name vocalists. In an early example of payola Al Jarvis got $500 in 1937 to feature Benny Goodman records immediately prior to that swing leader's arrival in L.A.

Before black communities had enough money to support (white-owned) r&b stations, and white attitudes toward black music had loosened a little, the only black music on the radio came from a few scattered rhythm and blues shows, such as Al Jarvis in Los Angeles, on otherwise pop stations. In the thirties the situation had been even worse. Black music of any kind, even by Louis Armstrong, was kept off virtually all stations in the country.

As the market for black music expanded, so did the number of stations playing it. At first the South was the core of the r&b sound. On white-owned "Negro stations," black djs proliferated in the late 1940s and early fifties, blues performers like Howlin' Wolf, Sonny Boy Williamson, B.B. King, and Rufus Thomas did radio shows in Memphis, and "Professor Bop" in Shreveport, Louisiana, "Jocky Jack" Gibson in Atlanta, and the great "Sugar Daddy" in Birmingham were all important in further popularizing r&b.

Gradually white music stations began to accommodate the potential black audience in Northern cities. White stations set aside time for r&b shows, usually late at night. In Chicago WEBC hired the first really major black disc jockey, Jack L. Cooper, who had a regular program of "race records" that began each night at 11 o'clock. Al Benson, also in Chicago on WJJD, WAAF, and WGES, was well known for his "Yo' Ol' Swingmaster" show. In New York black jocks like Jack Walker, Joe Boston, Hal Jackson, and Phil "Dr. Jive" Gordon were taken on for the "specialty audience" of blacks that white stations sought. Although there were many such r&b shows hosted by black jocks, they were still a minuscule percentage of AM radio personalities.

An important jock who made something of a transition to r&b material in the mid-fifties was Bill Randle in Cleveland. For years his popular music show had been the focus of record company promotion. He was first important for discovering and breaking Johnny Ray's "Cry," and later for introducing Elvis Presley to Northern audiences. (Randle had come to Cleveland from Detroit, where he proved no match for Ed "Bellboy" McKenzie, another local jock. Rumor has it that for years his mother sent him a copy of McKenzie's successful playlist, and that this was the basis of Randle's own popularity.) The most famous and important white r&b jock of all was another Cleveland-based dj: Alan Freed, the father of Rock'n'Roll.

Alan Freed as Moon Dog

Freed did his first r&b show in 1952 for station WJW in Cleveland. He had been hosting an evening "good music" show when Leo Mintz, the owner of one of the bigger record stores in Cleveland, asked him to come by and watch teenagers snapping up rhythm and blues records. He did; he told a British interviewer later:

> I heard the tenor saxophone of Red Prysock and Big Al Sears. I heard the blues-singing, piano-playing Ivory Joe Hunter. I wondered. I wondered for about a week. Then I went to the station manager and talked him into permitting me to follow my classical program with a rock'n'roll party.[12]

Mintz has said that Freed was not as enthused with the idea of a rock'n'roll show as he later claimed, that he did not want to devote his whole show to r&b, but was finally convinced by Mintz. Freed called his show The Moon Dog Show (later, The Moon Dog House Rock'n'Roll Party). The Moon Dog theme was from Todd Rhodes's record for King, "Blues for Moon Dog," and Freed would howl as he played the song over the introduction to the program. He dropped the name "rhythm and blues" and substituted "rock'n'roll." He did not invent the term, as he sometimes claimed. It had been used on quite a few r&b records before he popularized it.

Freed was a strange, strong character, perfect for popularizing rock'n'roll, or rhythm and blues, to a white audience. He had grown up in Salem, Ohio, where he trained as a classical trombonist and mechanical engineer. He had been a classical dj in Newcastle, Pennsylvania, and a pop disc jockey in Akron before coming to Cleveland. Along the way he became a heavy drinker. "He was always drunk," said Soupy Sales, the morning man on Freed's Cleveland station, "but he was on late at night and could always handle it." His gravelly patter was authentic, since his vocal cords had been damaged when some polyps had been removed from his throat. He would often howl during records, keeping time by beating his fist against a telephone book. The music became his life. "Anyone who says rock'n'roll is a passing fad or flash-in-the-pan trend along the music road has *rocks in his head, Dad!*" he said.

Freed's show became so popular that he was known outside of Ohio and was hired by WINS-New York in 1954. His show made WINS the most popular radio station among young people in the city. Later he moved to WABC.

In March 1952, before the New York move, Freed staged the Moon Dog Coronation ball with several of the most popular r&b artists of the time. It was held in the Cleveland Arena. He reportedly sold 18,000 tickets for the 10,000 seating capacity hall. When the crowd showed up along with some 10,000 others who had not been able to buy tickets, there was a near riot, and the show was canceled.[13] Charges of overselling were brought against Freed but were dropped, and he successfully staged the concert a few months later. Large numbers of white teenagers attended the concerts along with blacks, and Freed was criticized for "mixing the races." He staged a similar series of concerts in the St. Nichols Arena when he arrived in New York, and they were equally successful. The only advertising done to fill the 6,000 seating hall was made over his daily radio show. The performers were Joe Turner, the Drifters, the Clovers, the Moonglows, the Moonlighters, the Buddy Johnson Orchestra, Fats Domino, Red Prysock, and the Harptones. All on one bill.

Freed was one of the most important popularizers of rock'n'roll. Besides his eight years on major radio stations and his numerous concerts, he syndicated a radio show that played in St. Louis, Baltimore, and over Radio Luxembourg, sponsored a number of Top Hits albums, and appeared in movies such as *Rock Around the Clock* that proselytized the music worldwide. He was credited with co-writing fifteen rock'n'roll hits including Chuck Berry's "Maybellene," but he did little more than promote any of them.

Play It Again, Todd: *The Rise of Top 40*

The 1950s radio scene was characterized by decentralized independent broadcasting stations, which succeeded the networks as the leaders in programming innovation. They popularized a whole diversity of regional music styles, from hillbilly and country and western to r&b and the hybrid rock'n'roll. Gradually, however, the patterns of ownership in independent broadcasting shifted away from individual stations, toward chain owners, and changes in programming formats and regional radio soon followed.

The chain owners were usually businessmen who had made small fortunes in some other area of business and been attracted to radio as an investment medium in the late forties and early fifties. They had no illusions about the broadcast music business and sought to rationalize radio production much as they might have hired efficiency experts to increase the production in their factories. The president of Storer Broadcasting, which began in the Southeast in the fifties and now includes major stations in Atlanta, Detroit, Cleveland, Los Angeles, Toledo, Milwaukee, and New York, once compactly summarized his commercial philosophy:

> American radio is the product of American business! It is just as much that kind of product as the vacuum cleaner, the washing machine, the automo-

bile, and the airplane. . . . If the legend still persists that a radio station is some kind of art center, a technical museum, or a little piece of Hollywood transplanted strangely to your home town, then the first official act of the second quarter century [of commercial broadcasting] should be to list it along with the local dairies, laundries, banks, restaurants, and filling stations.[14]

Storer had made his first big money in filling stations. Following the success in radio, he kept expanding. The chain of stations became the basis for an empire that included heavy investment in widely diverse business ventures, including the Standard Tube Company, the Miami Beach Publishing Company, and Northeast Airlines. Local radio was being recognized as potentially big business, and attracted entrepreneurs anxious to solidify their ties into more stable conglomerate corporations.

The racist anti-Semite George Richard was another early chain owner in radio. He owned WJR in Detroit, from which Father Coughlin had held forth for years, WGAR in Cleveland, and KMPC in Hollywood, Station of the Stars. Elsewhere the Starr, Balaban, Plough, Bartell, Storz, and McLendon chains were all begun by single businessmen, who gave them their names. Storz and McLendon, in particular, were heavily identified with the surge in teenage pop music.

Todd Storz began his air empire with KOWH in Omaha in the early fifties, then expanded to the powerful WTIX in New Orleans in 1953, then on into Kansas City with WHB, and Minneapolis station WDGY. The chain currently owns additional properties in Miami (KQAM), Oklahoma City (KOMA), and St. Louis (KXOH), but has dropped the old Omaha station. Gordon McLendon, like Storz, started in the South and West, away from the old time Northeast business center that financed and owned the networks. McLendon's first big station was KLIF in Dallas, Texas, then KTSA in San Antonio, and KILT in Houston. Today, the "Old Scotchman" has sold many of his Texas properties although he still owns stations in Los Angeles (KOST), Chicago (WNES), Buffalo (WPHD), Dallas (KNUS), and Pembina, North Dakota (KCND). Storz's and McLendon's spectacular growth in the fifties was at least partly attributed to a programming innovation they made that influenced the other chain broadcasters and shaped the future of AM radio.

In search of stable audience and advertiser money, the various regional stations had tried for a long time to distinguish themselves from one another and develop a unique "sound" that separated them from other stations. One approach to this problem of identification was specialized music programming, be it strictly r&b, country and western, or some other more specific regional style. Program specialization, however, undermined the overall business strategy. Stations ran a risk of cutting back on audience size, ratings, and advertiser dollars in their quest for uniqueness. The chain owners found a much better solution in the concept of Top 40 radio.

For a long time Lucky Strike had sponsored the Hit Parade on NBC affiliates. The show was a weekly broadcast of the top hits and enjoyed long-term popularity that stretched back from the middle fifties to the early 1940s. Top 40 radio made the weekly broadcast a daily programming concept, which extended not only to broadcasting only the top hits of the day, but developed a tight and distinct radio *sound* for stations. Top 40 programming meant strictly limiting the station playlist to mainstream market pop singles, repeated station identifications, jingles, weird sound effects, extensive use of echo chambers, integration of hourly news broadcasts into the music format, and the use of promotional gimmicks and contests for the audience. Many of these "innovations," especially jingles and special effects, had been around in radio since well before the mid-fifties, but the Top 40 concept put them all together.

Storz put the formula into effect first, at his Omaha station, and is credited with first developing the "rotation" pattern of programming hits. This means that not only is the sum total of programming taken up with only forty songs, but that the Top 10 of those songs are played much more frequently than any others. Storz got the idea of Top 40, and rotation, when he and his program director Bill. Stewart were out drinking one afternoon in a bar in Omaha. They had been talking about radio all afternoon, and grew irritated that the same song kept coming on the bar's jukebox, again and again, for hours. Finally there was silence in the bar, until a cocktail waitress went over to the jukebox to make a selection. She picked the same song, and played it another three times. Storz and Steward were convinced, then, of the power of endless rotation in building hits, and the attraction of a limited playlist.

Gordon McLendon contributed the "instant news" concept to Top 40. He stole Storz's idea of rotation and limited playlist, but first distinguished KLIF from other stations by its band of roving reporters on the streets of Dallas. Anytime anything happened in Dallas that was considered newsworthy it was broadcast, virtually right away. In later years as formats have become more rigid, the "instant news" concept has been modified to be news on the hour and, in a twist from Bill Drake and other late sixties radio programmers, news at twenty minutes before or after the hour. The important point is that Top 40 did away with drawn out, hour-long evening wrap-up news programs, and tried to make the news as topical and immediately entertaining as the music.

The man most often credited with developing the wild promotional antics of Top 40 stations is Chuck Blore, who worked at different points for Storz and McLendon. One bright afternoon in the 1950s Blore startled a Southern Californian radio audience by announcing that an amoeba monster had landed on the outskirts of Los Angeles. Through the rest of the day he used his station KFWB to broadcast deadpan announcements about the amoeba's progress to the inner city. Fun-loving area college students joined in the obvious prank and called the station with reports of "sightings of the monster." Many hundreds of more gullible people in L.A. were terrified by the news. (Years later another dj tried exactly the same stunt in Arizona and was threatened with arrest and fired for his efforts.) Whatever the mass psychology of the event, it certainly helped to establish KFWB's image as lively radio.

Top 40 had immediate effects as a programming innovation. It largely did away with the personality jocks and their large salaries, which were no longer needed since the overall sound of radio was now a formula. In rationalizing pop radio Top 40 also had the short term effect of driving out r&b artists, who seemed to fit better in looser formats, with their proselytizing dj counterparts. Djs were reduced to an element in sound formula, rather than a creative force in their own right. Radio was integrated in a more specific way into the fabric of the music industry. For records to become hits, they had to get airplay, and with repeated and constant airplay available on Top 40, records were made into hits.

At the same time, the innovation was the beginning of a narrowing in the range of AM radio, and of a catering to the current tastes of listeners, that eventually stunted AM's willingness to play unknown music, or break open regional hits into a national market. This tension between contracting playlists and sound formula on AM radio, and the record industry's desire to move new products and use radio as a promotional vehicle, provides the frame for understanding the record promotion system to this day.

Top 40 was fabulously successful. From their original base in the deep South and West, Storz and McLendon expanded into coastal and Northeast markets. Other chain owners, also originally centered in the Midwest, West, and South followed them into city centers where they bought up classical, foreign language, or disaffiliated network stations and brought in Top 40 music.

Payola Week

As radio's role as hitmaker was clarified and enforced by the Top 40 concept, the record industry began paying djs on the side, to get them to play specific songs occasionally, but most of all to create a happy continuing climate of cooperation between regional promo men and local jocks. In much the same way that other sorts of corporations give regional salesmen added incentives and extensive expense accounts for wining and dining top clients, giving them gifts and other forms of subtle bribery, record companies began by supplying multiple free copies of current releases that could be converted to cash. Hi-fi sets were popular Christmas gifts. By late in the 1950s, a more orderly system of direct cash contributions to djs was worked out. This payola system was exposed during the 1959-60 congressional investigation of rigged quiz shows on daytime television, and heads within radio began to roll.

One of the first to go was Alan Freed, father of rock'n'roll and as the top paid jock on New York's WABC radio station, still the most visible dj in the business. Over the years Freed had accumulated a small fortune from his ample $30,00-plus salary, promotional gimmicks, concert promotion, and record company payoffs. Just a few months before he was pressured out of big time radio, in fact, he reached something of a peak in his own money making when his Broadway Paramount Christmas show grossed over $300,000 for a twelve-day run. In the summer of 1959, however, Freed got into some trouble at a Jerry Lee Lewis concert he ran in Boston. Some small crowd problems were exacerbated when police stopped the show. By night's end a number of people were badly hurt, and Boston authorities charged Freed with inciting to riot. The dj was working at WINS at the time, but quit when the station refused to help him defend himself against charges that were eventually dropped (but not before be bankrolled losses from the remainder of the canceled tour, and bankrupted himself in the process of paying off creditors). It is possible that WINS had wind of what was about to happen in Congress.

Freed got a job with WABC, but was dismissed in November when he refused "on principle" to sign a statement saying he had never received money or presents to promote records. At the time, he was hosting a rock'n'roll dance show like American Bandstand on local New York TV station WNEW. A couple of days after the ABC firing, WNEW also dropped his contract. Freed left New York City and went to work with Mel Leeds at Los Angeles station KDAY. In 1960 he was indicted for accepting $30,000 in payola bribery and two years later, after a partial guilty plea, was fined and given a suspended sentence. Then in 1964 he was indicted again, this time for evading income taxes. He died early the next year, ruined, humiliated, and drunk.

Others went too. Dale Young and Tom Clay at Detroit's station WJBK were fired. Clay admitted taking more than $6,000 from small record companies during the previous two years. When station manager Jack LeGraff defended payola as "part of American business," he too was thrown out of the Top 40 station. WWDC in Washington used the scandal as the slogan for a children's charity show. During the station's "Payola Week" listener requests were taken in exchange for contributions ("You pay, we play," said the jocks). But payola was no joke for others within the industry. Hearing dates were set in 1960 for the House Legislative Oversight subcommittee of the Commerce Committee (Chairman, Owen Harris, a Democrat from Arkansas) to probe the misuse of free records, payola to disc jockeys and other station personnel, payola to company A&R men, chart rigging via dealer payola, conflict of interest between music and broadcast interests who used radio to promote their own product, and kickbacks at all levels of the record industry. While widespread malpractice was found, it was the jocks who took the punishment. As with the scandal and legal action surrounding network TV quiz shows, the corporate sponsors (in this case the record companies) were virtually untouched.

Professor Bernard Schwartz of the NYU Law School reports in his *The Professor and the Commissions* that in fact Harris himself was deeply involved in corrupt practices and conflicts of interest. Schwartz had been brought to Washington a couple of years previous to investigate the functions of the regulatory agencies. He soon found out that Harris, who was connected with the Federal Communications Commission, had gotten a 25 percent share in television station KRBB in El Dorado, Arkansas, which before Harris' chairmanship of the Commerce Committee had been having some troubles with license renewal. When the Schwartz finding was exposed in the press, Harris was pressured successfully to sell his share in the station, but stayed on as chairman of the committee with overall responsibility for investigating broadcast corruption.

Schwartz also found that the Federal Communications Commission members themselves were in the pockets of major broadcasting powers and could be counted on to look the other way when it got to the really big payola of the time, namely the trading in licenses, price fixing agreements between the major networks on advertising rates, disguised rate cards, and special kickbacks to advertising agencies buying spot time. FCC Commissioner Doerfer was once paid by the government to take a vacation on Bimini Island with media mogul George Storer. In fact the commissioner's travel expenses were fully covered three times: twice by Storer and other important broadcasting groups the commissioner addressed during the vacation, once by the FCC. With such double dealing in high places, it is small wonder that the payola investigation was essentially a whitewash job that moved quickly from TV investigation to attack the smaller independent broadcasters.

It remains an open question just how much the jocks of the period were influenced by payola. Boston dj Stan Richards suggested at the time that the record companies paid the jocks "in the hope that something good would happen," but did not make direct demands. Richards admitted taking a lot of payola money during his years at WILD, but claimed he was never influenced by it. Alan Freed admitted taking payola. "But not in front. If I've helped somebody, I'll accept a nice gift, but I wouldn't take a dime to plug a record. I'd be a fool to; I'd be giving up control of my program."

The duplicity of the investigating committee and of all the payola hearings is pointed up by comparing the treatment of Alan Freed with that given Dick Clark, the host of American Bandstand. Clark emerged from the payola hearings intact. In fact he was strengthened and made more secure in the industry when his image as a clean businessman was vindicated. At the end he was congratulated by the investigating committee chairman as "a fine young man." There is something hateful and pure about the man. An eternal teenager, he somehow epitomizes the clean cut, money-making, straight-shooting, ultimately corrupt, and ultimately pardoned side of America. He is a good example of how go-getters get into high places, and how money makers are protected.

The $263,245 in payola money that the Harris Committee identified as being paid to jocks represents only a small part of total industry payola. Certainly it did not include the money that Dick Clark made from ownership in some thirty-three companies connected with the music business, including ownership in three record companies, a management firm, and a record pressing plant. During the two year period dating backward from April 1960, when he appeared before the Harris committee, Clark made some $500,000 in salary and increased stock value in these companies. At the time of the hearings he held copyright to 162 songs, many of which he helped popularize on his TV show. Between 1958 and 1960, for example, Clark played Duane Eddy's eleven records some 240 times on his show, promoting many of them into national hits. Clark also managed Eddy, owned stock in his record company, and owned all his publishing rights. The *New York Times* estimated that had Clark been required to pay ABC their going advertising rate for songs he had a financial interest in that he plugged over the air, he would have owed the network some $25 million.

Early in 1952 Clark had teamed up with Philadelphia jock Bob Horn for a daily afternoon show on WFIL in Philadelphia. The show then was called simply Bandstand. Clark got the job full time for himself in 1956 when his co-host was hauled in for drunken driving just when the station owner, the *Philadelphia Inquirer*, was conducting a strong editorial campaign against the offense. (Horn was also accused of income tax evasion and, along with some prestigious members of Philadelphia's business community, of involvement with a teenage girl vice ring. This last charge was dropped.) The show went national for ABC in 1957. By the time the payola hearings came, Clark was toting up annual billings of $12 million on the show.

His economic clout protected him through the hearings. Compared to the $200,000 in yearly billings that Alan Freed brought ABC radio in New York, Clark was a sounder investment. The network stuck by him through the investigation, helping him connect with lawyers and never canceling his show. At the end, the investigating committee made Clark divest most of his publishing and management holdings, but he kept Bandstand.

ASCAP vs. BMI: *Gershwin Does Not Like Bad Music*

At the heart of the payola investigation was a long-standing rivalry between ASCAP and BMI.

The success of disc jockeys in the late thirties increased the perennial tension between broadcasters and Tin Pan Alley. ASCAP had hated radio from the start. Its members depended on the sale of sheet music, piano rolls, and individual recording discs. Radio cut back drastically on the market for sheet music and the tradition of home entertainment. It also cultivated the public's taste for pop music that could be easily packaged, consumed, and quickly cleared out of the way for new products. Saturation airplay, it was found, could make a hit out of the most unlikely song, but the average duration of a song's popularity declined. Tin Pan Alley men were exasperated by the development. Song hustling had never been a quiet business. Now it became a frantic search for big hits. To make things worse, broadcasters in the early years of radio were notorious for shafting alleymen on their legitimate performance royalties for airplay of their songs. As early as 1931 the broadcasters paid ASCAP $1 million for the use of its songs, but it was too little too late.

In 1924 the broadcasters had formed the National Association of Broadcasters (NAB), which handled negotiations for royalties with the ASCAP people. Payments were made through the twenties. In 1930 a long-term agreement was negotiated that called for ASCAP royalties on overall radio billings to increase from 1 to 5 percent over a five year period. By the late thirties ASCAP claimed that the 5 percent ceiling on royalties was an unfair percentage, and announced that when the agreement ran out at the end of 1940 they would be demanding that the rate be increased to anywhere from 7½ percent to 15 percent, representing a 50-200 percent possible increase. In response the broadcasters formed their own licensing organization, Broadcast Music, Inc., in 1940. In spring of 1940 ASCAP released a more official statement of its demands, which called for a 100 percent increase in the royalty rate, from 5 to 10 percent of overall radio billings. The percentage spread represented a difference of between $5 million in annual royalties and $10 million.

Many observers feel the real quarrel between ASCAP and BMI was not over mere percentage points on royalty payments for air time play of records, but represented a much more pivotal struggle between the two entertainment giants of the time: movies and radio. Since the invention of the talkies and the movie *The Jazz Singer* in 1927, Hollywood studios had been interested in New York publishing companies. Many studios had bought up the rights to top ASCAP writers and music publishing firms. Warner Brothers, for example, had the rights to all the songs of Victor Herbert, Jerome Kern, Cole Porter, Noel Coward, George Gershwin, Sigmund Romberg, and Rodgers and Hart. The showdown in 1940, then, was also a showdown between the multimillion dollar movie/publishing business and the threat posed by radio entertainment.

Negotiations between ASCAP and the broadcasters were deadlocked through 1940, largely because of ASCAP intransigence. (A former NAB executive recalled going to an announced negotiation session with the ASCAP people, and being told they had all left for Florida for a brief vacation.) When the agreement between the two groups finally did run out at the end of 1940, all of ASCAP's music was taken off the air. For a period of ten months in 1941 radio stations only played songs by new BMI artists (there were also a couple of defections from the ASCAP camp) and old standards that had passed into the public domain, beyond the reach of copyright law, like "I Dream of Jeannie with the Light Brown Hair." Eventually a new agreement was reached between the two groups. Significantly enough, ASCAP finally settled for a 2.1 percent royalty rate on overall radio revenues, a setback from the previous 5 percent rate. BMI remained as a licensing organization and grew during the remainder of the 1940s.

BMI differed markedly from ASCAP in its structure, system of royalty payments to its publisher writers, attention to local radio airplay as well as network exposure of material, and policy of prompt payment and even advances offered on songs. It was fully identified with the rising tide of independent local broadcasters and diverse regional artists. For once, it was possible for black r&b artists and country and western musicians along with any number of songwriters who were unfamiliar with the intricate ways of the New York songwriting and publishing establishment to publish their material and get airplay and royalties. By the early fifties, of course, those regional styles of c&w and r&b were popular, and their proponent artists were largely licensed with BMI. ASCAP was, if not losing money, then losing its hold on music publishing. It struck back.

In 1953 thirty-three prominent ASCAP members, including Alan Jay Lerner, Ira Gershwin, and Paul Cunningham, filed a $150 million law suit against BMI. They cited antitrust law and accused BMI of fostering a conspiracy "to dominate and control the market for the use and exploitation of musical composition." Of course the broadcasters had no material interest in playing BMI music rather than ASCAP music. Virtually all radio stations had blanket licenses from both publishing organizations that had them pay royalties based on their gross advertising sales. Whether they played more of one organization's music than the other, they made no more money for themselves. Although the radio stations owned stock in BMI, to this day the company has never paid a dividend.

The law suit lingered. Then in late 1956 ASCAP moved again. This time it got a congressional investigation of BMI led by Emanuel Celler and the Antitrust Subcommittee of the House Judiciary Committee. Some of the testimony at the hearings held by that subcommittee was mentioned earlier. In 1958 ASCAP introduced a bill into Congress that would have barred the broadcasters from owning any stock in BMI. There were more committee hearings, with Celler again playing a conspicuous part. Finally there came the payola investigations of late 1959 and 1960, which began as an investigation of TV and moved to radio. At the time *Variety* reported that it was "ASCAP songsmiths who take credit for switching the spotlight from the TV quiz rigging to the disc jockey payola."

Payola itself had been in the music business for years and years. Gilbert and Sullivan paid money to get their hits played as far back as the 1880s. In the days of the pre-fifties publisher dominated industry, bandleaders or lead singers were often the focus of payola. These people were bribed to use one song or another in their personal appearances and recording, in an attempt to boost sheet music sales. As radio showed its power as a merchandising mechanism for the music, it became the focus of payola. This payola was carried on by many ASCAP publishers. In 1932, in radio's early years, ASCAP took pains to notify its members of the laws against the practice (in New York, anyway, a law against commercial bribery), and warned them of using money to get their songs played.

After the 1959-60 payola hearings the BMI-ASCAP battle went on. In 1960 ASCAP appealed to the FCC to rescind all operating licenses for stations that owned shares of BMI. Nothing came of the move. In 1962, after an antitrust suit ASCAP had brought against BMI was settled in favor of BMI, ASCAP suggested that TV stations be given an incentive for getting out of BMI membership. The incentive was to have come in the form of kickbacks on royalty payments. In 1964 there were more FCC hearings prompted by ASCAP.

Seen in this way, the payola investigations of 1959-60 were simply a highlight of a long-running argument and legal controversy between

ASCAP and BMI. The music industry has moved squarely from publisher domination that favored ASCAP writers to record and radio domination that uses a looser structure, like BMI's. In recent years ASCAP itself has come to recognize and accept changes in the way music is produced and marketed. It now offers advances on royalty payments, a practice for which it once bitterly attacked BMI. In the late sixties ASCAP even took out full page ads in *Rolling Stone* to attract young songwriters.

The 1959 hearings were the last gasp of Tin Pan Alley music, but not of ASCAP, which has continued to make money through the years. Still it is interesting to consider why a weakened ASCAP had power at all in 1960 to turn a congressional investigation of TV quiz shows to a heated investigation of radio payola. ASCAP's strength at the time is partly attributable to the Hollywood powers behind it. Hollywood was a much older institution than independent broadcasting, and had a more extensive lobbying system that carefully protected its interests. Another source of ASCAP power was the real threat posed by rock'n'roll music. 1960 was an election year. Many conservative congressmen were connected with legions of public decency back in their home districts. They saw themselves as moral guardians who represented parents back home who were quite simply appalled by the loud sexual music.

But the independent broadcasters were clearly a coming force in the business community, and rock'n'roll music would emerge even stronger with the Beatles invasion in 1964. It would provide the main source of radio programming on into the next two decades. Entering the sixties, the chain owners in fact were consolidated in their power, and Top 40 was the major rock'n'roll format. Local radio stations begun in the late 1940s or early 1950s were major business institutions. Rock'n'roll was here to pay. The payola investigations were some of the growing pains of the new business, in which a couple of hundred expendable djs were fall guys for a level of malpractice that approached, but probably did not surpass, that found in every other big business in the country. In the popular mind, the hearings receded almost immediately to the level of myth, pitting one music against another, with the main figures being well-bribed congressmen who tried to save American youth from itself.

One concrete result of the investigations, however, was a law clearly banning payola once and for all. The program director usually became a responsible agent for all music played at the radio stations. If there was any question that payola may have affected the exposure of a certain record, the program director was held answerable. Thus the hearings centralized and routinized rock'n'roll radio one step further. At first formula Top 40 radio did away with broad music selection and personality jocks; now power over all material played was centered in a single person, and djs were a weak adjunct. As the former vice president for sales of Capitol Records comments:

> The establishment of central programming resulted in a new manufacturer-radio relationship. Suddenly all new music had to be cleared through a central source. The program manager, or director, was now responsible for the station's "sound." He controlled on-the-air aspects; hiring and firing of disc jockey personnel, jingles, public service, contests, gimmicks, promotions and music were all under his autonomous control.[15]

With the additional responsibility of screening new releases and the flood of industry product in the early sixties, more and more of the program director's time was taken away from other tasks. Many radio stations divided labor and, while keeping the program director finally responsible for station affairs, developed a new job for a "music director." The music director then had exclusive responsibility for dealing with record company promo men and handling new releases.

Broadcasters genuinely worried about payola and FCC reprisals along with station owners who acted only cynically (and not stupidly), got rid of troublesome and interesting djs alike. Radio settled ever more comfortably into format programming. The Storz and McLendon concept of Top 40 was further refined and routinized by Bill Drake in the second wave of AM programming change that came after the Beatles Invasion.

MUSIC FOR
MUSIC'S SAKE
MEANS MORE
MONEY:
THE SIXTIES

The Record Business:
Getting It Right the Second Time Around

The Beatles made their debut in America at a time when the United States record industry was stagnating. The years 1955 through 1959 had seen retail sales increase as much as 36 percent each year. In 1960, however, industrywide sales were actually down (.5 percent) from the year before, and 1963 sales were up less than 2 percent from the year before. The general recession explained some of the decrease but a bigger problem was the music itself. With the exception of the "girl groups," the excitement generated by the r&b crossovers and the first wave of rock'n'roll had subsided; Philadelphia Schlock did little to bring it back.

The Beatles did not rejuvenate the industry singlehandedly. New styles of American music were emerging in New York and California, and the new type of record retailing, rack-jobbing, had been placing records before a broader spectrum of consumers. But the Beatles certainly signaled a new growth period for the record industry.

The Beatles, as everyone in the Western world must know by now, came from Liverpool, an industrial city northwest of London. They signed with the huge RCA-like electronic components firm EMI (Electrical and Musical Instruments, Ltd.) after George Martin, an EMI producer who had done mostly comedy albums, thought they might have something fresh. They had been turned down by most other British companies including British Decca, who picked a group called Brian Poole and The Tremoloes in their place. Their first contract with EMI gave them all of 1 cent royalties per single, 6 cents per album.

The group got off to a good start in 1962 with "Love Me Do" which made number seventeen on the British charts, followed by "Please Please Me" which hit number one. In 1963 for the first time in twelve years a British group, the Beatles, won the music poll of the British magazine *Melody Maker*. The boys were ready for the big time ("bigger than Elvis," hoped John Lennon), and they hit the States late that year.

Acceptance in the United States was not immediate but when it came it was hysterical. Ten thousand teenagers were waiting for the plane at the airport in New York. "I Want to Hold Your Hand" became the fastest breaking record that EMI's American subsidiary Capitol had ever released. By the end of the year the group had gotten twenty-eight sides on the singles charts and produced six top-selling albums. The record industry had never seen anything like it, not even Elvis. In the years 1963-68 the group sold an estimated $154 million worth of records worldwide.

The Beatles had more going for them than their light-hearted sexuality and wit, although both were new images for rock singers in America. Their manager, Brian Epstein, was extremely astute in promoting them. He was from Liverpool like them but had gone to private school and to the Royal Academy of Dramatic Arts before returning to manage the large record department in his family's department store. A customer's request for a Beatles record sent him to the Cavern, the sweaty, half-underground club that was the center of teen culture, or what passed for it, in Liverpool. He got the group their first contract, not an easy thing to do since they were so unorthodox for the time. Eighteen months later, having established the group in Britain he convinced Ed Sullivan to put them on his show even though British groups had usually failed in America. Sullivan gave them $2,400 for the appearance. The clean, suited image that Epstein built for the Beatles greased their way into the hearts of parents, as well as teenyboppers. Most significantly, Epstein promoted his act with coordinated press campaigns that emphasized the personalities of the Beatles as much as their music.

In addition to Epstein's packaging, the Beatles were also popularized by a $50,000 promotional campaign at Capitol. The money was spent mostly in New York since the company felt a success in that media center would spread to other cities. Although the Beatles eventually accounted for over 50 percent of Capitol's sales, the company was reluctant to back them until EMI insisted. Capitol evidently shared Sullivan's doubts about British groups. Before Capitol changed its mind, two independents, Vee Jay in Chicago and Swan in Philadelphia, put out singles based on rather minor agreements with the Beatles. The records engendered several lawsuits, but Swan's "She Loves You" still became the second best-selling single of the year. For its part MGM even pressed a single from a tape which an affiliate had made in Germany a year before.

Beyond their music, Epstein's promotion, and Capitol's belated push, the time was right for a new teen sound. Nineteen sixty-four was the year the postwar baby boom broke. Seventeen-year-olds became the largest single age group in that year.

The Beatles' success in the United States was followed to a lesser degree by a number of other British groups such as the Rolling Stones, the Dave Clark Five, the Hollies, the Animals, the Yardbirds, and Gerry and the Pacemakers, the last also managed by Epstein. The Beatles and the Stones continued into the seventies, of course, joined by a second generation of British groups led by the Cream, Led Zeppelin, and Jimi Hendrix.

New music was being developed in the United States at this time as well. In New York, Bob Dylan was moving from folk music into rock, adding electric guitars and a backup band to his traditional acoustic guitar accompaniment. He was soundly booed by condescending folk fans for his effort. "There was a lot of hypocrisy all around," he later told Anthony Scaduto, people saying "it had to be either folk or rock. But I knew it didn't have to be like that. I dug what the Beatles were doing, and I always kept [their success] in mind." Dylan's new style, quickly labeled folk rock, greatly expanded his audience, and gave him his first real commercial success; "Bringing It All Back Home," his fifth album, became one of the best-selling albums of 1965. Dylan was able to put an unsentimental concreteness about social situations into his singing, a rage against society and an ironic humor that was rare for the purely rock songs of the time. His synthesis influenced thousands of young people who were beginning to turn away from the norms of 1950s America. Other New York musicians like the members of the Blues Project and the Paul Butterfield Blues band from Chicago were beginning to electrify black country blues and to bring the Chicago blues to a new audience of white young people. The records of these groups sold with little publicity and virtually no airplay.

On the West Coast bands began to follow Dylan's move into folk rock. The Byrds were the most successful. They made hit singles of Dylan's "Mr. Tambourine Man" and "Turn, Turn, Turn." They were joined in Los Angeles by the soft-rock groups the Buffalo Springfield and the Mamas and the Papas, the Doors, a more electrified group, and the Mothers of Invention, probably the most experimental as well as satirical of the new California groups. The West Coast, along with a couple of city centers such as New York and Chicago, was producing a new white middle-class rock'n'roll music that drew from folk and earlier rock. It was inseparable from the new youth culture that was rejecting the consumer and goal-oriented patterns of adult middle-class America in favor of more free-living lifestyles involving shared communities and mind-expanding drugs.

The most developed center for the new progressive rock music and this new lifestyle was, of course, San Francisco. The major bands were the Jefferson Airplane, Big Brother and the Holding Company with Janis Joplin, the Quicksilver Messenger Service, the Grateful Dead, and Country Joe and the Fish. The Fish were from Berkeley, and often condescended to by critics and groups from across the Bay, but with their "Fish Cheer," "Vietnam Rag," and extreme psychedelic compositions, they had as much input as the others to the rest of the country. They were the only San Francisco psychedelic group to refer to part of their music as "rock and *soul* music."

The Airplane was the top band in the city commercially, but the Grateful Dead drew together all of the elements of the San Francisco scene and came to symbolize it to those outside California. The members of the Dead were mostly locals from Northern California cities. The group members had been influenced by a number of styles. Jerry Garcia had been involved in folk and bluegrass music, Phil Lesch had studied classical music and played trumpet, Pigpen (né Ron McKernan, the son of a white r&b disc jockey) was into electric blues. The name came in a moment of psychedelic inspiration: "One day we were all over at Phil's house smoking DMT," recalls Garcia. "He had a big Oxford dictionary, I opened it, and there was 'grateful dead,' those words juxtaposed. It was one of those moments, y'know, like everything else on the page went blank, diffuse, just sorta oozed away, and there was GRATEFUL DEAD, big black letters edged all around in gold, man, blasting out at me, such a stunning combination. So I said, 'How about Grateful Dead?' and that was it."[1]

Members of the Dead hung around with Ken Kesey's crowd in Palo Alto in the early days, and then played in the Acid Tests a few years later. They also played free in the parks and in Haight Street.

The music was reinforced by several dance ballrooms where thousands of turned-on kids went every weekend to see the groups and the light shows the ballrooms initiated. FM rock radio got its start in San Francisco at the same time, pioneered by several disc jockeys who, after dropping out of AM to take LSD and think things over, decided to develop a looser format to air the new music.

San Francisco musicians mixed with the new bands in Los Angeles.

David Crosby, first of the Byrds, then of Crosby, Stills, Nash, and Young, was central to this process. He lived in Venice (Los Angeles) with David Freiberg and Paul Kantner who became part of the Airplane, and hung out with Dino Valente who later joined Quicksilver.

The year that the various elements of the San Francisco scene seemed to jell, and to attract national attention, was 1967. In May the Beatles' "psychedelic" album was released—Sergeant Pepper's Lonely Hearts Club Band. The album, as had Revolver before to a lesser extent, helped to popularize acid and Indian music, as well as the less positive, more general trend toward Eastern *kitsch*. The power and popularity the Beatles had assumed in their straighter period was enabling them to lead millions of young people through a series of changes. In June came the Monterey Pop Festival. Attended by 30,000 people, it was the first large rock festival. Although it was initiated from Los Angeles and was co-produced by Lou Adler and John Phillips, both key L.A. music figures, it showcased the San Francisco musicians, along with Jimi Hendrix and The Who. The festival focused national attention on San Francisco. *Time* and *Newsweek* began doing their articles on "the hippies," and that summer thousands of "love children" descended on the city. The commercial possibilities inherent in such entusiasm were beginning to be noticed by record executives, many of whom, like Columbia's Clive Davis, had flown to Monterey.

As the various forms of the new white rock music appeared, an old controversy resurfaced: were the Beatles, Stones, and other r&b-influenced British groups, the Los Angeles-San Francisco psychedelic bands, and the white blues groups like Paul Butterfield or the Electric Flag, all nothing but further elaborations in the ever-continuing rip-off of black rhythm and blues music? Since the controversy is a complicated one, all of its ramifications will have to be saved for a later chapter. (See Chapter 7, Black Roots, White Fruits.) However, it is clear that in the big picture most forms of sixties rock (heavily folk-influenced groups like the Airplane and Dylan are partial exceptions) did have their roots in black r&b, along with country-influenced rockabillies who derived at least half of their inspiration from black singers and dancers, as well.

What is different about most of the white groups after 1967 is not their basic musical structure which is still largely blues/r&b derived, but rather the lyrics and the lifestyle that the groups represented. These groups were not simply presenting black music to a white pop audience that was unaware of it, as Perry Como and the other white cover artists had done in the fifties. The new groups represented an authentic white subculture that had been produced by the economic and social conditions of the sixties. It was not an extremely oppressed culture like that of the black ghettos, but it was a grouping that like blacks was differentiated from mainstream white America. Lyrics that concerned psyche-delic experiences and songs that lasted forty minutes were different from the techniques of both white pop music and black soul music.

As for rock music sung by white performers replacing, for the young white audience, rock'n'roll or r&b sung by blacks, the conclusion is clear. Says Ahmet Ertegun. "The little white girl in school loved to dance to Chuck Berry, but somehow John Lennon looked more like her dream, you know what I mean?"

Going to School with the Grateful Dead

Although record companies, especially the large ones, did not like the new rock music as music any more than they had liked fifties rock'n'roll, they were quicker to embrace it economically than they had rock'n'roll a decade before. In some ways the message was too obvious to miss. The Beatles, pushed by a British company, had created a commercial excite-ment unequaled in the history of the industry. Latching on to some of the other British groups was a simple matter. The distribution of some of them even fell automatically to American companies through joint licensing agreements with British firms. In other cases American groups were made to sound and dress like their British counterparts. Paul Revere and the Raiders on Columbia, who were from Oregon, and the Sir Douglas Quintet from Texas, on Tribe (Huey Meaux producing), were examples. White English singers also presented no racial "prob-lems" to bigoted executives and program directors. The folk rock groups were also easier for record companies to tolerate, at least at first. Major companies had been promoting clean folk groups like Peter, Paul, and Mary (Warner Brothers) and the Kingston Trio (Capitol) for several years, and the shift to folk rock was seen as a gradual one artistically. Columbia had signed Dylan when he was a pure folkie, although an outspoken one. With the Byrds the company got their first number one hit in the new wave—"Mr. Tambourine Man."

With two successful "sounds" just behind them, the industry was quick to move on the San Francisco music scene. Monterey had attracted a number of executives who recommended that various groups be signed. Columbia picked up Janis Joplin, RCA signed the Jefferson Airplane, Vanguard bought Country Joe and the Fish, and Warner Brothers on a tip from Tom Donahue contracted the Grateful Dead. Some of these groups had been signed before Monterey. A year later Capitol contracted the Quicksilver Messenger Service and the Steve Miller Band giving them quite a deal—16 percent royalties (based on wholesale prices) and $40,000 advances. "Some of the new groups are good," commented Max Weiss, one of the owners of San Francisco's Fantasy Records at the time, "but a little crazy. They are absolutely noncommercial and have to be taught to conform a little to make money." Others pointed out that the youth culture was so large in Northern California, that a San Francisco group could break even in that market alone.

Outside of the Bay Area, Los Angeles, and parts of New York, however, promotion was necessary—and usually a problem. Songs were too long or too "uncommercial" to be played on AM stations. "We found we couldn't sell the Grateful Dead's records in a traditional manner," said Joe Smith, president of Warner-Reprise. "You couldn't take your ad in *Billboard* and sell a record that way. We found that they had to be seen. They had to play concerts. We had to advertise on FM stations which were just emerging about that time. The packaging was important. The cult was important. Free concerts where you handed out fruits and nuts were important."[2]

The underground club circuit became an important avenue of promotion for acts that were seldom heard over the air. Companies would finance the tours, and assist in the bookings. Ads and reviews in underground papers were found to be extremely effective. "If they praise a record," discovered the Mercury promotion head, "the response is tremendous. If they put a record down, the lack of response is startling." Soon the bulk of advertising for many underground papers was coming from record companies. Columbia, followed by others, put out its own carefully written, "underground" news sheet called "Keep Your Ear to the Ground." It was directed at FM stations and head shops. CBS may have thought up the most outrageous corporate hype during the militancy of the sixties when it created an ad campaign for its new underground releases which tagged them "The New Revolutionaires." As FM radio quickly spread to the major cities throughout the country, record companies discovered that short radio ads, or *spots,* played over new music created quick sales. Radio soon outdistanced print in promotional importance. As college students joined hippies and sophisticated listeners in liking progressive rock, campuses became centers for record company promotions as well. Major companies established campus representatives (Warner Brothers had twenty-five), bought ads in campus papers and campus radio stations, and subsidized college concerts. By the end of the sixties record executives like Gil Frieson, then a vice president at A&M Records, spoke of a "Standard American Promotional Package" for new recording groups: "Billboards on Sunset Strip and Broadway, full page advertising in the underground press, the trades, and various other outlets; radio spots and a promotional tour with all expenses paid for by the label." "This package," he added, "is being used by practically every major label to lure in what the label considers to be 'heavy' talent."[3]

The underground groups caused new problems for record companies. Performers insisted on artwork that represented their music, and forced companies to spend more than they wanted to on covers. Of more significance, the groups spent far more time in the studio recording their albums. A&R men blamed the Beatles for starting this custom when they took hundreds of hours to record Sergeant Pepper. Warner Brothers considered dropping the Grateful Dead after they had spent $120,000 in studios around the country without coming up with a finished abum. (The group finally put together three albums from their tapes: Live Dead, Anthem of the Sun, and Aoxomoxoa.)

The controversy over studio time was one of goals: the company wanted commercial hits inexpensively produced; the new groups wanted musical creations. The tension over studio costs was always present, but when music for music's sake also meant commercial success as it did with the Beatles or Simon and Garfunkel, the group was indulged. Since recording costs were paid by the groups themselves out of royalty advances, record companies were hardly taking chances with successful groups, anyway. In the early years of underground music, "company freaks" were often hired to handle the clashes between long-haired musicians and record industry executives. Derek Taylor, the publicist for the Beatles, was in residence at A&M. Andy Wickham, another example, worked at Warner-Reprise.

The new rock music caused a shift from singles to albums. "The LP business really began with the advent of the heavier rock acts," said Don Kirshner in 1972. Since their singles were rarely played, albums were used to introduce the groups, who planned their albums as singles anyway, that is as conceptual units. The affluence of record buyers in the sixties also had a hand in allowing albums to sell like singles, and the switch was also forced by rack-jobbers who sold a selected number of best-selling albums in department stores throughout the country. In addition, albums afforded a greater profit margin, were less breakable, and cost only slightly more to handle. By 1969, 80 percent of the sales dollar was in LPs.

The record industry exhibited a number of different attitudes toward progressive rock. Most signed up a few groups and contracted with independent producers to supply them with new talent that they had difficulty recognizing themselves. Warner-Reprise and MGM probably represented two poles in the responses of the industry. Warner-Reprise made the decision to move on the music aggressively, creating a benevolent image for itself that was calculated to attract wary groups. Columbia used a lot of money and a certain amount of taste to sign Dylan, Joplin, Simon and Garfunkel, the Byrds, and Santana. RCA got the Airplane and several psychedelic groups that did not do as well but fared well with bubblegum groups like the Monkees and the Archies. Capitol rode with the Beatles.

MGM, however, followed a perspective pretty much its own, one usually the opposite of Warner-Reprise. It signed a number of progressive acts—the Mothers of Invention,Tim Hardin, John Sebastian, Eric Burdon, Laura Nyro, the Velvet Underground, and others—and then proceeded to alienate them. The company censored the Mothers' lyrics without consulting them and then released their records without bothering to tell them. They put out a record by John Sebastian that was recorded off a single speaker at a concert, in an effort to pressure him to adhere to their interpretation of his contract. They even released an entire album by the Grateful Dead (Vintage Dead) made from tapes initially intended for a one-song contribution to a "Sounds of San Francisco" LP proposed by another company but never produced. Legally, the Dead could do nothing. In the late sixties the company reportedly lost $4 million in a tasteless promotion of the Boston "Boss Town Sound." They hoped through hyperbole alone that Boston would become a second psychedelic record center to San Francisco. In 1970 the company turned against its progressive groups branding them "drug acts" and dumped eighteen from the label. "Hard drug groups," said company president Mike Curb, "come into your office, wipe out your secretary, waste the time of your promotion people, abuse the people in your organization, show no concern in the recording studio, abuse the equipment, and then to top things off, they break up."[4]

Curb was praised by President Nixon for his "forthright stand against drug abuse," but industry skeptics were quick to point out that Curb seemed more motivated by economic than moral considerations. Several obviously drug-oriented but strong-selling groups like Eric Burdon or Bobby Bloom ("You ain't been 'til you been high in Montego Bay") were to remain on the label while a number of completely unpsychedelic but poorly selling groups were among those getting the ax. The manager for Eric Burdon commented that he would be "ecstatic" if Curb would now let them leave the label because it was obvious, he felt, that the company president didn't understand rock music. Burdon left as soon as possible, followed by other acts, and the label soon changed its focus to clean teenybopper schlock like the Cowsills and the Osmonds.

Harnessing Creativity: *The Independent Producer*

An integral part of the record industry response to the new rock of the sixties was the growing utilization of independent producers. In the fifties the bulk of music was produced with staff producers who were assigned by the all-powerful A&R heads to record several of a company's acts. But these men often did not understand the new music. What's more, since many new groups wrote their own material, an A&R person was not needed to bring publisher and performer together. As conflicts between staff producers and groups increased, and as company A&R men proved for the most part unable to recognize underground talent, record companies turned to independent producers. In the fifties and early sixties a few independent producers had a practice of discovering and developing groups on their own, then selling completed prototypes or "masters" of single records to the companies. As the cost of a master rose from $400 to $500 to around $2,500, these producers often brought a group to a company for prior approval, signed contracts, and then with record company financing produced the master, which was turned over to the larger company for distribution. Often the new self-contained groups would stipulate in their contracts that they wished to work with a specific producer.

By the end of the sixties probably 80 percent of all records were being produced by independent producers. The arrangements usually took one of two forms: a simple arrangement with an outside producer who produced records for one of the acts at a larger company, or a more elaborate "label deal" or "joint venture" in which an outside producer formed a record label and contracted the material from the artists he produced on it to a major company for distribution. The arrangements were often done with a manager, or a group itself, like the Beatles, rather than just a producer and could also involve control over promotion and artwork in addition to recorded material.

Some of the more famous fifties independent producers were Norman Petty, who produced Buddy Holly from a studio in Clovis, New Mexico; Lee Hazelwood, who operated out of Phoenix, Arizona, before moving to Hollywood and was best known for his work with Duane Eddy; Jerry Lieber and Mike Stoller, who had careers as songwriters ("Hound Dog"), staff producers, independent producers, and owners of independent record companies. Besides their writing efforts for Presley, Lieber and Stoller were probably best known for their work with the Coasters and the Drifters. One of the best known producers in the history of rock has been Phil Spector, who has had as various a career as Lieber and Stoller.

Spector started out at age eighteen by writing "To Know Him Is to Love Him" (the title taken from the epitaph on his father's tombstone) and forming the Teddy Bears to sing the song. The single became a #1 hit in 1958 but Spector realized his main talent was not singing. He began to compose songs and help out on production with Lieber and Stoller and later at Atlantic and Liberty. He co-wrote "Spanish Harlem" in those years. Then, with PR man Lester Sill, who later became president of Screen Gems Pictures, he formed Philles Records (Phil plus

Les). Philles was a complete, independent record company which did its own distributing and promotion as well as production.

Spector developed his characteristic sound with the company—the Spector "Wall of Sound." The sound basically involved elaborate overdubbing, rare at the time, in which numerous strings, horns, drums, and so on were added to the basic singing track until it seemed that there was a rock orchestra backing the vocals. Brian Wilson of the BeachBoys, himself heavily influenced by Spector, called it "the Wagnerian approach to rock'n'roll." "Writing little symphonies for kids," said Spector. The one-mike-over-everything technique, a major component in the sound, was developed by accident when guitar sounds "leaked" from an unbuffered mike into the other microphones in the studio during the recording of, of all things, "Zip-A-Dee-Doo-Dah."

After "River Deep—Mountain High" sung by Tina Turner was poorly received, Spector retired in disgust returning several years later as an independent producer contracting several groups to A&M. He was eventually reintroduced to the Beatles by Allen Klein and started a new phase of his career, a rebirth, by producing John Lennon's "Instant Karma" and the Beatles' "Let It Be" album. Spector had met the Beatles in 1963 and even flew with them on their first trip to America. Always terribly afraid of plane crashes, he figured he would be safe flying with the Beatles since he was positive they would make it. He produced nearly all of Lennon's and Harrison's albums since the breakup of the Beatles until about 1974 and became the virtual A&R head at the Beatles' Apple label, somewhat in the tradition of fifties A&R men. At present he has made a label deal with Warner Brothers.

Although Spector was a seminal producer who virtually created the technological studio sound that influenced recording groups and companies, especially Motown, throughout the sixties and into the seventies, he was not really one of those independent producers that helped to solve the large record company's relation to creative rock music. His first heyday had been before the new wave. Though he was involved artistically with Apple and the Beatles, Allen Klein (the Beatles' second manager) and the Beatles themselves rather than Spector were instrumental in setting up the Apple label, which provided recorded material to Capitol. An independent producer who had a more direct role in steering major companies toward the independent producer as the link between them and the new groups was Lou Adler.

Adler was from the East L.A. ghetto, and like Spector he gravitated toward the record industry in his late teens. He and Herb Alpert worked up some demos that sounded something like rock'n'roll, and landed a job at Keene Records where they worked under Bumps Blackwell, and where Adler met Sam Cooke, who became a close friend. After a stint with a management firm that handled Latin acts like Tito Puente, Adler met Jan Berry and produced a record for Jan and Dean called Baby Talk. It was his first production, and acquainted him with the surfing scene. He formed Dunhill Productions around a Johnny Rivers album that became the first of the go-go records (Johnny Rivers Live at the Whiskey a Go-Go), and then turned the production company into Dunhill Records. Adler allied his label with ABC Records because he did not want to worry about sales and distribution, and did not have the money to finance the sessions. The second record Dunhill put out was Barry McGuire's "Eve of Destruction," a strange folk-rock smash that became a number one single. "I had a test on the first Dylan electric album and I gave it to P.F. Sloan ['Destruction' writer] telling him he ought to write some folk-rock stuff, which was just a label we put on it. . . . I didn't think it would get played."[5] McGuire introduced Adler to the musicians who were to become the Mamas and the Papas, and he turned out another series of hits.

At this point ABC realized Dunhill was a source of new music and that the Mamas and the Papas were an extremely valuable songwriting act and bought the company for close to $3 million. Almost immediately Adler formed Ode Records and contracted the distribution to CBS. It was the first time, says Adler, that CBS had agreed to distribute an independently owned label. CBS realized that a new music was being born, and felt that Adler, who had been a part of surfing music, the go-go fad, folk rock, and the West Coast scene in general, understood it. "Clive Davis had gone to the Monterey Pop Festival where he saw something happening, and he knew that I had put it on. But I had a great track record. He wasn't buying an unknown quantity."[6] After a time Adler switched distribution to A&M, which is co-owned by his old friend Alpert.

Adler's sound is different from Spector's. Instead of the elaborate overdubbing and the crescendo effects, records produced by him usually sound simple. Every instrument is clear, with no fogging. This is most evident on the Carole King records Adler has produced. Tapestry, which is at more than 13 million copies the highest selling album of all time, "was a very naked sounding album. I wanted it to sound like she was in the room playing piano for you." Although the records with Johnny Rivers and the Mamas and the Papas are more heavily produced—live effects preserved, strings added—the aim is to bring the artist out, rather than to create something new as Spector often seems to be doing by using the singer as only one of several variables in the total production.

Like a few other independent producers, Adler has always done more than produce the session. He usually coordinates the artwork and tries to design the ad campaigns. His contract with larger labels has been written to allow him to do this.

By the end of the sixties, various musicians and groups were beginning to form their own independent production companies to control artistic content and packaging while contracting with larger companies for distribution. Frank Zappa and the Mothers of Invention, fed up with the attitude toward progressive rock acts at MGM, left that company in 1968 when their contract expired and formed Bizarre, Inc. Bizarre was also a management company handling the Stone Poneys and Tim Buckley besides Zappa and the Mothers, but it was mainly a record label. Zappa and his business partner Herb Cohen signed with Warner-Reprise for distribution. Bizarre proved the value that independent label deals could have for a larger company. Zappa found and developed artists like Alice Cooper that probably would never have been recognized by a large company. The Cooper band was directed to Warner-Reprise several years later and became one of their highest selling acts.

Other examples in the late sixties were the Beach Boys, who founded Brother Records with Capitol distributing. The group later complained that Capitol was stealing royalties and that an independent label deal with the company offered them no more freedom than a standard relation. (Brian Wilson liked to call Capitol Records "Captive Records.") The Jefferson Airplane created Grunt Records but allowed their old company RCA to distribute. Like Capitol and other companies faced with an act that wasn't satisfied with their company, RCA found that doing a label deal was better than having the group leave the company altogether. Besides the greater creative freedom label deals usually offered, groups liked the fact that they could sign other musical acts to their new labels.

Although a few artists like the Tokens and Frank Sinatra had formed their own labels long before, the Beatles were the group that started the trend toward artist companies in the sixties. They used Apple as the economic unit to spring their ideas on the world. Set up with $2 million dollars after Brian Epstein's death in 1967, it had five divisions: records, music publishing, films, electronics, and retailing.

But Apple exemplified the possible pitfalls of an artist-run company. The Beatles lost hundreds of thousands of dollars through miscellaneous electronics inventions that never saw the market and through a boutique in London run by a financially profligate design group called The Fool. Liquor and side expenses by the staff were more than exorbitant and the Beatles were bled by an assortment of friends, some newfound, others old. By the end of the first year the company had lost a cool million. At that point John Lennon brought in music accountant Allen Klein who restored order. Paul McCartney preferred his new father-in-law, lawyer Lee Eastman, and separated from the group. Klein was a cigar-chomping entrepreneur who certainly exacted a percentage for his services, but he based fewer business decisions on the *I Ching*. Like most groups, the Beatles realized that as part of a money-making enterprise operating in a capitalist economy they needed a capitalist to handle business affairs. Groups that have felt otherwise, with the possible exception of the Grateful Dead, have unfortunately failed.

The Apple label was distributed by Capitol from the beginning. As Phil Spector pointed out the group would have been "fighting their old Capitol product" if they had chosen to distribute with another company. Capitol would even have been able to release tapes from sessions the Beatles judged inferior.

Merging

In the middle and late sixties a large number of companies in the music industry bought up or merged with other companies involved with music, or were themselves bought out by large conglomerates from outside the industry. Some of these mergers represented a response to new rock music or, put another way, a response to the continuing success of the independent companies.

But the merger movement in the music industry was also a "natural" process of centralization in which the successful companies joined to save expenses, to control prices and the market more effectively, and to amalgamate companies specializing in different types of music into one corporation that provided greater financing and simpler, central distribution. This centralization was no different than the process that had already occurred in older industries such as film, or for that matter, steel, rubber, and tobacco. Finally, the merger movement in the music industry was part of the unprecedented merger movement going on in the wider American economy of the sixties. Because the music business had become so profitable and because as part of the entertainment industry it was a high growth field, outside conglomerates looking for new acquisitions found music corporations attractive.

There were three types of mergers going on in the music industry. All were occurring simultaneously and were related to each other, but discussing them separately makes it easier to understand the different factors at work.

The first type of merger was "horizontal" involving companies that operated at the same level in the music industry: record companies buying other record companies, for instance, or distributors merging with other distributors. Horizontal mergers in the music business reduced competition where companies were operating in the same market—most often the case with distributors and rack-jobbers—and increased the spread over different audiences where the companies involved produced different types of music, as with record companies.

The most prominent horizontal merger of the latter kind involved Warner-Reprise whose parent firm bought Atlantic in 1967 and Elektra in 1970. (See pp. 204-205.)

Several large foreign record companies made horizontal mergers with American companies. EMI's purchase of Capitol in the fifties led the way. Phillips, the huge electronic and music concern in Europe, bought Mercury, and later MGM.

"Vertical" mergers were also proceeding throughout the middle and late sixties. These involved the integration of different levels of the industry—record companies buying up distributors or retailers for instance. ABC-Paramount became the first big record company to move heavily into distribution when it bought up the nationwide rack-jobbing/distributing/one-stop complex of New Deal Records, as well as several companies that covered specific regions. It was followed by Capitol in 1968, which acquired 53 percent of Merco Enterprises, a Long Island rack-jobber that serviced the Macy and Gimbel chains and 300 college stores in the East. In turn, several large distributor/rack-jobbers like Schwartz Brothers moved into the retail field. In 1969 CBS bought the Discount Records stores, a chain of youth-oriented, full-line stores mostly located near college campuses. CBS claimed that its purchase would allow it to experiment with new merchandising methods. Several years before, CBS had acquired the Fender Guitar and Amplifier Corporation. These purchases allowed them to make use of the financial, promotional, and advertising structures they had already developed in other areas of the music industry.

Vertical mergers allowed companies to keep middleman profits for themselves, and to control the selling as well as the manufacturing end of the industry. These mergers often had a defensive, snowballing effect. Other manufacturers moved to protect themselves from their competitor's monopolies by buying outlets of their own—distribution companies in the case of manufacturers, rack-jobbing firms or retail chains in the case of distributors.

The most important mergers of the sixties were the well-publicized "conglomerate mergers," initiated from outside the music industry. As the record and music business began to grow large, the companies in it were noticed by the conglomerate corporations involved in the large merger movement taking place in the American economy at this time. (Conglomerates are corporations containing companies involved in unrelated businesses, amalgamated into a financial and managerial unit.) The merger movement in the sixties was greater than any other merger period in the history of American capitalism, even more than the era of trusts at the turn of the century.

Although some of these mergers were brought about for standard reasons of efficiency, in which a conglomerate would put together a number of smaller companies in an unconcentrated industry or buy up manufacturer and retailer to achieve vertical integration, many of these mergers were made in order to drive up the stock of the parent conglomerate. Mergers were a quick way for conglomerates to expand overall sales and to increase per share earnings—two factors that were crucial in determining the value of the shares of the parent conglomerate, at least in the speculative investment climate of the 1960s in which other traditional valuation factors like net worth or debt to equity ratios were often overlooked. Financing the acquisition of target companies was made easy for the conglomerates by the federal tax structure at the time which made it possible to charge off most of the money needed to buy the companies as a nontaxable expense.*

Companies in the music industry were especially attractive to merger-hungry conglomerates. Earnings at music companies were high, 10 to 15 percent after taxes according to an Atlantic official, and the companies were part of the entertainment field which was growing in the affluent sixties. The industry also catered to the fastest growing and quickest spending segment of the population, people between twelve and thirty. "Frankly," said a spokesman for the Commonwealth United Corporation, a large conglomerate, "we've made marketing studies of the music industry and we see definite signs of an unlimited growth potential in the field."[7] "Brokers realize," said Arthur Mogull, president of Tetragrammaton Records in 1969, "that the return on capital is much more rapid than in, let us say, the motion picture business."[8]

Dozens of record companies, independent production companies, and music publishing firms, booking agencies, management companies, and even concert promotion companies were bought up by conglomerates in the 1960s. The scale of the merger activity was also illustrated by several proposed mergers that fell through: ABC with ITT, Imperial with Studebaker-Packard (back in 1958), and MCA with Westinghouse Electric.

Warner Brothers-Reprise was sold along with the film and other divisions to a small film distributing company called Seven Arts. (Again, see the separate Warner profile, pp. 201-209.) The company was then unloaded, for $350-450 million.

Gulf and Western, a conglomerate with $2 billion in assets ranging from real estate to zinc mines to ammunition production, bought the

---

*For an explanation of this complicated and extremely lucrative process see "The Merger Movement: A Study in Power" by Paul Sweezy and Harry Magdoff in *Superconcentration/Supercorporation*, ed. Ralph L. Andreano (Andover, Mass.: Warner Modular Publications, 1973).

Paramount record and film organization in 1967. A "business technology expert" was brought in from Litton Industries.[9] Gulf and Western added Stax Records to its list of companies in 1968 when Stax left Atlantic, which had distributed for them for eight years. Stax's president Jim Stewart remained at the head of the company. The great Chess company was sold in 1969 for $6 million and 20,000 shares of (GRT) stock to GRT, the tape firm.

Omega Equities, the highly predatory conglomerate, run by James Ling, one of the founders of the most active of the *new* conglomerates, Ling-Temco-Vaught (as opposed to *established* conglomerates like ITT), bought up Roulette Records, and also set up the North American Leisure Corporation (NAL) to manufacture tape cartridges. The conglomerate also acquired producer Snuff Garrett's labels. At the end of 1968 Omega's wheeling and dealing outside the music industry caused the company to run afoul of the Securities and Exchange Commission which suspended the trading of Omega shares. The SEC charged Omega with selling securities "on the basis of inaccurate and incomplete information relating to the company's financial condition, product line, and acquisition program."[10] Part of the reason for the crackdown was that older, more established conglomerates like ITT, General Electric, and RCA, who had begun to worry about competition from "upstart" conglomerates, had pressured government agencies to monitor loose merger practices more closely.

While the new conglomerates were beginning to run into trouble with regulatory agencies and their own overextension, they were faced with another sort of problem concerning their acquisitions in the music industry. Many of the music men like Al Bell of Stax (which had been bought by G&W) who had stayed on as executives under conglomerate management, often selling out their interests, became unhappy at the pressures on them to run their music companies like other subsidiaries of the conglomerate. Executives were told to maintain a certain stable growth rate no matter what sort of talent they had at the time. Faced with these directives, many executives and producers left to form their own companies or to join others. Since many of the smaller companies acquired by conglomerates were built around one or two key people, a company would become a white elephant, impossible to sell, when these men left.

To the better run companies and those interested in entertainment for its intrinsic commercial possibilities rather than as a means to manipulate stock prices, concentration brought certain advantages. Duplication could be eliminated and accounting centralized. Profitable, coordinated, multimedia promotion was possible for those companies that owned a combination of record, radio, television, and talent management companies. Concentration also further reinforced the stable pricing practices that the large majors, RCA and Columbia, had established long ago. In an industry dominated by a dozen or so large manufacturers any sort of price cutting only hurts everyone. (Competitive pricing would be welcomed by consumers, of course.) Like other U.S. monopolies the record industry rarely competes in terms of prices, and when one large company feels that market or profit considerations necessitate a price increase, everyone follows suit. Competition is confined to nonprice strategies for raising sales—to advertising, promotion, and innovations.

The linking of record companies to nonentertainment conglomerates raised a moral question that has bothered a few musicians from time to time: that the profits from their creations were being used to develop and manufacture war machinery produced by other subsidiaries of the parent corporation. In effect the profits of the record division of RCA and Capitol-EMI, for instance, from the records of the Jefferson Airplane, or John Lennon and George Harrison, go to finance the development of armaments in other sectors of the larger corporation. Keith Richard of the Rolling Stones told an interviewer how he felt about the situation:

> How can you check up on the fucking record company when to get it together in the first place you have to be out on that stage every fucking night, you have to get out there every night in front of the people saying here I am and this is what I do. You can't keep a check on it. Someone else is handling all the bread.
>
> We found out, and it wasn't years till we did, that all the bread we made for Decca was going into making little black boxes that go into American Air Force bombers to bomb fucking North Vietnam. They took the bread we made for them and put it into the radar section of their business. When we found that out, it blew our minds. That was it. Goddamn, you find out you've helped to kill God knows how many thousands of people without even knowing it.
>
> I'd rather the Mafia than Decca.[11]

Why did the owners of companies involved in the music industry sell? For most, selling was the easiest way to cash in on the enterprises they had built up. Since there was no market for the private stock of most of these companies, it was necessary to sell or trade control in the companies to large corporations that were interested. A man might be making many thousands of dollars a year in salary, but be sitting on assets of several million which could not be disposed of. Selling meant security, of course, since an owner would no longer have to worry about some crisis destroying his company. In most cases he was retained in his leadership position at an attractive salary by the acquiring corporation.

Most sales were actually trades. Owners would trade stock in their companies for the stock of the larger corporation. In effect the owner of a small company subjected to the vicissitudes of the specific music market was trading for stock in a diversified corporation spread over several market areas. No income or capital gains taxes needed to be paid on the trades as opposed to cash sales. Of course if the stock in the larger company went down over time as was the case with some big companies in the early seventies, the sale was worth less. For the small company itself, in addition to the owner, a merger provided a source of capital for expansion and, as part of a more powerful corporation, financial security in times of crisis. In the early sixties rising costs, especially artists' royalties, packaging, promotion, and producing, had opened many independent concerns to the idea of eventual merger.

The Last of the Big Indies: *Lonely Bulls and the Volkswagen Body*

By 1970 few independent record companies of any significance were left. Larry Uttal's Bell Records was bought by Columbia Pictures in 1970. Fantasy Records in San Francisco was attracting attention with Creedence Clearwater Revival, but essentially it was a one act company. The two important indies left were A&M and Motown.

A&M was formed in 1962 by trumpet player Herb Alpert (the A) and promotion man Jerry Moss (the M). Alpert had been a cohort of Lou Adler's and Sam Cooke's at Dore Records. (The three wrote Cooke's "Wonderful World" together.) The association began when Moss helped promote a record Alpert had produced with Adler. The two eventually took an instrumental called "Twinkle Star," gave it a two-horn lead, and added some "Ole's" and crowd noises taped in a bullfight in Tijuana. The song, renamed "The Lonely Bull," sold 700,000 copies and launched the new company. Alpert turned out a string of successful albums such as Whipped Cream and Other Delights, Going Places, South of the Border, What Now My Love, Lonely Bull (all in the Top 10!), that made the Tijuana Brass second in sales to the Beatles in 1966. The music seemed to cut across pop lines but was especially successful with middle-of-the-road listeners.

The company continued to do a huge volume with a small roster of "easy listening" acts like the Brass, Sergio Mendez and Brazil '66, the Sandpipers, and Bert Bacharach. After the Monterey Festival, however, Moss went to England and started to sign new rock groups like Procol Harum and Joe Cocker as well as Cat Stevens, who was more of a folk singer. The association with Cocker taught the company how to sell the new rock, much as Warner Brothers had "gone to school with" the Grateful Dead. The company tied in even more solidly to newer music by making a label deal with Lou Adler's Ode Records, which releases

Cheech and Chong among others. By 1971 A&M had sales of $32 million and a reputation for releasing a small number of carefully selected records that were then strongly promoted.

The first Motown label was started two years before A&M. It has since become in terms of sales the largest black-owned business in the United States. The Motown legend always mentions that founder Berry Gordy began as an assembly line worker in a Ford plant. Gordy did do that, but he got his start in the music business by opening a record store on a loan from his father who was a plastering contractor (his mother was an insurance agent). "I loved jazz—Stan Kenton, Thelonious Monk, Charlie Parker—and I wanted to let people know I was modern, so I called the place the 3-D Record Mart. People started coming in and asking for things like Fats Domino. Pretty soon I was asking, 'Who is this Fats Domino? What is this rhythm and blues stuff?' I listened and ordered a few records by these people and sold them. Still all my capital was tied up in jazz, but jazz didn't have the fact—the beat. I went bankrupt."[12] Then after working for his father and Ford, Gordy began to produce masters and sell them to record companies in New York. Soon an eighteen-year-old songwriter named William (Smokey) Robinson persuaded him to set up his own company, which he did, on a loan of $700 from members of his family. Robinson wrote "Shop Around" soon after and they released it late in 1960. A few months later it had sold a million copies. In the next two years the company had a series of hits by the Miracles, Martha and the Vandellas, and the Contours, including two that became number one singles—the Marvelettes' "Please Mr. Postman" and Stevie Wonder's "Fingertips," made when he was twelve. (See pp. 258-261, for detailed description of Motown's later years.)

Motown was a highly organized record company. "A factory-type operation," Gordy called it. To many the Motown sound of the sixties sounded similar on every record. "They have invented the Volkswagen body and there isn't very much that can go wrong with it," said Phil Spector. Motown music was designed and mastered for three-minute radio exposure.

By 1967 the company as a whole was grossing an estimated $30 million annually.* The figure reached $40 million in 1972. Sixty percent of singles and nearly 70 percent of albums were hitting the *Billboard* charts. It's hard to guess what percentage of Motown's sales were in the white market but the company estimated in 1967 that when a record sold a million copies at least 70 percent of the buyers were white. Partly in response to this but also to minimize the effect of racism in the industry,

---

*Motown rarely releases sales figures. It is the only large record company that does not even allow the RIAA audits that determine Gold Records.

Motown has had white executives handle sales and public relations, especially in the early years.

Wholesale Mayhem, Retail Madness

By the end of the 1960s the marketing of records had changed completely from the decade before—both in the type of outlets where records were sold and in the wholesale distribution patterns. The changes were brought about by some of the same factors that affected the rest of the music industry in this period, suburbanization, the merger movement, and the rise of progressive rock. The results were greater concentration of wholesaling and retailing functions with the elimination of the old independent distributors and the mom and pop retail stores, further integration of the different aspects of the record industry, and, most likely, greater overall record sales.

In the fifties, as explained before, records were sold for the most part in mom and pop record stores. Big discounters like Sam Goody in New York began to replace them in larger cities, but they were not put out of business *en masse* until the rise of rack-jobbing.

Rack-jobbing is essentially the servicing of shelf space or *racks* in retail stores with various products. A rack jobber buys the toilet articles, spices, or whatever, from a distributor (or direct from the manufacturer if he is large enough), places them in spaces reserved for them in supermarkets or drugstores, and replaces them regularly as they are sold.

In the fifties general retail practices in the United States were changing. The idea of self-service and the concept of "scrambled merchandising"—drug stores selling radios or grocery stores selling toiletries and some hardware—were beginning to spread. Supermarkets and large chain stores were growing at a great rate, replacing the mom and pop stores of every description. The suburbanization of America, which took place in this decade, was an underlying demographic cause of these marketing changes.

Record rack-jobbers started out as rack-jobbers of other products. Dave Handleman, now head of one of the two or three largest rack-jobbing firms, began by selling Kotex, condoms, and candles in drugstores throughout Michigan, then decided to sell 45s and 78s in the same way. Charlie Schlang was another early racker. He bought returned records that record companies no longer wanted in their catalogues and sold them as budget items in rack boxes. Record rack-jobbers made all selections, handled shelf displays, and provided store owners with 100 percent return privileges. Department stores began to use rack-jobbers to handle their record departments which quite often were losing money in competition with discount record stores. As rack-jobber expertise grew and costs were kept low by volume buying, discount chains began to turn to them as well as regular department stores. A variation on the standard practice was to lease a department in a discount store to the rack-jobber. The majority of companies that handle leased department stores are also in rack-jobbing.

Rack-jobbing quickly began to affect independent distributors. Since they operated on a regional or national level, rack-jobbers bought where the price was lowest, not necessarily from the local distributor where the store was located. As volume grew rack-jobbers began to bypass distributors altogether and buy directly from the record companies. The record companies were glad to give discounts to stable, high-volume customers. In some cases rack-jobbers set up paper distribution companies that bought at distributor prices and funneled the records to a rack-jobbing arm of the corporation. Furthermore, the success of stores and departments served by racks put the mom and pop stores out of business, and the independent distributors found themselves without customers. The independent distributor had become a superfluous second middleman.

The elimination of the independent distributor was accelerated from the other end by record company practices. Independent distributors reached their peak with the proliferation of independent record companies in the fifties, but record company mergers in the sixties created such large units that branch distribution operated directly by the manufacturer became more efficient and more profitable, as least as long as the companies turned out hits in sufficient numbers. In effect most big companies, with the exception of A&M and Motown, which stuck to independent distributors, were now distributing as Columbia had always done.

The development of progressive rock also played a hand in eliminating the indie distributors. Distributors had had an important role in promotion for the independent companies in the fifties, but with progressive rock, record companies began to design elaborate promo campaigns from new "creative services" departments within their companies. Independent distributors also seemed to have a hard time understanding the new music. Said Jac Holzman, whose Elektra Records became part of the Warner-Elektra-Atlantic branch distribution system, "When the manufacturers took over promotion, the handwriting was on the wall." Tight money in the early seventies was a final factor that did in the independent distributors. (It also hurt the rack-jobbers.) Many retailers stalled on their bills, and the distributors had to default on their accounts to the manufacturers.

Pressed by the rack-jobbers on one side and the record companies on the other, the independent distributor either went bankrupt, as many did, or expanded his operation to include rack-jobbing. Those that expanded quickly enough became large concerns. Other distributors were bought up by rack-jobbers. The "one-stops," those small distributors that serviced jukeboxes in the fifties, also expanded their operations to include those small stores, often variety stores, that were too small to deal with distributors. One-stops have mostly been bought up by rack-jobbers, too.

In 1961 racks had accounted for $47 million in sales and nonrack stores for $305 million, while in 1966, five years later, racks accounted for $365 million (40.9 percent) and nonrack stores $372 million (41.7 percent).* By 1970 rack-jobbers and the owners of leased departments (mostly rack-jobbing concerns) represented more than 70 percent of all retail sales in the United States. By placing records in outlets and locations that had not carried them before, rack-jobbers probably increased record sales. To what degree is impossible to say, but it has been estimated that rack-jobbing expanded the number of retail outlets carrying records by five times.

Rack-jobbing created some dislocations in the music industry besides its effect on small retailers and independent distributors. It hurt the singles business, for instance, since albums which yielded greater profits were naturally allotted most or all of the limited space in outlets serviced by racks. A greater problem for the entire industry was returns.

One of the strengths of rack-jobbers has always been that they carry only the hits, at most the 200 best-selling albums with perhaps a sprinkling of singles. Stocking only the hits removes the risk of choosing records that don't sell yet take up display space and cost money in labor time, especially in returns. Stocking "all the hits" means limiting selection, however, and in the early seventies "full-line" retail stores stocking close to the entire catalogs of many labels began to cut into the rack-jobbers' business. The full-line stores like Tower Records in California also tried to create a loose in-store environment with poster art, records stacked on the floor, and give-aways (retail madness or "organized chaos," Tower's owner Russ Solomon called it) that was in contrast to the standard displays of records in racked department stores and it appealed to many consumers. The full-line stores even offered a little hope to those independent distributors still in business. Some rack-jobber/distributors countered by opening their own retail stores. Schwartz Brothers opened a store in New Jersey with a half million dollar inventory. Pickwick International opened fifteen stores in 1970 and had some 130 free-standing record/tape stores by 1972.

---

*Jukeboxes represented 4.4 percent of sales in 1966 and record clubs and mail order houses, 13 percent. All sales are at list price figures for retail and are therefore at least 20 percent above actual selling price.

By the early seventies, then, wholesaling and retailing were often integrated and the business was concentrated in the hands of a few large corporations. ABC had bought up a nationwide network of rack-jobbers and distributors, as had Capitol and Transcontinental. Pickwick, originally a budget line, had merged with Heilicher Brothers, Handleman, the biggest rack-jobber/distributor, was still not aligned with a larger corporation. Together they accounted for a huge percentage of the retail and wholesale record business, several hundred million dollars in sales. (In 1973 Handleman and Pickwick/Heilicher netted $10 million each on revenues of about $100 million each according to *Business Week*.) Big discounters and full-line stores dominated the retail market along with the racks, and a few chains—one of the largest, Discount Records, being itself a CBS subsidiary. In some cases—CBS, ABC, and Capitol before they sold their racks—all facets of the industry including manufacturing and production, distribution, and retailing were united in the same company. In all large companies except for A&M and Motown all facets but retailing were under the same corporate roof. The music industry had come to resemble other monopolized industries such as tobacco, steel, rubber, and automobiles. The process of concentration had been similar. It had just taken place in a shorter time period: one decade.

How Concentrated Is the Music Industry?

The process of concentration in the music industry has not been the same in the different parts of the business—retail, wholesale, and basic production (the record companies). In retailing, the pattern is identical to most other industries. A large number of small retail units have been concentrated into a few super firms, either full-line chains or rack-jobbers. The dynamic with distribution has also been one in which a number of small firms have been put out of business by a few even larger ones. Distribution is different in that vertical integration has been more widespread. Most distribution is now handled by the record companies.

With the record companies themselves the story is a little different. The industry did not begin with a number of small companies and gradually come to be monopolized by a few powerful firms. From the beginning a few, two or three, large firms have accounted for a majority of industry volume. The major reason for this is that the two biggest record companies have since 1900 been linked to phonograph firms and since the thirties to large broadcasting and electronics corporations. A number of small companies operated in the twenties but they were eliminated or bought by the larger firms in the depression. In the 1947-57 period a number of small record companies again entered the market but the biggest firms still accounted for at least half of the business. In the 1957-67 period, as the old-line companies misappraised rock'n'roll, some independents did capture more of the market. But in the latest phase, 1967 to the present, most of these smaller firms were merged with older companies or amalgamated by conglomerates.

Statistics that can be used to make accurate comparisons are difficult to come by, but a reasonable picture can be put together from a look at the number of companies accounting for pop hits. In 1954 (when, unfortunately for a comparison, classical and country were more significant) the Top 8 record companies accounted for 85 percent of the pop and r&b market, according to *Billboard.*[13] (These were the seven "majors" plus Dot. The statistics were used by the magazine to compare "majors," meaning companies that did their own distribution, with the indies.) In 1973 the Top 8 companies accounted for 82.9 percent of *all* records and tapes sold (estimated from the records that made the *Billboard* charts.)[14] In other words there has been little change, except that the top record companies now control a market that is ten times larger than it was in 1954 ($2 billion vs. $213 million).

When compared to other American industries the record industry seems highly monopolized. In 1973 the Top 4 record corporations accounted for 52.8 percent of all records and tapes sold (again based on the *Billboard* charts). By comparison in 1962 (when figures are available) the four largest petroleum refining companies accounted for 50.3 percent of oil industry sales, the four largest rubber corporations accounted for 48.1 percent of rubber sales, the four largest primary iron and steel corporations for 40.2 percent, the four largest makers of food products for 12.5 percent, the four largest apparel manufacturers for 4.9 percent, and so on.[15] And of course when all parts of the music industry are taken together, record companies, distributors, and retailers, and when the degree of vertical integration is also considered, the music industry must be seen as a highly monopolized sector of U.S. business.

Finally, although the record industry is easier to enter than many other industries since, for example, several thousand copies of a single can be recorded and pressed for a few thousand dollars, it is still highly unlikely that a company starting from scratch, from a few hit records, can now become an industry giant. A&M and Motown were able to do this during the sixties but the tendency since then has been for successful small companies to be bought up by larger firms ever on the lookout for executive and producer talent. (Asylum Records is a good case in point: see pp. 201-209.) Most producers would now simply make a label deal with a larger corporation since distribution is so much trouble and so monopolized itself.

Tape

If full-line stores and numerous widely placed outlets served by rack-jobbers helped to increase sales among the record-buying public, the introduction of tape brought many new consumers into the music industry for the first time. Tape had been around for years in its reel-to-reel form but that mostly appealed to hi-fi enthusiasts. What opened up the mass market was the car playback system. RCA was the record company most involved in pioneering car tape systems, and their attitudes toward the new market shows that it was a carefully researched move on their part, typical of decision-making practices in a large corporation.

> The beautiful idea of eight-track stereo tape cartridges did not simply emerge one morning full-blown like a Venus on the half-shell. It evolved painstakingly, after several false starts, from a technological developments and careful consumer motivational studies over a period of years.
>
> These studies were especially important. They revealed that a new lifestyle had taken hold and was rapidly accelerating in our country. A lifestyle epitomized by the expression "A Generation on the Go." . . .
>
> These were people whose ideas of leisure went far beyond the confines of home and hearth, who sought diversion in travel to far away places, in participative sports, in expensive hobbies, in second homes; even in novel ways of feeding themselves with instant, frozen and powdered convenience foods which wasted little time in the kitchen and did so much to enhance the accelerated habit of dining out. Furthermore, these studies ranked the enjoyment of recorded music very high—especially with the young. But they also revealed that despite this interest and our ever growing sales of records, we were only doing business with half the population.
>
> Given this picture of the changing consumer, it was apparent that our market might eventually run away from us if we remained rooted to the living room phonograph; that we had better do something about making recorded entertainment as mobile as the consumer himself and that the auto was the obvious place to begin.[16]

While RCA went with the 8-track concept, car tapes were first pioneered in 4-track. George Eash and Earl Muntz were the major innovators. They licked the technical problem of how to get enough tape to go around in the cartridge without binding or stopping. The cartridge was simply two small reels enclosed in plastic. They opened Muntz Stereo Pak in 1963 and began selling installation units and tapes in Southern California. The idea took off by word of mouth with almost no advertising.

Although technically at least as good, 4-track was soon to be replaced by 8-track which had the backing of several major corporations. RCA and Lear Jet, who had been one of the distributors for Muntz 4-track, felt that 8-track provided longer playing time and more automatic operation. They sold the idea to Ford in 1965, and Ford contracted the manufacture of playback units to Motorola. RCA was to provide the initial software catalogue and Lear Jet, the cartridges. Ford then initiated a multimillion dollar advertising and sales promotion campaign to launch the 8-track system which it offered in its cars. Motorola conducted a campaign at the same time that convinced General Motors, Chrysler, American Motors, and Volkswagen to install 8-track exclusively. Faced with such large-scale competition, Muntz, which had initially tried but failed to interest car manufacturers, lost out to 8-track. By 1967 all the major record companies were committed to 8-track. By 1970 8-track cartridges represented 79 percent of the market and 4-track accounted for only 1 percent.

The cassette system had been considered but because it was mechanically more complex it was felt at the time to be less reliable in the automated environment of wide temperature changes, high vibration, shock, and voltage variations. The major companies involved also wanted the car system to be compatible with home systems in order to increase sales, and the cassette machine did not yet provide high enough fidelity.

Improvements in cassette operation were quick in coming, however, because its major innovator, the huge Dutch electronics conglomerate Phillips, waived all claims of royalty fees and licensing agreements to manufacturers who wanted to develop improvements on the basic cassette system or produce software for it. Phillips' move also enabled its system to eliminate competitive cassette systems pushed by RCA, Telefunken, and Grundig who required royalty and licensing fees. Cassettes accounted for 5 percent of the tape market in 1967 but climbed to 18 percent in 1969.

The growth of tape was matched by the growth in ownership of car, home, and portable tape recorders. The annual sales of tape players surpassed that of record players sometime in 1971, and reached $861 million in 1972, as compared to $577 million for phonographs.*

The effect of tapes on record sales is complicated. At first certain companies, especially Columbia, asserted that tape would be "an evolution, not a revolution." But tape sold so well that these predictions were proved wrong. Consumers, it was found in 1968, liked tape cartridges because of their convenience, ease of handling, high sound quality (this was incorrect: sound quality was inferior at the time), and, compared to records, their greater durability, and easier storage.[17] After growing from 10 percent of the market in 1967, tape sales leveled off in

---

*Based on factory sales plus imports.

1970 to about 30 percent of record music sales. Major industry market researchers have predicted, however, that tape purchases will equal record sales in 1976 and that by 1982 tape will represent 70 percent of music sales. RCA did a study on buyers of 8-track stereo systems which showed that 45 percent of playback purchases were made by people who owned no record player or if they did, had not bought a record for at least a year before buying their tape player. These people clearly generated new music sales. The others, however, were found to be buying fewer records and more tapes. RCA concluded that tape purchases would accelerate. A factor left out in industry surveys was the rise of "downer" drug use, primarily of methaqualones and barbiturates. Young drivers on downers found that heavy rock music played at high volume through car stereo systems sounded rather nice. Sales of some heavy rock groups like Deep Purple were reported to be 70 percent in the tape configuration.

The manufacture of tape cartridges prerecorded with music was initially done by several tape duplication companies. The three main companies were General Recording Tape (GRT), Ampex, and the International Tape Cartridge Company. These companies licensed music from the record companies. GRT paid them $7,500,000 for the exclusive rights to RCA's music for 1972-77. Ampex signed up many of the other large record companies. Record companies soon decided to manufacture their own tapes, or at least to handle distributing and marketing of their tapes themselves. The tape duplicators began to set up or finance independent production companies to assure themselves of a supply of music to duplicate. GRT financed Blue Thumb for instance.

In the first few years after tape cartridges took hold the duplicators did well. By 1971, though, the duplicators were beginning to be overextended, and were feeling the effects of the defection of some of the major record companies. Tape duplicators also had overestimated the market for music, which actually slumped in these years. Ampex lost some $12 million in fiscal 1971 and nearly $90 million in 1972, partly from unprofitable tape recorder lines but also from bad deals made in their tape duplication division.[18] Speaking with the smug perspective of the record companies, Clive Davis, former president of CBS Records, summed up what happened:

> Non-record companies have come into our industry—mainly in the tape field—and have made contractual deals that stagger economic common sense. What has this outpouring of money brought to them? Very little indeed. If the same money had been spent in carefully building an organization that understood and supported creativity, much better results would have been achieved.[19]

Piracy

The success of tape focused attention on one of the long time illegalities of the record business: unauthorized recordings, usually called bootlegging or piracy.

Tape was an easy market for illegal duplicators. It was growing so fast that it was hard to monitor, the tapes were compact, and they were sold in a variety of new outlets such as gasoline stations that had little regard for far-away record companies. "The bootlegger got 50 percent of the business," said Earl Muntz recently. "We were making guarantees to these record companies and the bootlegger didn't have to pay anything."[20]

Joe Smith of Warner-Reprise claimed bootleggers netted $130 million in 1970.[21] Other people placed the figure somewhat lower, but nobody doubted that it was a *very* big business. According to Henry Brief, the head of the record manufacturers' trade association, illegal tapes cost only 75 cents to turn out, and could be sold for $2 and up. Duplicating equipment could be had for $500.

Violators were usually only convicted with civil statutes if caught, and simply paid a fine of $500 or so. Smith claimed in an interview that only petty criminals were involved ("real garbage people") but others felt that organized crime might be involved. "It has reached the proportions today that we must conclude that this is a highly organized operation," said Henry Brief in 1970. "Does that mean the Mafia?" his interviewer asked him. "You said that, not me," Brief replied. "We're looking into it."

Record companies began to fight back strongly in the late sixties. They refused to sell to dealers who carried bootlegged records and tapes. They lobbied for a new bill in Congress and finally got the McClellan antipiracy amendment passed to the 1906 national copyright law. The permission of the record manufacturers was now needed to duplicate records and tapes. Music publishers were allowed to claim $1 per unit damages on the profits from the sale of bootleg tape. Before the new law they were only entitled to a few pennies.

The record industry trade association still complained about off-the-air recording done for home use, and even of large numbers of tiny transistor radios that teenagers listened to all the time instead of buying records, but the big money problem, pirate tapes and records, seemed to be on its way to being licked.

Even so in 1973 one estimate placed the total value of bootlegged tapes and records that year at over $200 million. In 1973 *Billboard* in conjunction with the American Federation of Musicians and AFTRA conducted a three week investigation of bootleg recordings in retail outlets in New York City that proved embarrassing to a number of record stores. Unauthorized releases were discovered in Colony, King

Karol, Record Hunter, Dayton's, and Doubleday's Fifth Avenue outlets as well as Sam Goody's stores. Jeff Teitlebaum, a buyer for Goody, denied the charge.

The sixties were a decade of tremendous change for the music industry. A new music had arrived, or resurfaced in a different form. New ways of promoting and producing this music had been developed that integrated it into the financial and corporate structure of large companies while preserving enough creativity to keep record buyers happy. And the music industry as a whole had grown up. Retail, wholesale, and manufacture had joined in many instances, and the overall industry had been discovered and made a part of the larger corporate establishment in America.

The major institution which popularized the new music of the sixties, at least from 1968 on, was FM radio. Suppressed by corporate decision makers for thirty years, it made its comeback simultaneously with San Francisco rock. AM radio also made changes in the sixties, but adapted more slowly to the new music.

AM and FM Radio

The post-Beatles flowering of rock eventually expanded the radio business and made it more sophisticated, much the way it did the record companies themselves, in the development of FM stereo broadcast. Its immediate effect on AM, however, was to tighten up formats even more than in the heyday of Top 40. The main innovator in AM during the middle and late sixties was Bill Drake.

Drake Does Battle with Dead Air

Bill Drake learned much of what he knew about radio at station KYA in San Francisco in the early sixties. After the payola scandal had hit Philadelphia, ace jocks like "Big Daddy" Tom Donahue and Bobby "The Great" Mitchell had left WIBG for the Bay Area, doing a lot of old r&b material on the "jingle free" Top 40 station. In addition to having a varied playlist and some of the best djs in the country, KYA was distinguished by its insistent musical call letter identification ("Radio KYA!!! Boss of the Bay!!!") that substituted for a formal station break, and an endless series of promotional gimmicks. Drake took the more strident parts of KYA's formula with him when he went to KYNO in Fresno, California, as program director in 1961. There he perfected his Boss Top 40 format, which promised "More More Music!!" by reducing the commercials per hour from the maximum allowed (18) or the usual number (14-16) to a rigid 12 sets per hour. He also cleaned up the sound of the previous Top 40. He shortened jingles, made the contests simpler, got rid of most special sound effects and, perhaps most important, held disc jockeys to rigid time sequences between songs and commercials.

Drake radio was airtight radio. He eliminated pauses, which he termed "dead air." He perfected what is now the stereotype of the incredibly fast-talking dj. As he once put it, a jock should feel "free to talk if he has anything to say—anything as far as content or anything else. But if you're going to say nothing, say it in as few words as possible." Drake djs said "nothing" faster than anyone else. One of the most famous was "The Real" Don Steele, who might be heard any afternoon over KHJ in Los Angeles sounding something like this:

> Three o'clock in Boss Angelese! And gey HEY, thitz me, The Real Don Steele, a billion dollar weekend there, and you're looking out of sidewalk call; I got nothing but those groovy golds. We're gonna fit Chuck out here on a fractious Friday boy, got to get a set outside that (unintelligible word resembling blowing bubbles in a glass of water) jumbo city. (Pause) Take a trip. When you chase 'em, daylight.[22]

That particular Steele monologue was clocked at some sixteen seconds, unusually long for a Drake station, where jocks usually kept their comments to about eight seconds of screaming over a song introduction.

Drake's formula of more more music did in fact clean up Top 40 sound and inject more minutes of music into each hour. But the music tended to be even more homogeneous than before. The adoption of Drake style programming was usually accompanied by reduction in playlist at a given station, from forty to thirty, and sometimes fewer, records. Drake completed the depersonalization of AM radio by reducing the role of the dj to robot. He made AM radio a continuous wall of raucous noise punctuated by a repeating series of songs. Actually he had done little more than tighten up Top 40 in an especially rigorous way. As RKO General Radio president Bruce Johnson later commented, "He was like a chef. He found a new recipe for the old ingredients."[23] But the formula was fabulously successful and until every other major station in the AM market closely copied him, Drake programming was distinguishable, and he was personally in great demand.

KYNO became the hottest station in its market in six months. During the next couple of years, in 1964 and 1965, Drake established himself as a "programming consultant" for KGB in San Diego, and the RKO stations KFRC in San Francisco and KHJ in Los Angeles. In 1967 General Tire and Rubber Company (which fully owns RKO as a subsidiary) president Tom O'Neill, who was impressed with what Drake had done for his West Coast stations, gave him control of the rest of the radio chain. Among the thirteen stations to come under his power was progressive format WOR-FM in New York, which Drake changed to a golden oldies format in his first real clash with the growing FM radio movement.

A more refined version of the oldies formula was tried successfully in

1972 at KRTH ("K-Earth") FM in Los Angeles, and then at WFYR-FM ("Fire Radio") in Chicago, WAXY in Miami, and WROR in Boston, all RKO stations. The original WOR-FM oldies show had real djs. The later ones were automated formats, another important programming feature that Drake helped popularize in rock radio. A series of tapes were simply played on the various stations, with breaks for announcements of the weather, time, and some local and national news. The jocks used in the syndicated RKO-Drake package of oldies tunes recorded the tapes in Los Angeles or New York, then mailed them out to the various stations. The small additions to the format were made by local station personnel, but required virtually no thought.

Thus power was centralized in Drake and the RKO-General national offices to an unprecedented degree. Even with the live jock AM stations he programmed for the chain, Drake had absolute control over the style and content of dj performance. During his time with RKO he kept in touch with his air empire of thirteen stations via a red "hot line" telephone in his house in Bel Air, California, that connected him directly with the control booths of his different stations. At any point, Drake could monitor a broadcast and, when he wanted to make a correction in a disc jockey's style or change the records being played, call up the station right away. The hot line was a sort of Big Brother that was one more factor in keeping Drake jocks to a rigidly stylized approach, and kept the Drake sound absolutely uniform.

Drake not only did programming for RKO, although they were certainly his most important account. His services were available to whomever could afford them. He routinely charged $100,000 for program consultation, and usually collected a steady retainer from a station even after he left, should they keep many of his programming changes.

In 1970 Drake recognized the inroads on the music market being made by progressive rock FM, and recommended that RKO-General cut back on the number of commercial breaks in the average hour of airplay to four "commercial clusters." He also suggested they integrate album cuts in with the singles. Johnson reports:

> It didn't seem to work very well, or at least the rating at our stations started to drop at the beginning of 1971. I think that many AM stations switched to the four cluster because they felt the FM stations were a threat. And because FM stations weren't playing Top 40—they were playing more the new music—but it turned out to be a disaster. In the case of our New York station WOR-FM, which had the oldies market completely wrapped up and at the time was Number 2 and 3 in the city, they started feeling the pressure for some reason from the WPLJ's and WNEW-FM's, the progressives in New York, and they started playing album cuts instead of oldies. It drove the

format from, I think, 80,000 listeners per quarter hour to 10,000 per quarter hour in about six books, six reports (rating reports). So when we came in last year, in July of '72, after a lot of thought and after all kinds of information that we had, we decided to return to the basics again, back to Top 40.[24]

This time RKO did it largely without the help of Drake, whose contract with the chain was severed in August of 1972. There were extensive legal wranglings over his rights to his programming style, and the rights to the syndicated automated oldies format that had brought RKO-General such success with loser FM stations all over the country. All these disputes have either been muted or settled on terms generally favorable to RKO. Drake has gone on to syndicate his various other automated formats. He still programs some 150 stations, although they are much smaller than the RKO chain, and his overall influence within the industry has dropped off sharply.

Syndication and Automation

Drake's oldies shows with RKO reflected two major trends in sixties AM radio: a revival of the concept of syndication (or the same show carried on a number of different stations) and automated formats that eliminated disc jockeys and resulted in even more uniform and controlled sound in radio. Syndication goes way back to the early days of radio. Martin Block had his show syndicated in 1940, and Alan Freed had a syndication deal working with WINS for years.

Watermark Inc. and Stereo Radio Productions are now the biggest firms dealing with taped formats. The first is headed by Tom Rounds, who produces the lucrative American Top 40 show that is aired on 400 stations in the United States and abroad each week. Stereo Radio Productions is the leading firm in automated format radio. They specialize in "wall to wall" or "beautiful" music, meaning light classical and background. Their WPAT in New York is an example of the genre, which uses stereo FM in creating a totally bland environmental radio.

Top Fifteen?

AM radio expanded in the 1960s, as it had the decade previous. Both periods saw an additional thousand stations formed. But the overall picture of radio powers changed relatively little in the 1960s, especially compared to the fifties.

There are only about 181 important AM stations in the national market. Fifty-one of these are considered "primary" stations because they are located in those twenty-four cities which account for 54 percent of overall record sales. An additional 130 are "secondary" stations, located in regional, or auxiliary markets. The secondary stations are important in their own areas, of course, and can be used through "back door promotion" by record companies to help build a song on the primary stations.

The most powerful radio chains today, like RKO, Bartell, and the ABC network stations, are the ones that own the primary stations, have the largest ad revenues, and the most power in influencing other stations and their audiences to make hit songs and sell products.* All of these and the secondary chains and networks have extremely tight playlists which are centrally controlled. WRKO in Boston, for example, takes elaborate pains to pick records. The music director for the station, Marie Wright, listens to the hundred or so new records she receives each week and then, by calling local retailers, checks on the popularity of those few songs she likes. She notes whether secondary stations in outlying towns are playing any of the records, whether they have been included on the playlists of major stations in other cities like New York and Philadelphia, and whether they have reached the upper levels of the Hot 100 charts in *Billboard*, or are specially scored on the latest Bill Gavin report or other radio trade tip sheets and rating charts. Next she gets on the phone to the RKO-General national music director in Los Angeles, who has been duplicating the research process on a national level. Together they decide which two or three songs to "go on" for the week.

Promotion men from record companies and radio personnel at other stations in Boston claim that RKO is really programmed completely from L.A. Marie Wright tends to emphasize her local autonomy, and it does seem plausible that regional tastes can make a difference in the RKO system. But in practice this autonomy is tightly controlled, anyway, because centralized hit selection has certain other advantages.

"There is no way," comments Bruce Johnson, "for payola to get involved in our setup because the jocks can't pick up a record, nor can the local music director or program director unilaterally go on some record without having actual substantive proof that the record is going to be a hit." Under such control, playlists have contracted from the legendary Top 40 to around 27 on RKO general stations, and even less at WABC, one of the most important AM properties in the country. The New York station regularly plays only about fifteen records at a time.

---

*ABC AM stations include WABC New York, WLS Chicago, KGO San Francisco, KABC Los Angeles, WXYZ Detroit, and KQV Pittsburgh; Bartell stations include WOKY in Milwaukee, WADO New York, KCBQ San Diego; Metromedia AM properties include KLAC Los Angeles, KNEW Oakland, WCBM Baltimore, WIP Philadelphia; RKO-General has WRKO Boston, WGMS Bethesda, WHBQ Memphis, KFRC San Francisco, KHJ Los Angeles, WOR New York.

Concern over payola and the continuing quest for uniform sound are two reasons for shortened playlists. The main reason, however, is a simpler one. Stations playing fewer records and adopting the "all hits" formula have proven more popular.

The popularity of radio stations is judged by three nationwide survey organizations, to which radio stations ordinarily subscribe. One of the organizations, the American Research Bureau, runs the Arbitron survey, in which a "diary" is sent out to all the members of sample households above the age of twelve. The different diaries are filled out by cooperating households, and register the listening habits of the different members of the household. The survey usually lasts four weeks, with each cooperating home filling out the diaries only for a single week of the four. In major markets Arbitron is conducted four times a year. It provides radio stations with a complex set of demographics (statistics indicating correlations between age, sex, and location and radio listening habits) on their audience. The Arbitron diary system is supplemented sometimes with telephone interviewing. Significantly, the households participating in the survey are originally contacted by telephone. The Pulse Survey uses personal interviews instead of the diary forms as the basis of its sample, and keeps track not only of standard demographics and estimated audience size, but also the racial and ethnic balance of the audience. Many radio personnel feel that the Pulse Survey is particularly useful in locating the black radio audience. The Hooper survey relies exclusively on telephone interviews, although it takes the limits of this method into account, and projects figures for the poorer black audience that is less easily reached through telephone. In the Hooper sample, people are simply called up and asked if there is a radio in their home, if it is on at the time of the telephone call, what station is playing if it is on, and what station the respondent listened to the day before.

There are more sophisticated survey techniques now available to social scientists, and these too may one day be used in radio programming research. One broad area left to explore is the field of "psychographics," or what the psychological reaction of the listener is to different songs, commercials, jingles, or news material. Methods of psychographic research have been developed in laboratories, using electronic sensors attached to the listener's skin, something like a lie detector. There are a lot of bugs in the system, however, and of course there is the problem of duplicating, or taking into account in some statistical way, the difference in reaction between someone driving along and listening to the radio in their car, and sitting in a laboratory with a lot of electrodes hooked onto them. For the time being, then, the Pulse, Hooper, and Arbitron surveys suffice.

Radio stations are absolute slaves to the demographics of these three surveys. Advertisers make their buying decisions based on them, and program formats are changed to suit them. What has been found, basically, is that no one listens to AM radio for long, so the trick is less to attract an audience with a balanced and diverse format than to keep the fickle "quarter hour audience" from tuning out, or switching radio stations. A recent RKO survey indicated that the average eighteen- to twenty-four-year-old male listens to 5.2 radio stations a *day*. In most cases, no one station is listened to for more than a few minutes. With such a fickle audience, an extremely tight playlist of only the most popular songs seems to make sense. The hits keep coming.

Radio stations are organized top down, like other corporations, with a definite hierarchy and division of labor among employees. This is particularly true of the big AM stations. At the RKO chain, for example, at the top of each station is a general manager who makes all final decisions. The general manager is also the link to overall chain management. Under him are a program director, sales manager, chief engineer, and comptroller or business manager. The program director is responsible for the overall sound of the station. Anything that goes out over the air is tied to him. He supervises the work of the news director, the public service and community affairs director, and the music director or librarian. In chains, as noted earlier, the programming director and music director are limited in their power to determine the musical content of what is programmed. The sales manager handles selling time to clients. He often has several assistants who do the same thing. The salesmen work on a part salaried, part commissioned basis. Large stations have regular sales staffs of between five and ten people. The chief engineer also has a number of people working under him in maintaining the station equipment. The business manager or comptroller handles the accounts at the station. He keeps track of bills, receipts, the general cash flow, and other financial matters.

Beneath the program director, who is himself restricted by the chain management, are the disc jockeys. Their jobs are now automated and as routine as that of the station accountant, and allow as much initiative. Djs should have seen the writing on the wall back in the 1950s when the Bartell and Plough Top 40 chains began copyrighting different station dj names, like Johnny Rabbit, Bob Rollins, and Johnny Holiday, and getting interchangeable people to fill in air time behind the names. Through the rest of the rise of Top 40, Drake, and post-Drake contracting playlists and automated formats, disc jockeys have become steadily less important. Although they are paid as well as station general managers (at big AM properties anywhere from $30,000-$70,000 on the average) they make far fewer real decisions. Once the popularizers of a new music, AM djs are now cheerful robots whose personality and musical taste are predetermined by packaged formats and rating demographics.

The important personnel in AM radio today are national executives and national music directors, who outline the broad policy of the chain, and make determinations on specific songs. It is the national office that connects the local stations into the real powers in the record industry.

RKO-General, like other chains, has a policy of censoring songs with blatant drug lyrics, or some sexual content in songs. In the national office the chain has evolved a long list of criteria for judging what is obscene, or in questionable taste, or politically dangerous. Whatever an individual program director's feeling about a song, the decisions on censorship come from the corporate headquarters. If, says Johnson, there is a particular word or phrase that is objectionable in a song, "we will take it out, or we'll go back to the record company and ask them to take it out before we play it, and we won't be playing that record until they do." Record companies are also asked to provide shortened versions of album cuts to AM stations, and to modify the artists' product in various other ways to make it suitable for AM. They often oblige, simply because of the commercial importance of the medium. If WABC or KHJ goes on a song, for example, it has been proven again and again that that means a minimum of 50,000 units of additional sales, almost automatically. If a major chain makes a commitment to a song nationally, sales will be boosted several hundred thousand units.

In its lumbering and conservative ways, AM appears dead to the latest developments in music, but it is by no means dead as a huge and profitable industry. In 1976 national AM radio billings in the United States ran to around $1.4 *billion.* (See Charts 3.1, 3.2.) A single station for RKO-General, WOR-AM in New York, recorded more than $10 million in sales. A minute of time at KHJ-Los Angeles for a multispot buyer is around $135, at WABC-New York around $205. Specific AM properties do not compare to television station billings where a network buy* of a minute's time often runs upwards of $50,000, but that is only

---

*Television advertising more than radio is divided between network and spot buys. A network time purchase means an advertiser is willing to commit money for a long period of time, usually well in advance, to a national show, and evolved out of the old sponsor system in TV packaging. A purchase of spot time is time bought on a particular network affiliate, and is scheduled during "adjacency" positions; before or after the show, or during station identifications. In fact it is not unusual for spot time on a local TV station to be as low as $200, which makes it directly comparable to AM radio. Since network time buys are still a very important factor in television production, however, to suggest that time buys on television and AM radio were roughly equivalent would be misleading.

Chart 3.1
Radio Advertising Revenues 1959-1974
(millions of dollars)

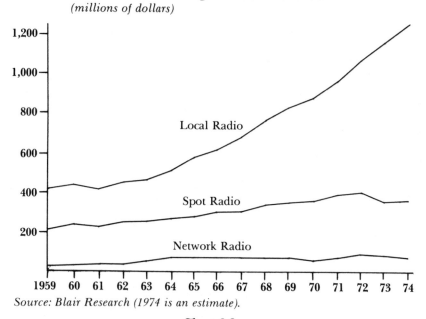

Source: Blair Research (1974 is an estimate).

Chart 3.2
Radio and Television Advertising Revenues 1959-1974
(billions of dollars)

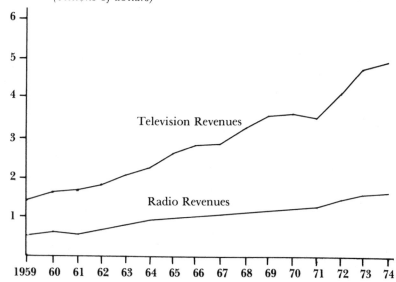

Source: McCann-Erickson (1974, Blair estimate).

because they do not reach a mass audience in the way the TV networks do. Taken as a whole the AM radio business is of staggering size and is still turning a healthy profit.

Frequency Modulation

AM radio in the sixties, because it was such a capital intensive operation with its own history, protocol, and advertising philosophy, did not adjust to the progressive rock sounds of the post-Beatles era. Even as Drake was accumulating a small fortune from his RKO programming in the late sixties, radio was beginning to take another turn. In 1965 the FCC had ordered stations in the top 100 markets (cities with more than 100,000 people) not to duplicate AM-FM programming for more than 50 percent of their daily schedule. The costs of partially separated programming in effect forced station owners to divide AM and FM completely, using the latter to break into new markets, sustained by its own, independent advertising base. Many stations were therefore divided into two essentially different stations, often for different audiences. Other joint station owners released their FM properties, creating a mild buyer's market immediately after the 1965 decision. (See Chart 3.3.)

Chart 3.3
Number of Authorized Radio and Television Stations 1922-1974

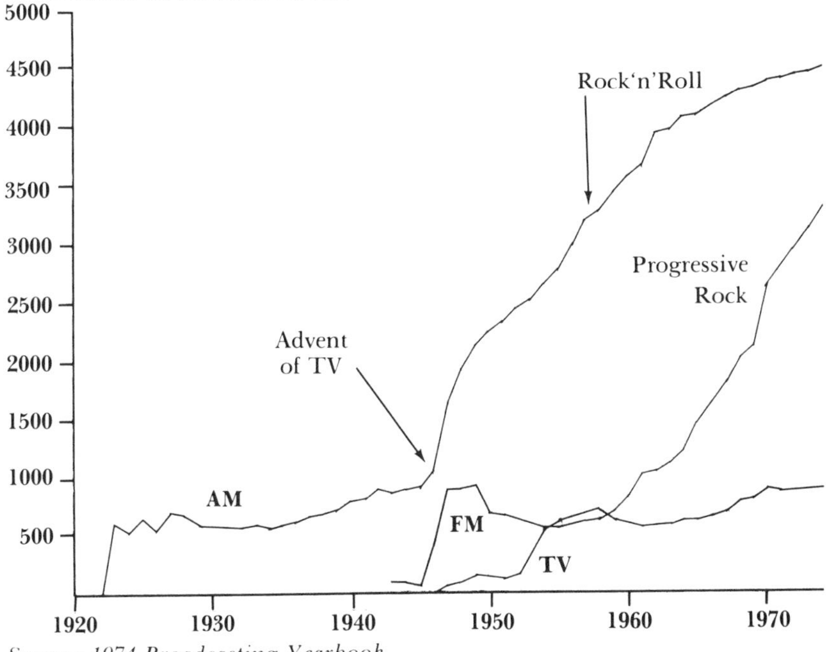

Source: 1974 Broadcasting Yearbook.

In the late sixties flowering of L.A. based folk rock, San Francisco psychedelia, and a continuing stream of British imports, FM rock radio first emerged as a commercial force. Beginning in San Francisco, it spread throughout the West Coast, into a few major Eastern markets, the college circuit, and finally into suburbia and the Midwest. In many important markets, rock FM came to rival Drake-style AM radio for the teenage and young adult audience. Advertising dollars soon followed.

Tom Donahue Throws a Rope to a Drowning Man . . .

One of the earliest experimenters in FM was Tom Donahue, whose career has spanned the history of progressive rock radio, and can be used to focus on its origins, initial promise, and commercialization. Donahue was a veteran AM jock who left a long standing job at WIBG in Philadelphia in 1960 following some heat from the payola investigation. He worked at KYA in San Francisco for a couple of years as a colleague of Bill Drake, playing mostly old r&b records from the fifties, then left AM to dabble in promoting (including San Francisco's first Beatles concert in Candlestick Park in 1964) and producing some early San Francisco bands, and forming Autumn Records.

He was highly successful. Over a four-year period, of the twenty-four singles the label released nationally, eighteen made the national charts and two were Top 10 hits. Autumn recorded the Beau Brummels, an early American Beatles imitation, as well as The Great Society with Grace Slick, and Sly and the Mojo Men, the first Sly Stone group. In fact, Sly (Sylvester Stewart) was resident producer for many of their acts. Despite its early success, the record company had real management problems. Donahue decided to abandon Autumn in 1966. As he explains:

> I had discovered that my partner in the enterprise was dying of Hodgkin's disease, and so was losing a lot of his interest in it. All he wanted to do was forget about the fact that he was dying, and find something that would help him do that. I was taking a tremendous amount of acid. You know, you're taking acid three or four times a week and it's very hard to talk to 37 distributors, and ask them the first day where your money is, the second day what they're doing about your records, and the third day, where your money is. So that wasn't working either, you know. I didn't get back to radio right away. I didn't do anything for about a year and a half. I was a geriatric drop out. My old lady and I got an apartment on upper Grant, and we took acid and laid back for almost a year and a half. And tried to keep it all in the air, somehow, I don't really remember how.[25]

The year and a half of thinking and lying about and listening to music convinced Donahue that Top 40 AM radio was estranged from the real music scene. At first he thought of going back to some AM station, and shaking it up some with more varied programming. Then one day:

> A friend of mine . . . was talking to me . . . about stereo FM which I knew nothing about because I didn't even have an FM radio. The more he talked it, the more fascinated I became with the idea, and I knew there were a lot of FM radios in San Francisco because it was a heavy ethnic market. I knew all those Chinese kids had FM radios in their houses, and a lot of Latin kids. So I started calling FM stations in town. I called KMPX and the phone was disconnected so I figured: "Ah, now I've got one." A drowning man doesn't care who throws him a rope. I went over and talked to them. At first they wanted to sell me all of the air time, and then have me go out and peddle it. Well, I knew I didn't want to do that. We finally came to an accommodation because the guy, the Chinese guy who was doing the 8 pm to Midnight show hadn't paid his bill in about six months. They said OK, I could have from 8 to Midnight, and then I would sell time within it and we'd get to keep half or a third of what I sold. This was the idea that if my shows worked, they would let me expand them to the rest of the time on the station.[26]

This was April 7, 1967. Within a few months the entire station was programmed in Donahue's freestyle way, the first progressive commercial FM station. Later in the year, writing in *Rolling Stone,* he denounced AM radio as "A Rotting Corpse Stinking Up the Airwaves," and explained the success of KMPX:

> For the past six months KMPX in San Francisco has been conducting a highly successful experiment in a new kind of contemporary music programming. It is a format that embraces the best of today's rock and roll, folk, traditional and city blues, raga, electronic music, and some jazz and classical selections. I believe that music should not be treated as a group of objects to be sorted out like eggs with each category kept rigidly apart from the others, and it is exciting to discover that there is a large audience that shares that premise.[27]

MPX was owned by Leon Crosby, although Donahue brought in his own financial backing and advisor Lew Avery. Together they expanded and opened up another progressive FM station in Pasadena, KPPC. They were the starting points for the movement to FM progressive rock that swept the country in the late sixties, and that, in the suburban markets, continues to this day.

The spectacular growth of FM is attributable to its technical superiority to AM, and relative cheapness as an investment medium.* In the

---

*For a more ample discussion of FM's technical superiority to AM, see Chapter 1, The Early Years, pp. 9-13.

late fifties, it was found that the great range of FM channels could not only sustain a higher fidelity for single signal transmission, but could in fact also be used to broadcast two separate signals simultaneously in a process called "multiplexing." This discovery made possible stereo musical broadcast. Stereo broadcast was particularly attractive to those audiences discriminating and wealthy enough to prefer high fidelity music, and by 1961, some fifty-seven stations were multiplexing largely MOR and classical music. As the rock audience grew in size and sophistication, it came to demand the same sound quality which it could get from records at home (reflected in a tremendous increase in the middle and late sixties in the stereo component market), but could not get from AM radio.

By 1970, three years after the introduction of progressive rock FM, there were 668 multiplex outlets. Because FM had initially been discouraged as an investment medium by a series of FCC and major network moves against it in the late 1940s and the expense of receiver parts, the FM stations that became so attractive to rock'n'rollers in the late sixties were much cheaper than the high pressured and well-endowed AM counterparts. FM attracted a new crowd of venture capitalists, a sort of businessman's avant garde on the edge of the counterculture, which invested heavily in the new medium. FM's growth dovetailed with other hip capitalist enterprises, like the ballroom circuit of concerts and the first widely successful underground newspapers.

As unique as Donahue's KMPX programming was, it had in fact been anticipated in radio's more open days during the rise of independent local stations broadcasting r&b in the fifties, and some maverick broadcasters in the sixties before Drake and the "Drake effect," mechanized programming on major AM stations. As Donahue commented, "At KYA I can see a lot of things that were developed there were ancestors of what we did later at KMPX. We didn't get into categorizing the music. We just tried to play what we liked." But as playlists tightened, the music scene continued to expand. The popularity of the Beatles was a seminal point in developing American folk rock and psychedelic bands. The Beatles' appeal required djs for the first time to play parts of albums along with the endless hit singles. American groups like the Byrds started in 1965 putting out albums that were all carefully produced from start to finish, with no filler or rejects or anything but polished cuts. But the freedom to respond to this music explosion was not available on AM, where, as Donahue put it:

> Somewhere in the dim misty days of yore, some radio statistician decided that regardless of chronological age the average mental age of the audience was twelve and a half, and Top 40 AM radio aimed its message directly at

the lowest common denominator. The disc jockeys have become robots performing their inanities at the direction of programmers who have succeeded in totally squeezing blips and bleeps and happy, oh yes, always happy sounding cretins who are poured from a bottle every three hours.[28]

. . . But the Networks Move In

In the late sixties FM became *the* exciting medium for rock. The new radio expanded beyond its initial base of dropouts and West Coast hippies to student and Eastern markets. It was found to be a good marketing medium for the big record companies, especially Warner Brothers and Columbia, whose creative service departments and promo men were anxious to market the relatively freaky San Francisco bands and English groups who had potentially substantial audiences, but little AM radio airplay. In the same way the rock'n'roll radio of the 1950s promoted the rise of new record companies, solidifying the strength of different r&b independents, the rise of FM radio in the late sixties, along with the expanded concert market, was crucial in popularizing and commercializing progressive rock music. Its commercial potential attracted a new relatively small bunch of entrepreneurs who in many cities virtually monopolized both the concert and radio arms of the progressive rock promotion machine.

In Boston, the FM rock station (WBCN), ballroom (The Boston Tea Party), and underground newspaper (The Phoenix) were all first owned by the same person, a clever former trial lawyer named Ray Reipen. In Detroit the Ballroom was long managed by WKNR dj Russ Bibb. In other cities a small clique of concert promoters and FM radio people worked naturally toward the same end, cooperating with each other in the development of local music markets. FM is still the main advertising arm of concert promoters, who in cities like San Francisco have close relationships with FM radio programming directors and djs that stretch back almost ten years. Local advertiser supported FM has continued as an important force, particularly in the suburban markets. From 1967 to 1972, the annual growth rate in local advertising sales was close to 17 percent. And national advertisers, especially since 1969, have invested heavily in the medium. The pattern of ownership of FM stations has tended toward consolidation of network and chain power in the major markets.

Outside the main student and freak city centers, some of the earliest stations to pick up on progressive rock FM programming were the college broadcasting outlets. In some spots on the East Coast, in particular, college FM radio preceded commercial FM by several years. For a short period of a couple of years, the college operations were treated by the record companies as commercial outlets. Their djs were given payoffs, under-the-counter ad rates, and all the other privileges of big-time radio. The college stations lost out to commercial local FM outlets, however, when they failed to come up with necessary capital to increase their transmitter power, and stuck to a free form radio approach long after it had been abandoned by the commercial FMs. The record companies followed the growing regional FM station chains, with their bigger broadcast range and larger adult audience.

The network and chain owners did not have a uniform response to the burgeoning FM market. Drake-programmed RKO converted progressive format WOR-FM to an oldies format in the late sixties. The Metromedia chain has had consistent success with the most progressive commercial formats in top markets like San Francisco (KSAN), Los Angeles (KMET), New York (WNEW). The ABC network recognized radio's trend toward more specialized adult audiences and in 1968 simply divided its programming up into four separate services for its affiliates: "contemporary," "information," "entertainment," and "FM" radio. ABC developed the FM packaging of "Love Radio," fed by tapes to network stations in New York, Detroit, Chicago, San Francisco, Pittsburgh, L.A., and Houston. Stations exchanged tapes and added local djs to announce contests and the time and weather.

"Love" programming was never a great success. The network dropped the feature a year and a half later, and hired Larry Yurdin from progressive Upsala College station WFMU and Tony Pigg from KSAN to redesign their FM packaging. Before they did, however, Love was heavily sold to the advertisers. They sent out brochures to the major corporate accounts. As *Rolling Stone* explains:

> On the brochure was a photo of a huge carton with the Love logo on the front. Inside the box, four youngsters who appear to reside safely in the 18-35 age range broadcasters like for their demographics. One is a black with a moderate natural, one is a chick, one cat has Donovan length hair, the other early Bobby Sherman. And if that don't get you, the copy will: "Like any successful business, we invest in new products, too. One of our latest ones is called LOVE . . . it communicates to a new kind of audience . . . that audience that thinks, feels, and buys in the same way. A group with whom the buying power of the country rests. And LOVE is the only concept on radio that's effectively reaching them . . . As marketing and business men, we anticipate the needs of the changing market. That's why it took almost a year of research and development to launch the LOVE format. A process similar to the way you market your new product. And though you won't find our new products on supermarket shelves, at least we can help you move yours off them."[29]

The long passage is interesting not only for illustrating the selling of the counterculture, but the duplicity of *Rolling Stone*, which would use exactly the same techniques to sell itself to advertiser markets.

Meanwhile, all was not well in the counterculture. After Lew Avery purchased KPPC, Donahue spent more and more time in Southern Cal, jockeying live there and setting up the new station, while fans were treated to tapes of him over KMPX. There were tensions between Crosby and Donahue and the rest of the staff. As Donahue later remembered it, "Avery was in the hospital and Crosby and his attorney were making a big power move to take over control of the operation from him in L.A. and part of that was to try to shut us out. And the same time the checks were bouncing which at the time was of moment to us, because we were all half starving working at the stations."[30] The situation quickly went from bad to worse. After a collective meeting the staff decided to strike, in the spring of 1968.

> At three o'clock in the morning on Monday, March 18, the entire staff of the best national rock and roll station walked out on strike and into the midst of an impromptu block party. The employees of KMPX, who began work as volunteers for minimum pay, claimed they had been censored, spied on, denied a fair share of the station's profits and persecuted because of "the whole long hair riff." The moment for the strike was selected by Philip Mannond, station janitor and astrologer, who counseled that at the position of the moon at that time "there were no bad aspects."[31]

Shortly after, the workers at PPC walked out. The strikers formed a union: the Amalgamated American Federation of International FM Workers of the World, Ltd., but insisted that artistic freedom was the issue at the root of the strike, and bad pay only secondary. Support for the strikers at KMPX and PPC came from benefits by local bands like the Jefferson Airplane, Grateful Dead, Country Joe McDonald and his Fish, Blue Cheer, Joan Baez, and Judy Collins, a telegram of solidarity from the Rolling Stones, and record companies like Warner/Reprise, MGM/Verve, and A&M who, along with 95 percent of other advertisers, temporarily canceled their accounts at the station.

By May the issues in the dispute, whatever they were, were not resolved. Donahue took his crew over to Metromedia owned KSAN. He also took his advertising budget with him. Donahue left briefly in 1969, but returned as station manager when the ratings started to slip in 1970. In April 1975, Big Daddy Tom Donahue, "the 46-year-old Perfect Master" and father of FM Rock, died of a heart attack.

In the mid-seventies KSAN was the biggest station in San Francisco, leading in the ratings among men aged eighteen to forty-nine (an incredibly healthy range of audience) *and* among women. Donahue said, "We are Number One—for what it's worth. And what it's worth to us is that it keeps the economic heat off our backs and lets us play around with the other things we want to do."[32]

The heat presumably would come from the management of Metromedia, the large chain of AM, FM, and TV stations that, along with ABC, leads in the commercial experimentation in FM radio. Metromedia is happy with progressive rock formats. They long ago converted KMET in Los Angeles to progressive rock, and WNEW-FM in New York is the leading FM station in that market. Vernar Paulsen, long time Metromedia executive who is vice president of the overall corporation, and general manager of WNEW-AM, worked at KSAN as general manager during the formative 1967-68 period, and at WNEW-FM as general manager from 1970-74. He has no illusions about the aesthetics or politics of FM radio, which, he says, "like any other product has to serve a need, like toothpaste."

Paulsen attributes much of the success of Metromedia in FM to the flamboyant willingness to gamble exhibited by the corporation president and chairman of the board, John W. Kluge, who made his first fortune in food brokerage, speculating in commodities trading, before making a commitment to Metromedia in 1958. His early stations were in Buffalo and Oklahoma, but like other chain owners he moved toward the larger markets in city centers. Before making a lot of money on the FM surge, Metro dropped a good deal following another idea: telephone radio with personalities like their successful L.A. talk show host Joe Pyne. Metromedia converted several of its FM properties to rock after the success of KSAN. KMET was programmed progressive in 1968, as was WMMR in Philadelphia. The New York station, WNEW, took longer to convert, but starting with Bill "Rosco" Mercer, they picked up a number of djs from the disbanded WOR rock FM, and have grown steadily since 1968-69 there, too.

Metromedia and other chains were quicker than the big networks (the exception here is ABC) in seeing the money value of FM properties. But while Donahue and friends have found happiness with chain radio, the story of KMPX is still the classic of the underground. It went from a dream of the counterculture to a ghastly greedy set of wrangles over a lucrative commercial property.

KMPX was initially fueled by the energies of people caught up in what they were doing, the music, the idea of progressive broadcasting, and the rock scene. They were willing to work for slave wages, and were pushed out when they asked for a larger share of the profits and for continuing control over the station. It's ironic, but not atypical, that the final solutions for progressive FM radio should be found with liberal corporate sponsors who eliminate all the politics of the experimental FMs, but keep the music and record ads.

Metromedia, for example, has quietly and not so quietly canned a number of jocks over the years. When they do so, station managers throw up their hands to the staff, express sympathy for the victims, but blame the corporate owners. After a while, the good vibes of the music and easy money return, and the threat is killed. Through the years a number of people have left Metromedia under pressure for political reasons. They include KSAN dj Roland Young who too obviously supported Black Panther David Hilliard in an obscenity wrangle, Larry Bensky, and Scoop Nisker, who was blamed by a Berkeley police chief for "inciting" anti-war rioters with his lively news collages; and at WMMR in Philadelphia, Robert Brinkley was fired for playing a mild Lenny Bruce cut. Elsewhere, KPPC had mass political firings, directed particularly at the Credibility Gap, one of the few remaining informative news shows whose format satirized each day's events, and a strike for control of programming at KZAP in Sacramento was ended when the owner told the staff he was willing to let them run things their way (collectively), as long as they didn't lose money. At the time, his position was welcomed as a great victory for the counterculture.

. . . And the FCC and the Devil Claim Him

The depoliticization of FM continued in 1970 when arch-Republican FCC chairman Dean Burch issued a warning against obscene or druggy song lyrics. Metromedia, along with the networks and other chain owners, used the "warning" to purge stations of some political djs and songs. WNEW in New York banned Steppenwolf's "The Pusher Man," an anti-dope song. *Rolling Stone* took the occasion to run a special review section on the underground radio, where it had gone, and gone wrong, with Ben Fong-Torres (himself a dj) commenting, "It appears that underground radio under the regressive nursing of network and/or corporate ownership is becoming just another spinoff of commercial, format radio."[33]

When John Lennon's "Working Class Hero" came out in 1970, it combined both feared elements: politics and obscenity artfully used. *Rolling Stone* commented, "that the progressive FM stations around the country say they want to play Lennon's song, but they're all too fucking scared." George Yahraes from ABC-FM commented, "if we try to make a test case and get hauled up to Washington the left would say 'Well, they've been ripping us off for years anyway,' and the right would say 'We're glad they took that station off the air.' It's the people who must decide what they want to hear on FM radio." Yahraes didn't suggest any ways "people" could make their desires heard in the corporate decision rooms. CBS-FM was a little more frank, although just as lame in saying, via Jim Smith at WBBM-FM in Chicago, that "either you have the balls to play it unedited or you don't play it at all. We don't have the balls."[34] One of the appropriate lines in the song, you'll recall, goes "You think you're so clever and classless and free, but you're still fucking peasants as far as I can see."

The stir over FCC pressure was exaggerated by the major powers in broadcasting. In its forty years of operation the commission has lifted only one radio station license for something said on the air. If the commission really tried to shut down a station for obscenity or drug lyrics it would lose in court. Almost anything set to music, even if pornographic in print, will be judged as having some artistic value and be protected (despite the recent Supreme Court antiruling on localized obscenity standards). The FCC does have power, however, in its ability to harass a station to death with warnings, short term license renewals, and other moves that stop short of decisive action, but tie stations up in mounds of legal red tape and expense.

It applied these tactics against a number of community service and nonprofit radio stations. The FCC slapped a fine on radio station WUHY in Philadelphia when Jerry Garcia said "Shit!" over the air, despite the fact that no one had registered a complaint with the station, or the FCC, about the incident. In handing down the fine, liberal FCC commissioner Nicholas Johnson filed a dissenting opinion which, said he, "found it pathetic that we always seem to pick upon the small, community service stations like KPFK, WBAI, KRAB, and now WUHY-FM. It is ironic that of the public complaints about broadcasters' taste received in my office, there are probably 100 or more about network television for every one about stations of this kind. Surely if anyone were genuinely concerned about the impact of broadcasting upon the moral values of this nation, he ought to consider the ABC, CBS, and NBC networks before picking on little educational FM radio stations that can scarcely afford the postage to answer our letters, let alone hire lawyers."[35]

Yale connected WYBC and Philadelphia station WDAS eventually challenged the dope lyric warnings with the free assistance of liberal media lawyer Terry Westein, a former assistant to Johnson. After years of wrangling, they stalemated the commission's warning.

The FCC worked effectively with the major networks and other commercial interests in discouraging innovative or interesting FM programming. Along with the antidope warning, several small political stations were harassed for possible violation of the Fairness Doctrine, an antiquated and ineffective legal concept first fought for by civil rightists and then consistently used against them, that insists on balanced editorial content in programming. The most immediate problem with the Fairness Doctrine of course is that the FCC is judge of what is and what is not fair, and what constitutes program editorializing. All commercial broadcasting reaffirms the status quo of values, political parties, and power alignments and culture simply by never challenging it. One popular argument suggests that any station that is violently and one-sidedly political (which in fact none of the harassed stations were) performs a social service by offsetting the oppressive and homogeneous, apolitical programming of other broadcasters, and so fits into a broader interpretation of the Fairness Doctrine.

With more and more FM stations turning to rock programming (approximately one out of every eight), the political promise of the underground radio is largely a joke. Most FM stations are supplied with news analysis by the same network services that contract out to AM stations and the largest commercial broadcasters. A significant exception to this is the string of Pacifica Stations, KPFA-Berkeley, KPFK-Los Angeles, WBAI-New York, KPFT-Houston.

Pacifica is a listener sponsored chain of radio outlets first set up in 1949 by the Pacifica Foundation. Despite their many problems, the Pacifica chain remains the best example of alternative (truly underground) radio. Their community oriented news coverage and programming have often resulted in dramatic repression by local police and right-wing lunatics, in addition to continual FCC harassment. The general manager of WBAI, the Pacifica station in New York, was jailed after playing tapes from inside Attica prison after the uprising there in 1971. The KPFT outlet in Houston was bombed twice in 1970 by local Ku Klux Klansmen. A station worker commented, "After the first bombing we built a concrete bunker around the equipment. For the second [bombing] they put the dynamite right on top of the bunker, and it collapsed down on the equipment."

For many of the commercial FM stations, having given up on radical news analysis and community service reporting, "politics" was reduced to screening advertisements from certain sponsors. WBCN in Boston had a longstanding policy of not advertising cigarettes, oil companies, or the products of particularly conspicuous war-making corporations (a policy since dropped), and many of the college stations important in FM's early days wouldn't touch any major corporate advertiser outside of the record companies. Other stations, like the ones in the Metromedia chain, were from the first open to all sorts of national advertisers, but turned some down because of their "sound" on taped commercials, which did not program neatly into a laid back dj style and progressive rock musical format. As Scott Muni, program director at the successful WNEW in New York, explained their reasoning:

> You cannot argue product. You know sometimes we get a letter from a listener saying "Why would you advertise a bleach blonde product? It's not true that blonds have more fun." Well, if you don't want to dye your hair blond, that's fine, but what about the person who does want to be a blonde? Or McDonald's hamburgers, "Why do you advertise McDonald's hamburgers?" Well doesn't everybody eat hamburgers? It's the sound, the *sound* that creates the problems. I remember last year we turned down a Mobil Oil

ad that would have been worth about $20,000 because the commercial had been designed for T.V., and had a visual going along with a really harsh noisy soundtrack, and just listening to the thing on radio was too much.[36]

Because of sound problems, says Muni, WNEW turned down more than $200,000 in ads last year. On the originally more independent West Coast KMPX, there was a long struggle to get any major advertising accounts other than record companies. Donahue recalled:

We did ads with small places. The first sponsor we had was a ski and climbing shop called the North Face. And we had a lot of record companies 'cause they recognized immediately that that was the right place to be. But I was so restrictive at the time that I wouldn't take a record company advertisement unless we were playing the record. If we weren't playing the record, I wouldn't let them advertise. The first national ad we were ever offered was Pepsi Cola. I remember we had a four hour meeting of everybody in the place about whether or not we were going to take the Pepsi Cola ad. It was too plastic sounding. We wanted to run one of their old jingles, the one that goes "Pepsi Cola hits the spot!" the one they had in the forties and fifties, but they wouldn't let us do that. And then finally it was resolved because one of the dudes stood up and said, "Hey man, I don't know what the hell we're all talking about. I drink Pepsi Cola and so do the rest of you." And it sort of evaporated on that particular issue.[37]

Most big FM stations now work out arrangements with national advertisers allowing the station to redo ads, or read copy rather than play a strident little cassette. The more intelligent advertisers comply with the FM request, since they came to realize it was in their interest to have hip djs selling to a hip young audience in their own familiar sound and style. Donahue told advertisers:

We're not trying to change it [the ad] purely because aesthetically we don't like your approach, we're also interested in your being around with us. If you use the wrong approach, you're not going to be around, 'cause you're not going to sell your product.[38]

The first national advertisers were the record companies, who quickly demonstrated a real feel for the FM medium and its audience. As early as 1968 Reprise records provided stations running ads for the John B. Sebastian LP with a choice of two taglines. The first had the announcer say, "John B. Sebastian. We think the B. stands for beautiful." If that wasn't hip enough, the alternate was "John B. Sebastian. We think the B. stands for . . . ballsy."

Staffers at some stations protested the change to high-powered national ads, but they were overruled by salespeople and station management. When newscaster Larry Bensky complained that KSAN should refuse an ad for the Standard Oil additive F-310 because independent tests showed it did nothing to improve auto performance, Tom Donahue laid out the basic truth: "Radical community stations are supported by advertisers with money. If you get in bed with the devil, you better be prepared to fuck."

FM radio advertising is a classic case of selling the counterculture, and using the counterculture to sell big business. Where there are still faint mutterings of protest from jocks with a conscience, advertisers and station managers effectively silence them. One time at WBCN in Boston, ace morning jock Charles Laquidara commented after an ad for Honeywell Pentax cameras that the parent firm was a major war-making corporation that had helped "kill all those Cambodian babies." He was suspended without pay for a week.*

Chart 3.4
AM and FM Radio Revenues 1962-1974
(millions of dollars)

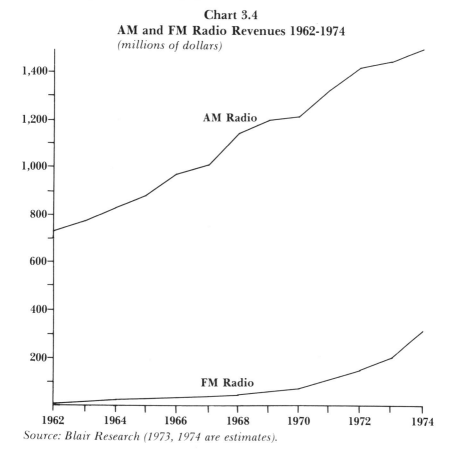

Source: Blair Research (1973, 1974 are estimates).

*Laquidara's-suspension for an aside on a page of advertiser coy could be contrasted with the earlier days at the station, when he took on the owner himself and won. A relatively new disc jockey named John Brodey was doing a show one Sunday

(continued on page 120)

As FM radio has continued to grow, expanding from overall revenues of $40 million in 1967 to more than $260 million in 1975. (see Chart 3.4), the stations have come to recognize their dependence on advertisers, and on getting a consistent audience to keep up their ratings. Donahue reported that early KMPX djs were paid almost nothing, then $100 a week, and now a regular $350 a week for jocks at KSAN. WBCN has moved to new multimillion dollar offices atop Boston's most prestigious Prudential Tower. The station, which is the most politically Left of all major commercial stations in the United States, pays much more attention to advertisers than in the past. One new service it offers to local promoters is heavy play of records of groups being brought into town for concert or club appearances.

As it approaches and surpasses AM radio audiences in many markets, FM must also begin to play the rating game that first prompted Top 40. During the past two years, in particular, progressive rock stations have tightened up on programming and are battling to get a broader and broader audience of listeners. They have given up on much of the free form dj and programming style of early years. Program directors have told jocks to play more commercial material that will keep the "progressive format" station in competition with AM and, what is more often a threat, conservatively formated "Top 40" FMs that play virtually all hit songs although many are culled from albums. Even WNEW, the progressive Metromedia station in New York, has worked to routinize its programming. "We've put together a 'ready rack' of top albums, the newest albums by people like Carly Simon or the Stones, and try to work mostly from that," says Muni.[39] It's less likely now to hear Donahue's proclaimed mixture of "rock and roll, folk, traditional and city blues, raga, electronic music, and some jazz and classical selections" than a tasteful selection of best-selling white rock. Often a single cut off particular albums will be encouraged.

Outside the major city and student-freak markets, FM is tighter still. Many stations have several songs they try to regularly work into a day's

(continued from page 119)

afternoon and was in the middle of playing Blind Faith's "Do What You Like" when feisty Ray Reipen called him up on the station "hotline," a telephone that rang right inside the control booth. Station djs had asked Reipen not to use the hotline to make comments on programming, since it only angered and disrupted whomever he called to get a personal comment on a line designed strictly for emergency use. But he persisted. "Hey Hotdog!" he boomed at a startled John Brodey. "Nobody wants to listen to a drum solo on a Sunday afternoon!" When Laquidara followed Brodey with a show of his own, he retold the incident in detail over the air, then put on one of his "favorite records," the long version of Ginger Baker's drum solo on "Toad," and followed it with other drum songs, like Aineslee Dunbar's "Mutiny," and some

(continued on page 121)

programming; others use the "ready rack" or "emphasis rack" idea, but make it much more selective than the hundreds of albums used at Metromedia. Many have extensive but tight playlists. FM has not exactly become another "rotting corpse stinking up the airwaves," but it has regressed from its days as free form access to the best new music. Its personnel and investors have grown with the medium and are willing to bend its promise a bit to keep the business profitable. As Ben Fong-Torres, who in addition to writing for *Rolling Stone* now does a show for KSAN on Sunday afternoons, recapped the process:

> The typical FM station goes on with waves of good vibes, building an audience of loyal listeners by playing album cuts unheard on AM, by talking with, instead of to, listeners, and by opening up the station to the community. As the audience builds, however, the ratings, "the numbers," climb, and the station owners suddenly have a marketable commodity. Suddenly the air is filled with increasingly uptight advertisers, administration takes over, and everything is sterilized. Suddenly there are playlists; certain records have to be banned. No more interviews—can't stop the flow of music. No politicizing—remember the Fairness Doctrine. Got to have that license in order to do your thing, you know. Suddenly there's no community out there, but a "share" of the "quarter hour audience." And in the end, FM rock stands naked. It is, after all, just another commercial radio station.[40]

Yes, it is.

The expansion of the rock music market not only changed the record industry and radio during this period in the late sixties, but also brought to the fore and developed the commercial importance of a number of industry-related businesses, particularly the business in personal appearances by rock stars. Concert appearances necessitated a rock concert circuit, with promoters working in various cities, and agencies to handle the bookings for rock acts. The managers of rock artists also came into their own during this period, simply because the properties they handled were worth so much money. And the music and youth culture that the industry traded off of generated its own press, which supplemented the traditional trade magazines.

We are treating a number of these secondary, supportive parts of the rock scene together, in a way that telescopes their particular histories, because the way they operate today has pretty much been determined by developments in the last few years, and because they all perform broadly

---

(continued from page 120)

selections from Buddy Rich. Laquidara was tripping on mescaline at the time, and may not have been so decisive in his protest if he hadn't been under the influence. But the action was a great success with BCN's listeners, who jammed the switchboard with congratulatory telephone calls for hours afterward.

similar functions, in being part of the grease that keeps the rock business rolling along. The discussion of their current operation precedes the discussion of the current scene in the business proper only because we have decided to treat them in this sort of integrated way, that deals with history and actual function today in the same discussion. It does not mean that they are anything but secondary to the moving powers and hard core institutions within the music business, namely the record companies themselves.

4 THE EXPANDED INDUSTRY

Agents and Managers

The two business people who work with rock artists day to day are agents and managers. Agents get acts dates. They usually operate out of New York- or Los Angeles-based agencies that represent entertainers and media celebrities in many fields other than rock, and are themselves part of larger corporate conglomerates. Agencies execute contractual commitments for the artist under the direction of management. In addition to telling agencies when an act or artist is coming into the country or going on tour and setting the commercial terms of that tour, management is generally responsible for the overall planning and career development of the act. The rise of rock in the 1960s and tremendous expansion of the music industry generated a nationwide market for personal appearances by "contemporary" artists. The structure for promoting personal appearances had existed since the 1950s, but it was considerably changed and consolidated in the late 1960s, during the ballroom era and immediately after. Likewise, the commercial potential of the music and special demands of its performers changed the accepted style of management while increasing its rewards.

Frank Barsalona: *Premier Handler*

The most important rock agent today is Frank Barsalona, president of the exclusively rock music agency Premier Talent. He began in the music business as a performer:

> . . . a country and western kid performer named Greg Mitchel, which is funny since I come from New York. Well, at one point in my career, just after graduating from college, I realized I was going nowhere. So I thought to myself, "What I should really do is go where there's the best chance of meeting all the people who are now standing in my way, where I can meet managers and publishers and agents and promoters." And I realized I should go to a booking agency.[1]

Barsalona went to the General Artists Corporation (GAC) which at that time was one of the largest talent agencies in New York. In the early sixties, he was assigned the rock acts, which were "the lowest of the low." Barsalona was the youngest agent in the business, and disagreed violently with his bosses over how the young rock'n'roll artists should be handled.

> I realized that all these people I'd thought so much of were pretty stupid, and the way they wanted me to handle my acts was pretty stupid. I wanted to guide their careers rather than exploit their success. And we wouldn't do that. We'd take an act that had a hit record, all the agents at GAC would look at *Billboard* every week and see the new acts coming up, and then we'd call the manager and try to get to see him and try to get to represent the act, and then we'd destroy the act.[2]

A Top 10 record at that time could keep an act on the road for about a year and a half of personal appearances.

Agencies extracted as much money as possible from promoters who were, according to Barsalona, arranged on a three-tiered system. At the bottom were young promoters "who were constantly going out of business because we were constantly fucking them up." A second level of promoters, for whom the agencies occasionally did favors, was financially unstable, but not as bad as the first. The third tier was the main promotional circuit, handling all important industry product. It was composed of "guys who had been around a long time, and wouldn't touch a rock act unless it was a sure thing," who made their money from middle-of-the-road acts like Tony Bennett, Steve Lawrence-Eydie Gorme, or Frank Sinatra along with an occasional rocker who had shown real staying power, like Elvis Presley.

In 1964 Barsalona watched crowds of teenagers mob the Beatles when they arrived at New York's Kennedy Airport, then at their hotel, their concert in Carnegie Hall, and another concert that he attended in

Washington, D.C. Looking back on his reactions to the GAC booked tour, he comments, "I realized then that rock might really have potential, and I remembered all that business about all the war babies growing up at the same time, and I decided then to start my own agency."[3]

He founded Premier Talent. The company has never had a losing year. It annually books at least $50 million in rock talent.* On every dollar, Barsalona gets 10 percent for his privately held corporation. Premier now represents most of the big acts in rock including British artists like Black Sabbath, Ten Years After, Procol Harum, The Who, Yes, Emerson Lake and Palmer, Jethro Tull, and Traffic, and Americans like David Crosby, Graham Nash, Neil Young, J. Geils Band, Johnny and Edgar Winter, and Black Oak Arkansas, among many others.†

Barsalona grew with the British invasion, the post-Beatles revival of rhythm and blues, and the rise of progressive rock in the late sixties. He started with acts he had known at GAC, like the Chiffons and Little Anthony and the Imperials (which he helped put back together), and then graduated to Herman's Hermits, which he got on a bounce back from the rapacious Dick Clark.‡ Experience with the Hermits led to contact with other British groups like Wayne Fontana and the Mindbenders and Freddie and the Dreamers. Premier was still a relatively small American agency, unable to compete with the other established agencies in the States. In England, however, its operation was as big as anyone's and Barsalona concentrated his talent buying there.

In the middle sixties he picked up a number of British acts, including The Who, Procol Harum, and The Animals, along with some secondary

---

*Barsalona is not the source of this figure. It is an estimate based on the grosses of other agencies, like CMA and IFA, and the relative importance of Premier in the rock field. An officer at IFA said that roughly 40 percent of their $100 million in billings represented rock concerts. Premier does more business than IFA by at least 25 percent. Thus, the $50 million figure which has also been confirmed as an accurate minimum estimate by a number of other industry figures. We may note too that the 10 percent Barsalona gets is skimmed before agency expenses.

†"Others" includes Bad Company, Maggie Bell, Brownsville Station, Joe Cocker, James Cotton Blues Band, Earth Wind and Fire, Focus, Foghat, Frampton's Camel, Golden Earring, Humble Pie, James Gang, Jo Jo Gunne, King Crimson, Lindisfarne, Little Feat, Mark Almond, Dave Mason, Montrose, Poco, Pousette-Dart String Band, PFM (Premiata Forneria Marconi), Roxy Music, Santana, John Sebastian, Sharks, Slade, Sparks, Spooky Tooth, Steeleye Span, Strawbs, Livingston Taylor, 10 c.c., Robin Trower, and Rick Wakeman.

‡The Hermits' manager was in New York before they broke in the United States, trying to line the group up with some agency. No major agency was interested; neither

(continued on page 126)

was a logical business decision based on his interest in an investment that would pay for years.

A few years ago George Harrison announced that tickets for an upcoming December concert tour were to go on sale in the early fall. The move would have taken several million dollars out of the fall concert market and hurt several acts then touring. Barsalona called Harrison's people and "just told them that if they went on sale with the tickets too soon, they might get away with it, at least this time, but they might have trouble getting support on later Dark Horse artists." Harrison begged off.

Barsalona is now considered by some to be the supreme handler in the industry, the premier broker between record companies and the talent-exposing concert system. Ahmet Ertegun recently introduced Barsalona to Wall Street Senator Jacob Javits. "Here is the most powerful man in the music business, bar none," he said.

IFA, CMA, William Morris

While Barsalona was building his Premier empire off money from the British invasion fad, other talent agencies were changing corporate hands and regrouping. In the fifties the most important agency had been the Music Corporation of America (MCA). It folded, however, when management was forced to dissolve its talent arm after merging with Universal Pictures in the early sixties. Many of the agents who left MCA took talent with them and formed their own businesses. None of these new companies survived into the middle sixties except the Ashley-Famous Agency, which was bought up at that point by the Kinney Corporation. When Kinney bought Warner Brothers, it had to dissolve its talent arm just as MCA had done.

Ashley-Famous was bought by Marvin Josephson Associates, a small management-agency specializing in TV packaging run by two veteran network TV lawyers. They renamed Ashley-Famous "International Famous." Shortly after the Ashley-Famous acquisition Josephson per-American groups like Sam the Sham and Mitch Ryder and the Detroit Wheels. From the beginning Barsalona took rock'n'roll's ability to make a lot of money seriously. His style did in fact differ from his mentors at GAC. He was a ruthless negotiator, but loyal to his acts and their careers rather than to the sham system of MOR promoters. His policy of not screwing acts and instead working with them to develop their careers

(continued from page 125)

was Barsalona, but the day before the manager was to go back to England, empty-handed, he arranged a meeting with Clark's organization. "It was clear that manager would have *given* the Hermits to Clark, if only to say he'd gotten some deal for them when he went back home, and the Clark people were really screwing him, so I sort of

(continued on page 127)

suaded Herb Spar to join his growing company. Spar had worked closely with Bill Graham in forming the Millard Agency, stocked with many of the important San Francisco bands and other largely West Coast groups. He dissolved Millard but brought many of his acts with him and linked Marvin Josephson Associates into the wellsprings of new rock talent. Today IFA is second only to Premier Talent in representing rock acts. Their clients include Aerosmith, the Beach Boys, Jefferson Starship, Loggins and Messina, Mott the Hoople, James Taylor, Stephen Stills, Seals and Crofts, the Mahavishnu Orchestra, and many others. While Premier represents almost exclusively young audience acts, IFA is a traditionally diversified agency that draws revenue from a wide area of entertainment ventures. It agents for clients in publishing, television, film, commercials, and even news broadcasting (John Chancellor, Harry Reasoner).

IFA president Ralph Mann stressed in an interview that while the concert division is growing, a relatively small percentage of their total revenues comes from the rock business. Last year International Famous made some $1.6 million in profits.

Barsalona's own alma mater, GAC, went through a couple of different owners and emerged as Creative Management Associates (CMA). CMA continues today in the pop music field, with acts like Cat Stevens, Carly Simon, Electric Light Orchestra, and Grand Funk Railroad. Its concert division is headed by long time agent Norman Weiss, who has a somewhat sleazy reputation as an "old style" backroom wheeler dealer. But the real glamor at the agency lies with its middle-of-the-road acts and movie division, the latter led by Sue Mengers, one of the few important woman agents in the business. The William Morris Agency is another old theatrical firm that has survived through the years. It is still one of the top three overall entertainment booking operations, but has never had a reputation for strong representation of rock acts. Less important still are Associated Booking Corporation (ABC), Agency of Performing Artists (APA), and American Talent International (ATI). The three largest agencies are William Morris, CMA, and IFA, which among them dominate the New York-Hollywood film-television business. The three most important agencies in rock are IFA, CMA, and at the top, Premier.

"The Promoters Have a Responsibility to Me"

The rise of Barsalona paralleled the rise of rock, and with his

---

(continued from page 126)
stepped in and negotiated the deal." The Hermits became sudden successes, and Barsalona continued to represent the grateful manager and group in their U.S. dealings.

increased power he successfully enforced a "new" style of operation for agents and concert promoters. As the ballroom and commercial concert scene opened up in the late sixties, Barsalona used his hold over the important English acts to distinguish a small group of young promoters, who were given a virtual monopoly on Premier's talent and special favors in return for certain commitments to the agency. A clearly reciprocal relationship was established between the promoters and the agency. In return for access to headline talent, price breaks, preferential treatment in selecting dates and locations, and even special deals covering specific losses on Premier acts, the new promoters assumed responsibility for working with the agency's new, unestablished acts. Boston concert promoter Don Law, who of course is completely dependent on Barsalona for his business operation, provides one view of this "Barsalona system" of promoter-agency amicability:

> Frank was important in setting out a code of ethics in the industry. If a guy lost money on a date, you should try to make it up. If he's out there doing the best possible job, taking the risks and losing the money, then he should also have the headline acts. Now Frank really amplified that and made it much more of an industry way of doing business.[4]

Promoters who did not play by the new rules simply were not allowed to buy Premier talent. The company exclusively represented rock acts and had no obligations to the old MOR promoters. "We cut off a few people to get our point across," recalls Barsalona. "The promoters have a responsibility to me. If they won't exercise it, then I don't have to deal with them."[5]

Other agents, particularly Herb Spar at Millard and IFA, followed Barsalona's lead in working closely with young rock promoters. Over the years, as the promoters themselves have grown in power, this has increased the power of some agents at the expense of others. Again, Law recalls:

> There were certain guys you knew would fuck you, do you in. I remember a guy at IFA who really beat a number of us, particularly Howard Stein, for a lot of money. And so I would stay away from him. I wouldn't buy from him unless I had to, and I'd be very cautious. Whereas Herb Spar was somebody who made a point about knowing a lot about my business and whom I knew I could trust. He knew the size of the hall, the problems, what the police scene was like, everything. So he wasn't going to shove a deal down our throat that would kill us. And I think that was true of a number of people, so we worked with them. And they weren't that important then, but have become more important since.[6]

The three tier structure of concert promotion was replaced with a new system of relatively few rock promoters handling both young acts and headliners. During the heyday of the ballroom circuit the promoters' dual functions blurred together. "Headline" acts were often bought sight unseen, and small unknowns were commonly elevated to headline status overnight. Nor were the commercial venues the only places where agencies could get work for their clients. The market for rock was expanding rapidly among older students. Those acts not getting booked into the ballrooms were sent on college tours. Over the years, however, college administrations got tighter with money and more worried about property damage at rock concerts, while the audience for headline acts outgrew the ballrooms. A single promoter now not only commonly controls a large geographic region, usually based around a major city, but also operates over a wide range of facilities including clubs, small and medium sized (2,000-5,000 seating) concert halls, and large athletic gardens and stadiums.

The "new" system of rock agent booking was built from the ground up, from the days when rock musicians were considered the "lowest of the low" to their present status as million dollar properties. Agents are wont to congratulate themselves on the morality of the system, but it is really a simple defensive structure based on a business judgment. Promoters and musicians have emerged as independent forces in their own right, and the interests of both have to be respected by the major agencies. The current rationalized monopoly in concert promotion cuts back on competition between the mutually dependent agencies and concert markets. The agency gets exposure of new talent as well as headlines in attractive halls by respected and consistent promoters. The promoters get all worthwhile talent, and in their area are commonly recognized by all the agencies.

The "ethics" that Don Law talked of vanish when the agency deals with less powerful promoters. It is not uncommon for a young promoter trying to break into the business to develop a new act into headline status, then have the act given to a major operator. Although less important now that they comprise only about 20 percent of all dates, college concert committees are also consistently ripped off (through inflated prices, pressure, last minute contract changes, cancellation with no replacement) by major New York or Los Angeles agencies, or the regional middleman firms that buy from the major centers and sell to colleges.

What is spoken of within the industry as a new way of doing business is only a better, more sophisticated and smoother way of doing business among established powers. In the same way that record companies have been willing to ease up on royalty rates with the assurance of continued stable profits from their main acts, agencies have adjusted their style. Even more than promoters, artists must be treated in a familiar, friendly fashion that reflects a commonality of interests. Rock'n'roll is here to stay, and pay, only if handled correctly. Herb Spar observed, "It only makes sense, it's good business. You want to stick with a certain product, relate to that product . . . that rock artist, that group, and develop it to your mutual benefit."[7] Agencies think of the acts as products to be gingerly handled, while the prized agents are the ones who can relate well to rock groups and their managers. "You know," confided IFA president Ralph Mann, "this is a very personal business. You get agents with personalities, with the ability to relate to people and be friendly and what not, and you make more money that way."[8]

The decision to add an act to a major agency roster is based on a number of factors affecting the act, including their stage presence and show, quality of record deal, commitment of the record company to do major promotion work, track record of the manager, personnel problems, and broadly speaking, "commercial potential." It is a business decision potentially involving hundreds of thousands of dollars in expenses or profit, and treated as such. At Premier, where there are only seven people working for the company (four agents) other than Barsalona, the roster is kept relatively small, restricted to immediately saleable artists. When a new act comes on with the agency it almost invariably is represented by managers who have worked closely with Premier over the years (like Dee Anthony) or already has proven, extensive concert experience. When a young act is signed to the agency roster, it's not unusual for it to go through a number of image alterations and changes in the stage show which are worked out between the manager and important people at the agency.

An agent's work is straightforward and routinized. He is assigned a number of properties, and represents them in a specific region. In IFA's New York office, for example, Herb Spar headed the concert division, but also had specific responsibility for promoters in Indiana, Kentucky, New Jersey, Michigan, and Ohio. Another agent handles colleges in the Midwest and New England areas; another handles the Southern promoters, and so on. In addition to covering all the bookings for a given area, agents are assigned to different artists for particular responsibilities, either assembling tours or representing the rest of the agency to the manager and working directly on tour control with road managers and artists. A couple of years ago all of IFA worked on an Elton John tour, but the Englishman was particularly grateful to one agent who had charge of tour direction, and awarded him a gold Rolls Royce for his efforts.

Agents spend their days on the telephone, making deals, deals, deals. They handle a lot of money, and have the ego as well as limited artistic satisfaction of building young artists and mixing with the stars. But the work is really comparable to selling encyclopedias by telephone. "It gives you ulcers after a while," said Spar. "I'm going to have to get out in a little while or get very sick."[9] (Spar died in 1976.) A few nights a week an agent will spend time scouting talent at local clubs or covering a concert he's arranged. When an agent brings a particularly successful artist to the agency, just as when a lawyer lands a big client for a corporate law firm, he can count on getting a little bonus or some sort of kickback commission deal. But most work-a-day agents with a few years experience booking rock acts make about $20,000, a small sum in comparison to their annual volume of business. They are on salary from the agency company. It is only the overall corporation that gets the legendary "10 percent of everything."

Dear Landlord: *The Managers*

The agencies were not the only ones to understand the demands of the new rock business. Managers too changed their style. With few exceptions, in the 1950s they had been a sleazy bunch of businessmen out to bilk their often black r&b clients for a few quick bucks, with little respect for either the artists as musicians or their rights in law. An exception to this general pattern was "Colonel" Tom Parker, Nashville based industry veteran and manager of Eddie Arnold, who came on his most valuable property in the person of Elvis Presley.

Parker virtually adopted the white r&b singer, with whom he enjoyed a twenty-one-year career, and devoted himself fully to planning the commercial life of the young star. He moved him in and out of a variety of entertainment music and media, from rock'n'roll to the U.S. Army, religious albums, and several movies. Two major factors in the colonel's career plan, of course, were Presley's really exceptional ability and appeal, and his willingness to work for an MOR audience. His career and manager presented an old style of entertainer and businessman in which young rocker, cum buck private, man of God, movie star, and legend is thoroughly (albeit benignly) manipulated by a much older, paternalistic adult figure. Finally, Elvis Presley was a single person, not a group, and was thereby an exception to the general pattern.

The first big rock manager who was really different from the fifties all too true stereotype was Brian Epstein, the extraordinary interior decorator, actor, record salesman, Beatles manager. Epstein was "new" in the sense of understanding and identifying with his clients, relating to them as human beings as well as lucrative properties, and giving attention to the career development of the group, rather than making a fast buck.

Epstein was an unusual person. He was totally absorbed in the Beatles, in understanding each one of them personally and directing their career down to the last detail, from their identically styled suits to an obligatory bow to the American audience during their first appearance in this country on the Ed Sullivan show. He was protective of the group. When John Lennon remarked that the Beatles were more popular than Jesus Christ, and Beatles records were being burned in the Bible belt, Epstein flew over to the United States to take care of the uproar. Arriving to a hostile gaggle of reporters at the airport, he confided to lawyer friend Nat Weiss that he would rather cancel the group's upcoming American tour and absorb the estimated resulting $1 million loss himself than expose the boys to any abuse.[10]

When Paul McCartney announced that he'd experimented with LSD, Epstein immediately backed him up and announced that he had used the drug himself. In fact, he had experimented with drugs well before the Beatles.

Epstein is remembered in some industry circles as a stupid business-man who made sweetheart deals with record companies and promoters alike and didn't get enough money for his group. With the exception of the last six months of his life when he was psychotically depressed and heavily drugged much of the time, however, it now seems obvious that he handled the group's career with a finesse never matched since.

Arriving in New York in 1964 for the first round of American concerts and Beatlemania, Epstein was met at the airport by Sid Bernstein, the promoter handling their Carnegie Hall gig. Bernstein drove Epstein from the airport directly to Madison Square Garden and suggested that the demand for tickets behooved the boys to do a second date in the much larger hall. Epstein looked over the huge hall, which certainly could have been filled with Beatles fans after a few days' publicity, and said simply, "Sid, let's leave this for next time."[11]

Epstein was gay. Nat Weiss has suggested that his physical attraction to the Beatles was the first and main reason for his wanting to manage them. But whether Epstein sensed the group's promise, or was only following a love of John Lennon, or both, by the time he O.D.'d on barbiturates in 1967 he had set the standards of top rock management.

In the United States, the most important new style manager was Albert Grossman, who started on the folk circuit handling acts like Peter, Paul, and Mary, then got interested in the young singer-songwriter Bob Dylan and followed him into national and world fame. After Dylan turned electric, Grossman picked up management rights to some of the underground American electric bands, including Janis Joplin and Big Brother and the Holding Co. He also got Dylan's backup group, The Band.

Grossman was an older man who along with partners Bennet Glotser and Bob Schuster had years of experience in the New York based folk scene. He was "new" like Epstein in fully understanding the commercial potential of his acts, including the commercial potential of their critical lifestyles and attitudes, and in openly identifying himself with his acts against the rest of the musical establishment. New York friends were surprised to see middle-aged Grossman wearing blue jeans and long hair tied in a ponytail. They should not have worried. Grossman was first and last a cagey businessman who plunked down the millions he made in percentages of his counterculture artists on land and restaurants in the Woodstock, New York, area, and took out $200,000 accidental death insurance to protect his investment on each of his top five acts. (When Janis Joplin died of a heroin overdose in 1967, a long, ugly court battle ensued between Grossman, who claimed the death was accidental, and the insurance company, which saw the O.D. as suicide. For Joplin's body, Grossman won a settlement of $112,000 which he split with his partners.)

It may have been a failing touch, or his removal from the main currents of the industry and attention to New York real estate deals, but Grossman gradually fell from importance in the rock business in the late sixties. Dylan satirized his manager (who got 25 percent of his most famous act) in the bitter "Dear Landlord," then dissolved their business ties. The Band also left him. Joplin died; Peter, Paul, and Mary and Paul Butterfield simply were not as big a draw as they once had been. A special label deal with Warner Brothers produced the latest Grossman corporation, Bearsville, in 1970. But the only major new talent to appear on it has been Todd Rundgren.

If Grossman was a transitional figure in the mellowing of super managers, Eliot Roberts represents the latest and current type. Roberts manages Crosby, Stills, Nash, and Young, all but Stills individually, Joni Mitchell, Jackson Browne, the Eagles, Joe Walsh, and a number of other L.A. acts. Along with David Geffen, he founded Asylum Records which, with the companion management firm of Geffen-Roberts, has come to represent the L.A. hip ideals of artistic freedom, and lots of money too. (The two principals are still good friends who talk together several times a day by phone, but G-R Management is now exclusively Roberts' operation. Geffen moved on first to full control of Asylum and the Elektra-Asylum label at Warner Communications, then to the Warner film division.) As Roberts said recently, he and Geffen realized early on that humane management of acts pays dividends. "People see now that they can become millionaires by doing it right. People used to think you had to beat someone for all their publishing to hit the jackpot. We showed them that it was the other way around. If you left the publishing there and did the right thing by the artist, and the artist was good, then you'd make it."[12]

The publishing rights, or right to royalties from songs artists compose, is one thing managers have traditionally stolen from acts they represent. The practice was widespread among rock managers in the fifties and sixties. It continues today, particularly at the lower levels of the industry, where musicians can still be persuaded to part with their publishing in return for getting a break into the business. Many of the people Roberts has worked with, including Graham Nash, Joni Mitchell, David Crosby, and Stephen Stills, had their publishing stolen in this way.*

Operating

Broadly speaking, managers handle relations with lawyers, record companies, agencies, and the act. A manager is finally responsible for protecting the act, stretching out its career, and giving it a certain freedom from business affairs to develop artistically. Discharging that responsibility means everything from making sure record company promo men hustle FM djs into playing new releases to functioning as wise father and guru to often divided and confused bands. Management differs from artist to artist. As Roberts suggests:

> Let's say you wanted me to manage you. Well, we'd have to get together. I'd have to find out what you wanted, what you're like, whether you're abrasive and hard, or soft and sensitive. I'd have to find out what you're capable of. Whether you can go on all these interviews or whether you would get shell-shocked. All this varies from person to person. It's all in the person. What do you want to be? Do you want to retire in three or four years? You know, that's all part of it. It depends on what the person wants.[13]

Day-to-day management activity might include getting studio time for an upcoming album, selecting recording material, arranging for backup bands for solo artists and road managers for groups, keeping an eye on the record company, negotiating the company contract deal, getting promotion work done for the artists, and getting the artists involved in planned programming of concert exposure, product release, and record company hype and publicity. Managers are in regular contact with record company publicity and marketing people to time product public-

---

*Managers rip off acts in other ways. Sometimes they hire press agents and charge it to the act, or charge the group part of their office expenses, limousine rentals, or whatever. Often managers make phony deals with agencies, getting a kickback by offering the act for a low price. This book deals almost exclusively with established powers in the industry who have already found success and have money behind them. They can "afford" to be honest. The other side of the music business, the underside, tied in less with the major record labels and more with hustling club dates, is full of young, naive, struggling musicians and a whole parade of 15 percenters. And even at top levels of the industry, unprincipled managers like Terry Knight (Grand Funk Railroad) are not really uncommon.

ity and availability around personal appearance schedules. They supervise agents, make the final decisions on concert pricing, and are the final link between company A&R men, independent producers, artists, and the maze of contracts that keeps the product rolling.

It takes a lot of money to manage a group from obscurity to stardom. One manager who has taken several acts along that route is Dee Anthony, who has routinely invested hundreds of thousands of dollars in the process for bands like Humble Pie, Alvin Lee and Co., and J. Geils. Once an act does start turning a profit, however, the manager stands to make a great deal off his investment. Managers get 15-25 percent of everything the artists get paid for, from personal appearances to mechanical royalties on record sales. Management-artist contracts often include an escalation clause that increases the manager's share of the action over time, as the group becomes more successful.

During the sixties the typical relations between artist and manager were broken down somewhat, along the lines suggested by Roberts. Most rock groups at least turned to their peers for career direction. Managers often became an extension of the bands—handling only one group whom they traveled and lived with. Bands sometimes became their own managers. Road managers like the Jefferson Airplane's Bill Thompson and the Doors' Bill Siddens took over business affairs for their acts. James Guercio, manager of Chicago, and Peter Asher, manager of James Taylor, started as musicians.

Many of the successful young rock managers seem almost to have drifted into the business out of simple love for the music, artistic frustration, or attraction to a particular act, group of people, or scene. Eliot Roberts describes how he met three of the most valuable properties in rock, David Crosby, Steve Stills, and Neil Young at a time he was managing only Joni Mitchell:

> At the same time I was with Joni, I was working with David Crosby, in California. David had just been "kicked out" of the Byrds—whatever expression you want to use—and was alone. We were all living at David's house as a matter of fact, Joni and I. At the same time that Joni began recording her first album, the Buffalo Springfield were in the studio next to us. This was at Sunset Sound here in L.A. Now Joan knew Neil from the old days in Toronto. Joan was an old Canadian and Neil was an old Canadian, and they both had done the folk circuit in Canada. So we went next door, and Joni introduced me to the guys. Neil knew Joni. . . . it was great. We all started hanging out while the sessions were going, and I became incredibly fond of the Buffalo Springfield. I had never been into that kind of group, which was writer featured, with Neil and Stephen. The group was really self-contained and was writing what I felt to be very important topical things. At that time they had just been doing "For What It's Worth"—

because of the Sunset riots—and they were . . . political's not the right word, but they were very involved in what was going on around them.[14]

Soon after, Roberts moved into a house with Stills; the Springfield broke up; he came to manage Neil Young; Crosby and Stills met Graham Nash at a party. One thing led to another.

Other important rock managers are much older. They have been in the business for a long time, either in management or law, and simply made an adjustment to rock. Allen Klein was an accountant for years before working his way up through a number of much smaller clients to handle the Rolling Stones' business, and from there on to the Beatles, where he effectively succeeded Epstein for all the band but Paul McCartney.

Nat Weiss, who now manages Mahavishnu John McLaughlin and his new orchestra, the remnants of the old one, Chick Corea and Return to Forever, and unknown Andy Pratt, and represents Peter Asher (and thus, James Taylor),was a divorce lawyer in New York whom Brian Epstein met at a party and called up one day for some advice. He got involved with Epstein's Nems Publishing Company, first scouted the Cyrcle, and now has his own label named Nemperor Records, in honor of the old friendship. Dee Anthony has been in music management for years. Before handling all the heavy metal rock acts he does today, he worked with MOR performers like Buddy Greco, Jerry Vale, and Tony Bennett. Led Zeppelin and John Denver manager Jerry Weintraub has also been around for years. He used to work with fifties singer Jane Morgan.

Even the young managers surround themselves with lawyers, financial advisors, and industry veterans to help them manage the money of lucrative rock acts while they concentrate on relating to the band and its album product. Weiss advises Asher. Barsalona performs the same general function for several managers whose acts are on Premier's roster. James Guercio produces Chicago's albums and has access to several lawyers, accountant Harold Kaufmann, and day-to-day manager Larry Fitzgerald in running the group's near empire.

The new managers, like the new agents, are not radically different from their predecessors. Although they represent themselves to their acts in a more honest way, and have shifted from a sort of anarchistic "take the money while the money is good" attitude to a more sophisticated analysis of artist development and staying power, they are primarily concerned with making money. Where there is not a direct economic dependence, or where they do not perceive that dependence, "new" managers still destroy weaker businessmen when they get a chance.

A few years ago Roberts violated his own "humanistic" creed and angered some real industry powers in the process. On the Crosby, Stills, Nash, and Young national tour, he put a number of promoters to the wall on price and percentage deals. Shortly after the tour the new Roberts group Souther, Hillman and Furay went on the road. Roberts called in all sorts of favors from promoters to help make the initial string of concerts a success. Despite the hype and good production, the band flopped in a number of cities and badly burned promoters. In this case, the mutual back scratching between top acts, the agencies, and the twenty promoters with a monopoly on the entire concert market seems to have broken down slightly with some probable results. One important promoter commented off the record that "next time Eliot goes out with a new act, he'll have some surprises. He won't get help. People will try to break his balls the way he did theirs."

In the area of personal appearances, the promoters take care of the "front lines" in producing concerts, the managers package and prepare the talent, the agencies are an effective go-between. While occasionally the self-regulation of the powerful breaks down, as with Roberts in Boston, most of the real rip offs are reserved for outsiders to the club.

Agencies preside over a multimillion dollar concert business. They perform a crucial function in the industry. Less stable and important than the major record companies, of course, and much smaller, agencies still provide the only means other than radio by which new product is exposed and sold. While broadly dependent on the record companies, they have a strength of their own. The super agents are at the center of daily industry operation.

It seems unlikely that the agencies will become a major power rivaling the record companies the way that some of the more diverse ones already rival the big studios in Hollywood, but they are a growing power within the rock machine. Managers have always been around and, as long as the industry lasts, they always will be, changing styles with their clients and getting a steady 15 percent. They are more decentralized than the agencies, not as important, and as individuals do a comparatively small dollar volume of business. They are talent scouts still essential in integrating artists into the overall business process and, as entrepreneurs, in first capitalizing and developing acts into commercial properties.

Concert Promotion

As long as there has been rock'n'roll, there have been rock'n'roll concerts. Alan Freed promoted concerts throughout his career. His first big date in Cleveland for a 10,000 seating hall brought in some 20,000 kids. When Freed went to WINS in 1954, he started doing concerts at the St. Nichols Arena, using many of the same people he had in Cleveland, like Joe Turner, Clyde McPhatter and the Drifters, and the Clovers,

Moonglows, and Moonlighters. Later that spring Freed went to the Brooklyn Paramount Theater. His first show in the large hall grossed the all time house record of $125,000, while his second concert later that year piled up another record breaking gross of $155,000. There was certainly money in rock concerts.

The success of Freed's concerts encouraged a number of dying nightclubs and dance halls to revive their status by booking rhythm and blues acts. Other disc jockeys and music personalities like Dick Clark (his famous Caravan of Stars) and Murray "the K" Kaufman from New York also got involved in concert promotion. Kaufman did shows at the Brooklyn Fox Theater. Clark toured his Caravan all over the East Coast in particular. Djs were naturals as concert promoters. They had unlimited access to the promotional power of radio, daily contact with managers and artists, and were in many cases celebrities in their own right. Freed, Clark, Kaufman, and all the other djs paid their acts virtually nothing. Freed seldom paid a headliner more than $200 a week, and Frank Barsalona, head of Premier Talent, reports that Clark was even worse. Percentage deals for unexpectedly high grosses were not worked out for artists. Most of the shows were packaged deals, with as many as five or ten acts in each show, each doing a few numbers and getting quickly off stage. Often the disc jockey tours would run five and six shows a day.

In 1964 and in 1965 Sid Bernstein promoted the Beatles in Carnegie Hall and Shea Stadium, the second event grossing well over $300,000. Years later Bernstein was the first promoter to use Madison Square Garden for a rock concert. He was an old style impresario who had been in the New York entertainment business for a long time, and simply by following the English music magazines like *Melody Maker* realized what a popular phenomenon the Beatles were. He has had uneven success since his contacts with the Beatles.

The early sixties had seen two parallel booking systems develop, which handled two different types of concerts for two different sorts of audience. One of the booking systems processed the rock'n'roll acts of the time, who were usually pretty desperate kids trying to make it, hoping for a hit single and the chance to get packaged, with some other one-hit groups in a celebrity tour. Rock promoters were sleazy links between celebrity djs running the tours and the cut throat New York agencies that booked them. The second booking system was linked into the Boston-New York-Philadelphia folk scene and was anchored with people like Manny Greenhill from Folklore Productions and Harold Leventhal. The folk circuit booked its acts into clubs like Gerdes in New York, Club 47 in Cambridge, the Troubador in L.A., Mainpoint in Philadelphia, and Cellar Door in D.C., and a series of small colleges and club dates in the Southwest. There were real class differences between the acts and audiences. The folk crowd was largely white middle-class students. Rock'n'rollers, particularly during the pre-Beatles period, were largely white working class kids and some blacks, and were treated as such. The rock and folk movements were largely antagonistic, until exceptional artists like Dylan loosened up some of the class biases of the folkie purists and intellectualized rock in an overpowering series of concerts with what would become The Band during 1965 and 1966.

It was really not until the late sixties with the flowering of West Coast L.A. based folk rock and the San Francisco psychedelic sound, coupled with the continuing British invasion and widespread revival of rhythm and blues bands here and in England, that the concert circuit as it exists today began to take shape in the evolution of the ballroom circuit. Although the ballrooms sprang up quickly in other cities, San Francisco was their birthplace. The history of concert promotion in that city is representative of what went on elsewhere. It is also interesting as an example, since San Francisco was a tremendous music market as well as the starting point for the counterculture music scene. More than elsewhere, musicians were a real cultural force in San Francisco, and for years they unsuccessfully fought against the commercial music establishment, and the rising hip music business establishment in the city.

Bill Graham Makes the Trains Run on Time

Central to the San Francisco story is Wolfgang Wolodia Grajanka, who at the time he started the first and most famous ballroom was a thirty-five-year-old German emigré. He had been born in Berlin in 1931 of Russian parents, kept in an orphanage in France until 1939, left Paris at the time of the Nazi invasion to walk to Marseilles, then on to Lisbon. He got on a boat there and sailed via Casablanca, Dakar, and Bermuda to New York City, where he was adopted by a family in the Bronx, changed his name to Bill Graham, and proceeded to grow up in America. Graham was drafted into the Korean War, where he was decorated, and court-martialed twice for insubordination. When he got out in 1953 he went to school, got a degree from City College in business administration, worked odd jobs, and toured Europe as an actor.

He found himself in San Francisco in 1965 as regional manager for Allis-Chalmers, the farm equipment firm. In 1965 he quit the company to manage the San Francisco Mime Troupe. Needing money for the Troupe, he got a rock group to do a benefit. The following January, Graham, the Grateful Dead, and spin-offs of the Merry Prankster crew organized the Trips Festival, one of the electric kool aid acid tests. The same year Graham opened up a small hall in the Fillmore district for producing rock'n'roll shows. It was a fantastic success. Paying the bands relatively little, Graham had soon made a small fortune, and expanded to New York, where he opened up a Fillmore East in 1968.

Meanwhile in San Francisco the rock music scene was burgeoning, and other people were getting into the concert business. One bunch of resourceful theatrically inclined hippies set up a corporation called the Family Dog to produce dances. They had a couple, the kickoff being a memorable affair with the Jefferson Airplane, and then split to Mexico. Management of the Family Dog Ballroom, also known as the Avalon Ballroom, passed to Rock Scully and Danny Rifkin, part of the Grateful Dead entourage (and now managers of the band) and then to Chet Helms, a mysterious but likeable fellow from Texas. Helms nursed the Avalon through its ups and downs (mostly downs) in the late sixties.

The Grateful Dead themselves set up the Great Northwestern Tour in 1967 with Quicksilver Messenger Service and Jerry Abrams Highlights. They handled everything from tickets to posters to concert security themselves. "No middlemen, no bullshit," said Rock Scully at the time. "We did it all, posters, tickets, promo, setting up the halls. All the things the promoters say you can't do, we did, man, and 'cause we weren't dependent we felt free and everybody did. That told us that however hard it is, it can be done, you don't have to go along." So began the Dead's long saga of confused politics and tension between their growing popularity and search for artistic control of their performances and product. Soon after the Northwestern Tour, the Dead, Jefferson Airplane, and a number of other San Francisco and Berkeley groups announced that they were no longer willing to be promoted by Bill Graham, who was accused of ripping off the Bay Area youth community and its culture, and putting nothing back.* "I'm not a freakout," said Graham. "I'm not a hippie, I don't sell love, I sell talent and environment."[15]

The protesting groups activated the Carousel Ballroom, a huge old Irish dance hall in downtown San Francisco. The Carousel was opened with two spectacularly good concerts, featuring the Dead and the Airplane, but quickly fell on hard times. The hall's rent was prohibi-

---

*Since his early days as a hip capitalist, Graham has tried to incorporate and blunt the Left's criticism that he ripped off the community. He has done a lot of benefit concerts, more than any other promoter. On some of them he got paid for his services but took no profit. On other occasions he has operated wholly at his own expense. What is surprising in all of this is not that Graham has thrown some of his time in for charity, but that other concert promoters have not been forced to do likewise. It may be, as Don Law suggests, that "Graham creates his own problems by being so dramatic all the time," or as Barsalona observes, "by trying to identify with his audience and wear blue jeans and all that." (Barsalona moves around in a chauffeured limousine, and has never been attacked as a rip off pig.) For whatever reasons, Graham is an exception that proves the rule, and not much of an exception at that. His middling contributions to

tively high, and the facility demanded considerable upkeep, but there was no steady supply of bookings. None of the San Francisco groups fully took over as managers and booking agency for the hall. Eventually the project went bankrupt. Ironically, during its last months Bill Graham wanted to share the Carousel with the Dead and others, which may have provided a temporary solution to their business problems. During the spring of 1968 the assassinations of Bobby Kennedy and Martin Luther King had hurt business generally and toughened the mood around the Fillmore West, which was located in the middle of a black ghetto. Graham was looking around for an alternate hall, and would have welcomed proposals from the rock bands for joint management of the Carousel. But they held out, and folded. Soon after, Graham bought up the lease and renamed the hall the "Fillmore West."

Other ballrooms sprang up in 1968, including the Electric Factory in Philadelphia, the Boston Tea Party, the Kinetic Playground in Chicago, and the Grande Ballroom in Detroit, along with the other Fillmore and the Electric Circus in New York City. "It was so easy to promote an act back then," said Herb Spar from International Famous Agency; "you had six or seven halls in as many cities. You got the weekend dates at those ballrooms, and the off days just outside the cities, and within seven weeks, you had good exposure in the seven major markets."[16] The ballrooms operated out of old warehouses or abandoned factories, with low overhead costs and little in the way of atmosphere except what was provided by the music and the enthusiastic fans who came to hear it. The Electric Factory in Philadelphia had some coffin-shaped boxes along its walls where people could lean back and rest. Most ballrooms had no permanent seating, however.

The ballrooms all folded in 1970-71. They fell apart for a number of reasons. The rock concert scene had grown enormously in the last few years and audiences for top acts were far greater than ballrooms (usually big enough for about 2,000 people) could accommodate. There had been dozens of successful festivals and much larger concerts that proved this fact. The increased expense of getting higher and higher priced groups cut back on the easy profits, police continually harassed the ballrooms for their crowded mob scenes on top nights, and the operators themselves were anxious to get into big money doing much larger concert promotion.

---

charity amount to a few hours of his time. The money is all from the audience that goes to the benefits. Seen as a percentage of his overall profits and time, the charity work is a minuscule part of his total operation. Graham's benefit concerts are comparable to the pro bono ('for the good of the people') legal services offered for free, in a limited way, by Wall Street law firms.

All the ballrooms had been started by young entrepreneurs with little risk capital. Many of them made overnight fortunes and, more important, developed standing relationships with the important New York agents who controlled the flow of rock talent. After the decline of the ballrooms as a venue for rock concert promotion, most of these entrepreneurs went on with much larger concert promotions, and today they form a network of promoters who control the personal appearance business and monopolize rock promoting in their particular area. Graham still controls San Francisco, as well as doing national tours. Don Law from the Boston Tea Party runs the Boston rock concert business, Larry Magid from the Electric Factory does all the important concerts in Philadelphia, and so on. As noted earlier, these city or regional monopolies are respected, and in fact encouraged, by the agencies.

When Shelly Finkel of New York-based Cornucopia Productions tried to go into the Boston concert market in the early seventies, Herb Spar and Frank Barsalona asked him to leave. As Spar explained, "You try to do what I think is ultimately fair. Don Law doesn't go into Connecticut, where Cornucopia operates, and Cornucopia shouldn't go into Boston. He's lived in Boston, he's worked the market, he was one of the starters of the Tea Party, he's worked with the local fire and police departments, he's worked with the local vice squad . . . he's *made* the market what it is. So to me it's offensive for a guy to get on a shuttle plane and come in from somewhere and steal his business, and I won't allow it."[17] Of course, the monopoly extends to include locals who might be interested in promoting in their home town, too. As Law says:

> Rock is like the classical music business that way. You just don't have a lot of people promoting shows. You've got someone who represents Columbia management and then in each town there's probably only one person who promotes the concerts. The reason for that is that because of the amount of traffic you've got, it doesn't work to have three or four people trying to follow the traffic together. It doesn't work that way. It's like banging heads. If there's one or two people up there who are very good, you know you also expect they will try to give the act the best possible shot and that they won't run smack up against somebody else who's going to take their business away. The situation tends to encourage a limited number of promoters.[18]

It certainly does. Today only some twenty-odd promoters or promotion companies control more than 90 percent of the money made in rock appearances. These various people include Bill Graham, Concerts West, Pacific Presentations, Concert Associates; Ron Delsener and Howard Stein in New York, Bob Begarus in Detroit, Steve Glents in Detroit, Ron Powell in St. Louis, Frank Freed in Chicago, Larry Magid in Philadelphia, Don Law in Boston, John Scher in New Jersey, Mike Belkin in Cleveland, Marty Anode and Donald K. Donald in Canada, Jack Boyle in Washington, Allen Dolberg in Milwaukee, Alex Coolie in Atlanta, and a few others. Virtually all of them have been in the rock concert business since 1968, the year of the ballrooms.

Does the Aquarian Age Breed Sympathy for the Devil?

The first of the rock festivals was at Monterey in June 1967. The idea originated as a commercial venture with Ben Shapiro, an L.A. promoter, Derek Taylor, ex-publicist for the Beatles who is now working for Warner Brothers, and Alan Pariser, another interested businessman. After a visit to San Francisco to get bands, and under pressure from Ralph Gleason, the *Rolling Stone* columnist and long time jazz critic for the *San Francisco Chronicle*, Monterey's concept changed, however. It was made into a benefit concert for the Diggers (the socialized relief committee of the Haight) and pop conferences and other means of popularizing rock music. There was even some talk of giving the money to some explicitly political groups, but that was quickly canned. John Phillips and Lou Adler were taken on as co-producers, Pariser was forced out.

As the first of the great rock spectaculars Monterey was probably also the most significant in getting record company recognition of relatively new acts like Janis Joplin and Jimi Hendrix, who were pushed "above ground" in the show's publicity. But there were a lot of problems with the way the event was handled. Had it not been for the very profitable sale of television rights on the event to the ABC network for some $288,843 the project would have wound up $77,392 in the red. The money, instead of going to the Diggers and other representatives of the San Francisco youth scene that pretty much supplied the core talent for the event, went to the staid American Negro College Fund. As Michael Lydon commented in covering the event in *Rolling Stone*, "Months after the Mamas and the Papas closed the show, a bad taste remains. What was a festival to some was a free ride to others. Most artists got there with talent, some with pull. A festival which should and could have been all up front still leaves questions asked and unanswered."

Rapid advancements in the technology of portable public address systems, particularly the use of transistors and printed circuits, have made rock a possible outdoor event, as well as presenting the possibility of minutely timed, grueling concert tours. In the summer of 1968 there were several other festivals, but the second one planned for Monterey's anniversary, at the same site, never came off.

In 1969 there were huge rock gatherings in Atlantic City, Seattle, Dallas, and "Woodstock"—Bethel, New York. Dairy farmer Max Yasgur got $50,000 for loaning his 600 acres of land for a couple of days, and announced to the crowd the second day of the rained on, world famous festival, "I don't know how to speak to 20 people, much less all of you . . . you are the largest group of people ever assembled in one place at one time . . . we had no idea there would be this many . . . and you have proven something to the world. That half a million kids can get together for fun and music and have nothing but fun and music."[19] They had little else. No food, scant medical supplies, no ready john, but lots of dope and music and good highs. *Rolling Stone* was ecstatic in its coverage of the event, announcing:

> Nine days after the passing of the ABM bill by the United States Senate, an act that brings total destruction that much closer to being one man's temperamental reality, an army of peaceful guerrillas established a city larger than Rochester, New York, and showed itself immediately ready to turn back on the already ravaged city and (its) inoperable life styles, imminently prepared to move onto the mist covered field and into the cool, still woods. And they will do it again, the threat of youthful dissidence in Paris and Prague and Fort Lauderdale and Berkeley and Chicago and London criss crossing ever more closely until the map of the world we live in is viable for and visible to all of those that are part of it and all those buried under it.[20]

The festival promoters were all twenty-six or younger. The real driving force behind the event was John Roberts, twenty-four, whose family owned a drug and cosmetic business. In addition to being independently wealthy from his father's exploits, Roberts had his own investment counseling firm. He financed the $2.7 million festival out of his personal inheritance and holdings. How he managed to spend $1.3 million in excess of receipts remains a mystery, since the performers' fees (with Jimi Hendrix paid a high of $18,000) added up only to around $150,000. After the event Roberts talked about a string of additional expenses that were bankrupting him. There supposedly was some $600,000 for helicopters, food, and medicine, $500,000 in duplicate costs in moving the festival from Walkill to Bethel, and $200,000 for advertising. But on the last day of the fair, members of Woodstock's publicity office were talking about expenses totalling only around $1.5 million. Somewhere along the line they doubled. Woodstock was dreamed up by former dope dealer Michael Lang, a friend and advisor to Roberts. After the dust cleared at the festival site, Roberts sued Lang, and vice versa, for damages and rights to the Woodstock name. Albert Grossman, who managed many of the acts that appeared at Woodstock and lived in the actual town of that name himself, offered to pick up all rights to movies and soundtracks along with the supposed debts of the groups for $1 million. The different law suits went ahead anyway, and dragged on for years.

Woodstock was both a festival of youth culture and an example of its commercialization and control. At the time radical journalist Andrew Kopkind commented that:

> The promoters must have sensed the responsibility they carried. They tried every aspect of cooptation theory. SDS, Newsreel, and underground papers were handed thousands of dollars to participate in the festival, and they were given a choice spot for 'Movement City'; the idea was that they would give hip legitimacy to the weekend and channel their activities within the system. They bought the idea.[21]

Woodstock was a good example of the counterculture feeding off the counterculture, a few wealthy kids who never distinguished hip culture from hip capitalism. In their memoir of the event, *Young Men with Unlimited Capital,* the promoters make the (believable enough) argument that in some way they identified with the cultural rebellion Woodstock represented, even as they moved to make a profit off it in their position as businessmen/entrepreneurs. The real money of course was made after the festival, after it had become a mythic event for young people everywhere, on the rights to the Woodstock albums and movie. The audience for the concert played out its role in a way that eventually proved profitable. In a sense, the half million people who attended and had a good time were the largest unpaid studio audience in history.

If Woodstock was generally regarded as the confirmation of a counterculture of love, cooperation, and nonviolence, Altamont was seen as its opposite moment, a dark underbelly of panic and violence. The December 1969 Rolling Stones free concert at a deserted speedway east of San Francisco started as the British group's Christmas present to their United States audience at the end of a long and profitable tour. It was badly planned and produced, however. Concern about security led the Grateful Dead to call in their friends, the sadistic thug Hell's Angels, to act as guards for the Stones and other groups that played. The Angels themselves developed into a major problem at the concert. Marty Balin, the lead singer for the Jefferson Airplane, was knocked unconscious during their afternoon set by an Angel. Several other people were beaten with pool cues. By the time the Rolling Stones came on stage, there was a steady stream of blood and violence in the front ranks of the audience. A black man, Meredith Hunter, was eventually stabbed and killed by an Angel, on whom he had apparently drawn a gun.

Much of this was lost on the bulk of the crowd. The four days of notice for a free Rolling Stones concert had brought hundreds of thousands of people to the desolate site. Most of them could not see what was going on up near the low-slung stage. Several newspapers also missed or ignored the gruesome side of the Altamont story. Nearly a week after the concert *Variety* headlined "Stones Create Another Woodstock, 300,000

Flock to Boffo Bash." But the cinema verité documentary film of the Stones' tour released later by the Maysles brothers as *Gimme Shelter* graphically uncovered the horror of Altamont for a mass audience the next year.*

There were other nasty concerts, run-ins with the police, bombings, and gate crashing at benefits. Concerts did not seem the guaranteed good time high they once were. A spokesperson for the disastrously crashed Rainbow People Ann Arbor Blues Festival in 1970 said, "This town is dead for entertainment as far as next year goes. We lost 25 to 30 thousand dollars. People have ruined it for themselves. They can't gripe about it. This is the age of the rip off and this seems to be the zenith of asshole rock in this country." In New York a guy named Ishmael Brown bombed the Electric Circus, for no clear reason. He injured seventeen people, then blew himself up in his own apartment a week later. The Toronto Peace Festival that John Lennon and Yoko Ono worked on wound up losing thousands of dollars instead of benefiting the antiwar movement. The Aragon Ballroom in Chicago was repeatedly busted by cops for dope when the owners failed to come up with a suitably sized bribe to get "protection" by the police. When Sly Stone was late for a concert in Chicago's Grant Park in 1970, concert goers used the occasion for a violent riot against the repressive city police.

Elsewhere politics and random violence were more confused. As colleges opened up to rock concerts—probably the single biggest boon to concert promotion, along with the ballrooms—in the late sixties, the stage was set for a great deal of property damage. In Washington, D.C., the entire city was gradually shut down for concerts. The Post Pavilion closed its doors to rock after a riot at a show by The Who. American University stopped producing concerts after a crowd ripped open their gym to crash the Allman Brothers. Another crowd did the same at a Traffic concert at George Washington. Baltimore Civic Center stopped after a soul show there got delayed and led to a little violence. Constitution Hall shut down after Sly told a sedate crowd not to feel bashful

---

*The Grateful Dead were at first traumatized with guilt over Altamont. Later, in "New Speedway Boogie," lyricist Robert Hunter tried to extract some folk wisdom from the event, with indifferent success. One verse of the song is "I spent a little time on the mountain/Spent a little time on the hill./Thing went down we don't understand/But I think in time we will," and another repeats the first two lines but ends with "I saw things gettin' out of hand/I guess they always will." The Dead were originally scheduled to follow the Rolling Stones and close the concert. They had plenty of time to look at what was going on in the hills of Altamont. Hunter rejects the idea of Woodstock and Altamont being the beginning and end of the counterculture. They are simply different events that reflect different stages of the same movement: "One step's done, and another begun." But just where to go from here,

about dancing in the aisles, on the seats, and so forth. The ultra-conservative owners of the building, the Daughters of the American Revolution, did not appreciate his good cheer. Finally, there were dozens of fights at a Grand Funk Railroad bash at Robert F. Kennedy Stadium. Civic auditoriums started insuring their audiences against obscenity. In Oklahoma City at a concert with the Jefferson Airplane, promoter Leonard Jay had to post $1,000 for Grace Slick saying "bullshit" on stage. Jim Morrison of the Doors was continually busted from 1968 on for obscenity, indecent exposure, inciting to riot, and other stage antics. He often said: "The cops have fun, the kids have fun, we have fun. It's kinda weird."

Between 1967 and 1970, more than 2.5 million people attended some thirty rock festivals (out of forty-eight that were announced and planned). Most of the festivals were overattended and badly managed, but people's basic humanity allowed them to enjoy the communal gatherings, however dismal the weather and long the wait at the portable johns.

Ballroom Blitz and the Rise of the Current System

Late in 1970 Bill Graham announced that he was shutting down his Fillmores East and West. Within months the Playground, Electric Factory, and Tea Party had also closed their doors. Graham made a typically stormy exit from the San Francisco rock scene. Typically enough, he made no real exit at all, and returned the next year to establish his hegemony over the city's rock entertainment with concerts in the old Winterland Ice Palace and the Berkeley Community Theater. Towards the end of the ballroom days, however, when profits were wearing thin, the grumpy millionaire was given a hard time by Bay Area community organizations who wanted him to put money back into the San Francisco community. In New York, the Motherfuckers, a local street gang who disguised their violence with political arguments, attacked him physically.

The official announcement of his leaving the Fillmores was made at the end of a long meeting with art groups in San Francisco, who were discussing Graham's obligations to support the people who put on psychedelic light shows at his concerts. Graham did not want to keep the shows, which he said were not demonstrably profitable. That was enough of a rationale, he felt. "This town has never stopped rapping an

---

and how to understand the violence of Altamont still eludes Hunter, who ends with a hopeful prayer for redemption: "One way or another/One way or another/One way or another/This darkness got to give." Analysis of the Dead's critical role in the festival gives way before charitable mysticism.

147

honest businessman for four fucking years," he told the assembled group. "I leave here very sad. . . . I may be copping out, but your attitudes have driven me to my conclusions." But *Rolling Stone* reports that:

> Graham really blew his gnarled top only after Steve Gaskin, a resident communications lecturer at the Family Dog (involved in the light show talks) told him, "When you started, you had to make a choice between love and money. You've got our money, so you can't have our love. . . . You've used dramatics today to fuck over a lot of heads with your emotional trips."

Graham replied (as recorded verbatim by *Good Times,* a local newspaper):

> I apologize, motherfucker, that I'm a human being. I fucking apologize. Emotional—you're fucking right. Fuck you, you stupid prick! Do you know what emotions are? Stand up and have emotions. Get up and work. Get up and sing. Get up and act. You think I'm an actor? You're full of shit, man. I have more fucking balls than you'll ever see! You want to challenge me in any way about emotions? You slimy little man. . . . YOU SLIMY LITTLE . . . MAN (to a musician who tried to calm him)! Don't get peaceful with me! Don't touch me!![22]

It was a great exit, and it is too bad really that he could not have stayed away longer, but Graham and all the other "honest businessmen" of rock, the captains on the front lines of entrepreneurial capitalism, came back within months: Graham at Winterland; Magid at the Shubert Theater and Spectrum; Law at the Orpheum Theater and Boston Music Hall and Garden.

The increased expenses of the ballrooms point up the expansion of the rock concert business. In its heyday the Boston Tea Party, for example, had a capacity of no more than 2,000 people. One show was performed a night. Tickets were scaled at $3.50. The cost of top acts plus overhead on the hall ran only to about $4,000-$5,000 a night, and Law says he and partner Ray Reipen made a weekly profit of around $5,000 for three nights. By 1971, however, a $7,000 gross simply could not support English acts like Jeff Beck, Eric Clapton, or The Who, all of whom would have played for a couple of thousand dollars only two years before.

By contrast today Law scales his tickets at around $5, $6, and $7, and even higher with certain acts. He works two medium-sized halls seating 2,860 and 4,200 people, and insists that to break even he needs to get an 80 percent paid house for either one. For the small hall that comes out to roughly $15,000 and for the bigger one about $20,000—just to break even. To get into the biggest local hall, the Boston Garden, Law needs more than $50,000 simply to open the doors and stage the show, let alone buy talent.

Rock concerts have grown into a multimillion dollar business. Although he is a powerful businessman and has a tight hold on Boston's concert market, Law is only a medium level promoter in grossing more than $3 million yearly. Howard Stein, the New York promoter who operates all over the United States, grosses more like $15 million annually. A single group, Crosby, Stills Nash, and Young, grossed $6-10 million on their last tour. *Billboard* reports that acts spend more than $30 million on travel going from gig to gig. Figures like these suggest that concert promoting is at least a $150 million annual business for the rock industry.

The amount of capital needed to break into the promotion business has increased proportionately. Law, Magid, Graham, and Stein all started with a few thousand dollars. Presently, even if a young promoter finds a good concert area that is not picked clean or controlled by an established promoter (which is extremely unlikely), he will need hundreds of thousands of dollars to set himself up and stay in business long enough to start turning a profit. Gary Perkins and Sepp Dona-hower, who are partners in one of the most successful rock promotion firms, Pacific Presentations, started in the concert business in 1967. They began with $10,000 in backing, and produced the first Grateful Dead concerts in L.A. But because of management problems and a few misjudgments, the initially profitable venture was abandoned. The partners came together again in 1971. By that time, "needed operating capital amounted to approximately $25,000. In addition we very obviously had our ideas developed on paper. We borrowed money from people who were interested in investing in such an operation. We now use four times the initial amount as working capital."[23]

Perkins and Donahower think that young promoters have virtually no chance of breaking into the locked-up concert promotion industry. In addition to needing about $50,000-$100,000 in operating capital, new promoters must be prepared to lose money for a long time before major agencies start consistently feeding them profitable talent. As detailed in the discussion of agencies and managers, the promotion monopoly handles new acts by "packaging" them as a second bill to the headliner. If the new act makes it, or as, in the case of Black Oak Arkansas, the agency is firmly committed to making the act make it, the promoter gets first shot at the new star next time around. According to the Frank Barsalona "new system," agencies deal with people they already know. They give them the best acts, so those promoters can afford to do the agencies the reciprocal favor of developing new talent, which then goes to the same promoter. It is a cycle that is hard to break.

The first rock promoters were dropouts from other parts of the industry, or young people who identified with the music and could see its potential profitability. Over the years, promoters have become more obviously businessmen, and businessmen have become more interested in promoters. Perkins and Donahower both attended UCLA business school before getting involved with rock'n'roll.

Promoters everywhere are working closely with banks on special projects that need short term financing. The banks recognize the promotion business as relatively stable and enjoy getting a cut of the pie. Don Law does his business with the First National Bank of Boston. Shelly Finkel from Cornucopia Productions, who promoted the mammoth Watkins Glen Summer Jam, gets financing from Marine Midland Bank in New York City. As Finkel comments, "People who are in banking and finance realize it is a big, big money business, and they're more open and receptive. When we went to our banker the first time and said, 'We're going to do a big show,' he said, 'Sure.' We says, 'You're going to read about it all over.' He says, 'Sure.' I says, 'It's going to make a lot of money.' He said 'Sure' again. When the money came in and he saw it all over the papers, he realized it was real."[24]

Finkel and his partner Jimmy Koplik used the Watkins Glen concert not only to make money, but to establish themselves as national promoters. The concert involved $1.5 million in financing and drew 600,000 people, which was 450,000 more than the expected paid admission of 150,000 ($10 tickets). The event came in July 1973. After months of negotiations, arm twisting, and possible bribes, Cornucopia got the Grateful Dead, the Allman Brothers, and The Band to do a single show together. It is rumored that The Band and Allman Brothers both got about $140,000 for their three hour sets, and the Dead around $117,000. In any event, talent fees were approximately $400,000. Additional expenses included some $30,000 for medical supplies, $50,000 for special off-duty New York police, $100,000 for advertising, $100,000 for the rental of 1,000 portable toilets, $40,000 for the cleanup, $40,000 for water, and $200,000 to Bill Graham and his FM Productions, who handled lights, sound, and staging. Everybody made money, and Finkel and Koplik got their desired publicity.

Afterward Finkel commented that Watkins Glen was not the last of its kind, "We're going into bigger events, extravaganzas, as we look at them, or spectacles. We view ourselves as modern day P.T. Barnums. That keeps our ego filled."[25] The disadvantages of the rock spectacular approach were shown up the following summer, however, when Cornucopia dropped an estimated $100,000 for a poorly attended concert at Ontario Speedway in Ontario, California, that featured Crosby, Stills, Nash & Young. A few days later the promoters, who had failed to get insurance for bad weather, were rained out in a concert in New Jersey, and lost an additional bundle. They went bankrupt temporarily, but got some new financing and are now back in production.

Festivals are not the base of the concert business. Day-to-day business is a routine of booking and combining dozens of acts over a seasonal period, usually months in advance. Once the deals are made, each concert promotion goes into a pipeline of making arrangements with the appropriate hall, buying radio and print advertising, printing tickets and putting them on sale, and making specific arrangements with roadies and the agency on details of production (special stage requirements, light and sound, et cetera). Most of the monopoly promoters have bought up outright, or have virtually complete access to several different halls in their cities. Don Law, for example, actually manages and rents space in the Orpheum Theater in Boston, in addition to using it whenever he wants for his own promotion purposes. Larry Magid has a long-term deal worked out with the Spectrum in Philadelphia whereby he gets first choice on all dates and a special rental rate. Likewise the major promoters get kickback deals and special advertising rates (like any large corporate sponsor) on radio. Sales manager at WPLR in New Haven Dick Kalt is more honest than some in admitting this as standard practice: "If you buy from us over a period of time, naturally, we give you more than the rate card says you're going to get."[26] FM radio and underground and sea-level press are particularly dependent on local promoters' advertising. Law puts more than $2,000 a week into Boston area newspapers and FM radio stations.

Each day promoters are in touch with the major New York and Los Angeles agencies, confirming old dates, finding out about new tours, picking up industry gossip and the latest word. Formally at least, acts have an asking price, a guarantee plus percentage of the net, and promoters bid against that. The promoters deal largely with the agents, of course, and not the managers of the groups. The same agent will sell a promoter several different acts and the promoter, to be successful, must have a workable and stable relationship with the agent. The bidding on a particular artist, then, is less important than the overall treatment of the promoter by the agency. Their relationship reduces on the one hand to mutual occasional favors, and on the other to a fairly routine system of talent buys. One promoter explained how he mechanically figured out which acts should go in what halls, and how much he could afford for them:

> A safe way to base a deal is if you have a hall and you have a group, you give the group the guarantee and add onto the guarantee the expense of the hall. Then you take a split—that's *your* profit. Then above that figure you each get a percentage. Say it's a $100,000 gross; the group gets $20,000 upfront as a guarantee; the hall expenses are another $20,000, which makes it $40,000. Then you have your miscellaneous advertising and outside expenses, which bring the show right there to $45,000, which is low. You should usually figure on 60% of your gross to break even.

Now say we use the figure we just did, $45,000. I would take on $5,000 which would be my profit going into the split. Then it would be a 60-40 split, the act getting 60%, I would get 40%, above $50,000. At $50,000 which is the half-way mark, I'm into $5,000 profit, the act is making $20,000, and the hall expenses are paid.[27]

Promoters make an incredible amount of money, and the way they figure deals is just as this one says, but the split usually occurs at a later point in approaching the ticket sellout. Usually terms are not quite so favorable to promoters, who make their money on a great *volume* of business, rather than on individual concert dates.

Many acts demand a guarantee in excess of $20,000 and ask for a percentage of the gross sales, rather than the net profit. Promoters are currently bemoaning the terms of the 1976 David Bowie tour, which many of the monopoly concert producers passed up. It demanded a large guarantee plus 90 percent of the gross. A common industry compromise is a guarantee *against* a percentage of the gross, meaning that an act will not go into percentages until the promoter has at least cleared enough to cover his basic expenses in ticket sales.

There are, of course, many rock artists who get considerably less than $20,000, and there are many who consistently get more. At International Famous Agency, for example, a range of artists with varying prices are represented. The Beach Boys, Doobie Brothers, and Chicago all get at least $25,000 guarantee a night; Grand Funk Railroad, Gordon Lightfoot, and James Taylor a minimum of $15,000; Mahavishnu Orchestra, Fleetwood Mac, and the Kinks at least $7,500-$10,000; Jesse Colin Young and Leo Koetke a minimum of $2,500-$3,500. All these figures are approximate—a framework for negotiation rather than absolutely fixed.

The biggest of the top twenty promoters are Graham, Concerts West, Concert Associates, Frank Freed in Chicago, and both of New York's top promoters, Ron Delsener and Howard Stein.

Stein is a relative latecomer, who emerged after Graham left the city in 1971. He had been around hustling odd jobs for a long time, however. At one point he was a $200 a month janitor at Columbia Records in Nashville. At another he had a T-shirt concession stand and hocked mementoes of rock idols outside Madison Square Garden. After Graham closed the Fillmore, Stein began producing concerts at the Academy of Music, an old opera house in the city, and broke into bigger money. Now he claims he and his subordinates are "the biggest promoters who go into regions on a regular weekly basis, with regional offices and regional employees, and continuously promote not only the superstars but are continually building new stars. We are creating new opportunities of exposure for new talent. We have more major cities running on a continuous basis than anyone else."[28]

But Stein, who was confidently plowing along with his bookings, looked up in the fall of 1974 to see that the rock concert business was inflated. There were no lines at the ticket booths. For the first time since the beginnings of serious rock promotion, the concert market was, and is, being challenged. TV probably has something to do with it. All promoters hate TV rock concerts, "and so should acts," said Spar, "because it hurts their record sales and makes them look like fools."[29] Or it may have been simply the summer of expensive tickets that preceded the fall season, or another reflection of the sagging, inflated economy.

Promoters have begun to tighten up on their booking schedules, packaging acts together that would have been billed as separate headliners a year ago. They are naturally less willing to back new acts. This is an important problem in the industry right now. Along with the increased commercialization of FM "progressive" and diverse rock programming, and the restricted AM radio playlists, it will slow down the influx of younger artists. Promoters criticize the bands and agencies for demanding simply too much money. The rock stars argue back that they are entitled to charge whatever the traffic can bear. Both ignore responsibilities to other musicians and the audience. The rock audience has had to endure an incredible escalation in ticket prices in the last several years, and will likely be in for further price hikes in the near future, as promoters preserve their high profit margins on established headline acts with higher and higher guarantees.

Stein sees the concert market "collapse acting as a purge and leading to a healthier future."[30] It will be a future of growing consolidation of the concert business; as profits drop off on individual concerts there will be further moves toward monopoly. This direction is already suggested by Bill Graham's recent practice of working with a single artist over a national market area. The approach simplifies bargaining and accounting procedures for the act, provides an absolutely uniform production job, and obviously is attractive to the selected promoter. While the idea has been limited thus far to people like George Harrison and Bob Dylan, it could be expanded to take in an increasing number of headline acts, and if so would be the first important split within the promotion monopoly of largely regional entrepreneurs.*

If the current slump in concert attendance is left unchecked, says

---

*Recently several important East Coast promoters met on Long Island at Howard Stein's estate to discuss possible action against Bill Graham and his national tours. Stein himself works in a number of auxiliary markets, as do several other promoters with a secure base in some major city or region. Still they felt that Graham was getting out of hand in his complete control of the Bob Dylan tour. "Look," Stein reportedly told the assembled businessmen, who were anxious about their status and future, "your dicks aren't going to fall off if you don't do the Dylan date in your town." After Stein's consolatory remarks, the promoters decided to weather the Dylan tour with little protest. They had no choice. A few months later, Graham did the same thing with George Harrison.

Stein, "it could all just keep sliding until it's too late. And then it's over—because we all ate too heavily off the hog."[31] The complete demise of rock concert promotion seems less than likely. But if the market does collapse, the big promoters will get out before the crash. Stein, who has no fondness for rock music (he calls it a collection of "pimple tunes" and prefers the slightly decayed sound of Tin Pan Alley classics), might profitably turn his talents to promoting something else. Don Law is probably not alone in making plans to make investments in "some altogether different kind of business," now that he has accumulated enough money from rock concerts to be a powerful venture capitalist.

Rock Press

The Trades and Their Charts

The music industry is a large complex of corporations, people, money, and varied products. It requires its own structures for internal communication. A number of newsletters, tip sheets, and magazines directly servicing record companies, record retailers, djs, and station managers. The most important of these are the so called "trade" magazines: *Cashbox*, *Record World*, and *Billboard*. *Cashbox* has been around for years and years. It gives basic coverage to industry events, and charts the hits. *Record World* was started in the early 1960s by Bob Allston and Sid Parnes, who had been editors at *Cashbox* until they were one day thrown out. It does the same thing a little better, and is a magazine rising in importance and circulation. Along with the Bill Gavin report (a venerable tip sheet by a venerable man) and Ready On Records (a tip sheet that is connected with *Record World*), *Cashbox* and *Record World* give radio personnel a guideline to programming. But the most influential, largest, and oldest trade is *Billboard*, whose charts are followed diligently by the mass of industry executives, and which speaks with what is considered *the* editorial voice of the business.

Billboard was started more than eighty years ago as a newsletter for the outdoor entertainment industry of fairs, livestock expositions, traveling road shows, and carnivals. It grew over the years into a huge empire, a publishing company that also turned out serials like *American Arts*, *Amusement Business*, *Gift and Tableware Reporter*, *High Fidelity*, *Merchandising Week*, *Modern Photography*, *Photo Weekly*, *Vend*, and other magazines, and was subdivided into two separate publishing firms: Watson Guptill and Whitney Publishing. In the last few years Billboard Publications Inc. has abandoned some of those magazines and consolidated its corporate structure, but publishers William Littleford and Jules Novick have invested heavily in industries quite removed from the music business, like cable television.

154

Billboard has a number of offices in the United States, the most important ones being in Los Angeles and New York, and a number abroad as well, in Milan and London. Like the other trades, *Billboard* chronicles general news within the music industry and financial community, with particular monitoring of interesting new corporations or executives within the business, new artistic talent, campus markets, developments in recording studio technique and business, radio-TV programming, classical music, the country music scene, jukebox programming, tape and audio-video research, development, and marketing, international news, and the Canadian market. All of the editorial copy, however, is a mere backdrop for *Billboard*'s most important and saleable feature, its charts of record sales.

Over the years their charts, which started as a listing of the top tunes in radio, have become more sophisticated. They are now split into several different indexes or listings. There is a chart, for example, for AM radio singles which is subdivided into coverage of eight different geographic regions. And there are separate listings for National FM Action, Hot Soul Singles, Soul LPs, Easy Listening, Hot Country Singles, Hot Country LPs, and for international business, Hits of the World. *Billboard* also features Top Album Picks in the pop, soul, country, jazz, classical, disco, and comedy categories, with special notes to rack-jobbers and record retailers on how to display the different new records, and which ones to push hardest. Likewise, for radio djs, there are Top Single Picks. To wrap it up, there are the *Billboard* Hot 100 Singles, and the 200 Top LPs and tapes.

The ratings systems at *Billboard* and the other two trades are forever getting revised in one small way or another, but they all involve checking on the sale and airplay of records in some twenty-plus major markets in the country. *Billboard* has probably the tightest system. They call about eighty (out of a cooperating sample of 100) record stores and dealers a week, in twenty-two metropolitan regions. The chart compilers also call 125 sample radio stations each week, and get copies of their playlists. These two sorts of data are then weighted according to a sliding scale formula, fed into a computer, and programmed out as the weekly listings.

Although the trade system for keeping tabs on record popularity is serviceable, it does not always accurately reflect sales. Reporting stores and dealers are supposed to simply state which of their record products are selling best, but they are under constant pressure from distributors, and their own good business sense, to emphasize certainly heavily backed releases at the expense of others. Chart "action" on the *Billboard* listings is a measure of change in ranking of individual songs. A star marking next to the song will indicate a large percentage increase on the charts since the previous week. Chart action is widely regarded as a measure of a song's or album's popularity, but is deceptive. In *Clive*, Clive Davis' account of his exploits as president of Columbia Records, he notes that many of Columbia's best selling artists never had good chart action. They might make the Top 100, and hover in its lower reaches for months, selling slowly and consistently. Bob Dylan, on the other hand, had a relatively small audience that was more devoted. As soon as a song or album of his was released, it would shoot up the popularity charts because it triggered a dense but short buying spree. Chart action becomes important when used by program directors and djs to introduce a new song onto a radio playlist. Davis' comments suggest that Dylan got a disproportionate amount of radio airplay, if one were to judge and play a song strictly on the basis of its overall popularity and market.

In his caustic book on the industry, *The Music Machine*, Roger Karshner details the "trade bugging" and bribery used by the major companies to get favored treatment for their artists:

> While at Capitol I appointed a full time trade liaison. All the guy did, all day long, all week long, was to whine, dine, and wine the trades. He was instructed to get favorable listings at all costs. I offered him handsome incentives to achieve prescribed chart assignments. Five hundred dollars for maintaining a "star" or "bullet," for moving selections into the Top 20, or for obtaining a local "breakout" was not uncommon.[32]

What exact effect chart bugging or bribery, like any other sort of payola, really has on the industry overall is open to question, but certainly the charts are not prepared in splendid isolation from the real pressures and corruption within the business. Still, along with some of the tip sheets, *Billboard*, *Record World*, and *Cashbox* are religiously followed by thousands of retailers and djs.

The Music Press and Their Judith Crist

In addition to the trade magazines and tip sheets, which deal largely with the music industry and its structure and operation, and not with the content of its product, there grew up around rock'n'roll a number of magazines that treated the personalities and music in the rock scene.

The rock press really began with *Hit Parader*, a comic book-like pulp magazine edited by Jim Delahunt, now working for Atlantic Records. It circulated in the middle sixties, up until about 1967 or 1968, when it was surpassed by *Rolling Stone* and other more slick magazines. In between the words of the latest pubescent hits Delahunt put articles about people—rock'n'roll musicians and their influences from 'way back. *Hit Parader* provided a sort of running history of rock'n'roll and rhythm and blues that was devoured by the more serious fans of the period. Many of the established rock critics were weaned on the tabloid.

Crawdaddy appeared in spring 1966. It was a labor of love of rock put together by Swarthmore English student Paul Williams. The early issues of the fanzine were mimeographed sheets stapled together. It had a fervidly enthusiastic prose style, and long articles on the roots of rock in blues and black music. Later in 1966 Greg Shaw and David Harris got together in San Francisco to write about the music there in the *Mojo Navigator News,* a lively rag with cartoons, record reviews, and discographies. In New York *Cheetah* magazine was the meeting place and watering hole for Bob Christgau, Ellen Willis, Richard Goldstein, and many others who would become the New York pop critic establishment. *Cheetah* folded quickly enough. Goldstein went on to do a regular column for the *Village Voice* and began editing *US,* a book magazine published by Bantam, that also folded after a few issues. Meanwhile *Crawdaddy* author/editor/publisher Williams had graduated from Philadelphia's mainline college circuit and moved to Boston, where his magazine attracted area writers of the time like Peter Guralnick, Bob Somma, Sandy Perlman, Ed Ward, and most important, Jon Landau.

At the time he started writing for *Crawdaddy,* Landau was also writing for *Hard Times, Eye,* and *Vibrations* magazines, less successful period attempts to capture the market. He was soon the standout critic at *Crawdaddy,* as informed and far more popular than Williams. He was the first person, as *Real Paper* music editor Jim Miller puts it, "to write about the music without gushing about seeing God and purple colors everytime he listened to Country Joe and the Fish, or whatever the latest group was."[33]

In the years since *Crawdaddy,* Landau has established an unmatched reputation as the longest running, most popular, most powerful critic in the country. He is really so much more important than any other critic, at least from the standpoint of the industry, that there are no comparisons. Landau is a person regarded with respect who has consistently recognized commercial potential and talent. He is the only writer on rock who could rave about Bruce Springsteen ("I have seen rock and roll future, and it is Bruce Springsteen") when Columbia was about to drop the artist after he cost them some $300,000, and change the label's mind. Recently Landau approached several record companies to sound out getting a job in A&R. "Everybody I shook hands with made me some kind of offer. But wouldn't you know that?" he laughs. "They know I'm hot!"[34]

Landau is a charming power broker who enjoys toying with the industry and its plans for using him. His writing tends to be narrow, locating records in the context of the artists' previous work alone, and not in a more general social perspective. Referring to this narrow range of criticism, he likes to compare himself to Andrew Sarris, the famous *auteur* film critic who writes for the *Village Voice.* But other critics tease the film conceit. They call Landau the Judith Crist of rock criticism, alluding to the powerful and artistically conservative *New York Daily News* film critic, whose approval was wooed by major studios.

Many rock critics who later wrote for national music publications first worked for the underground papers. In San Francisco, for example, the *Express Times*, later renamed the *Good Times*, was originally edited by Marvin Garson and some other Berkeley graduate students, and had writers like Greil Marcus and Langdon Winner and other Bay Area writers who would later work for *Rolling Stone*.

Rolling Stone

The most important of the new magazine-newspapers to emerge from the sixties and the pre-eminent journal of the hip "new" record industry is *Rolling Stone* magazine. *Rolling Stone* editor Jann (pronounced Yahn) Wenner never had identity problems with his publication, which has been commercial from the first, and has over the years continued to work closely with record companies and hi-fi manufacturers in advertising a consumer youth culture. Wenner was asked if he had ever considered *Rolling Stone* part of the underground press and its tradition. He replied:

> No, I never did. We never joined the underground press syndicate and never participated in its reprint thing. We felt we were going for a different audience, with an entirely different approach. We were trying, from the beginning . . . to run on a very solid, commercial basis. We also want to make money. We are in business, and not ashamed of it, and we are covering music. Music is the greatest definable part of the youth culture, the thing more people were interested in and, most importantly, was the method by which people communicated.[35]

Wenner was accurately described in *Rolling Stone* ad copy some years ago as a "small, fleshy, often ferocious man about whom little is known and less is asked." He attended the University of California at Berkeley during the Free Speech Movement uprising, which he covered for the *Daily Californian* and as a stringer for NBC news. By 1967 he had dropped out of college and was doing freelance music writing, and was fully plugged into the developing music scene on the West Coast and elsewhere. He traveled to London for a few months, then lived in New York, and then came back to San Francisco to work on *Sunday Ramparts*, a weekly supplement to the long standing Bay Area radical magazine, as arts editor. There he worked closely with *San Francisco Chronicle* music columnist Ralph Gleason, whom Wenner had met during his U.C. days. As Gleason recalls:

> After that paper folded, an early warning of the troubles that eventually beset *Ramparts* itself, Jann came over one day and said, "Do you think

there's a place for a magazine on pop music?" I said there sure as hell was, and we started to conspire that afternoon. It was Jann's idea. I had a lot of miscellaneous experiences with various periodicals and I suggested that one way to launch it on a shoestring was to get the printer to give us office space. And so the printer who handled *Sunday Ramparts* printed *Rolling Stone.*[36]

Wenner moved quickly to get experienced people involved with the paper. *Newsweek*'s Michael Lydon came on as assistant editor. Gleason was there from the beginning as an advisor and regular columnist. And Jon Landau, first of the rock critics with a real reputation, also went over to *Rolling Stone* from *Crawdaddy*. In an interview in 1970, Landau recalled that, "I could see that *Stone* first of all was a serious professional magazine. Especially from a business point of view, it was a professionally run magazine and there was a sense of excitement with *Stone* that I remember from the early days."[37]

The first issue of *Rolling Stone* came out in October 1967, featuring a piece by Michael Lydon investigating the background of the Monterey Pop Festival ("done for a cost plus songs, not for a song plus costs"), a picture of John Lennon in army uniform from "How I Won the War" on the cover, and an editorial from Wenner inside that said:

> We have begun a new publication reflecting what we see are the basic changes in rock and roll and the changes related to rock and roll. Because the trade papers have become so inaccurate and irrelevant and because the fan magazines are an anachronism, fashioned in the mold of myth and nonsense, we hope we have something here for artists and the industry, and every person who "believes in the magic that can set you free."
>
> Rolling Stone is not just about music, but also about the things and attitudes that the music embraces. We've been working quite hard on it and we hope you can dig it. To describe it any further would be difficult without sounding like bullshit, and bullshit is like gathering moss.[38]

The first press run of 40,000 copies did not sell well; thirty-four-thousand were returned, but within months *Stone* was a financial success. It was making a modest profit and had the best writers around. There were more staff shuffles. John Burks from the *Chronicle* came on as managing editor. Greil Marcus came over from his other writing (for the *Express Times* and elsewhere), bringing Langdon Winner. *Stone* was recognized as authoritative within the industry. An article praising the then obscure Texas blues guitarist Johnny Winter led to a several hundred thousand dollar contract with Columbia Records, for example. Circulation grew. Wenner was determined to reach the rest of the world with the news of rock and *Rolling Stone*. He took out a full page advertisement in the *New York Times* to announce that, "Rock and roll is more than just music, it is the energy of the new culture and youth revolution."

But the magazine began to fall away from its editor. Sloppy accountants misinformed Wenner of his magazine's finances, leading him to invest disastrously in a London version of *Stone* (along with part-time venture capitalist Mick Jagger), which never came into being. He plunked down a lot of money on new, $7,000 a month office space in 1970. As Wenner learned of the shaky condition of his operation, he made sharp cutbacks. The move to the new offices on Third Street was the occasion for a bureaucratization of office structure in an effort to cut back on expenses (except the biggest one, rent) and improve production and efficiency. As Langdon Winner remembers:

> They replaced the haphazard, more or less communal office routine, where there were just desks scattered around and people talking to each other, and very little partitioning, with partitioning, departmental organization. Where before people had felt pretty much equal, and even with divided tasks able to talk to each other, a kind of organization of the flow of information was imposed. Who got to use telephones, handle mail, and who got to talk to whom became very important.[39]

The demand for "efficiency" was then also a rationale for the consolidation of power.

There were political differences at the magazine. Most of these were expressed as tensions between the Bay Area writers who felt a part of the many intense university and community struggles that wracked Berkeley and San Francisco in the late sixties and early seventies, like the People's Park demonstrations and the campaign against police brutality, and Wenner, who had always been suspicious of radicals and radical politics. At first *Stone* ignored political movements. Then it began to cover them, but only the most spectacular ones, and in a largely negative way. The magazine's coverage of the Yippie invitation to disrupt the Democratic party convention in Chicago in the summer of 1968 was violently antiradical. The demonstrators, said Wenner, used "methods and means as corrupt as the political machine they hope to disrupt."

By the following spring *Rolling Stone*'s editor was at least willing to talk about politics at more length, however grudgingly. Introducing a special issue devoted largely to "The American Revolution" in April 1969 he intoned:

> Like it or not, we have reached a point in the social, cultural, intellectual, and artistic history of the United States where we are all going to be affected by politics. We can no longer ignore it. It threatens our daily lives and daily happiness. . . . The new political movements we feel all around us can no longer be left at the periphery of the artistic consciousness. . . . The blacks and the students are our brothers and they are doing something which we must have awareness of. And we must participate in it because they are fighting a fight *against our enemies,* even if our participation is just by the fact of awareness itself [emphasis ours].[40]

Much of the coverage in the American Revolution issue was still negative. Ralph Gleason summarized the discussion by attacking radicals as the unconscious victims of their own "death wish" and baited them with violence: "You better figure out how to make a revolution without killing people," he suggested, "or it won't work."

Within the office Wenner hated political discussion. He was away from the office during the early days of May 1970, however, when the Kent State and Jackson State massacres occurred. While he was still on vacation the rest of the staff, led by the "radicals," put out a political issue on the Cambodian invasion, student protests, and police repression. When Wenner came back, he was met by a united bloc of writers who wanted the magazine to do political coverage consisting of Winner, Burks, Marcus, and a few others. Although what followed has never been made clear, it seems that Wenner was personally threatened by the political independence and apparent unity of his best writers. He claimed to the staff that he was getting a lot of mail from irate readers regarding the Kent State issue saying essentially, "I read *Rolling Stone* for the music. Don't bother me with politics." Wenner felt that the radicals were out of touch with *Stone*'s real audience, and argued that the wishes of the readers should be followed pretty closely in what the magazine covered.

Shortly afterward, Greil Marcus was frozen out of his job as record review editor. After a number of Marcus' departmental decisions had been ignored or overruled by Wenner, who sometimes did not even run Marcus' column any more, Greil called Jann up one day and asked, a little hurt, "Jann, am I working for this magazine or not?" To which Wenner replied, with utter calm, "I guess you're not." After Marcus, Wenner fired Burks, another rad named Michael Goodwin left, and Langdon Winner also decided he did not want to work for the magazine, in that atmosphere, any longer.

By the fall of 1970 the magazine was still in trouble from Wenner's investments, but the radicals were effectively out and the paper moved into a second phase of growth and consolidation. Wenner found some people interested in investing in *Stone*. Most important was Max Palevsky, computer wizard and self-made millionaire who had risen to be chairman of the board of Xerox Data Systems and chairman of the Executive Committee of the Xerox Corporation. Palevsky had founded his own company, Scientific Data Systems, in 1961. When it was bought up by Xerox in 1969 he moved into the parent company's corporate hierarchy. He had read *Rolling Stone* at the suggestion of a friend and been "impressed with its brilliance." Palevsky gave financial advice to Wenner on how to run Straight Arrow (the parent firm for *Rolling Stone*) "more like a corporate business enterprise rather than running it by the seat of their pants."[41] Another important corporate executive in

Scientific Data Systems, well-known financier Arthur Rock, also got involved with the magazine's corporate management.

Linking into extremely sophisticated and newly rich corporate executives like Palevsky and Rock solidified *Rolling Stone*'s finances during this shaky period in late 1970. It also spelled out the direction the magazine would take in the future. Although *Rolling Stone* was never taken seriously by people on the Left, even before the 1970 purge, it had for some time been the most creative of the commercially successful sea-level (not quite underground, not really establishment) newspaper/magazines. For people who were not content with the lonely outposts of rock criticism and political writing found in the underground press or entrenched establishment media, it offered a flexible environment to explore ideas, music, and youth culture. The removal of the radicals was not a dramatic event, in part because by writing for *Stone* they had already isolated themselves from the larger radical community, in part because the purge was carried out over an extended period of time, and the politics of the situation never became absolutely explicit, even within the *Rolling Stone* offices.

Still it remains an interesting juncture in the institutionalization and cooptation of the counterculture, a triumph for hierarchy and hip capitalism, that was symptomatic of what was happening elsewhere. "When we were first writing for the magazine," Langdon Winner commented afterward,

> and when the movement was still going in the direction of rejecting middle-class lifestyles and values, I think there was a series of attempts to try to pose an alternative to that lifestyle, to find other forms of life. A lot of the cultural explosion was really a frantic attempt to find new forms of all sorts of things—food, clothing, housing, social organization, new forms for experience—and I think that whole direction was cut off and what you have now is a legitimated, slightly hip, American consumer lifestyle which *Rolling Stone* sells in every issue, which is arguably not that different from any other American consumer lifestyle that one can point to, except that the products are slightly different, and different in the way they're presented.[42]

Winner's comment is correct. One way it is supported is found by looking at how *Rolling Stone* sells *itself,* as an advertising medium, to other corporations interested in selling youth culture. In a recent advertisement in *Billboard* magazine, for example, Wenner announced the results of "A scientific, impartial, accredited research study . . . based on 5,700 interviews with *Rolling Stone* readers" which discovered that the "average reader (and there are more than 2 million of them) buys 61 LPs a year, and 27 tapes. And they spend 1 hour and 26 minutes with each issue! 82% own tape equipment, 69% reported that someone asked their advice in purchasing hi-fi equipment in the past 6 months, 84%

own musical instruments, 95% own playback equipment."[43]* Or, as a *Rolling Stone* advertiser kit spelled it out a couple of years ago:

> Young people spend a *lot* of money on music; rock record sales now total $700 million annually . . . and half of that is spent by *Rolling Stone* readers. . . . *Rolling Stone*'s editorial coverage presents hi-fi as the normal and necessary part of our readers' lives they tell us it is. Not like the men's magazines where it is regarded as just another luxury to be collected and displayed or the general magazines where hi-fi is either held in awe or else is just one more household commodity. Because music is vital to the readers of *Rolling Stone*, so is high fidelity.[44]

The selling of high fidelity equipment and records are only two obvious examples of the *Rolling Stone* consumer lifestyle.

In the years since 1970, *Stone* has grown ever bigger. A standard issue now runs 104 pages. It is still published bi-weekly, with a paid circulation that approaches half a million, and a new syndicate deal worked out with King Features that distributes one *Rolling Stone* feature story, one record review, and one profile a week through a number of papers into some 33 million additional homes. The corporate structure has become more complex as *Stone* has diversified into other fields. In fiscal 1974 *Rolling Stone* alone grossed over $6 million, with a 10 percent profit, and claimed an $8.5 million gross for fiscal 1975.

The corporate board of directors has changed and expanded, integrating *Stone* into a web of high finance. As the *Los Angeles Times* recently observed in no uncertain terms, "In case anyone still believes that *Rolling Stone* is a hippie rag produced in a haphazard manner by a few wild-eyed freaks, he has either spent the last three years as a prisoner of war in some remote land or has just returned from an extended trip to outer space."[45] In addition to Arthur Rock and Max Palevsky, the board of directors includes people like Richard Irvine, a former executive with Walt Disney Productions. Late in 1974 Irvine was named president and chief operating officer of Straight Arrow Publishing. Before his new job he had run the Disney-owned Educational Media Co. and had been Disney's director of marketing. Jerome Hardy is also on the *Stone* board of directors. Hardy is the former publisher of *Life* magazine and currently president of the Dreyfuss Corporation, the blue chip investment firm. And Edwin L. Berkowitz, who formerly ran the MJB Co. in San Francisco and is another investment broker, is also on the board.

Wenner's own politics have been stated from the beginning of the

---

*Wenner's claim here is a little incredible. If each of an estimated 2 million readers buys close to 100 albums and tapes a year, each priced at roughly $5, *Rolling Stone*'s audience accounts for a full $1 billion in record and tape sales annually, or fully 50 percent of the industry *total*, and an even larger percentage of the rock sales.

magazine, although more recently his personal ambitions have become a bit clearer. He has talked extensively of starting another publication, devoted exclusively to politics, and in the meantime has integrated *Stone* into the left wing of the Democratic party. Such an integration should come as no surprise to readers of the magazine. Wenner's view of culture and political change has been as consistent as it is confused and shortsighted. He has never, for all the rhetoric, been a radical. In 1969 he told *Time* magazine that "Rock and roll is now the energy core of change in American life. But capitalism is what allows us the incredible indulgence of this music."[46] In 1971, on the occasion of *Rolling Stone*'s fourth anniversary, when profits were climbing again and the staff dissidents were out, he defined his position once and for all:

> If you're doing public art and communication in America—even if you live here—you're dealing with money, and you're in business. One of the cardinal rules of the commercial side of one's life (as an individual, a family, or a corporation) is to be profitable. If you're not, you can go quickly bankrupt, and then you're on the street again. (Unfortunately most American businesses become so carried away, they make that rule the game itself. And in that process, the material and spiritual needs of the people get fucked.) If you pay bills, whether for yourself, for your own family or for your business, you are a capitalist. The choice is whether you're going to be exploitative or whether you will be honest and maintain human dignity.[47]

The purpose of all capitalist structures is to generate profit. It *is* the entire game, and not any rule within a larger picture of benevolent business. Certainly the last 300 years of capitalist development would indicate that. Wenner changes the definition of capitalist from those who own factories, equipment, or magazines and use them to make a profit by exploiting the labor of other people to anyone who ever has contact with money, or receives a paycheck, or has to make a rent bill. He does away (incredibly enough) with all class distinctions between capitalist and worker, and is left with a sort of intuitive moral judgment on the "material and spiritual needs of the people" with which he apparently distinguishes one sort of capitalist (meaning *any person* in his definition) from another.

Wenner's strategy is to preserve the main structure of capitalism, while closely regulating those corporations that do the most obvious damage to life and property. He says:

> One is also tired of the eager attacks on any music enterprise (whether a group, ballroom, newspaper, or record company) because it makes money. The music business, corporate and otherwise, has spread more pro-life propaganda in the last five years than any other commercial institutions that quickly come to mind. Isn't it time to focus on the real problems, companies that do real damage?[48]

There is no room in Wenner's analysis for criticizing "liberal" industries like the pop music business for blunting the progressive potential of the music in its very method of packaging and marketing, nor does he recognize the integral connections between the record business and the rest of American capitalist enterprise (see Chapter 6, Who Owns Rock?).

The connections with Max Palevsky have eased *Rolling Stone*'s integration into the mainstream of party politics in the United States. During 1972 *Stone* gave so much coverage to the heavily Palevsky financed McGovern campaign that "National Affairs" editor Hunter Thompson assembled a full length, laudatory* book from his clippings. It was published by Straight Arrow. Wenner, once concerned that he might be alienating his audience by covering the movement has now, after the death of an identifiable movement, opened up a whole section in the magazine for "Politics." The section was first headed up by Richard Goodwin, an ex-speech writer for John Kennedy and Lyndon Johnson. Now it is run by Joe Klein, a reporter for the Boston sea-level *The Real Paper* who came to Wenner's attention after winning an award from the Kennedy family endowment for his coverage of events in that city.

Meanwhile the music section, still the most highly touted feature of *Rolling Stone* in its commissioned audience surveys and self-advertising copy for other corporate sponsors, is shrinking. "Today *Rolling Stone* is stronger in music than ever" reads a *Rolling Stone* ad in *Billboard*, which claims the magazine "reviews more records and reports more music stories than ever."[49] It is a specious argument, as even Jon Landau, the music editor, points out. In the old sixty-four-page format, record reviews usually ran some five pages. In longer issues, the record section sometimes got as long as seven pages. Now with an additional forty pages in the average magazine, reviews run an average of only four pages.[50] One reason for this is Wenner's lack of interest in most music produced today. Years ago he virtually stopped listening to rock, and has since urged Landau to shorten the reviews and increase the number of records covered in a shorter space. *Rolling Stone* has made a clear move away from "serious" criticism and toward a more advertiser-oriented reviewing philosophy.

The understanding that has grown up between *Stone* and the record industry is that product will get covered. The hierarchy within the music business realized that good coverage necessitates many unfavorable reviews as well as enthusiastic ones. What is really important between

---

*McGovern was the subject of a bitter article by *New Republic* publisher Marty Peretz (who has his own many, many skeletons in closets). He replied by saying that Peretz clearly didn't like him, and referred readers interested in a more favorable treatment to Thompson's book.

the industry and *Stone* is simply the magazine's implicit promise to give material consideration. *Stone* is covering only as many records now as it did in the days of much longer reviews under early record editor Greil Marcus, but in a relatively smaller space. It is fulfilling its minimum obligations to record industry and audience, and insuring ad revenues.

The Press and the Industry

The relationship between most rock papers and their underpaid writers and the music industry is a dependent one. *Zoo World* and *Phonograph Record* are completely dependent on record company advertising to stay alive. Their critics are also dependent on the record companies. They subsist from one lavish press luncheon in L.A. to the next, and pay their rent with album "freebies." It is a standard practice for critics to be put on the release lists of record companies, meaning that they get free copies of all product "for review purposes." Of course, no critic can review all the new releases, or would want to listen to them. Most of these albums go unused in this way. But they can be cashed in at a local record store. This practice has been a source of much spare change for many a hungry writer. Introducing his "Consumer Guide" to rock, Bob Christgau once admitted that upon receiving all his free records in the mail, he immediately sorted them into "a sell pile and a listen pile."[51]

Jon Landau reportedly gets a lot more than spare change from the practice. Warner Brothers, along with its Asylum and Atlantic subsidiaries, supposedly sends him six copies of all their releases. That represents about $10,000 worth of new records per year from a single large label.

The economic dependence of writers on the industry, more than on their magazines, is further illustrated by the common practice of critics writing liner notes for record company albums. Jerry Wexler pioneered this practice with the new generation of music critics when he got an enthusiastic Jon Landau to write album note for Otis Redding. Now many critics do it regularly, usually not identifying themselves. All of the important rock critics, with the possible exception of Christgau, have done it at one time or another. That includes people like Marsh, Bob Palmer, Bob Blumenthal, Chet Flippo, Jimmies Isaacs, and others.

Writing liner notes can be defended on the grounds that the critic at least is contributing to the understanding of the material by the audience—certainly in the extensive liner notes that often accompany jazz or classical releases there is some educational function being served. A practice that cannot be defended, however, is that of writing publicity releases, in-house record company organs, and working as a publicist. Many of the recognizable names of rock criticism, from the *Village Voice, Rolling Stone,* or *Creem* are now or have been connected with record companies in this way. Stephen Holden does A&R work at RCA.

Bud Scoppa does publicity at A&M. Gordon Fletcher, Todd Everett, and Gene Sculatti all did a lot of writing for Warner Brothers' now defunct *Circular.* Marty Cerf and Greg Shaw, while still building up *Phonograph Record* as an in-house publication at United Artists, did writing outside. Paul Nelson does A&R and publicity work at Mercury, and writes for the *Voice.* Wayne Robbins used to write for both *Creem* and the Columbia Records in-house flack sheet *Playback.* The list goes on and on.

In addition to questioning the conflicts of interest that writers connected in such direct ways to record companies might have in writing about rock, it is also important to consider the quality of their criticism. Even at *Rolling Stone,* which is not dependent on record company support to stay alive, things have drifted into an almost automated routine in the record section. Different stringers have different categories of music that they enjoy, and they are assigned records within these categories. Gordon Fletcher, for example, is the heavy metal specialist assigned most hard rock albums. Stephen Holden does the singer-songwriter types. Ken Barnes does the pop kinds of English rock, Beatles imitations, and the like. Ken Emerson does the same. Russell Gersten does soul, and so on.

There are of course real questions about the economic value of favorable record reviews. Lou Adler points out that he has had a string of hits that were panned by *Rolling Stone* in addition to the 13 million selling Carole King record *Tapestry,* which many rock critics credit Jon Landau with breaking into a big hit. Likewise with the Warner Brothers release of Maria Muldaur's first solo album. Although it was a strongly produced pop rock record, many critics argue that it would have been destined for a small loyal jug band audience (she used to sing with Jim Kweskin's jug band) had it not been for Landau's lead review in the *Stone* record section.

Warners' Stan Cornyn has said that ad copy and print reviews do not sell records, that radio is the only real promotional vehicle for product. Landau himself disclaims the importance or complicity of *Rolling Stone's* selling records for the business. He correctly points out that most of the reviews in *Stone* are negative. For years, successful rock artists like the Doors, Janis Joplin, the Who, the Rolling Stones, Cheech and Chong, Emerson Lake and Palmer, Grand Funk Railroad, and Black Sabbath have been given terrible reviews on million-selling albums. What Landau says seems to contradict at least in part the experience of Richard Goldstein, who reports outright attempts at bribing him. "I maintained my illusions about the value free purity of rock," he says,

> until the day in 1969 when my agent informed me that a large music publisher would pay me $25,000 for three presentations on the state of

popular music. It was understood that I would favor this company's artists in my reviews. I was shocked, but also puzzled. It never occurred to me that my writing carried any real commercial weight, just as it never occurred to me that a sensitive lyric poet like Paul Simon could be as essential to the American economy as Harold Geneen (former Chairman of the Board of ITT).[52]

Goldstein's case is exceptional. The system of economic dependence on industry functions, freelance assignments for liner notes, and odd jobs working in publicity and the aesthetic and critical compromises made in the actual writing about rock converge in a total system. On the one hand, rock critics do not seem important in shaping audience reaction to specific records. They do not perform the same function, at as high a level, as do theater, dance, or film reviewers. But they are useful to record companies at least as an index of possible audience trends, and a source of consistent, basically snappy superficial copy that can be used to help sell records, if the product is good. Most industry payola is not given for specific deals, but is supplied on a continuous basis. It creates an atmosphere of cooperation between the critics and the business that suggests a more fundamental corruption of the writers' stance *as critics*.

Rock critics are welcomed into the music family. They get test pressings of new records well before their friends can get the album in the stores. When the albums are released, they get them for free, and they can be cashed in for money. They get taken to fancy hotels where new artists are showcased at bounteous luncheons. They get endless free tickets to concerts, clubs, private industry bashes. On a personal level they begin to identify with the record companies patiently trying to promote their product, rather than with the audience for rock. They have so many favors done for them by the industry that when the time comes, they do favors necessary to keep the promotion system rolling.

In a broad sense all the popular writing about rock is part of this corruptive system of freebies and favors, personal acquaintances, and promo men. Within the industry, which is on the surface so open, there is in fact a tightly controlled flow of information.

The best paid writers are ones with access to inside dope on the business. Some of this information is pure gossip for the fans about what star is fucking whom, or the personal tastes and habits of rock idols. Some of it is hard data, like when an album will be released, how much money is being spent to promote one artist or another, details of record deals, or whatever. But all of it sells rock newspapers and magazines. Writers privy to these crucially important industry "secrets" are the ones who make the most money, and they are given access to those secrets only if they show they can operate in a system that protects the business and serves its basic needs. One such writer is *Rolling Stone's*

Ben Fong-Torres, who has done excellent reporting on TV rock, underground radio, and the FCC, but can always be counted on by record companies in a crunch. They can trust him to sit in the back seat of a limousine with a major rock star and do a profile on him that's a puff job. He generates promo, while serving the record company's interest in protecting their client from hassles and embarrassment. There is a closed cycle of information in the industry and the rock press. Those who are allowed to handle the "inside stuff" are people trusted in advance to be either so stupid, pliable, or sycophantic as not to expose that stuff in a way that will harm the music business or enlighten readership.

Agents, managers, concert promoters, and rock press are all essential to the modern music industry, but the core of the business, of course, is the record companies themselves. Although other sectors of the music industry—agencies, management, concert production, and especially radio—are operated autonomously, the source of music is the record company.

Since the record company has control over what kind of music will be produced, it fundamentally determines what will be heard on radio and TV and, to a lesser degree, at concerts. Radio, television, and personal appearances are tools used by record companies to sell records; taken together they function in effect as a promotional infrastructure to the main business of selling records. While dependent on record companies for music, radio is of course not controlled by them. Government interest, expressed through antitrust and licensing surveillance and payola inquiries, has maintained a separation of the two media that is expressed as a constant tension. Nevertheless, the *function* of radio in the overall music industry is to sell records.

The focus of the next chapter is the record companies themselves: how they operate, what they do day by day.

5 SOLID GOLD: THE RECORD BUSINESS TODAY

From Rockefeller Plaza to Sunset Strip with a Stopover in Burbank

Music vs. Television

Music—the vast majority of it rock music—has become *the* pop culture in America. Its audience is still skewed to those under thirty-five, but the revenues it generates from young people make it financially more important than other entertainment industries. Whereas record and tape sales in 1973 were over $2 billion, movies accounted for only $1.6 billion in revenues, and all sports events for only $600 million. In many cities more people go to rock concerts than to sports events.

Television is still more important commercially than recorded music. According to 1973 figures, records/tapes surpass network ad revenues which are almost exactly $2 billion, but when sales from local ($1.1 billion) and what are called "national spot" ($1.4 billion) ads are included with network revenue, television accounts for $4.5 billion, still much more than combined record/tape sales.[1]

Even if radio ad revenues were added to the music figure, as they should be since most radio is programmed with recorded music, television comes out commercially more significant: $4.5 billion for all TV advertising as compared to $3.7 billion for recorded music plus radio advertising.

Looked at in terms of the impact the two mediums have on young people (those under thirty-five), music is more important. Although television may well have more *potential* for influencing people's lives in this country since more complete images and roles can be presented over television than through audio records and tapes, this potential is not realized under current TV programming.

To get an idea of what music means in the United States commercially, one would have to try to add all software and hardware music industries together. In 1972, the latest year when figures for all factors are available, the result would be: record/tapes, $1.924 billion; radio ad revenues, $1.575 billion; concert production, $150 million; tape recorders (excluding office dictating equipment but including car tape players, and commercial recording and playback equipment), $861 million; phonographs, $577 million; radios (table, clock, portable, and car but not commercial), $983 million; and musical instruments, $1.306 billion. The grand total is $7.376 billion for 1972 alone.[2]

Considering the often loose and sometimes differing methodologies used to calculate these statistics by various corporate research firms and trade groups, the total television ad revenue plus sales of TV sets for the same year equals $7.574 billion which is only slightly higher. Much of the hardware and peripheral music industries is oriented toward rock music in the same way that the record industry is. About 80 percent of recorded music is rock music. An exception would be musical instruments; the figures here include instruments used in school bands and orchestras and instruments like pianos used primarily by older people.

When Elvis Presley began recording for RCA twenty years ago record sales at $400 million were less than a fifth of what they are now. In the year of the Beatles they reached $862 million, or about a third of current sales.

The steady growth of the industry has been caused by a number of musical, technical, marketing, demographic, and social factors. In a characteristically dry manner Leo Strauss, a leading industry accountant, summed them all up: "The American figures are due to high population, lower cost of manufacture, and a consumer attitude of accelerated obsolescence." So much for Elvis, the Beatles, and Bob Dylan as far as Mr. Strauss is concerned. The sixties had seen a postwar baby boom that yielded a 43 percent rise in the eighteen to twenty-five age group. And in 1970 teenagers alone were spending $20 billion, twice what they were in 1959.

While recorded music, movies, and television, as well as sports and books, compete for consumer dollars, these different media are now often controlled by the same few corporations. The corporations operate music or films or television as subdivisions of huge media/entertainment/education enterprises.

CBS, the parent firm of the leading U.S. record company in terms of world sales, operates a broadcasting division, a publishing division, and a "creative playthings" operation, in addition to its music interests. Until 1973 CBS also owned the New York Yankees. Warner Communications operates publishing, television, and movie divisions. MCA and RCA deal in TV and movies as well as in records, and so on.

The record companies have become increasingly important within their parent corporations. In 1973, for instance, the CBS Records group accounted for about 20 percent of CBS' total sales (compared to the broadcast group which accounted for about a third) and about 26 percent of total profits. In 1971, the record, tape, and music publishing division of Warner Communications accounted for 65 percent of the corporation's internal profit. What about the record companies themselves?

How a Record Company Works

Since the purpose of a record company is to make money, an understanding of the costs and profits involved in making a record is a prerequisite to understanding how one works. (See Chart 5.1.)

Chart 5.1
What It Costs to Make a Record

Payments to publisher (2 cents per song)	.24
Musicians union trust fund fee	.08
Manufacturing cost	.35
Jacket, inner sleeve	.15
Artist royalty (includes recording fees)	.60 (variable)
Freight to distributor	.03
Advertising	.10
	$1.55

Sources: **Business Week**, *7/27/74; independent research.*

For a large company like Warner-Reprise the cost of administrative overhead can be divided and computed for each recorded unit. This would come to about 33 cents bringing total manufacturing cost to $1.88 per record. The record is sold to a distributor, depending on who it is, for about $2.51 so that record company profit is 63 cents. (All figures are based on costs in 1974 when an average record retailed for $5.98.)

This breakdown of costs is only approximate. The costs of jackets, royalties, and advertising may vary considerably, especially between new and established acts. This formulation is also based on a *successful* record. With an unsuccessful record, the company must pay recording costs and an artist advance. If the album is a success, both recording and advance are paid by the act through their royalties. "All the recording costs are charged to the artist," points out Joe Smith, president of Warner-Reprise. "So out of his fifty or sixty cents [the royalties] we recover until he is even. If he spent $50,000 making an album, and is getting fifty cents an album, we take his royalty for the first hundred thousand albums to pay it off."*

A company usually needs to sell as many as 25,000 singles or 85,000 albums to break even. Profits also vary according to the number of albums sold. If an album sells hundreds of thousands of copies, unit costs are reduced. Mike Maitland, president of MCA, has estimated that the profit on an extremely high selling album can reach $1.50 per record.

Looking at costs and potential profits for a single album is instructive in some ways, but a company does not really approach these problems on a per unit basis. Since beginning artists often do not even break even until the third or fourth album, (and many are dropped before this point), and since the majority of the 4,000 albums released each year are unsuccessful, a company must take into account all the records it is releasing in a given period to figure costs and profits.

"The economics of the record business is such that a few winners pay for most of the losers," says Smith. Although the ratio of hits to records released is somewhat higher at some of the more selective smaller companies such as A&M and Motown, 70 to 80 percent of albums released in the industry are probably "losers." They don't even break even. However, says a former West Coast director of business affairs for CBS Records:

> When you win, you win big. You can afford to take a 70% stiff ratio. On the three that make it, you more than make up your cost and profit on the entire ten. And if you spend on ten records, say a million dollars, and seven of these records earn back $50,000, but on the other three you earn back one million dollars, you still have a $100,000 profit over the million. That's still a ten percent profit.[3]

---

*Record companies can deduct more than studio costs from royalties, depending on the contract. In the first place the royalty (say 7 percent) is usually on 90 percent of the suggested retail price (the other 10 percent is supposedly for promotional copies and giveaways). Then a packaging allowance of 6-20 percent of the retail price can be deducted. Records sold through record clubs often yield only *one-half* of the royalty rate. The same is true for foreign sales. Finally, a "Reasonable Reserve" clause allows record companies to withhold payment pending returns. Reasonable Reserve clauses were especially abused in the fifties, when some companies simply used the artist reserves as operating capital.

An artist's income is more than royalties from record sales. If he/she *wrote* the song they get—currently—1 cent per song every time the song is included on a record or

The basic functions of a record company are to find artists, record and produce them, and then promote and market their records. The company is structured to carry out these tasks. The job of finding acts is ultimately up to the executives who also handle relations with parent firms and oversee the entire operation of the company. The A&R department takes care of producing. Promotion is part of a more general "creative services" department as at Warners or is handled separately. Sales and distribution departments take care of marketing. Art work and artists relations are either under creative services or operated as autonomous departments. The purpose of an integrated creative services department is to make it easier to build unified images of artists or groups.

"The mechanics of a record company," said Joe Smith in 1974, "are just that—the mechanics. Sales, promotion, advertising: they all require ability and they require top people. You try to hire the best people you can, but they can't do anything unless you put something in the machine. It's my job and Mo Ostin's job to put things into the machine."[4] Clive Davis, former head of CBS Records, told *Billboard* that he spent about three-quarters of his time trying to find and sign talent for Columbia and Epic. The highest executives must pay attention to the overall profit and loss figures for their companies in addition to acquiring talent, but often they use financial assistants to keep abreast of the bottom line. Mike Maitland at MCA is well known for his concern with the economics of his corporation, but for many years he also retained sole power to sign acts.

How does a record company go about acquiring acts? Established artists are a fairly simple matter. Based on an estimation of their future potential one company can simply buy them away from another company. The larger companies with the greatest financial resources, especially RCA and CBS, often follow this route. RCA bought the Everly Brothers and the Kinks from Warner, for instance. Columbia has acquired Delaney and Bonnie, the Association, Crazy Horse, and Loretta Lynn among many others. They paid $4 million to buy Neil Diamond

---

tape. The publisher, who often is the record company or the manager and not the artist, also gets 1 cent per song. These composing royalties are called "mechanicals." "Performance royalties" go to the composer each time the song is played on the radio or theoretically each time the song is performed live. As of a few years ago the writer got 2½ cents *each time* the song was played on the radio. The publisher, which as should be stressed may or may not be the composer, got *4 cents* for each radio play. Certain established concert promoters and clubs pay similar performance fees on a blanket basis for songs sung in their shows. The composer or writer also gets 5 cents for each copy of sheet music, while the publisher gets 25 cents per copy. None of these royalties go to the *performer* but only to the composer and publisher of the songs the

(continued on page 176)

away from MCA. Warner lured the Beach Boys from Capitol. By buying an act away from another label, a company is usually assured of some stable sales. It is costly, however. Companies would often rather find a group at the beginning of their career, sign them for little, and then try to build them into a successful act. RCA and MGM have reputations for buying rather than building acts, either because they find it quicker, or because they have difficulty recognizing talent.

Companies find artists in several ways. Davis did a certain amount of scouting by himself. He saw Janis Joplin and the Electric Flag at Monterey Pop for instance. Staff producers brought artists to him. Loggins and Messina were put together this way. John Hammond, a staff producer and now a talent director, found Bob Dylan. Outside "friends" with a managerial or legal interest drew his attention to new acts. Bill Graham asked him to come to San Francisco to see Santana and It's A Beautiful Day. David Geffen, at that time a booking agent, brought Laura Nyro by to play piano and sing a few tunes for him. A few artists, usually those with some kind of a track record, simply called up the company—Davis cites New Riders of the Purple Sage and Eric Anderson as examples.

Bands often become known in a particular region by playing at concerts, and are then signed by some manager who secures a contract with a record company. Some clubs in Los Angeles like the Troubador and the Whiskey A Go-Go are frequented by record company executives and managers in search of new talent. Ahmet Ertegun first noticed Eric Clapton in a similar club in London. He had gone to England with Wilson Pickett's band which was on Atlantic. With his back to the stage he complimented Pickett on the band's guitar player who he thought was playing on through a break. Then he turned around and noticed that Pickett's sideman was not playing but drinking at the bar, and that a "little thin kid" was playing blues American style. The kid was Clapton.

Independent producers constantly locate new acts and bring them to record companies. Production companies that are in exclusive label arrangements with larger labels often have power to sign new artists who are then distributed by the larger firm.

(continued from page 175)

artist records or sings live. In this sense an artist never receives a true *royalty*, which really accrues only to the composer/publisher who own the copyright, but only a per unit percentage fee.

Mechanicals are collected by an organization called the Harry Fox Agency through other publisher organizations. Performance royalties are tabulated by performance rights organizations. The two main ones are BMI (Broadcast Music, Inc.) and ASCAP (American Society of Composers, Authors, and Publishers), both of which are discussed earlier in the book.

From the outside it seems that record companies often try to create trends with the new acts they sign, but the question of who creates trends is a complicated one. Certainly companies can popularize a type of music by heavy promotion and subsidized exposure. The music itself, though, is usually already there. Various new lifestyles or reactions to certain cultural conditions produce a type of music which is then latched onto by record companies. Middle-class alienation and hippie alternative culture brought out the various San Francisco bands, for instance. When Joe Smith signed the Grateful Dead or Clive Davis contracted Janis Joplin, they weren't creating trends, only discovering a regional movement that they felt could be profitable throughout the country. The same is true of RCA's "discovery" of Elvis or for that matter of David Bowie. "David Bowie!" scoffs Smith. "RCA didn't know if they had it or didn't have it. It just happened."[5]

There seem to be two poles in the record business. One group of companies, RCA and MGM, for example, seems to believe that popular music runs in trends that can be consciously created and exploited by record companies. This approach has proven commercially valid in the most manipulatable area of pop music—bubblegum. RCA made millions on the Monkees and the Archies which were executive fabrications from start to finish.

The other approach, represented by Atlantic and Warner, seems to be to try to sign the musicians felt to be the most talented, still keeping within a broad spectrum of potentially commercial music. This way, the record company stays closer to basic musical change because it has a hand on the best musicians who are living at "street level."

Both attitudes are probably present to one degree or another at all record companies, and it can't be overestimated how incapable most, but not all, record company executives are at judging talent, and how much they rely on others with more ability to make recommendations to them. Commented Ahmet Ertegun, one of the few company executives who has been able to recognize good musicians through the years:

> We're always in the middle of a trend. The trend changes a little bit. You hope to be riding the crest of the wave at all times. We make daily evaluations of the talent that's available to us to see if we want to record them or not. Of course it's based a great deal on what's been selling over the last two years, and the sales of the last two years create the taste for tomorrow. We have two tastes here: our own personal tastes and the public taste that you try to acquire.[6]

"We never said," he commented a few minutes before, " 'Oh, let's go and sign up a bunch of English acts.' That's like saying, 'Let's go sign up some California groups.' You have to sign up *a* group—although people have done that. I remember when there was a Boston rush.

Everybody went up and signed anything in Boston. As you know, that's a synthetic approach to the problem."[7]

In the Studio

Production for a record company is a matter of matching the act with a producer who will bring out its commerciality if any. "Most A&R people don't know anything about music," complained Frank Zappa in the early days of the new rock music, "but look for the commercial potential." Commercialism is still primary now, but many companies have found that music made as the artist would like to make it is itself commercial. Most rock music is actually produced by outside producers, anyway. These producers often maintain formal ties with one company through an exclusive independent production arrangement. The arrangement provides artistic autonomy but gives the larger company control over distribution, marketing, and advertising.

With whom does a record company consent to make a label deal? "There are maybe a dozen people in the world you'd do it with," says Joe Smith, former president of Warner-Reprise. "Usually our criterion has been if there's one dynamite artist in there, but when you bet on Phil Spector, you're betting on Phil Spector. The artists come and go, the people stay. Whether it's going to be Foghat and Todd Rundgren now, or somebody else next year, Albert Grossman will still be there."

A label deal is usually set up in such a way that the record company agrees to a certain royalty rate plus a certain amount per album (a typical deal for an established artist who is not a "superstar" might be 11 percent and $30,000 advance per project) while the act in turn agrees to produce a certain number of albums a year for the record company. The record company recovers its advances from royalties before the act begins to collect its percentage. A more elaborate label deal is the "joint venture" in which the act and/or its management *owns* the outside label and agrees to split overhead expenses, usually fifty-fifty, *before* any royalties are realized. But once the album is successful the profits are also divided fifty-fifty. By sharing in the initial risk the label gets a bigger share of the pie. A typical joint venture is Chrysalis Records (Jethro Tull, Procol Harum, and others), distributed by Warner Brothers.

The actual production studio can be anywhere in the world, and often is. The growth of studios in places like Muscle Shoals, Alabama; Colorado; and Jamaica was made possible technically in the fifties. It was encouraged by sophisticated record companies which realized that recordings made in outlying studios often had a local flavor not attainable in New York or L.A. Session players with less standardized techniques were available, for instance. The bulk of recording, however, is still done in three traditional places: New York, Los Angeles, and Nashville.

The degree of control that producers exercise over a recording varies. Many bubblegum acts are given material selected by the producer and then told exactly how to sing it, just as if it were 1953. On the other hand, acts like Frank Zappa do their own producing.

The technical end of producing is getting the desired sound in the studios. Different instruments are recorded on different tracks of, usually, a 16-track tape. The sound going into one microphone makes a single track. The different tracks have to be integrated or "mixed down" to 2 for stereo, 4 for quadraphonic. Sound quality is essentially determined by how much of what instrument is kept—more or less bass guitar, drums, electric guitar, and so forth. Often the basic melody line is recorded first with the other instruments added to the tape later. The record must then be "mastered." Disparities in frequency have to be equalized electronically so that what are called highs and lows sound pretty much the same throughout the recording.

"If you think of what goes into a record," says Lou Adler, a producer who exerts more control over his artists (Carole King, Cheech and Chong, and so on) than most producers, "it's the hiring of the studio, the selection of the musicians—mating the material and the artist with the right musicians—regulating the flow of one song into another, mixing, and mastering. And then deciding on packaging, the type of album cover, the liner notes if any, the type of ads and radio spots."

Most producers leave packaging and advertising up to the record company, but such complete control over the process is not uncommon. Acts have a tendency to take over many producing duties themselves as they become more experienced.

Breaking the Act

Promotion is at this point pretty much everything that sells the records besides the music itself and certain backroom retailing practices. Decisions on advertising, promotion, and cover art are usually integrated at record companies so that a unified image can be created to sell the artist. The different areas may not be in one large department but they are at least functionally integrated by some executives assigned to each act.

What an act sounds like is important to the promo men assigned to radio but to the rest of the personnel in "creative services" what counts are a few superficial characteristics that can be used as a simplified market image for the act.

> Talent may be compared to commercial products—the cigarette you smoke, the TV set you watch or the car you drive. You select that brand of product that you have been convinced is the one you should buy. Similarly, talent must be given an identity, an image, and then it must be properly packaged.

This can only be done by carefully researching the talents of an artist and publicizing and promoting the image that best relates to these talents.[8]

The concept of building an act by building its image through a number of different promotional devices is clear in Neil Bogart's account of the Buddah Records campaign for Sha Na Na.

> One example of the development of this new promotion is our campaign with Sha Na Na, the satirical rock and roll revival group. To build this group, we created a music industry trend. We called it the rock 'n' roll revival. With slogans, stickers, buttons, industry and consumer contests, and even black leather motorcycle jackets for our promotion staff, we brought back the fifties. We took an active part in securing bookings for Sha Na Na at rock palaces such as the Fillmore West. We transported the group from coast-to-coast, making sure they were seen by their audience and their potential record-buying public. We flew radio men, promotion men, and distributors into New York and San Francisco to see the group.
>
> In all, our promotion went on for five months before the group's first album was released. Before that first record hit the stores, the entire country was aware of Sha Na Na. Before the first album, they had set a record for standing ovations at the Fillmore West. Before the album, they had appeared on the "Merv Griffin Show" and had been the subject of a feature in *Rolling Stone,* all of which led to their being invited to appear at Woodstock. In fact, by the time the Sha Na Na album was released, the Buddah office had taken on the aura of Orange Julius on Saturday night in Brooklyn.
>
> After initial development of the act by getting them seen and talked about, we began to concentrate on packaging the album. The double fold LP jacket was the result of weeks of research in *The New York Times* files to find the best rock and roll stories of the last decade. With the LP ready, we prepared radio promotion stickers, information on the group and the music they were singing, as well as a press kit that contained everything from Sen-Sen to a black plastic comb.
>
> Today an artist isn't developed overnight. With Sha Na Na we spent five months paving the way for their arrival. With other artists, a period of development must occur over a *longer* period of time. It has taken years for artists such as Judy Collins, Joni Mitchell, and Laura Nyro to attain their present success.[9]

Mr. Bogart exaggerated a bit when he claimed that Buddah Records brought back the fifties to America, but he was right about Sha Na Na. At least they made it as a new group.

Often record companies try to influence "opinion makers"—djs, program directors, reviewers, general industry figures—before taking the campaign to the general public. Warner Brothers and A&M, for instance, publish small magazines that describe what's going on at the company, give artists' backgrounds, and sponsor contests.

The Standard American Promotion Package developed in the sixties remains about the same today: billboards in L.A. and New York, ads in the trades and the not-so-underground papers that still cater to the youth market like *Rolling Stone* and the *Boston Phoenix*, radio spots, and an introductory concert tour.

The attitude toward how a tour should be sponsored has changed at some companies, however. Warner Brothers found that tours were just too expensive and that increased record sales did not justify the cost. "Warner Brothers being the leader of the industry," said Stan Cornyn, director of creative services at Warner-Reprise in 1973, "we made the mistake [of bankrolling artists' tours] bigger than anyone else—and we lured lots of other companies into following us just as we were bailing out. If the public wants to see an act, they will pay to see the act. If they don't want to see an act, they won't come even if it's free. It was sometimes costing us $5 [in promotion and tour expenses] to make a $3 album sale. You may recoup expenses down the line, but I don't know. Whether touring translates itself into album sales is a question, at least in my mind."[10]

Cornyn is not even sure whether a new group's album sales increase when the group tours with a name act. He cites the failure of Flo and Eddie (Howard Kaylen and Mark Volman) who toured with Alice Cooper. Warner is now wary of directly sponsoring tours, and believes instead in strongly supporting tours by buying radio and print ads for current records, timed to the arrival of the group at a particular city on the tour. The record ads are then tagged with a line that says something like "And be sure to see them at the Forum on November 29."

Nevertheless most companies still rely heavily on introductory tours as a vehicle to promote new acts. One of the things a record company looks for in deciding whether to sign an act is a willingness to go on tour. While not as important as radio exposure, the promotional tour gets the group seen before large numbers of people throughout the country, and establishes any visual image the company or the act may be trying, consciously or not, to convey. Since the act usually travels with an established group, the band is linked to a successful act in the same genre. The record company tries to coordinate all other forms of promotion with the tour. Local stores are sent the group's albums, radio spots are timed to the group's appearance in town, print ads are taken that advertise the band's album or single as well as the concert.

Singer-songwriters like Joni Mitchell tour clubs in the beginning rather than concert halls, but the importance to the record company is still the same. The company doesn't make bookings itself but has a hand in deciding where the group will go. The record company foots most of the bill for the tour, sometimes aided by the group itself or their management. The cost of the tour itself, equipment costs, hotels, and airfare for musicians and roadies, combined with the cost of the coordinated radio and print ads, and the expense of sending the albums to the stores, can be considerable. A twenty-city tour can cost $25,000 to $50,000 "easily," according to Mike Maitland, president of MCA Records. A really concerted push like RCA's David Bowie tour can cost over $100,000.

Most companies now have a separate artist relations department that supports the company's acts when they are on the road. The department arranges a number of things like radio interviews, transportation, and dope connections. "Their work goes on day and night," says Cornyn, "they're very hardy people." If the task is already being covered by local representatives the artist relations person just makes sure that everything is fitting together. Artist relations usually arranges for the promo bashes that the industry has become known for.

The most important thing in breaking an act is radio exposure. Progressive rock songs were played mostly on FM stations throughout the sixties, and broke many acts. At this point FM stations often sell records as well as AM stations, especially in large cities where more record buyers listen to FM, and for longer periods, than they do to AM. Many songs are still unsuited to AM play because of length, drug and sex lyrics, or "jangliness" as *Billboard* once put it. Even so, acts and their record companies currently try hard to find an AM single on a rock group's album, no matter how "jangly" the rest of the record sounds. "The key question" in determining whether a successful album will sell 100,000 copies or 50,000 copies, says Columbia's ex-president Clive Davis, "is whether there is a Top 40 hit in the album." If a single from an album is played on KHJ-AM in Los Angeles or WABC-AM in New York, the most popular AM stations in those cities, 50,000 more records may be sold in each town. An AM single isn't necessary to establish an act, but it certainly increases album sales. (An exception might be War's The World Is a Ghetto album which was the number one album in 1973 even though the "Cisco Kid," the most popular single taken from it, made it only to number fifty-five on *Billboard's* year-end charts. War has had top-selling singles from earlier albums, however.)

Some records take off with little promotion. "Soul Makosa" or most Beatles records are examples. "The reality," says Stan Cornyn, "is that if you have a good record, you can't kill it with a stick; if you have a terrible record, you cannot elect it Pope. If you have a middle-level record it helps to have promotion."

But with some 5,000 singles and 4,000 albums released each year, radio stations are glutted. Record companies feel it is at least necessary to bring records to the attention of program and music directors, if not to actively push them as well. The normal low-key procedure is for a radio promotion man from a record company to make an appointment with the music director or program director at a station and play his company's new releases for him (or her—there are probably more women music directors than there are promotion people). The promo man will take the radio person out to lunch or dinner if any sort of personal relation has been built up.

That's the procedure according to public relations people at record companies and radio chains. How much a part does payola play? Because of the high salaries paid to key radio personnel and the insulation of the disc jockey at major chain stations, probably a much smaller part than ten years ago. Roger Karshner, former vice president for sales at Capitol, claims, however, that "payola is still the industry's little bastard. No one will admit to him, but everybody pays child support, and the little devil keeps coming back for more—not openly, of course, but quietly in sneakers. The greedy little bloodsucker has gone underground."

In the last several years as radio playlists on Top 40 stations have been reduced, the job of a record company promo man has gotten harder. "Radio is no longer Top 40. It's Top 15—and it's cutting off the heads of the record industry," bellowed Jay Lasker, president of ABC-Dunhill, in March of 1974. ABC felt obliged to triple the number of radio promotion people it had, bringing the total to fifty. A few years earlier tighter playlists had moved record companies to space out singles releases. They wanted time to concentrate on one or two records, and to visit "secondary stations" located in suburbs or smaller towns. Larger stations often wait for these secondary stations to test out new, not yet broken records, before they will add them to their own playlists.

Cities where records first begin to be played and sold are known as "breakout" areas. Breakout cities seem to change year by year, but they are usually those places where some major music scene is developing or where certain stations are more willing to play untested records. New York was a key breakout area in the Freed era. Boston and San Francisco became more important in the heyday of psychedelic rock. Detroit was especially active before Motown moved to L.A. and is still a breakout city. Towns that are regarded as "typical" sometimes become breakout areas because stations in other cities figure that a record which becomes popular in the demographically typical town will also be listened to in other cities. East Lansing, Michigan, was once an example. Once a record breaks out in one locale, promotion men try to spread it to other cities. The head office is notified immediately when a record breaks so that promo men in other regions can tout it: "Hey man, look, it's already on the pick list at . . . ."

With the arrival of network concert shows, television has also become an important means for promoting records, although some companies feel it is more suited to increasing sales rather than to breaking new acts.

Once an act is broken—and the majority are not, they fail and disband—record companies try to increase sales album by album until sales are automatic. Warner-Reprise pegs its acts at a "plateau," and then tries to move them to a higher one with each album. An artist selling between 100,000 and 250,000 albums is at the first plateau—Bonnie Raitt, for instance. "We *think* we can take her to three hundred, three hundred and fifty thousand if we do certain things," says company president Smith, "if we advertise, if she's got a [new] tour, if the album is good, if we get a single out of it, all those elements. If we spend some money and some time with her, if she gets interviewed more, then more people will buy her. The next thing is to get an artist into a gold record class, that's four hundred and fifty, five hundred thousand albums. And beyond that, it's a crap shoot. I mean nobody can call an Elvis Presley. Nobody can call a Herbie Alpert. Nobody called the Beatles. You could have never called the Allman Brothers."[11]

Sometimes there is a conflict between building an act and selling records. A musician may become more successful in the long run, for instance, if he or she is not forced to put out the standard two albums a year, and instead grows at his or her own musical pace. A greatest hits album released by a company can also hurt an artist by saturating the market or breaking the conceptual flow of his or her albums. A record company "can't say—due to the economics of the record business—that they'll build the artist for three or four years," points out manager Eliot Roberts, "because in the fifth year, when the contract expires, [the act] may say to the record company, 'Fuck you, I'm a big star now and I want a 2 million dollar advance.'" If they were just concerned with building the act, "they would be in constant danger of being held up by managers and stars." The goal of the record company is to sell as many records of an artist as soon as possible.

Promotion can even be extended to the branch distribution outlets of the larger companies. Warner Brothers has shown multimedia slide presentations of its new releases to local distribution personnel in order to acquaint them with new "products." The company would like the shows to motivate people against dropping cartons and stealing albums, too, but it's unclear how successful they've been.

Promotion has changed as musical tastes have changed. Promotion departments are naturally set up to sell the type of record that is most popular. For some time now the most popular records have been rock or soul. (See Chart 5.2.) Starting in 1975, a record was certified Gold when it had sold 500,000 units (tapes or records) provided sales reached at least

$1 million. The dollar minimum is included to prevent high-selling, $1.98 budget albums from going Gold. Before 1975, when prices were lower, an album went Gold at about 400,000 units. At any rate, certifications are sometimes inaccurate, since records considered sold to stores may be returned later.

The distinction between soul and rock is vague. Albums that sold exclusively in the black market were probably considered soul records. Humor records could also overlap with rock, as in the case of Cheech and Chong.

Based on another survey of record manufacturers, *Billboard* reported the following percentage breakdown for 1972: "popular" 66.1 percent, soul 13.6 percent, country 10.5 percent, classical 6.1 percent, jazz 1.3 percent, and all others 2.4 percent.[12] The problem with their survey is that popular records includes the easy listening category. By most informal estimates rock and soul account for at least 80 percent of all records sold.

Chart 5.2
Gold Albums by Repertoire 1968-72

	1968	1969	1970	1971	1972
Contemporary	36%	42%	60%	69%	76%
Rock	24	27	43	54	41
Teen	9	10	9	10	23
Folk/Folk Rock	3	5	8	5	12
Easy Listening	33%	37%	28%	16%	4%
Pop Vocalists	25	27	24	14	4
Pop Instrumental	8	10	4	2	—
All Other Types	31%	21%	12%	14%	20%
Country	11	10	5	8	6
Original Cast/ Soundtrack	9	5	5	3	2
Soul	7	1	—	2	8
Jazz	—	2	—	—	—
Classical	—	1	—	—	—
Humor	1	1	1	—	3
All Others	3	1	1	1	1
	100%	100%	100%	100%	100%

Source: CBS Market Research.

Sail Away: *The International Market*

The record industry's highly systematized promotional and financial techniques have helped to expand the industry to the limits of the U.S.

185

market in less than a decade. The American market is far from saturated—the average age of active record buyers goes up each year, for instance—but the rate of annual growth has slowed somewhat. "If we were to continue at that rate" ($700 million to $2 billion in ten years), says Joe Smith, "the entire GNP would be in records inside of a decade."

Many executives, especially those affiliated with record companies whose parent corporations already operate on a multinational level, are increasingly looking abroad for the extra profits that quickly expanding markets can bring. "The immediate future will see an ever shrinking number of record companies as the competition stiffens for a more slowly growing domestic market," said Rocco Laginestra in 1973 when he was president of RCA Records. "It is overseas where the real growth opportunities lie. RCA Records' American operation will continue to be treated as a subsidiary, and the company's full scope of operations will be directed toward the entire world."[13]

RCA has already had years of foreign success with Elvis Presley. In fact foreign sales probably make RCA the third ranking U.S. record corporation even though the company has recently not done that well in the U.S. charts.

The move toward foreign sales has a long tradition in the U.S. industry, of course. Usually an industry begins to look toward foreign sales once it has attained a certain saturation of the U.S. market and enough size to handle overseas expansion. Since World War II profits from overseas operations of U.S. corporations have run some 20 percent higher than domestic operations.

The major foreign markets for records are in Japan, England, West Germany, and Canada. (See Chart 5.3.) Japanese retail sales of records and tapes are, at 570 million in 1973, second to U.S. sales, but because of restrictions put on foreign ownership of companies doing business in Japan, the market there has not been attacked by U.S. companies in a concerted way until recently. Columbia initiated a joint venture with Sony in which risk capital and profits were to be shared fifty-fifty. U.S. companies have long had a hold on the British and Canadian markets. Licensing its record catalogue to a manufacturer overseas is the simplest way for a U.S. company to make foreign sales. Increasingly, companies are doing more. They have been setting up foreign subsidiaries which manufacture and produce abroad. In non-English speaking countries it has proven necessary to create and manufacture local music in addition to U.S. hits in order to maintain sufficient volume.

The Bottom Line

A handful of large corporations control almost all of the recorded music produced in the United States. Based on all LP, tapes, and singles to appear on the *Billboard* record charts in 1973 the Top 10 corporations

Chart 5.3
Worldwide Retail Sales of
Records and Tapes 1973

	Country	1973 Sales (U.S. dollars)	Per Capita Expenditure
1	USA	$2,017,000,000	$9.70
2	Japan	555,200,000	5.14
3	West Germany	454,225,823	7.57
4	USSR	441,433,333	1.76
5	United Kingdom	384,000,000	6.86
6	France	248,761,009	5.08
7	Canada	110,140,100	4.91
8	Netherlands	93,949,056	6.91
9	Italy	79,124,174	1.41
10	Brazil	66,812,753	.66
11	Sweden	62,198,568	7.64
12	Mexico	60,477,439	1.07
13	Spain	45,622,000	1.35
14	Australia	44,533,000	3.36
15	Belgium	43,816,017	4.52
16	South Africa	34,548,990	1.53
17	Argentina	30,700,000	1.32
18	Czechoslovakia	28,940,172	2.02
19	Greece	25,575,766	2.84
20	Austria	22,754,000	3.03
21	Denmark	22,284,477	4.43
22	Finland	18,526,565	3.94
23	Poland	16,965,990	.51
24	Yugoslavia	16,133,333	.77
	Total	$4,923,722,565	

Source: Billboard 1974 Buyer's Guide.

accounted for 82.9 percent of the U.S. domestic market. The leading four corporations made up for better than half the market, 52.8 percent, and the top two alone, CBS and Warner-Elektra/Asylum-Atlantic (Warner Communications), accounted for 37.8 percent. As shown earlier in the section on mergers (pp. 82-87), the degree of concentration in the record business is as high as in any other heavily monopolized U.S. industry.

The *Billboard* figures, based on hit charts, are useful in showing the concentration of the U.S. record industry, but they cannot really be used to compare the performance of different record companies. They do measure the percentage each corporation has of U.S. hits but not total sales or year-end profits. Profits figures are especially necessary in ranking the commercial effectiveness of record companies, since the

Chart 5.4
Share of the Market by Label and Corporation 1973

How The Top 10 Corporations Shared
The Hot 100 Chart Action

0 10 20

Rank/Corp.	No. of Records	% Share
Warner Comm.	120	19.6
CBS	71	10.7
Capitol	53	10.4
MCA	24	6.6
RCA	36	6.3
Polygram	50	5.7
ABC	45	5.4
A&M	31	5.3
Motown	29	4.6
Arista	18	3.1

How The Top 10 Labels Shared
The Top LP And Tape Chart Action

0 5 10

Rank/Label	No. of Records	% Share
Columbia	88	9.8
Atlantic	47	5.6
Warner Bros.	43	5.6
RCA	47	5.4
A&M	47	5.3
Capitol	43	5.2
MCA	35	4.9
Elektra/Asylum	31	4.5
Epic	31	3.4
Arista	26	3.0

How The Top 10 Corporations Shared
The Top LP And Tape Chart Action

0 5 10 15 20 25

Rank/Corp.	No. of Records	% Share
Warner Comm.	221	24.9
CBS	140	15.5
Capitol	59	6.9
RCA	62	6.8
MCA	43	6.3
A&M	59	6.2
ABC	58	5.5
Polygram	51	4.5
Arista	30	3.7
Motown	31	3.5

How The Top 10 Labels Shared
The Hot 100 Chart Action

0 5 10

Rank/Label	No. of Records	% Share
Capitol	35	7.5
Columbia	38	5.5
Elektra/Asylum	23	4.9
A&M	27	4.8
RCA	29	4.7
Atlantic	27	4.6
Warner Bros.	21	4.3
MCA	22	4.2
Epic	14	2.9
ABC	28	2.9

How The Top 10 Labels Shared
The Hot 100 And Top LP/Tape Chart Action

0 5 10

Rank/Label	No. of Records	% Share
Columbia	126	8.9
Capitol	78	5.7
Atlantic	74	5.4
Warner Bros.	64	5.3
RCA	76	5.2
A&M	74	5.2
MCA	57	4.8
Elektra/Asylum	54	4.6
Epic	45	3.3
Arista	39	2.9

How The Top 10 Corporations Shared
The Hot 100 and Top LP/Tape Chart Action

0 5 10 15 20 25

Rank/Corp.	No. of Records	% Share
Warner Comm.	341	23.8
CBS	211	14.5
Capitol	112	7.5
RCA	98	6.7
MCA	67	6.4
A&M	90	6.0
ABC	103	5.4
Polygram	101	4.9
Arista	48	3.6
Motown	60	3.6

Source: **Billboard**.

business is full of labels that post large sales while at the same time they lose money. The condition has been called "profitless prosperity."

Sales and profit information, unfortunately, is impossible to get for many record companies. Some companies are part of larger corporations that do not break down figures for their record/tape divisions. Others combine record and tape figures with sales of related departments like musical instruments or music publishing. Motown and A&M are not publicly owned corporations and are not required to publish any sales and profit figures at all.

With all these shortcomings it is still possible to estimate roughly where the various record corporations stand in relation to one another. Although profit and sales give a different dimension, the share of the market chart (5.4) shows to an extent which companies are at the present capable of capturing trends and influencing taste. Chart 5.5 shows changes since 1969, broken down for singles and albums.

Chart 5.5

1970-73 Comparison of Corporations' Billboard
LP/Tape and Singles' Chart Action

	1973		1972		1971		1970	
	LP/Tape	Hot 100	LP/Tape	Hot 100	LP/Tape	Hot 100	LP/Tape	Hot 100
WEA	1	2	1	1	1	1	1	1
CBS	2	1	2	2	2	3	2	3
Capitol	3	3	4	8	4	6	3	4
A&M	4	7	3	9	5		8	
Motown	5	4	6	3	7	2	4	2
RCA	6	10	4	4	3	5	5	6
Polygram	7	5						
MCA	8	9	7	5	6	7		
ABC	9	6	10	9	8	4	6	5
London	10	10	8		10		7	7
UA			9				9	10
Bell		8		7	9	8		8
Apple							10	
Buddah								
Kama Sutra				6		9		9
MGM					10			

The two leading companies in the American record industry are CBS and Warner-Elektra/Asylum-Atlantic. Formed as an off-shoot of Warner Brothers films in the late fifties, WEA is a latecomer to the bigtime. A strong adaptation to rock music and a series of astute mergers have put it in a position to rival CBS's Columbia subsidiary which, with RCA, has been the leader of the U.S. recording industry since the twenties. Warner and RCA are discussed in detail at the end of this chapter, Warner as an example of a company that has exploited modern rock music in a sophisticated manner, and RCA as an old company that, while generating huge sales, has made a number of costly mistakes in adapting to the new era—mistakes duplicated by several other large companies.

Chart 5.6 shows a partial sales and profit picture for the major record corporations. Figures for sales and profits have been drawn from several sources, some more reliable than others. When no figures are available, we have estimated approximate rank.

CBS is different from its rival WEA in a number of ways. It is a large corporately structured record company with a chain of command flowing out of its New York offices while WEA is essentially three companies integrated financially and in terms of distribution yet mostly autonomous in regard to creation and production. CBS seems more diversified. It has large foreign sales with important subsidiary operations in Europe, Latin America, Australia, and elsewhere, and a joint venture with Sony in the important Japanese market. WEA is only beginning to make large sales abroad. CBS has an extensive classical division and a profitable country and western section. WEA has minimal classical sales through the Nonesuch label and only minor beginnings in the c&w field with a recent effort by Atlantic. CBS Records is a subsidiary of one of the oldest and most powerful media corporations in America and although obviously an integral part of it, only accounts for a quarter of CBS, Inc.'s total profit. WEA is the cornerstone of Warner Communications, which is itself a new and fast-moving media corporation without the old-line corporate and financial ties or the technological base of CBS.

CBS

CBS, Inc., has four main divisions—broadcasting, records, merchandising and manufacturing, and publishing. Sales from all divisions total a billion and a half a year. The bulk of the corporation's profits come from the broadcast groups, $70 million in 1973, which consists of TV and radio stations and national television and radio production networks.

Several years ago the record club and musical instruments division were lumped with records, but now domestic and international records and tapes are a separate division. In the merchandising and manufacturing group CBS operates the Pacific Stereo hi-fi equipment and record stores, the Discount Records chain, the Columbia Record and Tape Club, and a musical instruments division that manufactures Fender

Chart 5.6

Approximate Sales and Profits

Record Company	1973	1972	1971	1970	1969	1968
Sales						
(figures in millions)						
1. CBS[1]	362.5	312.3	276.2	247.5	207.2	
2. WEA[12]	235.9[2]	214.5	170.8	115.8	87.1	64.2
3. RCA		203[2]				
4. Capitol	142.3[6]	130[5]	143[5]	178[8]		
5. Polygram (est. position, combined co.'s)						
6. MCA		70				
7. ABC[3,10]		82.5	87.3	78.1	69.4	49.1
8. Motown		40				
9. A&M			56[9]			
10. United Artists (unavailable)						
Profits						
(figures in millions)						
1. CBS	25.0[1]	26.8	23.1	18.6	13.1	
2. WEA	22.2[2]	23.8	18.9	14.8	12.1	10.0
3. MCA		12				
4. A&M						
5. Motown						
6. Capitol	5.2[7]	1.4[6]	8[4]	8.7		
7. ABC[3,10]		1.0	6.4	3.5	4.6	3.9
8. RCA	"3rd quarter loss"					
9. Polygram						
10. United Artists		"small profit"	loss	loss		

---

[1] CBS Annual Report 1973, p. 17. Includes pressing plants

[2] NYT May 5, 1974

[3] Includes rack-jobbing/distributor division

[4] BB March 3, 1973, p. 3

[5] BB April 19, 1972

[6] BB August 25, 1973

[7] Net before extraordinary items

[8] BB August 28, 1971, p. 10

[9] "Company spokesman"

[10] BB April 18, 1973, p. 8

[11] 1972 report of parent company, Transamerica Corp.

[12] Includes music publishing; Warner has the biggest music publishing company in America

Chart 5.7
RCA

Sales and Net Profit by Segment

(Dollar amounts in millions)

		Sales and Other Revenue		Net Profit	
		$	% Total	$	% Total
Electronics — Consumer Products and Services	1973	1,149	26.8	48.0	26.1
	1972	1,098	28.4	57.7	36.5
Electronics — Commercial Products and Services	1973	644	15.0	25.8	14.1
	1972	531	13.7	11.7	7.4
Broadcasting	1973	684	16.0	47.7	26.0
	1972	611	15.8	36.0	22.8
Vehicle Renting and Related Services	1973	677	15.8	19.3	10.5
	1972	636	16.5	15.4	9.7
Communications	1973	165	3.9	18.2	9.9
	1972	137	3.5	13.6	8.6
Government Business	1973	381	8.9	3.3	1.8
	1972	396	10.3	3.4	2.2
Other Products and Services	1973	581	13.6	21.4	11.6
	1972	454	11.8	20.3	12.8
Total	1973	4,281	100.0	183.7	100.0
	1972	3,863	100.0	158.1	100.0

Profit information in the above table is after deduction of allocations to the respective segments of corporate expenses not charged directly to any of the reported segments.

Source: RCA Annual Report 1973.

guitars, Leslie speakers, Steinway pianos, Rhodes electric pianos, and Rogers drums. It is difficult to spend more than a few dollars on music in America without contributing to CBS's profits.

Rock music probably accounted for 15 percent of CBS's record sales in 1960, but had grown to over 50 percent by 1972. The change was implemented in large part by Clive Davis, a Harvard Law School graduate from a poor background who was president for over six years when he was fired for allegedly misappropriating company funds. Davis was able to move equally well at both the performance and the corporate levels, and was considered to be the unofficial voice of the industry. Davis signed Janis Joplin, Santana, and others after Monterey, and brought the horn sound of Blood, Sweat and Tears and Chicago into prominence in rock music. Columbia made the turn into new rock when it signed the Byrds. It had picked up Dylan earlier, when he was still a folkie. Dylan had been signed by John Hammond, Sr., a long time producer and talent scout for Columbia who also found Bessie Smith.

Once into rock music Columbia was able to use the financial resources of CBS to expand. The company bought Neil Diamond away from MCA for $4-$5 million, and paid Laura Nyro $2 million to go with them. The deal the company was willing to give Johnny Winter (estimates range as high as $600,000) seems to have been more than the fragile guitarist could handle. Columbia had long been accustomed to spending large sums on research to be able to control profit from innovations. The company allotted a minimum of a million a year to research "the disc concept." CBS has been able to make independent label deals with several successful producers such as Kenny Gamble and Leon Huff (Sounds of Philadelphia).

Columbia is also strong in the country field with artists like Johnny Cash, Loretta Lynn, and Kris Kristofferson. Country stars have the advantage of being long-lived. Audience loyalty continues much longer than it does in rock.

Probably the group that has provided the most money for Columbia has been Simon and Garfunkel, together and alone. As Paul Simon once pointed out: "Simon and Garfunkel was a much bigger phenomenon in general, to the general public, than the Rolling Stones."

The man who replaced Davis was Irwin Segelstein, a television network programming executive who, according to *Business Week,* is "a strong believer in cost analysis and market research."

Capitol

Capitol was a fairly prosperous company going into the era of new rock music in the mid-sixties. The company was hardly receptive to the new music, however, and was forced in 1964 by its parent firm, Britain's

EMI, to market the Beatles in the United States. The Beatles carried Capitol for five years, and masked the basic problems at the company: outdated financial organization, little understanding of rock music. The company "went from a $30 or $40 million business to $120 million with the Beatles." Artie Mogull, former vice president for A&R, told *Fusion:* "But they also had to make enormous overhead additions. Then when the Beatles broke up, they were left with the overhead." Capitol had also invested in a large rack-jobbing firm, Merco Enterprises, and had started a record club (sold in 1968). Both lost money.

The dam burst at Capitol about the time the Beatles broke up. The company had neglected its other artists (some of whom like the Beach Boys left in disgust), and had followed an indiscriminate pattern in signing new acts. Capitol was a company that would release anything. In fiscal 1971 the company lost over $8 million, even though they were $8.7 million in the black the year before.

EMI axed top officers and sent over Bhaskar Mennon, an Indian executive schooled in sophisticated financial techniques. The artist roster was slashed from 270 to 165, and the A&R department was cut from thirty to seven. Sales and promotion men were given less say in artistic decisions. Under Mennon's new controls the company inched back into the black, posting a profit of over $5 million in 1973. They got lucky with singer Helen Reddy, and sold a lot of albums by Grand Funk and Pink Floyd. Leon Russell and his Shelter label which Capitol distributes have helped to enliven the firm's image slightly, but reportedly have not contributed significant profits. Mogull, now at MCA, has story from the old days that sums up Capitol's position:

> "You could tell a good song plugger. He'd be on his way home with five dollars and a bill in his pocket from the electric company that says if he doesn't pay his bill tomorrow they're going to cut him off. He runs into some band leader like Guy Lombardo so he says, 'Let's go have a sandwich.' Now he knows he's going to have to pay for it, since he's the song plugger. But he knows if he does that, he's not going to have any money to pay the electric bill. So what does he do?" Mogull pauses in his anecdote. "For thirty-five years Capitol has been staffed by people who would go home and pay the bill."[14]

Polygram

In the early seventies the British electronics conglomerate Phillips and the Deutsche Grammophon company in Germany bought up several firms in the U.S. music industry. Through its U.S. subsidiary the Polygram Corporation in New York, the European group now controls MGM, Mercury-Phonogram, and Polydor Records, as well as the Chappell Music Publishing Company, a large old-line publishing house.

MGM had been wracked with problems before Polygram bought it out. It had lost nearly $18 million in 1968 and 1969 and barely broken even in 1970 and 1971. The MGM film company which dictated record division policy for a number of years set unrealistic sales quotas which were artificially met resulting in a huge record return problem. Large scale pilferage was discovered in one manufacturing plant. Several fiascos like the "Bosstown" campaign and deals with unreliable independent producers cost millions. The turnover in top executive positions was so rapid and in-fighting among directors so great that no effective control was ever exerted over the problems. It seems, as well, that several company officers seeing the ship sinking began to protect their own financial interests at the expense of the company.

Under Mike Curb, its last president, MGM had concentrated on bubblegum acts that appealed to the subteen audience. Under Polygram the company is attempting to move back into the mainstream of rock music.

Mercury was in a much more solid position than MGM. The company had been an innovator in computer techniques and rapid marketing devices. Mercury had several ties with British labels that provided it with successful acts such as Rod Stewart.

The intention of the Polygram Corporation seems to be to consolidate several record companies to save money on distribution and manufacturing, and to pool financing. It gives them a direct outlet for their European music product, and holds out the possibility of new American acts that can be marketed abroad. Their consolidation resembles the process that MCA went through in combining Uni, Kapp, and Decca (see below), but may not lead to the same profitable results. There are no American stars on the labels, except for Bachman-Turner Overdrive on Mercury-Phonogram (and they're Canadian), and few acts with potential, except for the Ohio Players. Several acts on MGM like the Osmonds seem to be leaving for other labels.

MCA

MCA Records in its present form is a recent creation. In the late sixties MCA, Inc., bought Kapp Records and formed Uni Records. MCA already owned Decca. The three firms were operated autonomously for a time and then consolidated under Mike Maitland who had been president of Warner-Reprise.

The companies were ripe for consolidation. Since each operated its own distribution network before the consolidation, they were "patsies," as Maitland remembers it, to independent distributors who could pay one of the three, the one whose product was currently the hottest, without paying the others. Consolidation put a stop to that and also enabled the company to shave its distribution points from 25 to 7, using company owned branches. Pressing plants were also consolidated, and Decca's scattered New York offices were centralized. Musically, the three fit fairly well together. Decca was traditionally strong in the country field and Kapp had a number of Broadway show records and middle-of-the-road artist Roger Williams, while Uni was active in singles.

MCA got two breaks during this period of consolidation. The Who's "Tommy," after selling a million, came back a second time, and "Jesus Christ Superstar," which was a project from out of left field, sold an amazing 4 million tapes and albums in its original form and became an additional Gold Record in the film score version. MCA, Inc., was able to cash in on the "Jesus Christ Superstar" road shows, too. Christian schlock was, for a mercifully brief time, as big as Eastern kitsch had been in the Beatles' Maharishi period.

Someone then brought an Elton John record to Russ Regan who was working for MCA at that time. The company was able to break him in the United States even though he was virtually unknown in Britain. In December of 1972 the consolidation was complete, and the new label, MCA Records, was launched with double Elton John, Neil Diamond releases in order to spread the name as quickly as possible. ("Decca" was a bad trade name since it was owned by British Decca outside the United States.)

Diamond was later bought away by Columbia, but MCA has kept The Who, even though they were dissatisfied with Decca's stodgy promotion, and Elton John. In the mid-seventies Elton John signed a five year, six album contract with MCA that guaranteed him $8 million on royalties of 20 percent—which, until a later contract between Stevie Wonder and Motown, was probably the highest deal ever made with a musician. John brought Kiki Dee to MCA on his Rocket label, and the company also had success with Olivia Newton-John and Lynyrd Skynyrd. The soundtrack from Universal Pictures' *American Graffiti* was another completely unexpected success. MCA has managed to break enough artists and luck into enough unusual music that it has become a success-ful company quickly.

Many of the successes at MCA Records have come from organizational and financial decisions. The company makes a bigger profit ($12 million on $70 million in sales in 1972) than several other companies doing more business. MCA under Maitland is conscious of finances: "Our A&R department regards a record as an artistic endeavor, our manufacturing division regards it as a 'product,' I see it as $1.00 to $1.25. 'Product' may be an improper name because this is a business that has an artistic side, but you can't ignore the fact that there are people working on our assembly line, just like Ford."[15]

Maitland is an old hand in the record business. He worked his way up to vice president at Capitol after the war, before becoming president of

Warner Brothers. Like most successful executives in the music industry, he is aware that there is a difference between the people that make music and those that sell it. He has few pretensions about his own ability to judge commercial talent, feeling it's safer to trust to high A&R people who do have that ability. "This company has turned around. Instead of Kapp and Decca it's MCA Records. We've cleaned up our manufacturing plants, our distribution; we're in business in Germany and England— we're making a lot of money. But I'm unhip."[16]

MCA, Inc., the parent corporation, is a conglomerate based in the entertainment industry. Besides owning the record division, the third largest music publishing firm in the United States (Rodgers and Hammerstein, and so on), and Universal Films and TV, MCA, Inc., operates the services at Arlington and Mt. Vernon cemeteries* and at Yosemite National Park, and owns the Spencer Gifts novelty store chain, and a bank in Colorado.

ABC

ABC has always relied on mergers with smaller labels to provide it with a source of talent. The company was called ABC-Paramount for a time, then ABC-Dunhill, and now ABC-Blue Thumb. ABC Records sales increased 150 percent the year it bought Dunhill, for instance, and besides getting the Mamas and the Papas the company signed Dunhill's business head, Jay Lasker, who is now the company president. The company was originally formed in 1955 as the record division of the American Broadcasting Company.

The acquisition of Lasker and Lou Adler's Dunhill label put ABC into rock, but not because anyone at ABC *liked* that kind of music. It was a case of giving the kids what they wanted in order to make more money. Larry Newton, the former president of ABC Records, tells the story in a way that makes ABC's attitude clear: "In 1966 four guys decided to start a company, Dunhill Records. Trouble was, they didn't have any money. We advanced them $75,000. Eight months later we bought them out for $2.5 million. What happened? The first record they made flopped. The next sold a million. They made a third. It grossed $4 million. You know what this record was? The Mamas and the Papas, four animals. They collected $268,000 in royalties, and we paid $2.5 million for the company just for that one act."[17]

ABC moved into rack-jobbing in a big way at about the same time as it bought Dunhill. Their rack-jobbing section has lost money for them, but the company holds on to it feeling that records are such a growth industry that their subsidiary will move into the black eventually.

---

*Record conglomerates seem to have a propensity for funeral ventures or *vice versa*. Warner Communications grew out of an extensive cemetery and mausoleum business, too. Music and death are both high yield investments in the United States.

Some of ABC's major acts in the past few years have been Three Dog Night and Steppenwolf. Currently they have, among others, Steely Dan, the Pointer Sisters, and Jim Croce, who with ABC's help turns out Gold Album after Gold Album from the grave. To record buyers, of course, record company identification means little or nothing. What counts is the sound and the artist.*

The Rich Get Richer, the Poor Do Label Deals

At this point the Top 10 record companies are seen as "big companies" with the exception of A&M and Motown. Bigness brings with it certain market advantages. Easy access to major financing means ability to expand when favorable situations arise and ability to withstand losses in bad times or when mistakes are made. A large catalogue of past records provides a base of steady sales that smaller companies don't enjoy. Distribution through company branches—so long as the company turns out enough successful records—means saving middleman profits and controlling distribution. A large company with total distribution can sell more of a hit because it can move the records into stores quickly. On the other hand bigness means higher overhead. Profit margins can be quickly trimmed when a company hits a dry spell but bigness brings a stability that prevents major fluctuations—usually. Exceptions like MGM and Capitol are glaring.

Whether or not a big company is a help to an act or a hindrance is a somewhat controversial question within the record industry. At bottom it is an unrealistic question since few small "artist-oriented" companies exist in the industry. "Independent" labels are usually aligned with one large company for at least distribution and usually promotion and advertising as well. Large companies are aware to some degree of the problem—after all it's unprofitable to alienate acts in the long run—and have often divided the overall company into smaller divisions or provided artists relations departments.

Still, many acts feel that they go unnoticed at large companies, that they never deal with anyone who can support them without approval from higher up. The Kinks have complained about Warner Brothers being "too big," and Poco has criticized Columbia for inadequately supporting them. On the other hand a large company simply has more money to spend to break an act or increase its sales.

Complaints are most often heard when a company decides that a particular act is not going to make it, or is not going to sell a lot more records, no matter what they do. After all it's in the company's interest to promote a group that *is* going to sell. Obviously, the decision on who to

---

*Motown and A&M have been profiled as "The Last of the Big Indies" in the preceding chapter. For Motown also see "Black Capitalism" in Chapter 7, pp. 258-61.

promote and whom to leave on their own has little to do with quality of music, and is made by the company, not the act. With these priorities, jazz and classical music, for instance, are rarely promoted (with a few recent jazz-rock exceptions).

Joe Smith of Elektra sums up the argument from the point of view of the large company:

> You've got Bob Krasnow and his Blue Thumb label [Blue Thumb was recently bought by ABC] which is an artist's company, but there are fiscal problems. They cannot make their commitments, they can't offer the same kind of guarantees, the same type of treatment, they just don't have the money to do it. They certainly are attractive, but I fear for the Bob Krasnows. Obviously companies like that are only looking out to get involved with companies like us to make distribution deals, to take that end off their hands. And they'll become independent production arms which is maybe where it all is: a half dozen big distributing operations and everything else. . . .[18]

There are pressures on companies to get bigger that don't come from the record business. More artists usually means greater sales and profits, provided signing and recording are not indiscriminate; and the greater the sales and profits a record company can show, the more power it gets within the larger corporate, conglomerate structure that most record companies are part of. Greater power to record divisions means that record executives can move to higher levels within the overall corporation.

Tangled Up in Red: *Eating the Returns*

The record industry has the usual problems of any capitalist manufacturer: rising operating costs, in the form of studio time and promotion expenses, materials shortages, in paper for covers and vinyl for records, and "labor" problems—in the form of increased royalty demands by artists. But the record industry has also followed the rest of America's monopolized corporate sectors in the time-honored solution to this problem: higher prices. And like steel and automobile corporations, record companies tack on a little extra profit on top of the "justified" increase needed to cover higher costs. Record manufacturers have found that record buyers will consistently spend more if they have to. They are even willing to pay an extra dollar for a superstar's record even though a guaranteed big seller actually costs the manufacturer *less* per unit to put out.

Two other problems are more specific to the record business: tightening playlists on radio and the costs involved in returning unsold records. Tightened playlists, as explained before, make it harder for new acts to be exposed.

Record returns have long cost the industry millions in profits. Unsold records come back to the manufacturers for full credit or exchange. The paperwork and labor and shipping costs have been estimated to cost 27 cents to 45 cents per LP or five single units. Of that amount, the retailer pays 2 to 5 cents, the rack-jobber 20 to 30 cents, and the maufacturer 5 to 10 cents. An average rack-jobber was shown to spend 18 percent of his operating cost on processing returns. The manufacturer's share is greater than the study showed because he is forced to recycle the returns as budget priced cut-outs or else to "eat them": to melt them down to make other records.

Industry spokesmen have railed against the policy of giving a 100 percent return privilege for years, but the practice is continued because it serves a purpose. It sells records. Most records by unestablished artists, a leading rack-jobber has pointed out, would never see the inside of a store if retailers were not able to return unsold copies for credit. The obvious compromise is to try to gauge response more carefully. "I've cut what I consider to be overly enthusiastic orders in half," says Ahmet Ertegun, and the WEA group now claims to keep returns at 16-17 percent, a level considered "manageable." RCA notes that additional copies can now be pressed and gotten into stores within ten days if necessary. Returns will always be a problem, because record companies as capitalist enterprises always need higher sales.

Rock Steady: *The Future*

Even though the growth *rate* for records and tapes is beginning to stabilize, the future looks bright for record companies. Records sell even in times of recession because as Sam Goody used to say, they are a "poor man's luxury."* They are also relatively cheap and long-lasting, when compared to movies, sports, and some other forms of entertainment. Furthermore, the top age of active record buyers, probably in the low thirties now, increases every year. A much larger proportion of the American population will be buying records fifteen to twenty years from now.

Rock music and rock stars will have taken over television by that point, too. The average TV viewer will have been raised on Presley, the Beatles, and Carole King, and won't stand for the fifties pop fare served on television now. Not that the emotional/political content of TV will change that much. We'll just have John Denver rather than Johnny Carson hosting late-night celebrities, and Grace Slick replacing Dinah Shore. Helen Reddy and George Carlin are already late night features.

---

*Jay Lasker, president of ABC Records, has his own theory on this. People continue to buy records because they "have been trained right," he once said. They have the buying habit.

Every network has its concert show. Even Cheech and Chong, according to their producer Lou Adler, are being groomed for a comedy spot.

Further increases in the record market will be aided by stronger merchandising and continuing technological development. TV advertisements for oldies packages have already opened up a virtually new business. Sixty-two million dollars were spent for TV ads of such packages in 1973, and millions of albums were sold. Quadraphonic sound, while taking longer than stereo to catch on, is becoming an important business. Columbia sold $6 million worth of Q discs in its first year of marketing them. But basically it is a boon to hardware manufacturers rather than record companies.

Even though sound coming through four speakers and approximating live concerts may sound better, it probably won't cause people to buy more records; when they buy a new record they'll just make it quad. The usual fight between leading manufacturers like RCA and Columbia for competing technical systems is occurring in the development of quadraphonic sound. CBS backed a matrix system that essentially combines the four recorded channels with some overlap. The "discrete" system, backed by RCA, keeps the four channels separate from recording to playback. Most hardware manufacturers now provide compatible equipment that makes it possible to play either system. Total record/tape sales may reach the $3 billion mark by 1980, with tape about 40 percent, assuming that the seventies recession does not become a thirties depression.

A technological threat to records may be posed by video cartridge development and the introduction of mural-sized, full color wall screens. However, the main software products shown on the systems will probably still be musical groups playing in concert. Also, the research and development for these new items are already virtually monopolized by the biggest record companies and their parent corporations—CBS, RCA, MCA, Warner Communications, and ABC. MCA has developed a video disc which produces the results of a video tape cartridge, but looks much like a record and can be distributed as one. Virtually all companies now try to assign video rights to themselves as well as standard tape and record rights when they make contracts with musicians.

Different Strokes: *Warner-Reprise and RCA*

The Warner Brothers film company had an interesting beginning. After losing several million yearly in 1925-27, when medium-sized motion picture companies that did not control first run movie houses were being squeezed out by well-financed monopolistic companies that did, like Paramount, Warner Brothers introduced sound pictures, "talkies," to the U.S. public. Operating with an exclusive equipment licensing contract from Bell Telephone which had developed the sound process, the company did an about-face. It moved into the big time showing a $17 million profit in 1927.

The capitalistic glories of the early Warner Brothers had long faded by 1958 when the film company formed a record division. It was the new rock music of the sixties that was to turn the company around a second time. The comeback that records made possible took only slightly longer than the change talkies had made.

The first four years of Warner Brothers Records were a disaster. Headed by Jim Conklin who had been president of Capitol and Columbia, the company tried to become a full-line record firm overnight, with a big catalogue representing too many kinds of music. The company had managed to sign Bob Newhart, a popular comedian, and the Everly Brothers, but it was still losing about $3 million a year when Mike Maitland became president in 1961. The film company thought of closing down the record division, but decided that it would lose even more money in unpaid bills owed by distributors. Almost immediately the company got lucky. They signed another comedian, Allen Sherman, and the folk trio Peter, Paul, and Mary who had enormous sales. The group made 15 million total unit sales over the next eight years. A third comedian, Bill Cosby, signed in 1963, completed the initial turn-around. For a time Cosby accounted for an inordinate percentage of the company's business, perhaps as much as 50 percent.

In 1963 the company bought Reprise Records which was owned by Frank Sinatra. The Warner Brothers film company made the deal in order to get Sinatra to do a series of four films for them. Sinatra was paid $22 million and given one-third ownership of the combined record companies, and of any record companies that might be bought later. The films failed, but Reprise suddenly became successful. Reprise had been a middle-of-the-road label with artists like Dean Martin, Dinah Shore, Sammy Davis, and Alice Faye. In a pop world that was turning to rock, Reprise had not been earning money. After an initial shake-up, however, the label underwent a resurgence. Dean Martin, Nancy Sinatra, and Trini Lopez began to sell.

Warner Brothers-Reprise was established, but it was hardly a contemporary label—rock music was where the big money was beginning to come from. The company began to move gingerly into the new music. Joe Smith, a Boston disc jockey brought in by Maitland as a national promotion man, signed the Grateful Dead after seeing them at the Avalon Ballroom in San Francisco. The company already had the Kinks on a licensing agreement from England. But now a series of moves to buy out Warner Brothers diverted attention from the growing involvement in rock music. Jack Warner sold out to Seven Arts, a small film producer and distributor.

"It was as if the *Pasadena News* bought the *New York Times*," said Smith later. Seven Arts, using merger financing techniques common in the sixties, bought Warner Brothers for "no money of their own, they borrowed it all, they leveraged it, and they went into terrible debt and proceeded to operate the company in a manner to try to raise that stock price to get some fast money turnover."[19]

Seven Arts, who had bought the company to sell it, made one important decision before they sold out. They bought Atlantic Records in 1967. The Erteguns and Jerry Wexler wanted to realize some capital gains and sold for $17-22 million. Atlantic was a solid company that had been a leader in r&b and soul for years, but now it too suddenly became even more successful. Several English groups that Ahmet Ertegun had acquired through personal visits, contacts with manager Robert Stigwood, and agreements with Polydor Records in England, became large sellers: Cream, Led Zeppelin, the Bee Gees. Jerry Wexler took Aretha Franklin who had been only moderately successful with Columbia and turned her into a million seller. The Stax-Volt label deal that included Otis Redding took off, and Atlantic began to latch on to new white progressive rock bands like Crosby, Stills, and Nash. Three years after Atlantic was acquired, it was earning pre-tax about as much as it had been sold for.

After the Atlantic purchase it was obvious what a great deal Frank Sinatra had made. He now owned one-third of Atlantic as well. The man who had called rock music "the most brutal, ugly, desperate, vicious form of expression it has been my misfortune to hear" was now making more money from it than he ever had from his own crooning. The one-third clause was subsequently scaled down so that Sinatra's interest was about 20 percent.

When Seven Arts put the company up for sale, the first few deals fell through. National General started to buy the company but was prevented by the antitrust division of the Justice Department. Commonwealth United, a fast-moving conglomerate, began merger procedures but sold its option to the Kinney Corporation, a funeral and cleaning services conglomerate. Kinney paid $350-400 million for Warner Brothers, depending on stock prices. "We were uncomfortable during this period," recalls Smith. "I know the Erteguns, Jerry Wexler, Mo Ostin, Mike Maitland, and myself were extremely unhappy. Here we were running two of maybe the half dozen successful top record companies in the world and they were footballing us around to people who had no feeling for us or touch."

The Kinney Corporation was an upstart conglomerate, not much older than the Warner Record division. It was run by an ambitious young man from Flatbush, Steven J. Ross, now 49. Ross had taken his wife's family business, large-scale funeral companies, expanded into rent-a-car agencies (initially employing funeral limousines), and then into parking lots (offering free parking to rent-a-car customers) and building maintenance companies.

The parking lots were originally owned by the Kinney Corporation, which was separate from the Ross family businesses. Since the Mafia has been heavily involved in New York City parking lots, garbage collection companies, and cleaning services *Forbes* magazine and others have speculated that Kinney and through them Warner have also been involved with organized crime. Kinney and Warner have denied such allegations. At any rate Ross became the leading figure in the merged companies which used the Kinney name.

In 1967 a friend introduced Ross to Ted Ashley, head of the Ashley Famous Agency, one of the biggest U.S. talent agencies. Ross exchanged $10 million in preferred stock to buy the agency, then realized that Ashley and his executives represented a pool of underutilized executive talent in the entertainment business. The Ashley men knew the workings of the film and record industries and had numerous contacts, yet they were heading an organization that made only $1 million profit in a good year, according to *Fortune* magazine. Ross decided to scout out the entertainment business to see if some good buys were available that would put the Ashley people to work. William Sarnoff, a nephew of RCA head General David Sarnoff, was told to put together a list of likely acquisitions, and Warner Brothers-Seven Arts, as it was then called, turned out to be near the top. Kinney acquired Warner Brothers in the same year it bought two big cleaning service firms both in Cleveland and the Hackensack Trust Company (now the Garden State National Bank). Ashley was subsequently made head of all of Warner Brothers. He now runs the film division and sits on the board of Warner Communications.

The merger with Kinney provided the record division with financing to expand. International distribution was set up, a domestic branch distribution was begun, and a third company was added for $10 million—Elektra Records. Elektra had been started by Jac Holzman the fifties as a folk label. The company had Judy Collins and, for a time, Tim Buckley, the Paul Butterfield Band, and Spider John Koerner, Dave "Snaker" Ray, and Tony Glover. It also built a classical roster, and in 1965 moved into rock music with Love. Elektra became an important label in 1967 when it recorded the Doors. Since the company was strongest in areas not covered by Warner Brothers-Reprise or Atlantic, it fit well in the Kinney scheme.

In 1973 the Asylum Record Company was bought by Warner Communications and amalgamated with Elektra a year later. The label's head. David Geffen, soon replaced Jac Holzman who had been of Elektra. Geffen was a young, extremely ambitious booking agent who built a certain reputation for servicing acts over a long period of time rather than just squeezing them for as much as could be gotten in terms of tours and so forth in as short a time as possible. He joined Eliot Roberts in the Geffen-Roberts Management firm after leaving the booking agency. The two men then managed many acts, like Joni Mitchell, Crosby, Stills, Nash, Young, and Jackson Browne, who did not want to be treated as acts usually had been before the sixties. The "nice" approach has made millionaires of both men.

According to Roberts, he and Geffen formed Asylum in order to minimize contractual pressures on singer-songwriters who wanted to work at their own speed. When the label got too big Roberts sold out to Geffen and returned to the management company. Geffen was able to lure Bob Dylan away from Columbia for a one album deal, and in 1974, six months after Elektra and Asylum had merged, the company had the three top chart albums: Dylan's "Planet Waves," Joni Mitchell's "Court and Spark," and Carly Simon's "Hotcakes."

Ashley and Kinney tried to integrate the three companies to end cost duplications long before the Asylum purchase, but except for distribution and overall financing the companies are still run essentially autonomously. A&R, advertising, promotion, marketing, and merchandising are all handled separately. Separate operations help to preserve the individual flavor of the companies and to limit bureaucracy to a degree, but the divergent personalities at the heads of the labels are probably the main reason why Warner has never been integrated along the lines of MCA.

A music committee exists to oversee the record division, however. It consists of Ahmet and Neshui Ertegun from Atlantic, Smith and Mo Ostin from Warner-Reprise, and David Geffen from Elektra-Asylum, who has replaced Jac Holzman. Geffen, thirty-two, and Ahmet Ertegun, fifty-one, are the committee's co-chairmen.* The committee makes general decisions like those involving distribution that concern the entire record division. None of the label presidents sits on the board of directors of the parent corporation Warner Communications, and Smith, until 1976 president of Warner-Reprise, maintains that there is almost no contact between the record people and the Warner board.

---

*In 1976 Smith became president of Elektra-Asylum and Geffen moved to the Warner film division.

Music and Image: *Stan Cornyn, Stan Cornyn*

While Warner Brothers was being traded between corporations and the record division was being expanded, Warner-Reprise in Burbank was beginning to involve itself in rock music. At the time, as mentioned above, it was recording mostly middle-of-the-road artists like Sinatra and Martin. Basic economics provided the motivation: while the company could push one of its MOR artists to sales of 300,000 or so, it soon discovered that a Jimi Hendrix could sell 2 million albums.

After the Grateful Dead, Mo Ostin (who is now chairman of Warner-Reprise) and Smith began to sign rock acts and singer-songwriters. Besides the Dead and Hendrix, the company signed Jethro Tull, Procol Harum, Deep Purple, Black Sabbath, the Faces, and the Mothers of Invention. Smith and Ostin, like Ertegun, were not satisfied with the small number of groups being provided by the English record companies they were affiliated with. They went to England to sign up some of these groups directly. Black Sabbath and Deep Purple have at times been Warner-Reprise's biggest sellers although they are rarely mentioned in the rock press. Though highly commercial, they are not bubblegum acts. Much of their sales are in tapes, and they appeal to young car owners who like to turn up the volume on their tape decks. Smith has a somewhat blase attitude toward hard rock groups:

> If I were to start a record company today and were looking for a sure thing, the surest thing would be a "high energy"—euphemism for loud—rock group. They seem to be faceless. You can change players in them, with the exception of Jagger or Rod Stewart. You can take three people out of Uriah Heep and put three others in, and it won't make a hell of a lot of difference, as long as they're people with musical competence. They seem to generate a sort of sex appeal for young people.[20]

As for singer-songwriters Ostin signed Joni Mitchell for $15,000 after she had been turned down by RCA and Columbia, got Neil Young who wanted to solo away from the Buffalo Springfield, and Arlo Guthrie. Smith signed Van Dyke Parks, Gordon Lightfoot (who had been with Liberty), Van Morrison, and James Taylor, who had been displeased with the lack of attention he had received at Apple. Randy Newman also joined the company. Warner-Reprise clearly felt that these primarily acoustical acts would become popular, since they lured many of them away from other companies, but Smith claims that they had no conscious policy to sign singer-songwriters, only that "their coming reflected the personal tastes" of Ostin and himself. The more general move toward acts that appealed to the young and expanding audience was a conscious one.

Progressive rock acts like most of these required a newer sort of promotion than the record industry was used to. As detailed earlier (pp. 74-77), Warner-Reprise learned the new techniques such as posters, T-shirts, apple give-aways, and concert tours with their promotion of the Grateful Dead. Coincidentally, at this time their advertising manager was changed, and the company adopted a new "hip" image that successfully identified Warner-Reprise with musical change and the new underground culture.

"Did you change the advertising at Warner-Reprise because you were faced with a new audience and because the company had recently signed new rock artists?" asked an interviewer of Stan Cornyn, then director of creative services at the company, now executive vice president. "No, you make me sound more intelligent than I was," Cornyn replied. "What happened is that the guy I was working for took a sabbatical for a few months to work on his law exam. I had to do the ads and I did them my way because I was rather tired of the way ads had been done before— usually a big face shot of Tony Bennett with sky rockets going off or something. I just wrote the only way I knew how, really: my way of communicating which is honestly with a sense of humor and self-deprecation. It comes out a little wry. This turned out to be astonishing to the record industry which is used to another kind of hyperbole."[21]

The series of ads included a "Win a Fug Dream-date Contest," a "Pigpen Look Alike Contest" (to hype the Grateful Dead), and an offer to give away dirt from Topanga Canyon where Neil Young lives: "Free Dirt!" Cornyn poked fun at the company's inability to sell Randy Newman's or Van Dyke Parks' albums, offering to give them away, while at the same time gave the impression that Warner-Reprise was willing to stay behind a new artist until he made it. The Newman give-away was referred to as a chance to see "capitalism crumble before your eyes."

The ads sold records but that was not their main benefit to the company. Cornyn has often said that print ads rarely help a new artist and only announce an established one. More importantly, artists not with Warner often felt that the company, as portrayed by the ads, seemed to be closer to the music. The image was successful in attracting new artists to the company. "They were a symbol that the behavior of acts did not have to be that of Peggy Lee to be acceptable to the management of this company," says Cornyn.

One group of ads for Joni Mitchell seemed to have backfired, however: "Joni Mitchell Is 90 Percent Virgin" referring to the fact that she had only sold a tenth as many albums as Judy Collins; "Joni Mitchell Takes Forever," talking about the long wait between her albums; and "Joni

Mitchell Finally Comes Across" announcing the arrival of the album, her third. Joni Mitchell and her manager Eliot Roberts thought the tone of the ads was demeaning, and they were one of the reasons why she left the company for Asylum Records. Her departure was not for long, as far as Warner Communications was concerned, because Asylum was bought out by Warner-Reprise's parent firm a few years later.

Ms., Mad, and Warner Comm. Corp.

A certain amount of criticism is now heard that Warner-Reprise is too big, that it is losing its artist-oriented image. The Kinks and Brownsville Station are two acts that have complained of being lost in the shuffle or of not receiving adequate promotion. Some rival executives have predicted that acts will go elsewhere.

The problems are present at most other record companies, too, however, and there are few companies where an act that feels neglected could turn. Out of the top ten the only small companies are really Motown and A&M. Motown limits itself to black acts for the most part, and takes few new groups anyway. A&M is limited, by choice, in the number of new groups it wants to sign. Conceivably, a disgruntled act could go to Asylum, as Joni Mitchell did, but profits would still remain in the Warner Communications Corporation since Asylum is a part of it. Warner Communications' strategy of three relatively autonomous record companies also tends to limit the type of bureaucracy that acts are bothered by, at least in comparison to an RCA or a Columbia. For its part Warner Communications has been able to stave off ossification in the proven industry manner: buying out a hot young independent label.

Although the Warner record companies are still outpaced by CBS in foreign sales and depth of catalogue they have been able to stay in the number one position in terms of U.S. chart albums for several years now. The music division at Warner Communications, which includes income from music publishing as well as records and tape sales, accounted for nearly $234 million in sales in 1973. Sales have risen an average of about 28 percent a year since 1969, although the rate of increase has been declining each year. Profits rose about 25 percent each year from 1969 through 1972, but fell 7 percent in 1973. The drop in profits that year seems to be industrywide. CBS's profit fell nearly 7 percent also. The Warner group will probably stay ahead of CBS in the domestic charts, and it shows signs of increasing its share of the foreign market. At any rate, the two companies will most likely be the dominant record corporations for some time to come.

The combined music division at Warner Communications is the most important part of the organization, accounting for 43 percent of overall sales in 1973 and 46 percent of total profits. The old Kinney organization of cleaning services, parking lots, and funeral companies with one or two entertainment companies has been changed to Warner Communications which except for several New Jersey banks and some real estate is primarily a media/entertainment conglomerate. (Much of .the old Kinney is maintained as a separate corporation.) The corporation is heavily involved in films and television, of course, and also in cable TV and publishing. Warner Communications owns a quarter of *Ms.*, all of *Mad*, and sixty-three regularly issued comic books. In fact *Mad* has the highest profit in relation to sales of any Warner business, $2.5 million on sales of $6 million in 1973. Warner Communications has learned how to commoditize pop culture more successfully than any other U.S. corporation in the last decade.

Radar, Refrigerators, and Records: *RCA*

RCA has been the butt of a number of jokes in the record industry over the years. The company is the corporate giant that "missed the boat," as it admitted in a self-effacing ad in 1970, on both fifties rock'n'roll and sixties rock. RCA latched onto Elvis Presley and the Jefferson Airplane, top sellers in their periods, but nevertheless estimated that both rock'n'-roll and progressive rock were just fads.

The history of the company is a history of typical industry reactions to new music. A profile of a company like MGM would give a distorted picture of industry reactions since MGM by stultifying its progressive rock groups, even to the point of eliminating some acts for drug lyrics, was so antirock as to be atypical, while a closer look at CBS would give the impression that any large company could make the turn-around. RCA was average in its structural adjustments. As a monolithic corporation the company also makes an interesting comparison to the Warner group of labels.

In the decades before rock'n'roll RCA was often considered to be the leading record company in America. Its only close rival was Columbia. It was strong in country and classical, each probably accounting for 20 percent of the business in 1955, and its pop or middle-of-the-road music sold well. They made some big mistakes—missing out on the introduction of the LP for instance (RCA even turned down the LP's inventor, Dr. Peter Goldmark, when he first came to the United States looking for a job—he went to CBS), but in the slow-moving industry of the forties and fifties, big money and standardized tastes seemed enough.

In 1956 with the rockabilly movement brewing on the edges of country music, Elvis Presley came to the attention of Steve Sholes, RCA's director of country A&R. Presley was signed for $35,000, well-promoted, and recorded for pop and even r&b in addition to country. His sales became immense. From 1956-62 he was responsible for 31 out of RCA's 39 million-selling singles, and from 1958-60 he accounted for nine of their forty Gold Albums. Industry sources have speculated that he accounted for a quarter of RCA Records' total business for at least a decade.

It would seem natural that the company would go after more rock'n'-roll performers, but they did not. Presley was regarded as a freak by most RCA executives such as George Marek, the opera buff who headed the company soon after Presley was signed. There may have been no pressure from outside the record division to limit rock'n'roll at the company, but record executives were bothered by establishment disgust with Presley's uninhibited performances. Besides, most company executives were more at home in classical music. Sam Cooke was with the company from 1958 to his death in 1964, but he was regarded as an r&b performer by the company. RCA made no real effort to promote him in other markets as they had Presley.

In the early sixties RCA had a strong MOR roster which helped the company believe that its lack of involvement in rock would not be damaging. The story goes that Bob York, a key A&R man for the company in this period, announced at a meeting that the company needed "a pianist, an instrumentalist, a male vocalist, a female vocalist, a foreign singer, and a folk group." He then signed Peter Nero, Al Hirt, John Gary, Ann-Margaret, Sergio Franchi, and The Limelighters. With these artists and Elvis, as well as Henry Mancini and Harry Belafonte, the company was able to plug its ears to what was happening around the country. Even the Beatles made no impression on the company's talent scouts.

In late 1965, the company signed the Jefferson Airplane. The decision seemed to portend that RCA would come back strong into sixties rock, but in fact it was much like the Presley signing. The company was still wary. They waited to see what would happen with the Airplane. The group took a couple of years to break outside of California, but they did. "Surrealistic Pillow" in 1967 became the first of six Gold Albums the Airplane made for RCA over the next six years. The company made more of an effort to follow the music up than they had with Elvis, but they only got their fingers burned. They introduced five progressive or psychedelic acts like Prism, Groupquake, and Joyful Noise, only to have them all flop.

The company, it seems, had only lucked on to the Airplane. The problem was that their A&R department could recognize a fad but could not pick out the quality music within it. Joe Di Imperial, RCA's A&R

man responsible for signing the Airplane, was reported to have said that a person didn't need to hear any of these new groups to tell which were worth signing, he had only to look outside of the clubs where they were playing to see if there were lines. The formula worked for the Airplane, but represented only "a synthetic approach to the problem," as Ahmet Ertegun put it in a related context.

The company also paid little attention to the singer-songwriters that were beginning to surface at the edges of the rock scene. Along with Columbia they turned down Joni Mitchell. "We brought them Joni's songs and demos," remembers manager Eliot Roberts, "and they said, 'That's nice, a girl and some songs, but it's not making it. We're looking for the Rascals or Wilson Pickett.' "

RCA was bumbling but it was still selling records. Elvis and the classical and country catalogues were always there to pay for the overhead and then some. A deal with producer Don Kirshner gave them two high-selling bubblegum acts, the Archies and the Monkees. The Monkees have hardly made a contribution to music, but RCA wasn't bothered. They didn't really need a Dylan, a Joplin, or a Miles Davis when the Monkees could sell 15 million albums in three years. They also had the Guess Who, a group that filled the same slot that Grand Funk did at Capitol.

The Monkees, however, did not have the staying power of a Dylan. The company could not go on for long finding quick hit bubblegum acts while missing out on the main rock market. Heads continued to roll in the A&R department. The art and promotion departments also seemed unaware of the demands of the new music.

The Youngbloods, who had put out one million-selling single for RCA, "Get Together," left the label for Warner-Reprise complaining that RCA forced album covers on them that they didn't like and restricted their recording style. "There was a very basic mismatch between RCA and the Youngbloods," their manager Stu Kuchins told *Rolling Stone*. "Their company policies are set up for an older industry. Their style is old and their ideas are old. . . . It's a very stale company. Lately, they've been making some efforts, but mostly what they've done is to update their vocabulary. They have a basic lack of comprehension of what the music's about and what the people who enjoy it are like. They don't know how to put an RCA artist across to the public. RCA operates basically on momentum."

In about 1969-70 the company signed two acts that straddled MOR and rock—John Denver and Harry Nilsson—but both took several years to break. A new A&R man was brought to the company in this period, Dennis Katz, who finally signed several acts that represented hard rock.

Katz was the brother of Steve Katz of Blood, Sweat, and Tears, and he had managed the group. He brought David Bowie, Lou Reed, and the Kinks to RCA.

Some people in the industry have charged that RCA acquired Bowie simply to change the image of the company and that they have lost money promoting him. The company denies this of course. Herb Helman, vice president for public relations, has said that the rumors stem from overestimates of the money RCA put into Bowie's original American tour. According to Helman the tour cost was high— $100,000—but not extravagant. Each Bowie album climbs progressively high on the charts, and it seems the promotion has paid off. Whether the company signed these three acts out of taste or simply to sprinkle a little glitter on their old-line image is hard to say. The company has said that Bowie's music was what had originally attracted Katz, and that the promotional hook Bowie's lifestyle provided was a lucky adjunct. "We didn't want the Kinks because Ray Davies was going to show his ass," protests RCA's Eliot Horn somewhat unconvincingly. "We loved the Kinks!" At any rate the company finally had a few acts that placed them in the mainstream of rock music.

RCA was not out of the woods yet. They had other problems. Although Katz and the RCA president he served under, Rocco Laginestra, had found several top acts, they had not signed many others that looked like they were going to make it. RCA is such a huge operation that a number of successful new artists in all fields are necessary to pay the overhead.

Furthermore, in 1973 the company was making the change to streamlined branch distribution. They had been distributing first through RCA appliance dealers, then in a mixed "dual distribution" system. The changeover cost millions, and required a strong roster to bring it about. RCA did not have that roster in 1973, and the company actually lost money in the third quarter. Rising costs that lowered profits to a certain degree at other companies like CBS and Warner, did not help the company during the year, either.

In 1974 RCA appointed yet another new president for its record division, Ken Glancy. Unlike Laginestra who had come from the financial side of NBC, Glancy was a "record man" who had been in A&R at Columbia during the sixties and headed RCA Records' British operations. Armed with Bowie, Reed, Denver, and Nilsson in its pop/rock field the company may become profitable again, but it won't happen overnight.

"Victor is an elephant," said George Marek twenty years ago. "You must not expect an elephant to behave like a gazelle."

Not a Gazelle

RCA Records is very much a part of a larger corporation. Sales and profits for the record company are not broken out from sales and profits figures for all "Electronics—Consumer Products and Services." The record division reports to a group vice president who is responsible for several other divisions besides the record company such as Random House and Global Communications. Day-to-day affairs are left up to executives in the record division but large financial decisions require consultation with the group vice president. Signings over a certain figure, or investments in Broadway shows, which require hundreds of thousands of dollars, are examples.

Headquartered in Rockefeller Plaza in New York, RCA, Inc., is of course one of the biggest corporations in the world. With sales in 1973 of over $4 billion, it is the twentieth largest corporation in the United States. The corporation is a prime defense contractor, manufacturing electronic equipment and managing ballistic missile early warning systems among many other things. At the beginning of 1974 RCA was working on more than a thousand government contracts. These contracts amounted to over $243 million for fiscal 1974. (It would be ironic although sordid if there were some tie-in between RCA's support of the Vietnam War and their promotion of Barry Sadler, whose "Ballad of the Green Berets" was both a Gold Album and a million-selling single for the company in 1966.)

The company also provides an elaborate automated communication system utilized by the 800-mile Alaskan oil pipeline, operates NBC radio and television, and manufactures hundreds of industrial and consumer electronics products such as TV sets and appliances. They own Hertz Rent-a-Car, Banquet Foods, and the Cushman and Wakefield commercial real estate firm. Like Warner Communications and CBS, they are involved in publishing. RCA owns Random House and Alfred A. Knopf. A look at the sales and profit figures for the years 1972 and 1973, gives an idea of the immensity of the operation. (See Chart 5.7.)

Record company presidents at RCA have traditionally left talent acquisition to the A&R departments. This has tended to insulate top executives from changes in the music, putting the company at a disadvantage compared to such companies as Motown, Atlantic, Warner-Reprise, and CBS (during the Davis reign). A record company can get by without chief executives directly involved with the artist roster, but the top people must be aware of their own weakness and must at least be able to recognize A&R people that have ears—as at MCA.

Production at RCA has tended to be more in-house than at many other record companies. As much as 40 to 50 percent of their recent records have been produced by staff producers. Since staff producers are often older and used to working within the structure at RCA, this situation has again often distanced the company from new music.

The decision to allow the Airplane to do a fairly autonomous label deal has been a wise one for RCA. Relations have been strained over certain censored lyrics ("up against the wall motherfucker" and a line about Jesus sleeping with Mary had to go), but the deal has kept one of the least corporately oriented groups in the country tied economically to one of the United States' most powerful corporations. Grunt has been a financial success and has also served as a window onto the San Francisco scene, providing groups that RCA probably would not have noticed on its own.

Advertising has been a weak point for RCA over the years. Until 1970 much of it was contracted out as at nonmusic companies. Outside advertising companies often had little understanding of rock music or its audience.

Catalogue and Fads

The strength of RCA has certainly been its catalogue and the breadth of its music. The catalogue contains around 2,000 records. Many of these never make the Top 200 charts but sell consistently in small numbers. Dozens of classical records have sold several hundred thousand copies over the years. The classical catalogue contains a basic Brahms, Beethoven, and Bach that never becomes outdated. Only two classical records have ever gone Gold—a Van Cliburn treatment of Tchaikovsky for RCA, and Walter Carlos' Switched On Bach for Columbia. *The Sound of Music* has also been a tremendous seller over time for the company. The record has sold over 8 million copies in the United States and 5 million more abroad. It ranks with Carole King's Tapestry for the best-selling record of all time. (The King record definitely has higher U.S. sales, and is probably the better-selling record overall.)

Overseas sales have long been important to RCA. As a subsidiary of multinational RCA, Inc., the record division knows how to operate abroad. At one point the company released records simultaneously in the United States and overseas. In fact RCA would show up better on the trade sales charts if its overall sales were tabulated, not just its U.S. sales. Country sales are often as steady and long-lived as classical. Country fans have proven to be loyal. Once an artist is established his/her records sell for years. These steady catalogue sales help cushion the company during times when no one area is hot.

An approximate percentage breakdown of current sales by type of music at RCA would be 50 percent rock (RCA calls this "contemporary"), 17 percent MOR, 20 percent country, 8 percent classical, and 5 percent jazz and r&b selling exclusively to blacks. This breakdown puts John Denver in the MOR category with Perry Como. The country field has often been dominated by RCA, and the company has such greats as Chet Atkins, Floyd Kramer, Bobby Bare, Skeeter Davis,. Waylon Jennings, Lester Flatt, Dolly Parton, and Charlie Pride. RCA had sixty singles on the country charts in 1974, more than any other label.

The three highest selling acts in the company have been John Denver, Charlie Pride, and Presley, Elvis had one of his best years in 1973 and was still near the top at his death four years later. The company has been extremely weak in r&b, although before World War II it dominated the market along with CBS.

The weakness of the company has been its inability to react to changes in mainstream rock music. Where the company has seen something brewing, it has moved to catch part of a commercial fad. It has never been able to regard significant new music as music. The rapid turnover of top executives, the underuse of outside producers, and the old-fashioned approach to advertising have reinforced the company's distance from the music. RCA represents the way old-line bureaucratic corporations deal with creativity.

Fundamentally, of course, there is no real difference between RCA and the looser, "hipper," and more successful Warner Communications. They both have the same goals: to commoditize music and musicians, to make the music as commercial as possible, to use different techniques, but to sell music as *well* as they would refrigerators, to abbreviate musicians into superficial images that can be stamped on to ads and sixty second radio spots, and to turn musicians into self-promoters who are in effect their own salesmen.

It's just that Warner is a lot better at doing these things than is stodgy old RCA. Warner has learned that if a company acquires some taste and treats its artists with a certain amount of sympathy, emphasizing long-run return, the company will show a greater profit. To paraphrase Joni Mitchell's sophisticated manager Eliot Roberts: "Be sensitive, you'll make more money."

6 WHO OWNS ROCK: THE POLITICS OF THE MUSIC INDUSTRY

Politics are integral to any discussion of popular culture. Critics of high art have long fostered the image of the artist as someone isolated from his time. The conservative tradition of criticism sees the problems and solutions of art posed in purely personal terms, much as the conservative or bourgeois artists have seen freedom as possible within a purely individual frame. When one considers folk art and culture, this individual interpretation of the artist and his work breaks down for both aesthetic and political reasons. The artist himself is not isolated from society the way classical artists were; quite the opposite, he draws his images and forms of expression from traditions long ingrained in the popular mind; his struggles and events are common to his community.

The conflict between high art and folk art is also a social dynamic. The classic position of the artist has been that of an isolated and castrate rebel, whose work has the progressive aspect of denouncing the social order, but is made impotent by the way it is practiced or expressed, and by the distance between the artist and masses of people. Folk art is often communal in its artistic form, as well as the way it is practiced, and because it arises in a familiar way from the community of people and ensemble of relations between people in which the artist himself exists, can break down the impotence of art's criticism of society. In many cases in American folk art and music, this connection of the artist to large masses of people with a shared experience has become explicit in political struggles, from Joe Hill writing for I.W.W. picket lines to Bob Dylan's importance to the student rebellion, civil rights struggle, and New Left in the United States and abroad during the 1960s. Most rock music has been much less political than Dylan's early songs, of course. But rock music and musicians have been a part of a broad movement for political and cultural change that had its roots in the stable repression of the fifties, and disrupted America through the sixties.

In rock'n'roll there are again dynamic artistic and social forces that converge. Rock'n'roll is black music, at its roots. Black people of course are an oppressed minority within the United States. Part of the reason they have developed such a creative and continuing music culture is precisely this oppression, which has forced the black community to look to its own resources in folk art as a source of identity and strength. The music industry is racist, like the rest of the United States, and many of the political forces that are exerted on blacks outside the business are duplicated within it. Since the music business has made much of its money in the last twenty years off the creativity of black musicians, it is important to look at the unfolding of that racism within the history of the industry.

Women are another outgroup whose oppression has not been as acknowledged as that of blacks, but is just as consistent. Women's culture has traditionally been relegated to those limited areas where women were allowed autonomy: in cooking and sewing and the raising of children. They do not have a strong musical heritage like black people, but have been exploited by the industry, which is sexist like the rest of American business. Women have always been the subject of rock'n'roll songs. Now they are beginning to write and play their own. Their current role is hopefully a transitional one, and a strong women's music will develop. It is therefore important to explore this dynamic in the context of the industry as well.

But probably the main reason why classical conservative criticism and understanding of the artist's role in society break down—along with the fact that the music is made by certain people, with their own histories, and reference to particular other people—is that this is the United States, a capitalist or business society based on selling and profits. Because it is popular, and can be marketed and sold, rock'n'roll music is, like most other music, or art, first and last a commodity that can be bought and sold. Its character as a commodity makes the music no different, *in this way*, from television programs, baseball bats, or shoes. The fact that the music itself is a product which like other products can be bought and sold and profited from (of course) ties into a broader observation. That is, the music business, the record companies and radio stations, are themselves integrated into a much larger framework of other businesses, sources of finance capital, and the general network of the business system which has an interest—a real, material interest—in reproducing and reinforcing the status quo.

This is an important tension in rock music, and understanding the tension is critical to having a real understanding of how rock music functions in American society. At the same time that the music itself, or the musicians, or the lifestyles they embrace may be, or appear to be, critical of the current system, they are in fact tied into that system in a material way. Through its operation they make their living and provide profits to numbers of corporations, many only vaguely linked to the music itself.

Many people feel that the business community surrounding the record industry is significantly different from the rest of the business community. At times, record companies have been linked in the public's mind to left-wing political groups and causes. In fact there is no real evidence for this connection, and in many cases record companies are owned by some of the most obviously reactionary and militarist corporations in the United States. But there are so many forms of the argument about the liberality and progressive character of the music industry, and the arguments are so pervasive, it seems important to establish the actual political character of the industry before launching the discussions of racism in the industry, sexism in the industry, and the overall cooptation of rock into the business system.

What, then, are the political dispositions of record companies and their chief executives?

The Wall Street Shuffle: *Bi-Partisan Is Best*

Three major record companies are owned by some of the oldest powers in American electronics manufacturing and broadcasting, and are politically indistinguishable from their parent firms: RCA, CBS, and ABC. RCA and CBS have long been part of a business establishment that supports both major political parties on a regular basis, but emphasizes connections with one or the other during specific political crises. This was not always the case, but dates from the Second World War. RCA, for example, was originally identified almost exclusively with the Republican party. Their experience points up the shortcomings of such unilateral party identification. RCA president General David Sarnoff had repeatedly and vituperatively condemned Franklin Roosevelt, before his election. Sarnoff considered Roosevelt a dangerous sellout to socialism.

With the coming of the 1930s depression and the rise of Roosevelt, many commentators observed an ebbing in RCA fortunes, as reflected, for example, in some critical rulings of the FCC. By the end of the war, however, RCA had learned its lesson and was back in favor with top Democratic government circles. The corporation enjoyed a close relationship with the conservative Democratic administration of Harry Truman, and the long fifties Republican regime of Dwight Eisenhower.

The Vietnam War was an important point in the evolving corporate community in America since after the protracted defeat of the United States, major business interests that had been working essentially in harmony since World War II and the death of Roosevelt, split on the subject. Most directors at CBS and RCA supported the war when it was backed by Republicans and Democrats under the Eisenhower, Kennedy, and Johnson administrations, but tended to favor disengagement, along with many other important multinational corporations, when the war began to take too great an economic and social toll (wild inflation, an unfavorable balance of payments, recession in the late sixties and continuing through the seventies, and student and ghetto riots). Establishment media organs like *The Wall Street Journal, The New York Times,* or network television reflected this change in position.

One dramatic example of corporate reevaluation of the American military commitment in Southeast Asia was the CBS retrospective documentary aired in 1971, *The Selling of the Pentagon.* It discussed the self-advertising arm of the military and specifically criticized the network's own lopsided pro-Pentagon coverage of the Vietnam War. RCA's fully owned network NBC also criticized the war, although it was even later than CBS in coming around, and always lagged behind the other network in its coverage. This is understandable. RCA did not want to fully alienate the defense establishment. It is one of the largest military contractors in the United States. During the Vietnam War buildup RCA had annual Defense Department contracts averaging $300 million, and still got some $243 million in DOD business in 1974. Clearly, it is not in the company's interest to stray too far from policies preferred by the Pentagon.

Although CBS had less directly to gain from propagandizing Vietnam and other wars, its directors have played a key role in the formation of U.S. foreign policy. Bob Lovett, for instance, is a CBS director immortalized in the novels of Louis Auchincloss as the consummately well-connected behind-the-scenes power broker in Washington. He was an advisor to more than four administrations of presidents, stretching back to Franklin Roosevelt. As a septuagenarian, he was invited by John Kennedy to be secretary of state.* Henry Schact, another corporate director, is a member of the Council on Foreign Relations a group of some 2,000 businessmen, government leaders, and academics that has

---

*For more detail on Lovett's extensive powerful career, see David Halberstam, *The Best and the Brightest* (Random House: New York, 1973).

been called the "secret and continuing government" of the United States. During the past thirty years a really astonishing number of executives in the State and Defense departments have been drawn from the council, whose chairman is David Rockefeller, also chairman of the Chase Manhattan Bank, trustee of the greatest of American fortunes, brother of the former vice president of the United States. The publication *Foreign Affairs* is the only access the general public has to the organization, which decides the most key foreign policy issues for the United States long before its conclusions are unveiled to the Congress and people in the form of "policy."

It should not be surprising that the directors of one of the biggest media conglomerates in the world should be of interest to foreign policy makers, since network television and radio have played a key role in popularizing different deceptive and illegal government policies over the years. During the 1960s CBS president Frank Stanton was courted extensively by the government. From 1957 to 1967 he was chairman of the board of the Rand Corporation, the infamous California-based, Air Force-funded think tank that has done extensive secret research for the military on subjects as diverse as counterinsurgency warfare techniques, effectiveness of prisoner interrogation methods, and police surveillance uses of cable television. Along with Harold Geneen, at that time head of ITT, Frederick Kappel, recent head of AT&T, and David Sarnoff, head of RCA, Stanton was a member of the Committee on Communications of the National Citizens Commission on International Cooperation, a five person ad hoc committee set up by Lyndon Johnson in 1965 to review the status of world communications, and future plans for the United States global media empire. Finally, Stanton was head of the committee that annually reviewed the activities of the U.S. Information Agency, a CIA-funded propaganda operation overseas, and he was chairman of Radio Free Europe, another propaganda outlet, financed through the CIA. The directors of CBS, RCA, and ABC are also on the boards of other leading American corporations. Taking CBS as an example, Frank Stanton is on the board of New York Life Insurance, Pan American World Airways, Atlantic Richfield, Diebold Venture Capital, and others; Courtney Brown is a member of the Chemical Bank of New York and a director of Union Pacific and Borden, Inc., as well as other corporations; William A.M. Burden, whose son Carter at one point owned *The Village Voice*, is a director of American Metal Climax and Aerospace Corp.; Lovett is president of the powerful investment banking firm Brown Bros., Harriman and Co., and sits on boards of a number of railroads; Schact is president of Cummins Engine Co., a trustee of the Committee for Economic Development, and a member of the executive council of the Harvard Business School Association. The list is endless. Old man and recently retired chairman of the board William Paley is also chairman of the Museum of Modern Art (founded with Rockefeller money), a trustee of Columbia University, a consultant/counsel to the North Shore Hospital, and president of the William Paley Foundation.*

Directors of several other music corporations have been connected more exclusively with the Democratic party. The sociologist G. William Domhoff has pointed out that principals in Gulf & Western (Paramount, and until recently Blue Thumb), 20th Century Fox, and MGM have been part of what he calls the "Jewish-Cowboy" fund raising clique that forms a significant part of the Democratic party's financial base. Arthur Krim and Robert Benjamin, key powers at United Artists and directors of the parent firm Transamerica, have been major Democratic fund raisers in New York. Benjamin has also been a member of the Council on Foreign Relations. MCA's Lew Wasserman has also long been an important behind-the-scenes figure in the Democratic party.

Who Owns the Old Line Companies?

In addition to interlocks with other businesses, institutions, and political parties, and ownership by larger conglomerates, the major networks and record companies are tied in with long standing banking interests. Many observers believe that final control of corporations in America is held by the huge banks, insurance companies, and other finance capital "groups" that have derived from the leading families of nineteenth century robber barons and industrial tycoons. Thus the Morgan banking fortune lives on in the Morgan Guaranty Trust Group, the Rockefeller oil fortune in the Chase Manhattan Bank and Chemical Bank of New York Trust, the Ford, Dillon, Read, and Harriman fortunes in the First National City Bank of New York, a more recent group of interests originating in canning, textiles, oil and construction clustered around the Manufacturers Hanover Trust, and a number of regional groups including the Philadelphia-Boston coalition in the Mellon National Bank and Trust and First Boston Corporation, a separate Boston grouping around the First National Bank of Boston (representing families like the Adamses, Lowells, Cabots, and others), the Maryland-based Dupont group, and so on.

In the interest of obtaining needed capital for expansion, most corporations have long gone "public," and issued virtually all their stock to thousands of unconnected share owners who get a cut of the profits in dividends, but can in no way affect the activities of the

---

*The list of institutional and corporate interlocks within the major network record companies extends to hundreds and hundreds of connections. Many are carefully outlined in a pamphlet available from Research Group One (Baltimore, Maryland) and reproduced in *The Insurgent Sociologist* Vol. IV, No. 4, Summer 1974. More can be found in standard corporate reference guides.

corporation. Since most stock is divided between divided owners, only a relatively small amount (that is, 1 percent) of voting stock may be needed to control the corporation. Control here is used in the sense of having the power to determine the board of directors of the corporation, long-term decisions about its future, major relations with other businesses and government, major capital investment decisions, such as sinking money into entirely new technologies, sources of finance capital, and overall policy direction. It has nothing to do with day-to-day operation or management of the company which is left to corporate officers.

In this way, one can say ABC is controlled by the Morgan group with its 65 percent of voting stock, and CBS by the Rockefeller and Morgan groups with some 47 percent of the voting stock. Many observers, however, feel this concept of control is a confusing one that exaggerates the power of the banks. The corporations, they argue, have found their own sources of capital, principally through their own huge profits, and therefore do not need help from finance institutions. And in fact the corporations are managed separately, make decisions day-to-day separately, and have a force and life of their own, quite apart from the banks. This counterargument seems an especially strong one when discussing family run corporations like Ford or RCA. Despite the fact that 30 percent of RCA's voting stock is owned by the Rockefeller, Morgan, and Manufacturers Hanover Trust groups, for example, the Sarnoff family has run the corporation with a virtually unchallenged iron hand for generations.*

No matter which side of this complicated argument proves to be correct, that is, whatever the exact relation between the finance groups and the big media-record conglomerates, their interests are broadly the same. The media-record company conglomerates work in tandem with the major continuing finance institutions in American business, which themselves are based on the first fortunes of the robber barons. There is a full integration of the media conglomerates into the fabric of U.S. industry and capital.

Are New Voices Louder?

Given their ties into big and bigger business, no progressive political

---

*For a more detailed discussion of the arguments within this debate see S. Menshikov, *Millionaires and Managers* (Progress Publishers, Moscow, imported by Imported Publications, Inc., 320 West Ohio, Chicago, Illinois 60610), for a discussion of the banking/financial group argument, and *Who Rules the Corporation?*, Robert Fitch and Mary Oppenheimer, for an update of same. For the counterargument see, generally, *Monopoly Capital* (Baran and Sweezy) and specifically the essay "Resurgence of Financial Control: Fact or Fancy?" in *The Dynamics of U.S. Capitalism* by Paul Sweezy and Harry Magdoff (New York: *Monthly Review*, 1965).

initiative will be coming from the parent firms of the record companies. One liberal theory that seems to be held to by *Rolling Stone* and is advanced by many industry spokespeople has it that as the record divisions become more and more important *within* the parent companies their officers (presumably hip, ultra liberal) will exert more clout with the larger corporation, be it United Artists or CBS. The firing of CBS Records president Clive Davis would indicate that this is untrue.

CBS claimed that Davis had conspired with David Wynshaw, who was director of artist relations at this time, "and others" to improperly obtain company funds for personal use. Specifically Davis was charged by Columbia with using $20,000 of CBS funds to sponsor a Bar Mitzvah, $53,000 for home improvements, and $20,000 in "unnecessary" hotel services in Los Angeles. The alleged misuse of funds occurred over a several year period during which Davis was legitimately earning some $350,000 each year in salary and benefits. People within the record industry naturally wondered why a man making that much money would be embezzling sums on the side, and more important why CBS would be so concerned since they were paying Davis far more legitimately and since Davis, who was considered one of the most astute corporate and music figures in the business, was making millions for CBS. Observers began to look elsewhere for reasons to explain the firing.

Wynshaw, it turns out, was linked to a crime figure who was arrested for allegedly running a heroin smuggling ring. A secretary at CBS was also accused of taking part in the smuggling scheme. The real reason for the firing of Davis seems to have been the presence of this more publicly embarrassing drug scandal in the record company. (Charges that drugs were being used as radio payola were also bandied about at this time.)

Why was this enough to fire the successful president of the country's largest record company? Because at the same time as the CBS developments, the Nixon administration was both continuing its harassment of the news media and looking for any possible scapegoats for the Watergate affair, which was beginning to make waves. The CBS board, especially chairman Paley, was worried that the licenses for the television stations that CBS owned would be challenged by the Nixon administration or corporations acting for it just as the license of a Florida TV station owned by the *Washington Post* had been. The record division would have to be cleansed quickly, and Davis would have to go if the TV stations were to be saved. In other words the $300 million plus record division was not as important as the five CBS television stations. It was rumored that Paley was urged to keep Davis on, but that he felt that the record division was not as stable a part of the corporation as broadcasting. CBS had made most of its money off of television, after all, although not so much from local stations, and records were a frenetic youth business that had really been important for only ten years or so. In this context, the malpractice which Davis reports he thought was being settled out of court, quietly, was only the focus of a larger struggle, in which the record division lost out.

Much of the resistance toward giving corporate or wider political power to record industry people probably stems from the attitude of older people to rock music. An exchange with Warner-Reprise president Joe Smith presents the situation:

> Interviewer: Do you think there's now a time lag between the huge current economic power of the record industry and its political power? For instance, the film industry in America had very little political power in the beginning but as it grew, as it became a huge industry, it was able to lobby for favorable economic rulings in California and Washington and was also able to turn out some politicians like Governor Reagan and Senator Murphy. It seems that hasn't happened with the record industry yet.

> Joe Smith: Yeah, we're five or ten years away from that. Because the record audience, people who buy records and are really into music, are under thirty-five for the most part. These are people who've grown up with Presley. Presley's been around from 1956 on. He's been around seventeen years. These people, assume they were teenagers, at that point, eighteen years old, now they're thirty-five. People in their early thirties do not wield great political power. Political power is wielded in your forties and fifties. And whatever clout will come out of the music business will come in the next ten years. Those people who are thirty-five or under now control a great deal of the buying power in the country—they buy two billion dollars worth of records, obviously. But their political impact will come later. Right now, the music industry and music stars are bitterly resented by people over forty, forty-five years of age. We're resented because there's this flamboyance, there's a cockiness and an arrogance as well as enormous amounts of money in this business. And it's a thing that most people over forty can't listen to. They can't tolerate it. It's so alien to their ears. And so not only do we not have any people with clout, ready to take over, but the people who do have clout resent us.[1]

Given the ten years Smith feels it would take, what would be the impact of politics on the record industry? Smith and Warner Communications are newcomers to the political arena compared to an RCA or a United Artists, and might possibly be seen as closer to the record buying audience than the more established companies. Still, Smith's personal preferences are only as liberal as California's Kennedyesque former Senator John Tunney, whom Smith helped put in office. ("We took one vote that I didn't ideologically agree with [George Murphy] and we put in John Tunney. I felt he was more in line or would represent more the thinking of myself and my friends.") Smith is certainly not outside the mainstream of Democratic politics: "I still am not discouraged with the political system in this country. I think you can turn things around. You know; maybe not drastically . . . ."[2]

Rolling Stone also represents a source of possible political change emanating from the music industry. But, again, its political views do not range far. The magazine was an explicit supporter of George McGovern, but plays down or ignores any political movements outside of the two party system or not backed by some sector of American business. Essentially the magazine treats politics as competition between individuals as individuals, not as representatives of different corporate and class forces. Their main political writers like Hunter Thompson add a "gonzo" stylistic edge to political journalism but rarely if ever talk about the economic determinants behind political issues. The magazine itself, while certainly autonomous, could not be as large and powerful as it is without the large volume of music industry advertising it carries. *Rolling Stone* is a lot like the *New Yorker* was forty years ago, the representative of a new sophisticated and literate, hip, middle class that is not without morality. Twenty years from now as that group of readers is in a position of established power, it will occupy much the same position as the *New Yorker* does now. With newer rhetoric, naturally.

By this time it is evident then that the record companies are linked in with big business in the United States. There are no indications from the parent firms, the separate power of the record divisions within the parent firms, or "youth" businesses like *Rolling Stone* that any of them will be responsible for, or support, fundamental political change in the United States. Only in the most degenerate use of the word is the record business revolutionary, or radical. (For a discussion of the related subjects of censorship, cooptation and the radical artist, see Chapter 9.)

"What Mafia? What Record Business?":
Corruption in the Music Industry

To the general public the music business seems to have a tremendous amount of corruption. Payola given between record companies and radio station program directors and disc jockeys, while more widespread ten years ago, is still present. Radio and television rating companies, important throughout the music and entertainment industries, were forced by the FTC in 1963 to sign consent agreements that would end unfair practices such as including "not-at-homes" as at home and overstating the number of viewers and listeners used as the basis for their charts. Several television variety shows have been cited for receiving kickbacks from record companies to cancel fees the shows have supposedly been paying singers. The American Federation of Musicians has complained about unscrupulous managers "stealing" audition demos from naive musicians through fast contracts. A rock festival in Powder Ridge, Connecticut, was backed by New York crime figures who had sold $20,000-$40,000 in advance tickets at $20 each. Glenn Yarborough complained in 1970 that the $100 million college concert business "has gotten very dirty with kickbacks being exchanged between subagents (mostly students sitting on college entertainment committees) and agents, and subagents and colleges." A major Alabama promoter was indicted in 1973 for allegedly extorting money from acts in exchange for favorable dates. Record companies have underpaid royalties by misstating sales. Artists' contracts now often call for the right to sales audit by outside accountants.

Within the record industry a number of illicit practices have been less known to the press and public. *Billboard* reported in 1972 that independent recording studios were being forced through internal competition caused by the overbuilding of studios in the 1960s to give 30 percent kickbacks on recording fees to both independent and staff producers. The kickbacks were "standard practice" in New York and Nashville, according to the article. Roger Karshner, the former vice president for sales at Capitol Records, has made similar charges about studio kickbacks and added that independent producers often exaggerate their bill to record companies, and also unfairly credit themselves as having played on sessions to get the standard AFM recording fee. Karshner has also charged, unfortunately without listing dates and names, that credit managers at loosely run record companies have canceled debts for a percentage kickback, that record company contract negotiators have made overly generous deals in return for money from the act, and that promotion men and salesmen often sell promo records under the table.

David Wynshaw told the Newark grand jury he estimated some half million dollars in payola had been charged to the CBS promotion budget during the last two years. Large-scale thefts were discovered at MGM record warehouses during the years the company was under chaotic management. An independent auditing firm charged Stax Records in 1973 with sending some $380,000 in free records and tapes to distributors in return for kickbacks, and also claimed executives at the company overpaid photographers $26,000 in several instances in return for kickbacks. Large retailers have often received kickbacks from record companies in the form of free records and payment for nonexistent advertisements and in-store displays. These kickbacks are essentially rebates and constitute unfair competition under federal trade laws. An interviewer asked New York record store owner Sam Goody in 1973 if "big retailers like yourself get better discounts from record companies?" "No, Sir!" replied Goody. "And they better not get caught, either."[3]

Some of these specifics may have eventually been proven false but they are representative of practices that go on throughout the music industry.

The music industry has certainly received an inordinate amount of publicity. Is it really more corrupt than the rest of American business? Probably not.

First, as Joe Smith observed earlier, the rock'n'roll business is resented for its arrogance and flash by established media. The attacks on payola and now drugola have in part been smokescreens for a dislike of sexual music, black music, and rock music. Second, the industry is just now passing out of its formative period. It has only become big business in the last decade. Many other American industries were equally, or far more, corrupt during the entrepreneurial periods when a few individuals and corporations were eliminating competition and centralizing control. Railroads were based on land giveaways that were pushed through Congress with bribery and further enriched through extorting cities and towns along the routes. (San Francisco had to pay $1 million to ensure that the railroad would not bypass the town.) Oil and mining companies benefited from illegal rebates from railroad and shipping companies. The rebates functioned as they do now with wholesale records in the record business, to penalize smaller concerns. Building contracts from subways to interstate highways to land development projects have often been based on kickbacks between contractors and government officials. The Maryland case involving former Vice President Spiro Agnew is only a particularly glaring and recently publicized example.

The point is that with American businesses still in their formative stages the form that corruption takes is often heavy handed and explicit. Once the industry becomes established corruption becomes formalized within the legal system. Much bigger sums are saved through manipulation of tax regulations and legal structures. In fact much of the penny ante corruption of low-level company officials and small businesses servicing the developed industry is stopped. Large companies employ outside management consultants, lawyers, and accountants to survey their operations to eliminate such practices. Finally, large corporations institutionalize "corrupt" practices. They spend millions annually to elect legislators and congressional representatives who will enact laws to protect their interests. The oil depletion allowance for instance is not a corrupt practice by the standard definition, but it probably brings in more money to the oil industry than any number of fraudulent schemes could. When scandals do break out, major corporations hire expensive public relations firms and media contacts to minimize the damage. Often these measures prevent corruption from becoming public in the first place.

The music industry is now approaching this institutionalized phase. Most companies are now part of larger corporations that are experienced in legally manipulating financial regulations and federal regulatory agencies. These corporations already have effective lobbies in state legislatures and in Congress. It is reasonable to expect that in five or ten years corrupt practices like payola will not receive the gross publicity they have in the past, and to the extent they do now.

Mafia or organized crime influence in the music business is somewhat different problem. Organized crime has proven capable of operating at a sophisticated corporate level as well as on the street in a smaller scale, individual manner. Ownership of multimillion dollar casinos in Nevada, control of huge union pension funds, and the near purchase by the Meyer Lansky organization of an operating interest in Pan American World Airways from the Chase Manhattan Bank are all examples.

Involvement in the music industry by organized crime is a difficult thing to measure. The jukebox business has long had mob involvement. Of fifty-eight underworld figures arrested in the 1957 national crime conference in Appalachia, New York, nine had openly declared interests in jukebox concerns. The jukebox industry, while peripheral to most of the recording industry since World War II, is a several hundred million dollar a year business. Much of the counterfeiting and record piracy, estimated at $250 million in 1973, has been carried out by organized crime as well. Certain pop singing stars of the fifties and earlier were popularized by promotion in mob-owned nightclubs. Often the club owners would exact a "manager's" percentage from the singer's salary that continued after the artist passed beyond the club level to records and movies. Frank Sinatra's contacts with crime figures have been widely publicized, and his Nevada casino license was revoked in 1963 after he associated too publicly with Chicago crime boss Sam Giancana. (Giancana was murdered in 1976.)

Plush nightclubs have played a much smaller role in promoting contemporary rock acts. High-living gambling sprees and the use of drugs by leading musicians, however, have brought record companies into contact with organized crime members. CBS reported in a television documentary in 1974 that their artist relations division had had to intercede with a mob figure to save Columbia artist O.C. Smith from a death threat placed on him for nonpayment of gambling debts. The mobster called in to protect Smith was Pat Falcone, now convicted of heroin smuggling and serving a prison sentence. Falcone brought in his influential loan shark friend Anthony "Fat Tony" Salerno, who was finally responsible for the shielding of Smith. After the incident Falcone became Smith's manager.[4] Other rock stars like Jeff Beck (whom Falcone also protected) have been threatened. One record producer cited these threats as almost common:

> I know that the—the Mafia, both the black Mafia and also the white Mafia, they are intimidating a lot of the super rock stars. They—are threatening—if he's a musician, they are threatening to break his playing hand, and if he's a vocalist they are threatening to slit his throat. And they, in turn—they are asking, and they're getting, 25% of the artist's fee in kickbacks.[5]

Mafia figures are also reliable sources of cocaine, the favorite rock drug. The drug connections are either paid in cash with the expense charged to the expense accounts of promotion and A&R men, or paid in album "freebies" (as is nearly everyone else in any way connected with promotion).

One of the most aboveground institutionalized mob involvements in the industry was suggested at Senate hearings in 1973, during the testimony of Gerland Zelmanowitz, a Mafia fanancier turned informer, who said Angelo "Gyp" DeCarlo, a New Jersey mafioso, and Tommy Eboli (alias Tony Ryan), another top-level mobster shot and killed in New York, were partners in Roulette Records. The label's president, Morris Levy, says the mob was never in Roulette, but acknowledged Mafia money in Promo Records, which he used to share with Eboli.[6]*

But how much control crime syndicates can exercise over large national entertainment corporations is still unclear. Many years ago labor racketeers did get a grip on the nationwide motion picture projectionist union, the International Alliance of Theatrical Stage Employees. They used their hold on the union to extort millions of dollars from the major studios. Legitimate union members never received any of the money, of course. They were as intimidated as the companies. At this point—making a guess—organized crime influence in the music industry seems less than mob involvement in the food processing industry, the hotel industry, the trucking business, or for that matter, the Nevada, New Jersey, or Rhode Island state governments.

The record industry is linked generally with the rest of the U.S. business community in its ownership and political character. Like the rest of American business it is racist. How its racism unfolds is particularly important to understanding the business, which depends so heavily on the art of black people.

*When asked by an interviewer what he knew about the Mafia in the record business, Phil Spector replied: "I wouldn't say anything I knew anyway. I just try to hire 'em, that's all. No, I wouldn't say a word about them. 'What Mafia? What record business?' Why must we do the interview on the night of Mission Impossible, man? That's a hell of a good program." (From *Rolling Stone Interviews Vol. 2*, pp. 247-48.)

7 BLACK ROOTS WHITE FRUITS: RACISM IN THE MUSIC INDUSTRY

Billboard reported 1955 as THE YEAR R&B TOOK OVER POP FIELD. Black rhythm and blues records showed a startling 200 percent sales increase over the previous year. As is typical in the trades, the headline was a bit exaggerated. Black artists recording top selling singles had increased only from 3-10 percent of the overall pop market. (See Chart 7.1.) Still the r&b surge had a major musical and cultural impact. Renamed "rock'n'roll" the loud music with its driving rhythms, slurred lyrics, and open sexuality took over the radio airwaves, first promoted by the independent radio stations, then gradually by the major chain owners. The apparent increase in popularity of black music was a mysterious phenomenon for the major powers within the record business. At a grass roots level, even preceding major radio play, white kids were buying up "race" records.

Rock'n'Roll: *A Plaque for Arthur Crudup*

In the 1940s black music was simply and nearly totally segregated from white music. *Billboard* still called rhythm and blues "race" music as late as 1949. The black music business existed as a separate and unequal counterpart to the white controlled major record labels. Except for the few black performers who were bland enough to sell to white

Chart 7.1

Percentage of Black Acts in the Year End Top 50 Singles (1950-1974) and Albums (1961-1974).

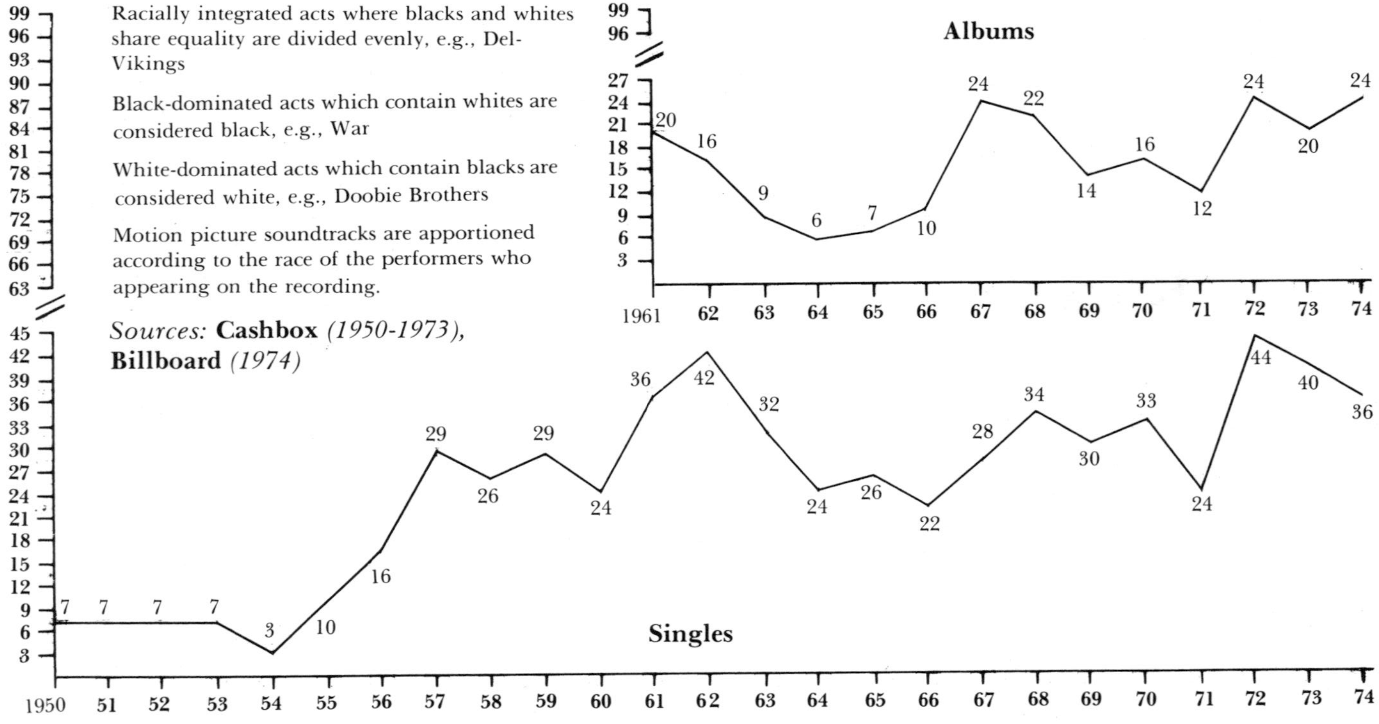

Albums

Singles

Racially integrated acts where blacks and whites share equality are divided evenly, e.g., Del-Vikings

Black-dominated acts which contain whites are considered black, e.g., War

White-dominated acts which contain blacks are considered white, e.g., Doobie Brothers

Motion picture soundtracks are apportioned according to the race of the performers who appearing on the recording.

Sources: **Cashbox** *(1950-1973),*
Billboard *(1974)*

audiences, like Nat King Cole and the Mills Brothers, black music simply was not played on network radio. Black records were sold in black record stores located in ghettos, and jukeboxes were similarly segregated.

By the 1950s, though, the situation had changed considerably. The decline in network radio (and the rise of television) had given independent radio station owners and the emerging small chain owners space to experiment with specialized record programming and cater to a diversity of musical tastes. Local radio was receptive to the grass roots popularity of rhythm and blues records among white kids, and promoted its commercial potential. From city centers to the rest of the country, the r&b craze broke down the segregated pattern of record sales and jukebox selections beginning in 1952.

The r&b these stations were playing, the forerunner of rock'n'roll, was itself a hybrid form. Rhythm and blues, as a category, had been picked up by the music business in 1949 as a more palatable catch-all phrase, replacing the designation "race" music. It encompassed styles as different as gospel, blues, and jazz. In the nationwide musical melting pot made possible by radio, a number of these influences converged to become rock'n'roll. R&b artist Johnny Otis, who had a touring road show and had started an r&b nightclub in L.A. in the early forties, watched the phenomenon on the West Coast. As he describes the process:

> In the early 40's a hybrid form of music developed on the West Coast. What was happening in Chicago was another kind of thing altogether. It was all rhythm and blues later but the Chicago bands, the people that came up from the Delta, came up with harmonicas and guitars—the Muddy Waters and the rest of them. They had a certain thing and we loved it and we were influenced by it to a certain degree. But on the Coast, the people who were there like myself and Roy Milton, T-Bone Walker, and Joe Liggins and the Honeydrippers, we all had big band experience. We all thought in terms of big bands but when it became impossible to maintain a big band and work and make a living we all had to break down and when we broke down, we didn't break down to just a guitar and a rhythm section. We still tried to maintain some of that sound of the jazz bands. We kept maybe a trumpet, a trombone, and two saxes—this was a semblance of brass and reeds and they continued to play the bop and swing riffs. And this superimposed on the country blues and boogie structure began to become rhythm and blues. And out of rhythm and blues grew rock'n'roll.[1]

By the time rock'n'roll was established as an independent style, that horn section had been reduced even further—first to a single saxophone, then to no horns at all, and the rhythmic base of the boogie structure had become even more dominant. Still it is important to note that the formative influences on rock'n'roll as well as virtually all its early innovators (for example, Joe Turner, a blues shouter from Kansas City; Muddy Waters, delta granddaddy of Chicago blues; urban harmony groups like the Crows and Chords) were black. As late as 1956, *Billboard* still referred to the music as "a popularized form of r&b."

The differences between rock'n'roll and r&b were real. They were often motivated by the tastes of the music's new white audience. As Otis observes:

> We found that we moved the white audiences more by caricaturing the music, you know, overdoing the shit—falling on your back with the saxophone, kicking your legs up. And if we did too much of that for a black audience they'd tell us—"Enough of that shit—play some music!" That's why Fats Domino and B.B. King would go over with the black audiences more than Little Richard—although Little Richard was big with the black audience. But still if he got into theatrics, you know, pretty soon the black audience would say—"No. Play some music."[2]

Many rock'n'roll performers exaggerated or invented theatrical stage antics for the kids. In addition to Little Richard's performances at the piano, Chuck Berry's "duck walk," the "animal gyrations" of Elvis Presley, and Bill Haley's sax man bending back during wailing solos to touch his head to the floor, are all examples.

The frantic style of djs promoting the Big Beat also helped define and in some ways caricature the music. For white kids buying records this was their first glimpse of black culture. It was easier for them to relate to it if it hit them in the face. Rock'n'roll was just that forceful. It is the difference, for example, between Elvis Presley's version of "Hound Dog" and the original sung by Big Mama Thornton. She was an old blues "mama" who knew what it was like to be put through the mill. Presley was a good ol' country boy having the time of his life shaking his tail feathers on the Ed Sullivan Show (even if they would not show *that* on network TV). The exaggeration of rock'n'roll made Bill Haley's cover version of "Shake, Rattle, and Roll" a pop hit. Joe Turner's original was certainly more authentic within the r&b genre. In covering Turner's song, Haley domesticated its sexual content, moving the action from bedroom to kitchen. But even with milder lyrics, Haley's exaggerated style intensified the forcefulness of the music.

In the fifties the major record companies were threatened by the rise of the independent companies, who had an almost exclusive hold on the new music, and an uncanny ear, it seemed, for predicting the bizarre tastes of American youngsters. In the battle between major and independent record companies, a battle between white run big businesses and white run small businesses, black musicians lost out. Saul Bihari, as you may recall, paid his musicians with a bottle of liquor. Big Mama Thornton recorded "Hound Dog" three years before Elvis Presley, and according to her the song sold over 2 million copies. But as to her royalties she says, "I got one check for $500 and I never seen another." Presley also recorded "That's All Right," written by Arthur "Big Boy" Crudup. Though the song was a big hit for Presley, Crudup was reputed to have received nothing more than an appreciative plaque from Presley and his manager.

"You're Paying Those People Royalties?"

The pillaging of black culture and mistreatment of black musicians did not begin with the sudden popularity of rhythm and blues in the 1950s. It has been part of the history of American music from the first minstrel shows through the present, and in fact is probably one of the most important forces in the continued innovation and experimentation of black music.

In the 1940s bebop or "hot" jazz emerged as a reaction to black swing bands getting ripped off by white bands. Instead of producing music strictly for dancing (entertainment), the bop musicians turned their energy inward and played for themselves. Bop music was threatening, particularly in its strict orientation toward the black community. Bop musicians talked "funny," did not seem motivated by commercial success, and were geared toward a verbal culture. "Head arrangements," coding technique which had evolved from New Orleans jazz, was a musical shorthand designed not only for musicians who read music but those who played strictly by ear. A brilliant parody of white culture, bop was a challenge to European musical form, melodic structure, and notation, and the beginning of a conscious black aesthetic in music.

But before the end of the 1940s bebop had been forced underground by a coordinated series of frame-ups and police raids on its best known exponent artists. Music sociologist Ortiz Walton suggests:

> Certainly, the invention of heroin cannot be attributed to Jazz or, more specifically, to bop musicians. The same holds true for its manufacture and distribution. Nor, one can be sure, were a few black bebop artists the only members of society who sometimes partook of the drug between the early Forties and mid-Fifties. Yet to judge by the number of arrests, convictions, and widespread publicity given to bop musicians for alleged possession of 'horse,' as it was called, one would conclude that the above statements were true. For practically *all* of the outstanding players of bop were arrested during this period, some, like Sonny Rollins, and Gene Ammons, receiving long jail terms [emphasis ours].[3]

With hot jazz under control in the fifties, r&b artists became the main targets of industry abuse. One of the factors that kept the music from expanding in popularity in its original form was the rapid turnover of artists working the field as *Billboard* reported in a retrospective article in 1952:

> On the whole, the older more established artists held their own throughout the year. Less than a handful of new names established themselves in the pop field, and less than that in the country and western division. The rhythm and blues department where artists turn over like leaves in the fall followed its usual pattern this year.[4]

The usual pattern of r&b turnover continued throughout the 1950s. Groups like the Chords, Charms, Spiders, Spaniels, Crows, and Four Tunes, all of which had hits in 1954, were nowhere to be found one year later. The reason is simple. While the mistreatment of performers was commonplace throughout the pop industry, it was particularly widespread among black artists. R&b artists had trouble getting honest lawyers, managers, fair deals in court, or straight answers to their questions about contract deals. Often taken right off the farm, or like Little Richard, out of a bus terminal kitchen where he was washing dishes, black musicians were routinely swindled out of their publishing rights, left unpaid for club dates, and denied representation by the American Federation of Musicians. While white artists were also ripped off during this period, they were not exploited as thoroughly, as an accepted practice, at the highest levels of the industry.

Ahmet Ertegun, the president of Atlantic, tells an interesting story about Columbia's royalty practices in the r&b field years ago. A Columbia representative came to see him.

> He wanted to make a deal whereby Columbia would distribute for Atlantic Records because we seemed to be very good at what he called "race" records. So I said, "Well, what would you offer us?" He said, "Three percent." "Three percent!" I said. "We're paying our artists more than that!" And he said, "You're paying those people royalties? You must be out of your mind!" Of course he didn't call them "people." He called them something else.[5]

The charting of hits in the national trade magazines also reflected and reinforced the racism of the time. The trade magazines like *Billboard* and *Cashbox* maintained segregated chart listings for pop, country and western, and r&b. The division between pop and r&b, at a time when much r&b material was moving into the pop market, reflected differences in the distribution systems for the two types of music. Pop music was music marketed by the major companies through their main distribution systems, which were national. R&b music was marketed by independent labels with independent regional distributors. Where major labels had r&b subsidiaries, the music was segregated in their catalogue listings and contracted out to independent distributors. R&b songs were first distributed to exclusively black retail outlets and radio stations. If they sold well enough the songs might be picked up by white stores and stations, and crossover into the white market. The black audience was separated as a secondary market, with different and inferior promotion budgets.

Even today the distinction between r&b and pop is based less on music than the race of the performing artists. In the 1960s white artists like Janis Joplin, Joe Cocker, and others performing almost exclusively r&b material were first listed on the pop charts, while blacks, regardless of style, were and are initially relegated to the r&b charts. As Curtis Mayfield described this process as it applied to his former vocal group, the Impressions, "No matter how deep they get into Beethoven or the symphony, that's an r&b product. And pop, that's the white artist."[6] Blacks performing in the country and western genre have even more trouble getting charted appropriately. In 1968, Charlie Pride became the first new black performer since Ray Charles to crack the c&w listings.

The distinct marketing of black and white performers also continues to this day, reflected in the trades by different chart listings (although now Hot R&B Singles has been changed to Hot Soul Singles in *Billboard*). Secondary markets still exist. In most cases, black songs must break out first in the r&b market before getting major attention from the pop promotion network. Many record companies still maintain separate r&b promotion departments. Their strategy seems to be that they are, with relatively little effort, assured of some sales in black markets with established black artists, but any venture into the white market would be risky. The record companies still reinforce and reflect audience racism, while officially arguing that the differences in music are real ones, worthy of distinct charting and promotion. The trades were more explicit when they first confronted the problem of popular black artists. In the 1940s their work was listed simply as "race music." When the music began to cross over into the white market, however, a more palatable term was needed. Record companies toyed with labels like "Ebony" and "Sepia" for a while, but these too were obviously distinctions of color, not musical style. Eventually "rhythm and blues" became the accepted term, until the late sixties conversion to "soul."

Another tactic used against black music was the widespread popularization of "cover versions" of black hits. Strictly speaking a cover record is usually a copy of an original recording which is performed by another artist in a similar style and released within the expected chart life of the original. Chart 7.2 lists some of the better known cover records. Included on the list are some songs that do not fit our strict definition of a cover, like the Beatles' version of "Twist and Shout" and "Roll Over Beethoven," which came several years after the originals, but reproduce them note for note with identical vocal style and arrangement. Other songs commonly identified as covers (for example, the Rolling Stones' recording of Slim Harpo's "I'm a King Bee" and the Cream's recording of Skip James' "I'm So Glad") are not included, since they exhibit some attempt at innovation and are performed in a more contemporary style. In the 1950s covers were used by major companies to recover the inroads r&b made into the white audience of the time. It was found that, at least during the early years of the r&b surge, the white teenage audience (and their parents) were happy enough to buy the white covers of black songs. Some of the early covers, like Presley's "Hound Dog," were artistically legitimate in their own right. But most of them lacked the feeling and sense of excitement that the originals conveyed. Often they were chorus-like sing-a-longs.

Several dozen songs were successfully covered by the majors in the early years of rock'n'roll. RCA began by covering "Cokomo" by Gene and Eunice with a version by Perry Como. Columbia covered the same song with a version by Tony Bennett. Columbia and Victor were so reluctant to have anything to do with rock'n'roll that they were rarely successful even with cover versions. Mercury's Crew Cuts, aptly named for the fifties teenage audience, did a cover of the Chords' "Sh-Boom" (originally on Atlantic's Cat label) that became the fifth best-selling pop song of 1954. They pillaged the r&b list after "Sh-Boom," covering hits like Nappy Brown's "Don't Be Angry" (Savoy), the Charms' "Gum Drop" (Deluxe), and the Penguins' "Earth Angel." Mercury's Georgia Gibbs covered Etta James' "Wallflower" with a cleaned up version called "Dance with Me Henry." The original version sold 400,000 for Modern and the Gibbs cover a million for Mercury. Decca used the McGuire Sisters (on their Coral subsidiary) to cover the Moonglows' "Sincerely" (Chess), and made it the #7 best-selling pop song in 1955, along with their cover of Joe Turner's "Shake, Rattle, and Roll."

Pat Boone, more than any other artist, built his reputation as a rock'n'roll singer by covering black rhythm and blues tunes. His label, Dot, was the most successful company at the practice. Boone recorded "Ain't That a Shame" (Fats Domino), "I Almost Lost My Mind" (The Harptones), and "Tutti-Frutti" (Little Richard), among others.

In order to obtain the far greater royalties from performances, record sales, and sheet music sales available in the white market, small record companies that consigned publishing and copyrights to themselves sometimes took their r&b songs to the big companies to be covered. Such practices kept the black version of the song out of the pop market and denied the original singer the royalties that would have come if the record company/publisher had pushed the first version as a potential crossover hit. By 1956, however, this initial suppression of black music

Chart 7.2
Cover Records and Questionable Revivals

Song	Original Artist	Cover Artist
1. Sh-Boom	Chords	Crew Cuts
2. Earth Angel	Penguins	Crew Cuts
3. Don't Be Angry	Nappy Brown	Crew Cuts
4. Gum Drop	Charms	Crew Cuts
5. Goodnight Sweetheart Goodnight	Spaniels	McGuire Sisters
6. Sincerely	Moonglows	McGuire Sisters
7. Dance with Me Henry (Wallflower)	Etta James	Georgia Gibbs
8. Tweedle Dee	LaVerne Baker	Georgia Gibbs
9. Kokomo	Gene and Eunice	Perry Como
10. Shake, Rattle, and Roll	Joe Turner	Bill Haley
11. Hound Dog	Big Mama Thornton	Elvis Presley
12. Money Honey	The Drifters	Elvis Presley
13. Lawdy Miss Clawdy	Lloyd Price	Elvis Presley
14. Ain't That a Shame	Fats Domino	Pat Boone
15. I Almost Lost My Mind	Ivory Joe Hunter	Pat Boone
16. Tutti Frutti	Little Richard	Pat Boone
17. I'll Be Home	Flamingos	Pat Boone
18. Little Darlin'	Gladiolas	Diamonds
19. I'm Walkin'	Fats Domino	Ricky Nelson
20. Party Doll	Buddy Knox	Steve Lawrence
21. Butterfly	Charlie Gracie	Andy Williams
22. I Hear You Knocking	Smiley Lewis	Gale Storm
23. The Twist	Hank Ballard and the Midnighters	Chubby Checker
24. You've Really Got a Hold on Me	Miracles	Beatles
25. Roll Over Beethoven	Chuck Berry	Beatles
26. Twist and Shout	Isley Brothers	Beatles
27. Money	Barrett Strong	Beatles
28. Do Wah Diddy	Exciters	Manfred Mann
29. Over and Over	Bobby Day	Dave Clark Five
30. I Like It Like That	Chris Kenner	Dave Clark Five
31. Cry to Me	Solomon Burke	Rolling Stones
32. Hitchhike	Marvin Gaye	Rolling Stones
33. Have Mercy Baby	Don Covay	Rolling Stones
34. Hang On Sloopy (My Girl Sloopy)	Vibrations	McCoys

Chart 7.2 (Continued)
Cover Records and Questionable Revivals

Song	Original Artist	Cover Artist
35. Just a Little Piece of My Heart	Erma Franklin	Janis Joplin
36. Cry Baby	Garnett Mims	Janis Joplin
37. Night Time Is the Right Time	Ray Charles	Creedence
38. Good Golly Miss Molly	Little Richard	Creedence
39. Heard It Through the Grapevine	Marvin Gaye	Creedence
40. Up on the Roof	Drifters	Dawn
41. Raindrops	Dee Clark	Dawn
42. I Shot the Sheriff	Wailers	Eric Clapton
43. Locomotion	Little Eva	Grand Funk Railroad

was less generally successful. R&b had merged and changed into rock'n'roll, which was becoming a dominant pop style, and the original versions of songs were in demand by a more sophisticated white audience.

The profitable practice of covering records was greatly helped along by the copyright laws. The appropriate law under which artists worked in the fifties was written in 1909 and does not include recorded material. To this day, it is impossible to copyright a particular recording of a song. One can only copyright the underlying sheet music. Thus while a publisher receives a royalty payment for the use of his publication, and a composer receives a royalty payment for the performance of his music, no royalty is derived from the actual recording. The performer gets paid only for the sale of his records. In a period of heavy cover activity it is the performer who suffers. Most of the performers whose songs were covered were black.

The wording of the copyright laws often led to other abuses. Even though the royalty payments on any piece of music are supposedly divided by the writer and publisher (usually fifty-fifty), many performers who wrote their own material did not get their royalties. According to Lee Berk, vice president and son of the founder of the Berklee School of Music in Boston:

> The U.S. Copyright Act speaks of a situation in which, in the case of an "employee for hire," it is the employer and not the composer who will have the right to be considered author or composer of the work. In such a case, then, the employer would also be the proprietor of the work by the fact of the employment relationship, and would have not only the right to

copyright the work and name himself as copyright proprietor, but also the right to name himself composer as well.[7]

The name which appeared on the record may not have been the actual author of the song. More important, even if the real author is credited on the record, it may not be his name that is registered with the publishing rights organizations (ASCAP and BMI) who collect the royalty payments for artists.

Fred Parris, for example, wrote "In the Still of the Night" and recorded it with his own group, The Five Satins. The record is a rock'n'roll classic and, according to Parris, has sold somewhere between 10 and 15 million copies. Taking the conservative estimate of 10 million copies, "In the Still of the Night" should have been worth $100,000 for the author in mechanical royalties alone (1 cent for every record sold), not to mention performance royalties of 2½ cents for every radio play. If Parris also owned the publishing, of course, the record would have been worth more than twice that figure. As to what really happened with the recording, Parris comments:

> I don't know about BMI. Okay, I used to see BMI on every label but I never knew what it meant. I didn't become a BMI writer—and this is very sad—until after the bulk of the plays on "In the Still of the Night." So what was happening was my name was on the label. So I just felt, "Well, look, my name was on the label, I'm the writer, I'm getting a fair shake. . . ." I'm not going to try and incriminate anyone but somebody else's name was in at BMI as the writer and that was where the money came from. When I got out of the service and went to them with my problem they said, "Okay, we feel sorry for you." And again, I still didn't have enough knowledge of the business and I didn't have enough patience, you know, to say, "Well, I'll see my attorney about this. I'll wait." Instead I wanted the money right then. They said, "Okay, we'll make it retroactive from such and such a date." But that "such and such a date" was nowhere near where the bulk of the sales were. So I came up with a figure of something like $783.[8]

A final factor that helped suppress black music and musicians was the technological innovations in the industry that required equipment changeover in the record buying public. The late 1940s saw the development of unbreakable 45 and 33 rpm records that required different playback equipment than what had been used for 78s. Because of a simple lack of money, the black record audience was slower to make this switch than the white. Victor and Columbia were marketing three speed record changers by 1952, but as late as 1957, r&b records were still sold in the black community as shellac based 78s. Independent producers could evolve formulas for predicting when a song would cross over into the white market on the basis of the demand for the song at the 45 rpm speed. Of course, to go into a separate 45 rpm pressing, an r&b record would have to show evidence of strong sales potential. The dual technology had the effect of diverting the white audience from many r&b artists. While not a conspiracy of the major record companies, the lock and key relationship of new and better records and the new record changers further isolated black music.

Rockabilly: *White or Black?*

The second wave of rock'n'roll performers to hit the charts were white. These were people like Elvis Presley, Carl Perkins, Jerry Lee Lewis, Johnny Cash, and the Everly Brothers—the rockabilly artists. Their music was widely regarded as an amalgam of r&b and country and western, the first tradition upheld by black artists and the second by predominantly white ones. As folk forms, both r&b and country and western exhibited spontaneity which differentiated them from the Tin Pan Alley "pop" of their day. But the relative contribution of each to the equally authentic rockabilly strain was more difficult to pinpoint. Johnny Cash's "I Walk the Line," for example, was closer to traditional country material, with country phrasing and with the bass line providing a steady country rhythm. The Everly Brothers' close harmonies were also characteristic of the country genre, but their unorthodox syncopated guitar riffs clearly established them as a rock'n'roll act. Similarly, Presley, Perkins, and Lewis often sang with a traditional country drawl, but in their up tempo tunes the lyric phrasing and driving rhythmic base came from the r&b tradition. That individual artists borrowed from various styles to different degrees, however, is not sufficient to reduce the rockabilly phenomenon to a simple formula of half white, half black. In fact, country music itself has black influences, and the rockabilly artists owe a far greater debt to black music than to white.

Country and western music is usually seen as having developed from the Scotch/Irish folk tradition. This is probably most true of those immigrants of Scotch/Irish descent who settled in the Appalachian regions. They had little contact with the slave culture of the Southern regions and its African music. In the South, however, where most of the rockabilly artists came from, there was a continuing interaction between the European and African cultures, despite the legally enforced separation of slavery. The blues was originally a form of rural folk music that was widely popularized by blacks. According to critic Peter Guralnick, "Blind Lemon Jefferson, a native of Wortham, Texas, travelled extensively all through the South. He is remembered as far east as Virginia and the Carolinas and he seems to have been a formative influence in the lives of nearly as many white musicians as black ones."[9] Once free to travel, the bluesmen spread the influence of black music all over the deep South. The banjo, for example, an instrument most readily identified with country music, is of African origin and was first popularized by black musicians. Even the word "banjo" is African derived.

The crossover between African and European music goes back even further. In post-Renaissance Europe, the music of the peasant culture, with oral traditions and highly improvisational styles, often existed quite separately from the "classical" music of the high court. Classical music was based on the rational tempered diatonic scale (a standard eight note scale). Composed only for performers who could read music, it was tightly disciplined and allowed little room for improvisation. The looser structure of peasant cultural forms rendered them more receptive to influence from neighboring cultures. Such crossovers were not limited by race. The Tarantella, a folk dance that swept medieval Europe, was originally brought over from Africa. When waves of European immigrants migrated to the New World in the 1600s, various folk forms came along with them, but the diatonic scale became the foundation for American popular music. Within this general framework, and not without significant deviation, the African slave culture exerted a profound influence on our musical development.

African culture can be seen as inherently more musical than European, since the meaning of words often depends on the pitch at which they are spoken. This quality gives African speech patterns their own musicality.

This heightened sense of language-as-music extends to African concepts of musical instrumentation. In African music, instruments are often used to approximate human speech. They are not simply external devices used to produce notes and "melody," as in European music. African talking drums, for example, did not send messages by using an abstract Morse Code-like system of tapping. They replicated the pitch and rhythmic patterns of the language; they really talked. Centuries later, Ray Charles said that it was this human quality that attracted him to country music instrumentation:

> I really thought that it was somethin' about country music, even as a youngster. I couldn't figure out what it was then, but I know what it was now. . . . Although I was bred in and around the blues, I always did have interest in other music, and I felt the closest music, really, to the blues [was country and western]. They'd make them steel guitars cry and whine, and it really attracted me.[10]

After the Civil War, the blues emerged as a distinctly Afro-American music in the folk tradition. At first the blues had no standard form or rhythmic pattern, being totally improvisational and derived from the Field Hollers. Interacting with the European diatonic structure, the blues soon became standardized into two or three common forms. The best known of these is called the "classic" blues. It has a twelve bar structure and follows a tonic, subdominant, dominant (that is, E, A, B⁷) chord pattern.

The musical notation of the European scale could not, however, accommodate the way bluesmen really sang. Their deviations from expected melodic regularity came to be known as "blue notes." To the Western ear, a blue note is a note which sounds a little flat, but not flat enough to be the next note down on the scale. In fact the blue note is an Africanism. In the European scale, the smallest interval between notes is a half-tone. In African song, which bears a close relationship to speech patterns, it is a common practice to "bend" the notes of a given scale to achieve a particular mood. Many of the bluesmen thus sounded as if they were singing in between the notes of the diatonic scale. They were thought to be "off key" by musically limited Western critics. In fact they were singing in their own hidden scale. Blue notes could be found all over rock'n'roll, in for example Elvis Presley's recording of "Hound Dog" and Jerry Lee Lewis' "Whole Lotta Shakin'," both of which also follow a classic twelve bar blues structure.

Another Africanism that found its way into rock'n'roll was the "call and response" style. Most commonly identified with gospel harmonies, the style was introduced to America in the work songs of slaves, and may have found its way into white culture through prison chain gangs. Repetitious work lends itself to the form, with a leader setting the pace and the rest of the group responding vocally. In African culture the call and response style was used in religious ceremonies as well as collective work. In America it found a new religious home in the Christian revival meetings where, denied the worship of their original gods, the slaves integrated it with European melodies and harmonies. In African music the call and response style exists not only as a lyric form where one vocalist answers another, but also as an instrumental style where an instrumental response reinforces and comes just after the vocal lead. Both forms were found in rock'n'roll. The black vocal groups of the fifties and early sixties used gospel styles as the basis of their sound. All of the blues based rock'n'roll music employed instrumental calls and responses. In the white dominated rockabilly style, instrumental calls and responses can be heard in "Whole Lotta Shakin' " and Bill Haley's "See You Later, Alligator" and in many of the Everly Brothers' tunes.

The most significant contribution black music made to rock'n'roll was its rhythmic base. African music is polyrhythmic, capable of sustaining more than one rhythm at a time. In America, where slaves were denied the use of drums (thought to be politically dangerous, since they could be used to signal an uprising), other rhythmic devices were developed. In revival meetings, call and response gospel music was punctuated by polymetric finger popping, handclapping, and foot stomping.

Polyrhythms are not found in European folk music forms, or their American country derivatives, which invariably accent the so-called "strong beats" and reinforce a single unsyncopated sustaining rhythm. The Big Beat that was rock'n'roll, in which the drummer accented the second and fourth beats of each measure on a snare drum while keeping the sustaining 4/4 rhythm on a bass drum and ride cymbal was derived from a basic African polyrhythm. It was found in virtually every up tempo rock'n'roll tune, including all the rockabilly tunes. (When he first broke, critics said Elvis Presley sang hillbilly in r&b time.)

In addition to the musical Africanisms which pervade rock'n'roll, including the rockabilly genre, the influence of black music and musicians can be seen in the personal lives and styles of the most memorable rockabilly performers.

Prior to the emergence of rockabilly, Sam Phillips' Sun label had been almost exclusively a blues label, Phillips himself having recorded blues giants like B.B. King, Bobby Bland, Howlin' Wolf, and James Cotton early in their careers. With Elvis Presley his dream of a white boy who could sing black came true and transformed Sun Records into an overwhelming commercial success. Most of the white artists who recorded for Sun had been living with and among black people all their lives. Jerry Lee Lewis talks about his growing up:

> I used to hang around Haney's Big House, that was a colored establishment where they had dances and such. . . . We was just kids, we wasn't allowed in. So we'd slip around to the back and sneak in whenever we could. I saw a lot of 'em there, all those blues players. No, it wasn't anything about us being white, we was just too young. See, it wasn't such a big deal like it is today. Somebody wanted to go down, it wasn't no big thing just because it was a colored place. Of course we was about the only ones down there.[11]

Carl Perkins, the son of a sharecropper, explains:

> I was raised on a plantation in the flatlands of Lake County, Tennessee, and we were about the only white people on it. I played with coloured kids, played football with old socks stuffed with sand. Working in the cotton fields in the sun, music was the only escape. The coloured people would sing, and I'd join in, just a little kid, and that was coloured rhythm and blues, got named rock'n'roll, got named that in 1956, but the same music was there years before, and it was my music.[12]

Elvis Presley, whose stage act bore more than a faint resemblance to Chicago bluesman Bo Diddley's, grew up in the Mississippi delta that produced such seminal blues figures as Muddy Waters, Howlin' Wolf, John Lee Hooker, and Jimmy Reed.

Having borrowed heavily from black culture, rockabilly was still a legitimate musical movement that integrated black based blues with country and western styles. It had its own identity and, obviously in people like Presley, Perkins, and Lewis, performers of real originality and talent. Unfortunately it is impossible to separate the popularity of rockabilly from a racist pattern that exists in American music, whereby a style that is pioneered by black artists eventually comes to be popularized, dominated, and even defined by whites as if it were their own. That is the history of black music in America from ragtime, to swing, to jazz, and rock'n'roll is no exception. Johnny Otis comments:

> Black artists have always been the ones in America to innovate and create and breathe life into new forms. Jazz grew out of black America and there's no question about that. However, Paul Whiteman became the king of jazz. Swing music grew out of black America—created by black artists Count Basie, Duke Ellington—but Benny Goodman was crowned king of swing. In the case of rock'n'roll, Elvis Presley—and in this case not without some justification because he brought a lot of originality with him—became king. Not the true kings of rock'n'roll—Fats Domino, Little Richard, Chuck Berry. . . . What happens is black people—the artists—continue to develop these things and create them and get ripped off and the glory and the money goes to white artists. This pressure is constantly on them to find something that whitey can't rip off.[13]

For this reason, it is possible to see someone like Elvis Presley as both the "greatest rock'n'roller of them all" and, as Margo Jefferson suggests in an essay on white musicians stealing from blacks, "the greatest minstrel America ever spawned [who] appeared in bold whiteface."

In a society where all races shared equality, it would be possible to judge the contributions of anyone on their individual merit. In a country where the enslavement of blacks was a founding principle and miscegenation remains a source of terror, it cannot be done. Ray Charles points out:

> When you get a guy who come up and say, like Elvis Presley, let's face it, man, you had more people goin' out and shakin' their asses and stuff like that. You know where Elvis *got* that from—he used to be down on *Beale* Street in *Memphis*. That's where he saw *black* people doin' that. Ain't no way they'd let anybody like us get on TV and do that, but *he* could 'cause he's white.[14]

Schlock Rock: *The Death of Rock'n'Roll*

If the rockabilly artists were not frauds, then the next wave of white heroes to make the rock scene certainly were. As TV exposure drew a final clear line between Presley and his black roots, the medium was used to promote the new teen idols. These were people like Frankie Avalon, Fabian, Ricky Nelson, Bobby Rydell, Connie Francis, Paul Anka, and Neil Sedaka. They were descendants of Pat Boone, and winners of Elvis Presley look alike contests. As a group they had a string of hits that would gag a maggot and glut a market: "Tiger," "Turn Me Loose," "Dede Dinah," "Gingerbread," "Venus," "Bobby Sox to Stockings," "Why," "A Teenager's Romance," "Be-Bop Baby," "Stood Up," "Poor Little Fool," "Lonesome Town," "Travelin' Man," "Kissin' Time," "We Got Love," "Swingin' School," "Who's Sorry Now," "Stupid Cupid," "Lipstick on Your Collar," "Lonely Boy," "Puppy Love," "Oh! Carol," "Calendar Girl," and on and on.

The schlock rockers. They had no identifiable ties to any musical form (except the elusive notion of pop) but since they had some semblance of rhythm and were young, they were marketed as rock'n'roll singers. They effectively gave rock'n'roll its final facelift of the fifties by whitening up the hit charts. The percentage of black musicians to make the year end singles listing had risen from just 3 percent in 1954 to an all time high of 29 percent in 1957. Schlock rock was never original or interesting enough to knock black music out completely, but it did contain its growth for the next few years. In the late fifties schlock emerged as the main trend in singles sales.

The beginnings of schlock in Philadelphia were linked with the rise of the Dick Clark TV show, American Bandstand. It was not only beautifully simple in design, but covered the market for music with a beat, while keeping black dancers away from white ones and providing a daily product acceptable to adults as well as kids. Clark's antics have been detailed. He was a second choice for the show, getting it after r&b disc jockey Al Jarvis turned down ABC on the grounds that the network wanted no black artists appearing. Clark willingly conformed to the racist network policy, however, and his loyalty to the network, and the tremendous success of Bandstand, kept him in a privileged position during the payola investigations.*

The second generation of schlock brought to the fore Chubby Checker, whose "The Twist" was the first in a series of dance crazes that swept the country in the early 1960s. His song covered the Hank Ballard and the Midnighters tune of two years previous. Ballard's version was

*ABC has stuck by Clark through the years. In the early 1970s the network decided they wanted to alternate Clark's Saturday Bandstand show with a black dance party show. The logical choice would have been the successful "Soul Train," syndicated out of Chicago, hosted by Don Cornelius. Clark announced that "It's my time slot, if ABC wants a black bandstand, I'll do it." He produced a bad imitation called "Soul Unlimited" which was then bought by the network.

much funkier. It sold extremely well in the rhythm and blues market, but there was little crossover into pop, and did not even hint at the national fad Checker triggered later. Checker was a real pop phenomenon. Like Bobby Rydell before him, he was created by a corporate decision in the offices of Philadelphia-based Cameo-Parkway Records. Even his name seems to have been manufactured, made to sound vaguely like Fats Domino (Fats-Chubby, Domino-Checker). Although Checker has since gone on to a certain amount of independent work, Charlie Gillett's assessment of his early years is still accurate. "To a greater extent than any previous rock'n'roll singer, Checker was a puppet who carried out the instructions of his producers."[15]

The twist itself is ambiguous socially. It was first successful at a time when the black liberation movement in the United States was surfacing, but its leading exponent was a harmless corporate controlled black man. It was essentially a frivolous fad welcomed by white audiences as a retreat from the worries of bomb shelters and missile gaps and an ever-imminent imagined war with Russia, but it released white bodies from their petrified stiffness, and anticipated more openly sexual dances. "The Twist" was a number one hit record twice, once in 1960 and again in 1962. Particularly in northern cities, it introduced dancing that was accessible to an older white audience as a commercial base for numerous discotheques. The twist was so powerful, particularly at pulling adults into the rock market, that major r&b artists and record labels had no alternative but to jump on the bandwagon. Sam Cooke recorded "Twist the Night Away" in 1962. Atlantic reissued an album of old Ray Charles material as "Do the Twist with Ray Charles."

A bright spot in the rock'n'roll drought was the so-called "girl groups" of the early sixties. The vocal harmony groups of the 1950s had roots in *a cappella* street corner society, and could not compete with the sophisticated musical backing and studio production that had since developed. The new vocal groups, almost exclusively black women, were products of the studio. Their work was excellent music, but after 1963 only the Chiffons ever had another Top 10 single ("Sweet Talkin' Guy" in 1966). Despite their sophisticated production, these artists simply faced too many obstacles; they were in many ways a throwback to a fifties style, they were women, and they were black. Their surge of popularity was more (pleasantly) surprising than their demise. (See Chapter 8, pp. 272-278, for more on the "girl groups.")

The English Invasion

All the factors limiting the popularity of the girl groups helped the growth of the Beatles, who were white males performing in a more contemporary style, as well as being very competent musicians and brilliant songwriters. But like other English invaders their music was hard driving rock'n'roll, and their inspirations and many early recordings came from black artists.

Shortly after their introduction to America in 1964, the Beatles re-released such classics as "Roll Over Beethoven" by Chuck Berry, "Twist and Shout" by the Isley Brothers, Barrett Strong's "Money," the Shirelles' "Boys," "Long Tall Sally" by Little Richard. Similarly, the Animals brought back Ray Charles' "Hit the Road Jack" (written by Mayfield) and Sam Cooke's "Shake." The Rolling Stones did Rufus Thomas' "Walking the Dog," "Hitchhike" by Marvin Gaye, a number of Chuck Berry tunes including "Carol," "Talking about You," and "Around and Around," and went deeper into the country blues genre with Slim Harpo's "I'm a King Bee."

The Beatles were open in crediting r&b artists as their early influences, especially the work of Chuck Berry, the Miracles, Chuck Jackson, and Ben E. King. But while openly and repeatedly acknowledging their debt to black music, and touring with black r&b greats like Little Richard, the Beatles along with the dozens of other English groups that quickly followed them were simply much more marketable than the black artists they imitated.

Within two years of the Beatles' arrival, there were no less than twenty English rock groups on the American charts; before them there had been none. In April 1964, just four months after their introduction to America, Beatles records were issued on five different labels and they had twelve singles in *Billboard's* Hot 100, including the top five positions. For about three weeks the Beatles accounted for 60 percent of all singles sold. Promo men complained that "Stations have been playing our records like spot commercials between Beatles tunes." Black acts in general showed a sharp decline on the singles charts from an all time high of 42 percent in 1962 to 22 percent in 1966, the lowest point since the initial surge of rock'n'roll in the mid-fifties. The girl groups had been treading water, but now with the Beatles' arrival, they were put under completely. On the album charts, only three of the Top 50 LPs for the years 1964 and 1965 were by black artists.

By 1965, deluged with the glut of English rock and the newly emerging folk-rock, even the r&b stations were playing white artists. The product was called "blue eyed soul." Along with performers like Presley, the Beatles, the Stones, and the Righteous Brothers, all of whom had some claim to the r&b market, such performers as Barry McGuire, Brenda Lee, Sonny and Cher, and Billy Joe Royale were also being played on black stations. Black stations were so squeezed for advertising dollars in face of the predominance of white groups that they had no alternative but to add pop material to their playlists and in many cases hire white djs.

Virtually the only black music on white radio, during this period, was produced out of Motown. It was clearly black but not harsh and, like the moderate Civil Rights Movement of the period, did not emphasize a separate black consciousness. Motown's president Berry Gordy trained his acts to appeal to a largely white audience (by the late sixties, Gordy would comment that any successful Motown hit sold at least 70 percent white), and exposed them in white run and patronized night clubs whenever possible.

The Great White Blues Controversy

By 1967 the British invasion had become virtually indistinguishable from a much larger cultural change going on in the United States.

The indigenous movement began musically with the rise of folk rock in 1965 and flowered with the growth of the San Francisco scene and its commercialization during the 1967 Summer of Love. Throughout the period of 1964-69, following the popularity of blues influenced British bands, there was also a revival in interest in blues among American rock'n'rollers. Groups like the Blues Project in New York City, Paul Butterfield Blues Band in Chicago, and later, the Electric Flag in San Francisco were able to successfully market blues albums with no hit singles to hang them on. In the second wave of English groups during 1967-69, the Cream stood out as a heavily blues influenced group. Ginger Baker, Jack Bruce, and virtuoso guitarist Eric Clapton included Skip James' "I'm So Glad" on their first album. At about the same time in America, Janis Joplin was conspicuous as the only white woman performing heavily r&b influenced material. Still with Big Brother and the Holding Company, she recorded "Piece of My Heart" (released by Erma Franklin a year earlier) and Mama Thornton's "Ball and Chain." Both here and in England a number of other white groups performed in contemporary r&b styles with considerable success. Most notable were Mitch Ryder and the Detroit Wheels, the Young Rascals, and, from England, the Spencer Davis Group.

The counterculture movement was largely a white-inspired, middle-class phenomenon, and reflected the growing separation of black and white struggles toward radical consciousness. In black popular music there was a resurgence of closer-to-the-roots hard driving rhythm and blues recorded in the Memphis-Muscle Shoals region of the South. Artists like Sam and Dave ("Soul Man"), Arthur Conley ("Sweet Soul Music"), and Percy Sledge ("When a Man Loves a Woman") were some of the new chart toppers. Aretha Franklin was crowned "Lady Soul." When James Brown had his first Top 10 hit in 1965 ("Papa's Got a Brand New Bag"), he was still "the hardest working man in show business," but now was King of Soul. In 1968 his hit single boasted "Say It Loud, I'm Black and I'm Proud." In the forefront of the new style was the Memphis based Stax-Volt studio, where production techniques were reminiscent of the simplicity of fifties production and Booker T. and the MGs were the resident rhythm section. Commenting on the different styles of Stax-Volt and Motown, Otis Redding said:

> Motown does a lot of overdubbing. It's mechanically done. At Stax the rule is: whatever you feel, play it. We cut everything together, horns, rhythms, and vocal. We'll do it three or four times and listen to the results and pick the best one. If somebody doesn't like a line in the song we'll go back and cut the whole song over. Until last year (1967), we didn't even have a 4-track tape recorder. You can't overdub on a one-track machine.[16]

During 1967 and 1968 black music of this type increased significantly on the year end charts.

Blacks seemed to have become more traditionally militant and directed in their political movement, while some whites dropped out completely from mainstream experience and, for the first time, tried to form an "alternative" to middle-class life. Into their cultural experimenting they carried both their parents' guilt over racism and fear of militancy along with a desire both to separate themselves from black experience and music, and not objectively rip it off. (Unlike the countercultural hippies, other white youths were as militant as political blacks.)

In an editorial in an early 1968 issue of *Rolling Stone,* self-proclaimed spokesman of the San Francisco sound Ralph Gleason sounded off in a piece called simply "Stop This Shuck Mike Bloomfield." Gleason attacked the former lead guitarist for the Butterfield Blues Band for forming the Electric Flag and persisting in playing blues. Both the bands that Bloomfield had played in were, significantly, integrated. "They keep insisting that the name of their game is chitlins and collard greens and its actually chicken soup, baby, chicken soup," said Gleason, who went on to praise the white San Francisco bands for being themselves:

> One of the most encouraging things about the whole hippie scene and rock music in San Francisco which grew out of it is that no one is really trying to be anything other than what he is. The white sons of middle class America who are in this thing are not ashamed of being white. They are the first American musicians, aside from the country and western players, who are not trying to sound black.[17]

Two weeks later the lead singer for the Electric Flag, Nick Gravenites, responded to Gleason in an article entitled "Stop This Shuck Ralph Gleason." Like Bloomfield, Gravenites was a veteran of the Chicago blues scene. He argued that in Chicago, blues musicians were mixed racially and that a white musician who was part of that scene could not simply be considered a prostitute or imitation. He touched on an important aspect of the controversy involving money in asking "Where are the mixed bands in San Francisco? . . . maybe . . . it's not profitable to have blacks in a band playing to a predominantly white audience." Gravenites had a low opinion of the white San Francisco groups, adding:

> Come on Ralph, say it. Pigpen [of the Grateful Dead] can't sing his way out of a paper bag. There's a Turkish born Greek dishwasher in a Greek restaurant in Boston that can sing circles around Grace Slick. . . . Ralph Gleason talks about originality being the 'key.' Originality is not the key, Ralph. Original shit is no different than unoriginal shit. It's all the same Ralph. It's shit.[18]

The puerile debate represents a high point in discussion among whites of what we call The Great White Blues Controversy, a debate which continues to this day. Unfortunately discussion of sixties white groups borrowing heavily from black sources often degenerates into one group of whites guilt tripping another, which only obscures the real economic dimensions of racism with purely aesthetic debates. When economics is considered as an issue, it is usually in the form of a reparations argument which does nothing to change racist conditions and is essentially reformist. Racism among musicians and their audience has a life of its own, but is most pernicious in the capitalist economic system, where songs and art are reduced to the same status as other commodities, and where the natural tendency for cultures to influence and borrow from one another becomes theft.

The aesthetic controversy has raged for years. Can whites sing and play blues, gospel, rhythm and blues, soul? Through the years, of course, they have, some not very well, some like Presley so well that their racial identities were a surprise to black and white audiences alike. Many producers and writers for black music have been white. Lieber and Stoller wrote "Hound Dog," virtually all the material for the brilliantly comical Coasters, and some of the Drifters' best work after 1959. Phil Spector produced a number of the black girl groups and then the most baffling blue-eyed soul group ever, the Righteous Brothers. In the sixties Stevie Winwood's interpretation of "Down and Out" when he was still with the Spencer Davis Group sounded exactly like Ray Charles, who himself comments:

> I remember one time a guy asked me, hey, man, do you think a white cat could ever sing the blues? Which is a legitimate question. It didn't hurt my feelings. I feel that *anybody*, if you ever have the blues *bad* enough, with the background that dictates to the horror and suffering of the blues, I don't give a damn if he's green, purple—he can give it to ya.[19]

252

Charles' view recognizes cultural crossover. As noted with such traveling musicians as Blind Lemon Jefferson, and the lives of the rockabilly artists, cultural overlap has been particularly true in the Southern United States.

A more sophisticated view of the aesthetic argument assigns merit to whites who borrow from black sources, but contribute their own originality of interpretation. Margo Jefferson explains:

> Borrowing itself is not the question, since music lives by eclecticism. Still if you borrow, you must return, and nobody wants an imitation back if they've lent out an original. Bonnie Raitt, Carole King, Bonnie Bramlett, Randy Newman, Joy of Cooking, Tracy Nelson, Bob Dylan, and some others have characters or traditions of their own to which they have joined blues and jazz. . . . But far too many white performers thrive and survive on personas and performances that are studies in ventriloquism and minstrelsy, careless footnotes to a badly read blues text.[20]

The middle sixties white groups were at least more honest in acknowledging and popularizing their blues roots than traditional fifties cover artists like Pat Boone, who simply diluted the r&b idiom in Dot's quest for a palatable white sound. The white blues groups of the sixties turned their white audiences on to a whole heritage of black music that might otherwise have been suppressed. Mick jagger, for example, once pointed out:

> We didn't want to do blues forever, we just wanted to turn people on to other people who were very good and not carry on doing it ourselves. So you could say we did blues to turn people on but why they should be turned on by us is incredibly stupid. I mean what's the point in listening to us doing "I'm a King Bee" when you can listen to Slim Harpo doing it.[21]

In addition to becoming aware of famous artists like B.B. King and Muddy Waters, white audiences heard of (and sometimes bought the old records of) more obscure blues and r&b musicians. The black blues turn-on had begun with the work of white urban blues folkies like Jesse Colin Young, Dave "Snaker" Ray, "Spider" John Koerner, and John Hammond. But the blues inspired rock groups, simply because they were electric and danceable, educated a much wider audience.

As blues became increasingly pop, of course, the aesthetic controversy became more clearly an economic one. It is hard to imagine Eric Clapton being severely criticized for playing blues guitar if he were not making millions off his music, while the bluesmen whose licks he copied are starving to death.

In the 1960s, artists performing songs by old bluesmen were more principled in paying royalties than Colonel Parker and Elvis had been. Thought Slim Harpo was already dead when the Stones recorded "I'm a

King Bee" his widow did receive some thousands of dollars in royalties, as did Skip James for the Cream recording of "I'm So Glad."

Even where the cover artists are more honest, the rest of the industry often is not. Arthur Crudup's "That's Right Mama" and "My Baby Left Me," for example, have been recorded by everyone from Presley to Elton John, Creedence Clearwater Revival, Canned Heat, Rod Stewart, and Tracy Nelson, among others. With a track record of performances like that, Crudup's songs should have been worth well over a couple of hundred thousand dollars. Crudup, however, never saw any of the royalty money. As he explained shortly before his death, "The company paid my manager but he didn't pay me. I was to get 35 percent of every dollar he received. Well, I failed to get it." Crudup's manager was Lester Melrose, who died a few years ago. After his death Crudup sued his manager's estate for the money. As of 1974, it appeared that a settlement of some $60,000 had been reached with the Melrose estate and the publisher of the songs, Hill and Range. Crudup and his family were flown up to New York to receive the check but at literally the last minute, while Crudup was waiting in the offices of Hill and Range's lawyer to finally get his money, he was told the matter would be taken back to court. Crudup died a few months later.

At the height of the blues revival Mississippi Fred McDowell recorded an LP called "I Do Not Play No Rock and Roll." It was released on Capitol and sold 25,000 copies. Dick Waterman, who later managed McDowell, arranged for the original Crudup suit, and may have done more than anyone else in the business to get work for the old blues men and protect them from rip offs, called the level of sales "Mindboggling. That's probably all of the Skip James and John Hurt and Sun House and Robert Pete Williams and Mance Lipscomb added together." Even in the middle of the blues revival the original country bluesmen rarely sold more than 3,000 or 4,000 copies of their albums, compared to the millions of covers.

The McDowell album was recorded at Malaco Studio in Jackson, Mississippi, and the masters sold to Capitol in California. Commenting on McDowell's cut of the album sales, Waterman hesitantly comments:

> I'm pretty careful what I say here because I don't want to get into libelous lines here. I think Fred was getting 3 points, 3 royalty points (3%). Based on the retail list price of say $4.95, $5.00 per album, 3 royalty points is 15¢ an album, which is very low, very very low. And I think Fred's deal was that he had to pay studio costs: the engineering, the tape, the mixing, the editing, the album art, the jacket, things like that. That's kind of a heavy handed deal, but its not that unusual. I do think, however, that there was a clause that when the Malaco people, several of them, went to California to try to market the tape that Fred's royalties ended up paying for the air fares and

the hotel and all of the expenses involved with the negotiation of the album. Now that's a little bit off the wall. That kind of strains credibility . . . you had to pay those off before you could go on to profit and at 3%, which was very very low, you just were not going to make it anyway.

Now when you consider that he was a solo musician, well of course they had a bass and drums sitting in on the session. But the cost of making the album . . . there were just no heavy expenses. This didn't have to be done on 16 track or 32 track with a heavy mixing schedule. It was simply not an expensive album to have brought in. The album could have been brought in for $1,000, $1,200, I don't know, something like that. . . On the other hand with Malaco producing the album in the studio, they could set their own studio rental fee as being $10 an hour, $50 an hour, $100 an hour, and to this day I don't know what it was, simply because they were paying themselves and then debiting Fred's account and at 3% he was simply never going to pay that off.[22]

Another way old bluesmen get ripped off is having their publishing declared in the public domain. Again, Waterman comments:

Sometimes you will run into a traditional bluesman who does a song and you honestly feel that its his song. So you apply for a copyright on it and they give you a copyright on it but then you try to collect the publishing money when someone else does it and the record company says "Well this is public domain," and you come back and say "No, I hold copyright such and such" and they say "This was done by Huddie Leddbetter in 1944, this was done by Tommy Johnson in 1927, this was done by Roosevelt Sykes in 1931." In other words they'll come back to you with three or four versions of the song and it may have a line or 2 or 3 or 4, it may have a verse or two, it may be virtually the whole song. And it's a way they can avoid paying. Somebody has to pay for a lawyer. If you don't have the money or the resources to go pay for a lawyer, lawyers are very expensive and copyright law moves very slowly, then you have to sit and weigh it and say 'Who's done that song? Is it on an Allman Brothers? Is it on a Rolling Stones?' And at that point you're going to sit and think about it and say 'Okay, I think it's worth going after.' If it's done by a new group, new label, new album, it's not going to be worth it at all. Record company lawyers work on delaying tactics and it becomes very cumbersome and very slow.[23]

Where industry people try to right the wrongs done to black musicians their proposals usually take the form of reparations for the past. Waterman suggests that:

Musicians who have attained powerful international popularity should realize that royalties on a "B" side would provide Skip James [who died in 1969] or Son House or Sleepy John Estes or John Hurt's heirs with more money that they could earn in months of coffee house work or small concerts.[24]

Ralph Gleason has called on leading groups to insist on work for bluesmen:

> Most blues originators have been betrayed, pillaged, and victimized by everybody, black and white, who dealt with them over the years. Their tunes have unclear publishing title even now. Who owns something that was recorded under ten different names in five years may never be settled. The argument over whether someone has stolen a tune or whether it's public domain has lots of ramifications. But there is surely one thing that can be done and this is to give these men work and it is really up to the leading groups themselves to insist on this.[25]

In some cases such efforts have been made. In 1969 John Mayall recorded an LP about J.B. Lenoir and donated the royalties to his widow. Of major white groups, the Young Rascals made probably the most sincere effort at getting black musicians work. They were a blue-eyed soul group that recorded almost exclusively r&b material, who were played heavily on black radio, and whose records consistently sold in the r&b market. In the late sixties the group announced that they would accept no more live engagements unless half the bill was black. At one point they turned down an appearance on the Ed Sullivan show because of what they felt were "racist policies." At present, medium level white blues guitarist Bonnie Raitt tries at times to include old blues people on her bill. She is managed by Dick Waterman.

Getting black musicians work may be a first step in balancing the economic inequities that flow from, and are at the root of, racism. But the effort does little to combat directly the racism within the industry and the audience. Reparations rely for their effect on the good will of white performers who have made it already by doing black material. There is no way around that contradiction, which is not overcome by charitable acts. As Jerry Butler said:

> The offensive part is that black music that has been denied can be accepted because guys in white skin are doing it. But to be copied—imitation is the first sign of greatness. So if anybody imitates something that I do, I feel a little flattered. For me, for a guy to say, "Wow, that's great music I want to learn how to play it," that's a compliment. But [for the audience] to accept it from him and not accept it from me is a putdown.[26]

Given the vastly expanded market for rock, the conditions present for the development of black music are not appreciably different now from what they were back in the 1950s. Black acts still get less money for personal appearances than whites, and the percentage of black musicians in the upper reaches of the pop market has not expanded with the increased influence of their music. Where black musicians make it big they are exceptions, usually uniquely accessible to white audiences or really extraordinarily talented. Simplistic arguments about public demand for white acts are undercut, at least in part, by the evident lack of access blacks have to network TV and other major broadcasting outlets (particularly true in the early and middle sixties) and the fact that it is black-rooted music that is usually being performed.

To preserve their artistic integrity, black musicians must innovate in a way that is not immediately cooptable by whites. Traditionally this experimentation has been in jazz music, which still attracts young black artists. Unfortunately, the experimentation is only marginally commercial. To be really successful at making money for what they do, black musicians are usually reduced to imitating their imitators. Jazz keyboard player Herbie Hancock scraped along for years winning *Downbeat* polls and critical raves doing jazz before giving in and cutting a million selling pop jazz-r&b album. The most successful black record company, Motown, consistently guided its artists away from harsh soul sounds, toward heavily orchestrated music that could cross over to the white market. During the height of the blues revival by white groups, a final irony was played out in the career of Jimi Hendrix.

Jimi Hendrix: *Psychedelic Bluesman*

Hendrix was a virtuoso r&b guitarist who started as a kid in the 1950s with steady backup work for groups like the Isley Brothers. But he never found an audience for his early American guitar playing, and went to England to develop a caricatured sexual image and a more commercial guitar style.

Eric Clapton described his rise to popularity:

> When he first came to England, you know, English people have a very big thing towards a spade. They really love that magic thing, that sexual thing. They all fall for that sort of thing. Everybody and his brother in England still sort of think spades have big dicks. And Jimi came over and exploited that to the limit, the fucking tee. Everybody fell for it. Shit.
>
> I fell for it. After a while I began to suspect it. Having gotten to know him, I found out that's not where he's at at all. That stuff he does on stage, when he does that he's testing the audience. He'll do a lot of things, like fool around with his tongue and play his guitar behind his back and rub it up and down his crotch. And he'll look at the audience, and if they're digging it, he won't like the audience. He'll keep doing it, putting them on, playing less music. If they don't dig it, then he'll play straight, 'cause he knows he has to. It's funny.

Clapton continued:

> He had the whole combination in England. It was just what the market needed, a psychedelic pop star who looked freaky, and they're also hung up

about spades and the blues thing was there. So Jimi walked in, put on all the gear, and made it straightaway. It was a perfect formula.[27]

Hendrix brought his English success back to the United States, where he made (and spent) millions of dollars, selling millions of albums, virtually all in the white market. Toward the end of his career, he tried to change his music, but the business interests surrounding him pressured him not to change from his commercial, psychedelic, oversexed black man image. The pressures of a situation that did not permit open musical growth and experimentation drove him to his Electric Ladyland studios after the breakup of The Experience. There he logged some 800 hours of tape (the Warehouse tapes) exploring the music he would have liked to do in public. Working with musicians like John McLaughlin and other avant garde jazz notables, he tried to fuse jazz, r&b, and contemporary rock styles. None of these tapes were released during Hendrix's lifetime.

Hendrix was one of the few black musicians with enough financial security to spend long periods of time in the studio creating concept albums rather than just hit singles. When albums came to provide a greater and greater percentage of total industry product in the sixties, record companies still tied their black artists to singles production. They were not confident that the large advances necessary for albums would be paid back in sales from the less commercially viable black groups. This fact may give a distorted picture of black success in the late sixties and early seventies. Whereas black artists generally showed a high percentage of hits in the singles market, peaking in 1972 with 44 percent of the year end Top 50, by this time singles sales accounted for only 13 percent of industry dollar volume. In LP sales, blacks have never accounted for even one quarter of the market. It is only relatively recently that leading pop black artists have had the necessary record company backing to put together concept LPs of the sort the Beatles and other white groups have been doing for ten years.

Black Capitalism: *Motown*

As the reformist Civil Rights Movement with its frequently white leaders and musical spokespeople evolved into a black liberation struggle in the late sixties, black music changed and experienced a renaissance. Riots in Newark, Detroit, Watts, and Cleveland and the emergence of militant political organizations like the Black Panthers were paralleled by a return to close-to-the-roots hard driving rhythm and blues, much of it originating in the Southern studios, mentioned above. The revival of r&b was symptomatic of the political changes in the black community.

It additionally focused the attention of government and the business community on the music industry as an ideal structure for coopting black revolt. It was thought that blacks should get more involved in the business, to let off a little steam in the artistic end, make a little money, and be absorbed into the still marketable American Dream. In May of 1969 Senator Jacob Javits gave a speech before an RIAA conference that was riddled with unintentional puns. In it he expressed "hope that the industry . . . will move forward . . . by striking a resounding note for black capitalism." Employing a variety of tactics that ranged from cajoling to rational appeal, promise to threat, government and big business looked as if different parts were going to get behind the program to make the music business a model of integration. *Billboard* wrote editorials urging the industry to hire more blacks. The FCC notified radio stations that they would have to integrate at the disc jockey and executive levels. Of course neither *Billboard* nor the FCC had much real power.

The idea of black capitalism has long been kicked around as a palliative for the inequities in the way wealth and power are distributed in the United States. In those areas where blacks are traditionally allowed achievement (precisely because they are fields penetrated by individuals, and not masses of people) like sports and entertainment, the idea is a particularly persistent one. It is also especially pernicious, since it seems less illusive and bankrupt a strategy.

Motown Industries is the largest black owned nonfinancial company in the United States. It was begun in the early 1960s by Berry Gordy, a middle-class jazz record salesman who realized that blacks preferred r&b styled music. Working closely with Smokey Robinson on an early string of hits, Gordy developed an elaborate, Spector-like production technique for his artists. He laid rich gospel harmonies over lavish studio work and came up with a perfect pop formula: music that was clearly black, but not threatening, and very danceable. Gordy built his acts from the groud up and groomed them for a long commercial haul. When he started he was a progressive force that provided a commercial frame for black musicians at a time when they had trouble getting any attention elsewhere. Gordy's concern with detail in career planning and management of his acts was unprecedented for black musicians.

But the strengths of the company were also its weaknesses. As his artists matured, they came to resent Gordy's constant interference with their lives and work. A number of important musicians left the label. As Martha Reeves explained it:

> The company grew, the tree got weak, and the limbs started falling off. The
> first limb that fell off the tree was Brenda Holloway. That's when it started

happening. Florence Ballard [of the Supremes]. Then the leaves started falling off, everybody felt it.[28]

What had begun as a haven for black singers and songwriters became oppressive artistically. In 1971 *Rolling Stone*'s Jon Landau wrote that, "Of all the major record companies, only Motown remains a completely in-house operation. One has the feeling, whether it's true or not, that Berry Gordy passes personal judgment on every single that comes out on his label."[29] *Fortune* magazine reported in 1967 that Gordy himself owned every single share of Motown stock. The company was grossing about $30 million per year at the time.

In addition to controlling artistic freedom, like any businessman, there is some evidence of financial malfeasance on Gordy's part. In 1968 Holland, Dozier, and Holland, the company's most successful writer-producer team, sued the corporation for $22 million in back money. They no longer produce for Gordy. David Ruffin of the Temptations was fired for asking "hard" questions about financial affairs. According to Ruffin, when the Tempts were earning $10,000 a night, the group members were only being paid $500 a week. Eddie Kendricks left the Temptations in sympathy for Ruffin, but he could not leave the label. "They have me," he commented in 1971. "I think they even own my face." (As to how much artistic freedom he was allowed, he said simply, "None.") Martha Reeves has complained, "I never handled my own finances. I always had a road manager who collected my money and took it back to Motown, with a green sheet. When the money ran out I couldn't pay the Vandellas any more and I lost the Vandellas."[30] Even during the height of her group's popularity, Reeves claims she was paid only $200 a week. In 1974 she got a release from Motown after MCA, her new label, paid Motown some $200,000 in past debts, and is now rebuilding her career. The Four Tops and Gladys Knight and the Pips left when their contracts ran out.

Important exceptions to the departure of name talent are Stevie Wonder and Marvin Gaye, both long time successful Motown artists who still work for Gordy. For both, the struggle to gain artistic freedom was hard fought. As soon as he turned twenty-one, Stevie Wonder reacted against Motown's restrictiveness by demanding his royalty payments, a sum of about $1 million (representing, on sales of some 30 million units, a low royalty rate of about 2½ percent) that had been held in trust for him by Gordy. "Stevie Wonder came to me," said Ewart Abner, then president of the Motown record division, "and said, 'I'm twenty-one now. I'm not going to do what you say any more. Void my contract.' I freaked."

Independent of Motown, Wonder then sank about $250,000 of this money into the production of his first progressive album, Music of My

Mind. Following its overwhelming success, he returned to the label, but under much more favorable conditions. Wonder now owns his own publishing and is the first Motown artist to do so.

Marvin Gaye has also come a long way from the days when Motown paid him "five dollars a side" for some early sessions. Always seen as a maverick, Gaye resisted Motown's formula music mentality right from the beginning.

> I didn't like the feeling of being made to do something, simply because a bunch of people said that this is what I should do, as though I'm a robot and couldn't think for myself or didn't know what I liked or disliked, and the biggest insult was that they always claimed they recognized me as a talent, but they never proved it by letting me do my own thing.[31]

Unlike Stevie Wonder, Gaye's sense of loyalty (he is married to Gordy's sister) would not permit him to leave the label. But years of stubbornness succeeded in getting the company to back his first concept LP What's Goin' On, followed by Let's Get It On, both million sellers in the seventies. Primarily through Gaye and Wonder, Motown is beginning to learn that loosening the reins a bit can add millions to their coffers.

Today's Motown Industries (based in L.A., not Detroit) is an international conglomerate which dabbles in a number of investment media other than music, especially film (*Lady Sings the Blues,* which starred Diana Ross as Billie Holiday). Gordy appointed E.G. Abner president of the record division. Before joining Motown in 1964 Abner had headed the old Vee Jay label in Chicago which recorded the Impressions, the Four Seasons, Jerry Butler, and others. Rather than be a progressive force serving the black community Gordy has marketed that community in a sophisticated way, to a largely white audience. He is no worse than other businessmen in the industry, but no better, as he uses his blackness to disguise his capitalism.

The Industry and Blacks

The advancement of the black capitalism strategy in other areas of the music business has followed a similar pattern, with little being really changed in the structure of power within the business or its effect on people. During the late sixties blacks broke into network TV advertising (usually one per ad) for the first time. In the early 1970s, a breakthrough of sorts came in the black movie. Films like *Shaft, Superfly,* and *Trouble Man* were for the most part black directed and produced, black acted, and black scored by the likes of Isaac Hayes, Marvin Gaye, and Curtis Mayfield. While generally more progressive politically than middle-of-the-road white adventure thrillers, the so-called "blaxploitation" flicks were really just another profitable business venture that took money out of the black community. Other films like *Putney Swope* and *Sweet*

Sweetback were distinct in their own way and more progressive, especially *Sweetback*, directed and written by Melvin Van Peebles, which was a startling left-wing film that innovated in production techniques as well.

Elsewhere in the music business, blacks made some inroads in production. Kenny Gamble and Leon Huff started with a $700 bank loan and rolled it into 30 million-selling singles in a five year period, with twenty-two records on the charts in 1968 alone. Along with West Philadelphia producer Thom Bell, they created the soft soul sound currently associated with that city, which they describe as "not as bluesy as the Memphis/Muscle Shoals stuff, not as pop as Detroit." In 1970 Gamble and Huff grossed over $1 million.

At a convention of black television and radio announcers in 1969, Stan Gortikov, then president of Capitol, publicly accused the industry of being "too damned white." Between 1969 and 1971 Stax-Volt and Warners, in addition to Capitol, responded by opening recording studios in ghettos, designed to tap local talent, much as Chess used to travel through the delta recording bluesmen. Nothing much has come of the studios. Many record companies experimented with black promotion men during this period, and kept them when they found they sold better to hip FM djs than their white counterparts, in part because they could subtly guilt trip white radio djs better, partly because they understood and related to the music. The secondary r&b radio markets have become all that more important in breaking black songs, too, and there again, black promo men are a better investment.

These innovations in production and promotion of records were not planned out in advance by the major white-controlled record companies. They evolved as a better procedure for marketing and creating new records. The slight changes and expansion of the racial base of the industry were profitable moves because records, as Sam Goody pointed out long ago, "are a poor man's luxury," and sell particularly well in black markets. According to Al Bell, vice president of Stax-Volt, "Statistics show that on a per capita basis, blacks, regardless of income, buy more records and record playing equipment, and spend more money on entertainment than anyone else in the major markets."[32] While black promotion men are used discretely to push records, the main avenues of talent promotion, the concert/club circuit and radio, are still fully run by whites.

As late as 1972, four years into the "back to black capitalism" movement, black artist Jerry Butler complained that there were only three major black concert promoters in the entire country: Teddy Powell in New York, Regal Sports in St. Louis, and Henry Winn in Atlanta. The concert market and promoter system that operates today (as detailed above in the section on Concert Promotion) grew out of the white freak ballroom circuit, then moved into colleges, and out into a broad commercial white market. The black community does not have enough money to sustain an entirely separate concert circuit, and many white promoters complain of racial tension when they've presented black acts. Black rock acts, both because of audience racism and promoter racism and fear of disturbance, are effectively excluded from the dominant concert network.

The overwhelming majority of concert acts touring today are white. The concentration of large crowds of people at rock concerts has always held out the possibility (sometimes realized) of violence and riots, but there is a double standard applied by white promoters as to what sort of crowd difficulties will be risked. Promoters and booking agencies have a special fear of interracial riots. For this reason promoters tend to avoid booking black acts popular enough to draw equally from white and black audience markets, while booking agencies have a standing policy of not packaging black acts with white. For these reasons it is difficult for growing black artists to get exposure in the pop concert field. Most black acts successful at selling their records in the pop market do not command commensurate concert audiences. Most acts appealing to a nearly exclusively black audience are relegated to clubs, usually marginal financial institutions whose heyday as mob decision centers and speakeasies has long passed. Clubs simply do not compare with the white concert market as a way to promote and build new acts.

The white-dominated AM radio establishment may in fact have marched backward during the period 1969 to about 1972. In 1969 *Billboard* announced "Soul Cut on Top 40 Stations." Commenting on the decision among many AM stations to drop black music, Jerry Wexler said:

> Radio stations who were serving their audience, or so they thought, didn't want to burden them with the sound of breaking glass in Watts or the sirens coming from Detroit, which was what R&B music meant at the time. In their opinion, R&B would be disturbing to their middle class listeners, so they took most of it off the radio.[33]

Throughout this period of objectively suppressing r&b, black music continued to sell. In its own inimitable style, *Billboard* reported that "with few or no picks or plays on pop stations soul product is parlaying heavy pop dealer sales with new sound sophistication to positions on the Hot 100." Jerry Wexler explained the phenomenon as follows:

> The old myth used to be that an R&B record could sell maybe 200,000 copies and, in order to get any real muscle in sales, had to sell pop (to whites). But now I think millions of sales are possible on 'secret service' hits—records that whites may not really be familiar with.[34]

In a period of ever tightening AM playlists many record companies, such as United Artists, have turned to FM stations to expose their black acts to the white market. In some cases, like War, this strategy has had considerable success. As always, however, r&b stations continue to be the major port of entry for black groups, and on Top 40 AM radio suppression continues. Commenting on Top 40 radio's general soul phobia, Jerry Butler complained that "They say their format is contemporary music and that they only play top hits and yet when there's a (black) hit that they're not playing it's either bad programming or prejudice."[35] Pop stations can be forced to pick up a soul single, but only if it becomes a breakout hit on an r&b station first. According to some program directors, the unofficial rule of thumb today is to add a soul record to the playlist only after it reaches the Top 10 of the *pop* charts *nationally*. And even this rule does not always hold true. One program director on a major station stated that "On and On" by Gladys Knight and the Pips received no airplay from any Top 40 station in Boston even though it had reached the Top 5 on the national pop charts. "Living for the City," Stevie Wonder's hit single, was picked up by Boston's WRKO only after it had sold 2 million copies.

Despite all the industry announcements about affirmative action in hiring black disc jockeys on pop stations, there has been really little increased representation of blacks in Top 40. Station managers told *Billboard* things like "We interviewed a lot of them, but we never heard back from them," and "We found lots of young kids, but they were too raw to even take and try to train." Even with the establishment of outreach and training programs blacks remain critically underrepresented in broadcast media. In San Francisco in 1971, for example, two coalitions—the Community Coalition for Media Change and Blacks in Media for Affirmative Action—joined forces to protest the "racist, insensitive" policies of local stations KGO, KPIX, KNBR, KFRC, KSFO, and KCBS. Yet as of 1974, FCC statistics showed that the proportion of blacks employed in Bay Area radio and television was less than 10 percent (149 of 1,589 employees). Jesse Jackson had a little more luck at Chicago's black-oriented WVON where he negotiated a contract change that nearly doubled djs' salaries.

While black radio sometimes provides blacks with entry level opportunities, many aspire to the larger white-owned networks and chains where the increased visibility can raise their salaries as much as $25,000 yearly. One of the most important AM radio chains, RKO-General, is ahead of the rest of the country with a token black ("and sometimes two," reports Bruce Johnson, president of the radio division) in all of the major markets. What soul stations remain are in bad financial shape. As then president of NATRA Del Shields complained in

1969, "There are men on soul radio stations being paid $65 a week, and how many black vice presidents are there in radio and TV?"[36]

Black djs on black stations are still poorly paid, which was one of the reasons NATRA attacked the current payola investigations as particularly hypocritical. There is a certain dishonesty in white businessmen attacking black djs for taking a little money on the side, when they hire so few blacks themselves and white djs, on the average, make so much more money than blacks (a standard AM salary running around $30,000, compared to a half or third of that for top soul stations). Jesse Jackson charged at the time of the first grand jury payola action of the seventies that "blanket indictments and rumors of payola are intimidating black oriented stations' music directors and removing playlists from (black) community accountability."[37] Rodney Jones, a dj with WVON, said in late 1973 that charges about payoffs to black broadcasters resulted in many radio stations across the country shortening their playlists to the point of eliminating the small and independent record companies producing black music.

Without AM radio exposure of soul and other contemporary forms of r&b, FM stations along with the traditional r&b outlets have become a major radio marketing medium for the music. A recent survey in Los Angeles showed that 80 percent of the black male radio audience listened to FM. And with the overall expansion of the music market, limited radio play and word of mouth still sell black product.

For those blacks who do make it through to stardom, as with whites, the pressure and necessary compromises to hit the big time separate them from their original community. The career of James Brown is a dramatic example of this process. In the fifties and early sixties he was a struggling r&b artist whose hard driving music was uncompromising, and unpopular in the white community. When he first broke into the pop market in the mid-sixties, his style was the embodiment of the brashness and anger felt by young blacks. "Say It Loud, I'm Black and I'm Proud" was a big hit, and an anthem for the less consciously political black cultural movement. In 1970 Brown was quoted in *Rolling Stone* as saying:

> Me and Nixon don't get along. He asked me to go along to Memphis in the campaign. I don't want to be his bullet proof vest. I didn't want to protect him from my people, deceive them. Make them think he's with me and I'm with him.[38]

But the years of success took their toll. In 1972 Soul Brother #1 became Sold Brother #1. For an alleged $200,000 contribution, Brown abandoned his "people" to endorse Nixon for the presidency. The move hurt his credibility in the black community and, more important for Brown, his record sales. Always an opportunist, as Nixon began to go down Brown recorded the hits "Payback" and "Funky President."

There are some suggestions of change within the industry. During the past few years United Artists records has distinguished itself with a roster of extremely talented and successful black acts (War, the Cornelius Brothers and Sister Rose, Ike and Tina Turner, and Bobby Womack) which it claims it markets right along with its white rock artists, and not in an inferior r&b network. The most spectacular of the UA success stories is War, formerly a backup band for Eric Burdon, after he left the Animals.

Having racked up their 6th platinum album (one million record/tape units) and more than $33 million in record sales, War is an important exception thus far to the rule that it is necessary to cater to white audience tastes in order to generate significant album sales in the pop market. *Billboard* magazine attributes the group's success to a young and more sophisticated black record buying public. The analysis is limited, however, since any album selling multimillions of units is selling in the white market as well. United Artists claims credit for their nondiscriminatory marketing technique. It is difficult to explain the staggering success of the band, but there is some evidence that UA is not all that it claims to be. In 1974 War initiated legal proceedings to buy their way out of their contract with the company, presumably because of its very low royalty rate. Another one of UA's major artists, Bobby Womack, who had a million-selling single with "Understanding," says:

> I think my company stinks. . . .They say, "Hey man, Don McLean is the one," and I say, "Yeah, man, but look how long he's been holding the ball and y'all done thrown the sink on him and everything, shit on him, and this nigger's still selling with nothing. You give me what you give him in terms of promotion and Bobby Womack would be a superstar.[39]

Conclusion

Africans were brought to this country in chains. Until the North sought to break the South out of its backward, plantation economic structure in the Civil War, blacks were held as slaves. Since the Civil War they have been maintained as de facto slaves, a bottom line in the economic order that stretches unbroken from the nineteenth century through today.

More than 300 years of ruling class, now largely corporate, oppression of black people has deeply ingrained racism as an attitude throughout white America. Historically, the way different ethnic groups have become assimilated into the mainstream workforce is by being replaced by another group on the bottom, a substitute marginal workforce. The

Germans and Irish were replaced by Italians, who were replaced by the Polish, and so forth. Blacks have not been "replaced" in this way, nor will they be. The great expansion of the United States economy that was fueled by the cheap labor of immigrants is now largely taken up by the cheap labor of workers in Asia, South America, the Philippines, and other areas of extensive U.S. investment. Racism at home is a fully conceived weapon in the hands of employers, who use it to keep the workforce divided against itself.

According to the U.S. census data, the percentage of the black population entering the labor force has been decreasing over the last thirty years, while the percentage of whites continues to climb. The number of blacks in trade unions is even more dismal. The absolute earning power of blacks has increased over the last fifty years, but declined relative to whites."

Black music performed by black artists accounts for about 20 percent of industry product, which corresponds to the percentage of the overall population that is black. But the contribution of black music to mainstream pop is far greater than its record sales would indicate, and the seemingly equitable percentage of black performers obscures the reality that blacks are excluded from most other important positions in the industry. Beyond these performers, the profits from black and black-influenced music still goes primarily to white executives, producers, agents, promoters, and, of course, stockholders. The current system of ownership and profit does little for the black community, or for the encouragement and growth of music within that community. In a continually expanding rock market, the demand for black performed r&b, in classic or contemporary style, has not expanded proportionately to the demand for white imitation.

The de facto segregation of whites and blacks and objective oppression of blacks by whites extend to every major aspect of the U.S. economy, including the music industry. The business is a particularly interesting and glaring example of this pervasive racism, since it has grown fat off the creative impulses and culture of black people. Through the years black music has been stolen, covered, and pilfered in more subtle ways, while its artists have been effectively suppressed and denied their due.

8 LONG HARD CLIMB: WOMEN IN ROCK

Women, like blacks, have always been important to popular music. But whereas blacks have developed musical forms that have been borrowed and popularized, women have most often been only the chief subject of songs, black or white. Only recently has a women's music begun to develop as a separate genre, autonomous from male pop music. The absence of women as creators in pop music can be called sexist just as the stealing of black music is seen as racist. Definitions should be made clear here, at the risk of sounding academic, because most people close to pop music have only recently given the issue any thought.

Sexism is the systematic discrimination against and degradation of women, and the denial of equal power to women in human affairs. Sexism is as pervasive in rock music as in any other form of music. It pervades the structure of the music industry along with the lyrics and instrumentation of the music itself.

Rock'n'roll and later rock music have reflected the image of women held by larger American society. Those images in rock have been grittier and often more realistic than those put forth by adult pop and classical/opera but the essential portrayal of men as aggressor/initiator/definer and women as passive-object/follower/defined has remained the same. As the general society changes, so do the superficial images: from woman as masochistic blues mama in the thirties and forties to teen angel in the fifties and foxy lady in the sixties. The more explicit sexuality of sixties rock helped tone down one more layer of romanticism covering relations between men and women, as did the wider movement for (male) sexual liberation, and thereby helped to force a reappraisal of traditional relations between men and women. But except for this backhanded effect the rock music of the sixties was no more liberating for women than the rock'n'roll and r&b of the fifties. The last few years have finally led to a women's movement in American society with a certain amount of force, and this movement has led to the first few changes in the standard rock view of women and to the beginnings of an expanded participation by women in rock music.

The problem facing women in popular music has been different from that facing blacks. Historically in America, blacks have comprised a culturally homogeneous nationality. Since the Second World War they have been integrated with whites at factories and work places in most parts of the country, but their ghettoization has preserved separate dynamics in black literature and music. Development of a strong cultural, often musical identity has been necessary for survival. Partially as a result there is an identifiable black American music. Racism in popular music and in the pop music industry can then be discussed as the stealing and suppression of black musical forms and the exploitation of black musicians.

A women's culture has existed historically, reflected in the art and artifacts of women in traditional roles such as housekeeper, mother, wife, and in the various attempts by women to break out of these roles and participate in the general power-giving institutions of society. Women have fashioned art from quilts and rags in farm sewing-bees, developed oral history in passing accounts of events from grandmother to granddaughter, assumed sole midwifery duties in certain epochs. Still, women's culture does not have the homogeneous, national character of black culture. Women have existed in relation to men and have held the class position of the men they are related to. Whereas in America black people have by and large been unified at the level of the poor and working class, women have been divided among all economic classes.

These factors coupled with denied access to musical instruments have kept women's music from making major contributions to mainstream popular music. Women's music, when it has surfaced at all, has been confined to hearth songs, and lullabies and nursery rhymes, to church choruses, and to noninstrumental lead singing. Arranging, composing, and instrumental work have most often been left to men.

Because of the content of the lyrics ("Under My Thumb," "Whole Lotta Love," "High Ball Shooter," ad infinitum), the macho posturing of male rock stars, and until recently the near total absence of women playing nonacoustic instruments, rock music has often been seen as a sexist *form* of music. Like any other form, however, rock is not inherently sexist. What makes it sexist is that women have been denied all of the essential power roles necessary to its creation: drummer, guitarist, songwriter (with few, mostly recent, exceptions), and on the industry side, producer and dj (again, with some recent exceptions). "Every once in a while," says Nicky Barclay, keyboard player for the all-woman band Fanny,

> people will lay it on us that we are playing male music. The only reason that's true is that because up until now it was always made by men. We're playing rock and roll. People would ask us if we're playing hard and loud because we feel we have to be like guys to be accepted. We're playing hard and loud because we are four musicians who like rock and roll and that's the band we're in.[1]

The sexuality of rock which gives the music its elemental energy is, in our opinion, also not inherently sexist but only sexist in its current mode. The sexuality of most rock music is clearly *male* sexuality, but it is not clear that it must, or will, remain that way as women begin to pick up electric guitars, which they are now doing, and as women begin to listen to female rock musicians, as they are beginning to do in larger numbers. Rock music's sexuality has the positive aspect of destroying puritanical sexual organization. Wherever it is controlled by women rock musicians, this liberation can be given a nonsexist character while preserving the high energy of the rock medium. Perhaps the long denial of women from any creative positions in rock music can be attributed to the fact that male society acts to prevent women from attaining positions which are sexually initiating.

For women to boycott rock music entirely would deny them a source of energy that cannot be had with nonelectric forms such as folk music. Folk and acoustic music can serve as a reflective retreat in which to hammer out more progressive lyrics and forge a women's collectivity, but in the context of modern communications technology, it can only remain an anachronism with a limited audience.

The history of women in rock music has been a difficult one. Dues have been high, successes rare. Gradually a small number of women artists have broken down many of the taboos and images that have kept them from developing a women's music. Whether a truly female perspective based on women instrumentalists, songwriters, producers, and disc jockeys will develop within rock music in the near future remains to be seen. In large part success will depend on the fate of the movement for women's liberation outside of rock music. It is this movement that has often led to the significant recent changes in the participation of women in rock music, and it is the women in this movement that will provide much of the audience and support for further changes, at least until American society, male and female, becomes less sexist and can as a whole support a nonsexist rock music.

The Fifties: *"He Hit Me (And It Felt Like a Kiss)"*

The revolution in music that was rock'n'roll effectively removed women from the pop charts for seven years, until the advent of the "girl groups." (See Chart 8.1.) Prior to the beginnings of rock'n'roll in 1955, female artists accounted for one-third of the positions on the year-end singles charts. Most of these women were pop artists like Patti Page, Doris Day, and Rosemary Clooney, who were not replaced by women singing rock'n'roll. By 1958 the proportion of women on the singles charts had declined to 8 percent.

Fifties rock was written and performed almost exclusively by men. Women did not sing; they were sung about. The most common term used to describe women was "baby," and the number of hit singles that refer to women as "baby" is staggering. Among the lyrics of the Top 50 singles in 1956 and 1957 there were "Bebop Baby," "Honeycomb, Won't You Be My Baby?," "Be Bop a Lula, She's My Baby," " Since I Lost My Baby," "Since My Baby Left Me," to mention a few.

An alternative to the "baby" theme was the "angel" theme—the idea that women were sent from the heavens ("Little Star," "Blue Moon"), that they were goddesses ("Diana," "Venus"), that they were presently in heaven ("Teen Angel," "Tell Laura I Love Her"), or that they were ethereal creations ("Dream Lover," "All I Have to Do Is Dream"). Women were almost never characterized as real people with developed personalities and emotions or down-to-earth (male) functions.

Where women were given personalities at all, they were "Butterflies," "Little Town Flirts," and "Runaround Sues" "movin' on down the line." The doublesided morality of the time allowed men this freedom to "shop around." As Gogi Grant sang in "The Wayward Wind" (1956), this was expected of men, even sanctioned. A woman who slept around, on the other hand, was branded a whore.

In 1962 Phil Spector produced a Jerry Goffin/Carole King song for the Crystals that might have summed up the preceding decade for women's music, if it had not been censored: "He Hit Me (And It Felt Like a Kiss)."

Leading the Pack: *The "Girl Groups"*

In the early sixties women became a recognized trend in rock'n'roll for the first time. Female vocal groups or "girl groups" as they were called at the time began to hit the top of the charts. In addition to the Orlons,

Chart 8.1

Percentage of Women in the Year End Top 50
Singles (1950-1974) and Albums (1961-1974).

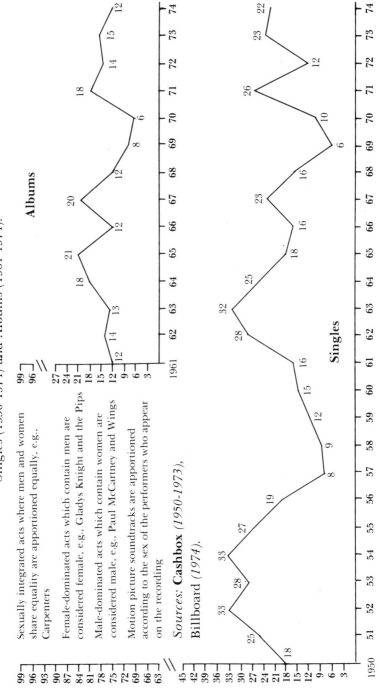

Albums

Singles

Sexually integrated acts where men and women
share equality are apportioned equally, e.g.,
Carpenters

Female-dominated acts which contain men are
considered female, e.g., Gladys Knight and the Pips

Male-dominated acts which contain women are
considered male, e.g., Paul McCartney and Wings

Motion picture soundtracks are apportioned
according to the sex of the performers who appear
on the recording

Sources: **Cashbox** *(1950-1973),*
Billboard *(1974).*

the Crystals, the Sensations, the Chiffons, the Essex, the Ronnettes, and the Jaynettes, there were the Shangri-Las and the Dixie Cups, and the Motown groups—the Marvelettes, the Supremes, and Martha and the Vandellas.

Prototypic of the "girl groups" were the Shirelles. The group first recorded for Decca, producing the hit "I Met Him on a Sunday." Decca had no faith in the group, however, and their next records were put out on Sceptor Records. Sceptor (now Sceptor/Wand) had been initially formed by Florence Greenberg, one of the few women ever to emerge as a record company executive. Mrs. Greenberg formed her company to handle the Shirelles, who had been classmates of her daughter in Passaic, New Jersey. Using a plaintive gospel call-and-response style laid over the big city studio technique of producer Luther Dixon, the Shirelles produced a string of rock'n'roll classics between 1960 and 1962: "Will You Still Love Me Tomorrow," "Dedicated to the One I Love," "Mama Said," "Baby, It's You," and "Soldier Boy." By 1962, the commercial appeal of the female vocal groups was proven and Dixon's production techniques, simultaneously developed by Phil Spector and Berry Gordy, had become a virtual science.

The reason for the popularity of the girl groups lies largely in what they were *not:* schlock rock. They were the diametric opposite of that other major trend of the time. Whereas the schlock scene was dominated by white male individuals (Neil Sedaka, Freddy Cannon, Bobby Rydell, Bobby Vee, Bobby Vinton, Brian Hyland, Paul Anka), the women's acts were black female groups. (The Shangri-Las were the only significant group in the genre that were white.)

The girl groups contributed the only really sexual music during the lull period in rock'n'roll. The fifties rockers were off the charts and the schlockers gave out a clean image that usually only appealed to teenage girls. There were no sexy white women singers at the time. White women were still kept on a pedestal in the days before the "sexual revolution." The only readily available sex objects, then, were black women. Remembering the Ronnettes, *Rolling Stone* wrote in 1968:

> They were the tough whorish females of the lower class, female Hell's Angels who had about them the aura of brazen sex. The Ronnettes were Negro Puerto Rican hooker types with long black hair and skin tight dresses revealing their well-shaped but not quite Tina Turner behinds. . . . Ronnettes records should have been sold under the counter along with girly magazines and condoms.[2]

The other female groups may have been less "brazen" than the Ronnettes but they were often received by whites in the same way.

274

In their role as sex objects for the largely white audience for pop rock'n'roll, the girl groups were treated in much the same way that the black blues women of the thirties had been. Although black male singers were often effectively confined to clubs, these black women singers were allowed to record because they posed no threat to previously white male sexual standards. As Ortiz Walton explained in *Music: Black White and Blue:*

> Mamie Smith was the first singer to make a Blues recording. It was so successful that record companies sought out a number of singers (female) hoping to get another Mamie Smith. Some of these "finds" were Eliza Brown, Ida Cox, Lil Green, Lucille Hegamin, Rosa Henderson, Victoria Spivey, Ethel Waters, and Edith Wilson. LeRoi Jones has astutely pointed out that the reason black women, rather than black men, were hired for these appearances is that America could always tolerate orgiastic interplay between white men and black women but could not stand white girls or white women being titillated sexually by black men.
>
> It is because of this sexual attitude that the Western white man has usually seen black music, especially the Blues, through blinders and has misrepresented the frank sensuality and expression of the life force as something licentious. This has led to an ambivalent attitude toward black music, an attraction for, and a threat to, what has been forbidden in the West—sex.[3]

Another reason for the emphasis on black women singers in the thirties rather than men was historical: black women were less transient than black men because they could get steady work as domestics and stay longer in one city. To be recorded a blues singer had to be in a major city, not traveling in rural areas, because portable recording equipment was unavailable until after World War II.

The female vocal groups of the early sixties were different from the schlock roster in another way. The Philadelphia crowd had few roots in anything that could be considered authentic rock'n'roll. They were image stars, rock'n'roll politicians, the creations of television. The female groups could be traced directly back to the r&b and vocal styles of the fifties, and, as in fifties rock'n'roll, the medium of their popularity was exclusively the record, and not television. Like the vocal groups of the fifties, the female groups of the early sixties were anonymous. Nobody knew that Martha's last name was Reeves, or who the "Vandellas" were. No one knew the names of the women in the Chiffons, the Shangri-Las, or the Crystals. These groups were only sounds, their members could never be cultural heroines because they did not have identifiable personalities. The Philadelphia schlock stars, on the other hand, had developed images. They were seen on television and their names could be matched with real faces. Their likes and dislikes, hobbies, and even their secret flames were written about in teen fan magazines.

If you were teenage and female at the time, you would have quite likely wanted to be one of those secret flames. Since men were the culture heroes, women by and large derived their self-esteem from the men they were allied with as wives or girlfriends. Women had no culture heroines of their own—no role models who existed independent of relationships with men. Social change was beginning in the early sixties, but in the pop market this was still the era of Saturday night dates, going steady, and nice girls who don't. Even the tough anonymous women in the female vocal groups did not sing about themselves but instead about their men who were "Rebels" and "Leader(s) of the Pack." Their songs sang: "He's So Fine," I wish he would "Be My Baby," when he called me on the phone I pleaded "Don't Hang Up," until "One Fine Day" he walked me home, and "Then He Kissed Me." I knew that if I played my cards right I'd be "Goin' to the Chapel" but of course, that was "Easier Said Than Done," "Da Doo Ron Ron Ron, Da Doo Ron Ron."

A Folk Heroine Emerges

Although much better than the schlock artists, the female vocal groups were pushed from the charts with them when the Beatles crashed onto the scene in 1964-65. Their tough, rebel image, although great rock'n'roll persona, was a throwback to the fifties and could not stand up to the much slicker image of the Beatles.

Joan Baez, the only woman to become a culture heroine in her own right, did not come from rock at all. Her traditional folk style made a brief impact on the popular market in the early sixties during the developing political activism of the Civil Rights Movement. The notion of social and political change demanded a relevance that the lyric vacuity of pop music was unable to deliver. In their search for a more substantial alternative, the activists discovered folk music. At the time, the distinction was made (often vehemently) between "ethnic" folk and "commercial" folk. In the image of the slick, college oriented Kingston Trio, Peter, Paul, and Mary were considered commercial. Joan Baez, by comparison, was considered ethnic.

Joan Baez must be seen as a positive step for women: she was politically active, outspoken, and controversial; she was not visibly dependent on a man, and she moved under her own steam musically. The victory, however, was not without compromise. It was no coincidence that the first woman to reach the status of culture heroine was a folksinger performing in a notoriously asexual genre. In a society founded on double standards, both racial and sexual, it is much harder for a woman than a man to project her sexuality in a way that contributes positively to her image. The "choice" at the time seemed to be one between the overt, often racist sexuality of black women with no names or the asexuality of a white female folksinger.

Although Joan Baez' talent and her impact on the period should not be minimized, it is still ironic that she rose to popularity, along with the rest of the popular folk movement, in the wake of what was essentially a black struggle. "In spite of its commitment to the Negro," Carl Belz has written:

> the popular folk movement was stylistically white, more thoroughly white, in fact, than the rock style it hoped to replace. For instance, it consisted almost exclusively of white artists. When it included Negro folk singers, they were Josh White, Leadbelly, and others who had worked in the folk idiom for many years and could be resurrected as safe, historical prototypes. The Negro songs that became popular with the folk movement belonged to an older tradition, and were appreciated like nostalgic glimpses of the past. Finally, the style of popular folk singers was radically different from the style of Negro folk blues. It was clean, elegant, and arty, and it possessed none of the raw immediacy of the Negro tradition.[4]

The demand for "Freedom Now" could only have been made less forceful by having an innocent white woman established as a major musical mouthpiece of the movement. As a spokesperson Joan Baez was effective, and as a musician she was true, but would the pace for change have been quicker if a black singer or black music had been promoted?

Women and the Beatles

The popularity of the acoustic folk genre was short lived. With the British invasion, the return to electric music was nearly total. The new electric style of the British groups, and soon of their progressive rock counterparts in the United States, signaled the beginning of a more or less steady decline for women on the pop charts. The participation of women reached an all time low at the end of the decade when they accounted for only 6 percent of the Top 50 singles in 1969. In 1970, only three of the Top 50 albums were by women.

The overwhelming popularity of the Beatles was the single greatest force responsible for the decline of women on the charts in the mid-sixties. Musically and to an extent personally, the Beatles were less sexist than many rock groups before or since. A number of their top selling singles dealing with relationships between men and women showed a surprising lack of heavy-handedness. Singing "Oh Please Say to Me You'll Let Me Be Your Man" was quite a turnaround: a man asking permission to belong to a woman. "I don't care too much for money,

money can't buy me love" was hardly the prevailing male attitude. Their general posture toward the love of a woman was one of appreciation ("She Loves You," "Thank You, Girl," "Love Me Do," "I Feel Fine"). In "Eleanor Rigby" and "Lady Madonna," they created real women who had personalities and substance. They had masculine limits, even so: "You better run for your life if you can, little girl/Catch you with another man That's the end of little girl."

After the Beatles broke up John Lennon continued to turn out songs that often were genuinely nonsexist, treating women as developed personalities and not as mindless bodies to be stuck between the sheets ("Jealous Guy," "Woman Is the Nigger of the World" with Yoko Ono, and others). Country Joe McDonald was perhaps the only other important male rock star to rethink his attitudes toward women and change the content of his songs (especially the Paris sessions, with songs like "Sexist Pig" and "Coulene Anne").

Despite any attitudes the Beatles themselves may have held, however, their popularity led the music industry to push a bandwagon of white male English groups. The few women like Nancy Sinatra, Marianne Faithful, Dusty Springfield, and Petula Clark who made the charts during the first wave of the British invasion were sometimes talented but overall, rather uninspiring. Dionne Warwick, a black woman with a name, was an exception and might have been a much larger success in less competitive times.

The Glass Cage: *Go-Go Girls*

By 1966 the proportion of women on the singles charts had declined from a high of 32 percent in 1962 to 16 percent.* Aside from the more pop-oriented women mentioned above, only two female vocal groups had survived the Beatle revolution, the Supremes and Martha and the Vandellas, both on the Motown label. In the rock market the new place for women was away from the microphones, supporting male singers as go-go dancers. Go-go girls became popular during the second generation of adult rock'n'roll nightclubs, the discotheque phase, and the role was institutionalized on two prime time rock shows, Shindig and Hullaballoo.

The first generation of adult rock clubs had grown out of the Twist craze. As the first rock dance to focus attention specifically on the pelvic region, the Twist was probably an early indication of growing but as yet

*That women continued to show a rise on the album charts during the first phase of the English invasion is explained by their participation on sound track albums of movies and Broadway musicals like *Mary Poppins, The Sound of Music, My Fair Lady, Hello Dolly, West Side Story,* and others.

unclear sexual discontent. Step by step, the string of novelty dances which followed—the Pony, the Mashed Potatoes, the Locomotion, the Frug, the Watusi, and the Monkey—became more explicitly sexual. The sexuality was agonized and incomplete. There was little sensual fluidity to these dances. The Monkey, for instance, emphasized an up and down movement of the arms and a back and forth movement of the torso that was indicative of a frustration which could only be dealt with by thrashing about. By the time Shindig and Hullaballoo had come along in 1964 and 1965, the most popular dance was the Jerk. The motions of the Jerk were a near mimicry of the sexual act. These dances provided the basic choreography for the all-female chorus lines on both TV shows. The shows gave the sanction of popular culture to an essentially bumps and grinds routine which had been previously limited to strip clubs.

In the discotheques the degradation of women was, if anything, worse. Here the go-go girls were fashioned much more explicitly in the mold of strippers. Clad in scanty bikinis, their only function was to titillate the males in the audience. In the posher clubs, go-go girls performed in elevated glass cages. As the male-oriented "sexual revolution" allowed for more daring displays of sexuality, go-go girls went topless. California was in the forefront of these developments, as usual, and it was no coincidence that the state which spawned the Sexual Freedom League also produced the first topless go-go girls. The "sexual freedom" provided by these falsely liberating changes was really only the freedom for more men to fuck more women more easily. Women were objectified by these developments, treated solely as sex objects without personalities. The development of an autonomous female sexuality that did not conform to male fantasies had to await the growth of the Women's Liberation Movement. This movement was in part itself a reaction to the dehumanizing exaggerations of the male-oriented sexual revolution.

Groupies: *Another Trap for Women*

As countercultural folk rock and rock groups began to be popular after 1967, the go-go girl phenomenon began to die out. Plastic boots and doll-like dancing just did not make it any more. Except for a few women singers like Janis Joplin and Grace Slick, discussed in the next section, women did not return to rock music as performers until the rise of the singer-songwriters beginning in about 1971. The bulk of the women surrounding the rock scene after the go-go girls were *groupies*.

Groupies were less ornamental than go-go girls—they fucked the stars and inspired a few songs—but they had about as little effect on the music. Like men in the counterculture, groupies were rebelling against

279

the plastic uptightness of straight American consumer society, but since no autonomous roles had yet begun to be developed by women their rebellion did not take them far. Instead of picking up guitars themselves, they became only adjuncts to male musicians. They openly slept with men but in reality they only carried over the standard dependent yet nurturing roles of their own mothers to a much flashier scene. As one woman told *Rolling Stone* in 1969:

> Being a groupie is a full time gig. Sort of like being a musician. You have two or three girlfriends you hang out with and you stay as high and as intellectually enlightened as a group of musicians. You've got to if you're going to have anything to offer. Musicians should pay more attention to the good thing they've got going for them—groupies, I mean. After all a groupie is a non-profit call girl. Like a Japanese geisha in many ways, and a friend and a housekeeper and pretty much whatever the musician needs.[5]

Status in the groupie world was determined by what stars a woman hung out with, just as the status of her mother, or any woman in straight society, was determined by the man she married. To most male rock musicians the groupie situation was idyllic, and to them of course it still is. "Used to be the soldiers who were the gallant ones riding into town, drinking the wine and taking the girls," said Jimi Hendrix once; "Now it's the musician."

The role of women in the wider counterculture was less mindless but still only a bit better. Probably the most popular image for women in the counterculture at this time was the "earth mother," especially in the couple of years after the breakup of the city communities when large numbers of white youths "returned to the land." Earth mothers got to be lustier and tougher than their own suburban mothers, but much of their lives were no more liberated than those of their grandmothers. Women on rural communes fashioned the handicrafts, baked the bread, and raised the children. Thinking and heavy work, as always, were done by men. For women, freedom in the counterculture was a trap.

In 1969, one of the great years for hard rock, there were fewer women on the year-end singles charts than at any time since World War II. The situation for both women album and singles artists was even worse than it had been at the end of 1966, during the height of the British invasion. "Girls are an ego problem," explained San Francisco producer Abe Kesh a little earlier. "There seem to be hassles with lead guitarists over volume levels."[6] Of a hundred and fifty or so bands in the San Francisco area, only a handful had women singers, let alone women musicians. Along with a few others around the country, these women singers were exceptions, but for the development of women in rock music, extremely important ones.

Breaking Out: *Grace Slick, Janis Joplin, Aretha Franklin*

Probably the most prominent women in rock music in the 1964-70 period were Grace Slick, Janis Joplin, and Aretha Franklin. The three were singers who essentially fronted male bands, Slick less than the other two. Their relations to women's consciousness which was only beginning at this time varied, but they all served as models of some sort.

Grace Slick, first as lead singer with the Great Society, then with the Jefferson Airplane, presented the "ego problem" that Abe Kesh had recognized as integral to women singers in the San Francisco scene. "Grace was obviously the most talented member of the group [the Great Society]," recalled Tom Donahue, who had signed the band to his Autumn label, "yet you could see the group try to push her into the background because they were afraid she would be too big a star."[7] With the Airplane she stood out less, sharing composing duties and audience attention with Paul Kantner. Her status was based on adulation from a male audience, and she seemed pleased with her role as psychedelic sex symbol. Her experiences never led her to rebel against the prevailing San Francisco concept of a "chick singer," and she criticized women liberationists. During the time when youth culture was not yet a coopted commodity, Slick and the Airplane provided a rebellious thrust in rock music, especially with their *Volunteers of America* album. As youth culture lost its critical impact and direction, the Airplane's science fiction reveries seemed irrelevant rather than helpfully utopian, and Grace Slick, the daughter of an investment banker, seemed more iconoclastic than revolutionary. The Airplane's status for a time as the highest paid concert performers in the United States, receiving $7,500 a night when that was top money, may have helped to isolate them.

Like Grace Slick, Janis Joplin was a symbol of rebellion to white middle-class youth turning from the ways of their parents. Always an outcast in conservative Port Arthur, Texas, where she had supported civil rights issues, written poetry, and played folk music, she headed for San Francisco after high school like so many others. A heavy dusk-to-dawn drinker who threw herself into lovemaking, Janis was an intense person. Her personal pain came mostly from a hatred of her body and from failures in relationships. Pain combined with a growing professionalism to produce credible white blues in cathartic songs like "Ball and Chain," "Turtle Blues," and "Combination of the Two." She may have had the power and understanding to become one of the greatest blues singers of all time but she died before she could achieve the needed control. She once told an interviewer that Aretha Franklin or Billie Holiday could express in two notes everything that could be said, but that she could not yet come close. She hoped to get there in time.

Janis Joplin was able to relate to other women, enjoying several lesbian relationships, but too often her love life seemed more self-destructive than liberating. She was aware of her oppression as a woman, much more than was Grace Slick, but was never able to express it coherently. She died before her life and career could be established. Even more than when she was alive, Joplin has become a symbol of the intense pain that was unavoidable to women breaking through in the confusion and experimentation of the sixties.

Aretha Franklin projected a much more conventional personal image than Grace Slick or Janis Joplin, but she probably experienced as much personal anguish as either. Her mother, also a singer, deserted the family when Aretha was young and died four years later. At age fourteen Aretha began to tour with her father's gospel caravan. The gospel circuit was demanding, although lucrative. Her father, Reverend C. L. Franklin, known as "the man with the Million Dollar Voice," received as much as $4,000 a sermon. She married her manager, Ted White, and had three children before she was twenty. White reportedly beat her. More recently she has had at least one nervous breakdown.

Aretha Franklin almost died as a recording artist. Columbia tried for years to make her into a pop star by encouraging her to sing songs like "Rock-a-Bye Your Baby with a Dixie Melody." Not until her contract was picked up by Atlantic did she begin to develop as a singer. Jerry Wexler produced her and the result was authentic r&b like "I Never Loved a Man," "Respect," "Natural Woman," and "Chain of Fools," which all became hits in 1967 alone. By 1968 she was "Lady Soul," the only black woman in popular music who exhibited the drive and forcefulness of the black militancy of the day. "Aretha did not pray like Mahalia for the endurance to make it on through," wrote Hettie Jones in *Big Star, Fallin' Mama,*

> nor make you believe her pain as Billie Holiday had. The statement black artists wished to make had changed, the blues had been transfigured by anger and pride. Aretha's music was a celebration, she was "earthmother exhorting, preacher woman denouncing, militant demanding, forgotten woman wailing." She was black, she was beautiful, and she was the best. Someone called that time in 1967 "the summer of 'Retha, Rap, and Revolt."[8]

Aretha's music was symbolic of the black movement but despite her background she never occupied a similar position to the women's movement. Most black radicals saw their primary task, especially at this time, in defending black manhood in white society. There was no room to include the women's struggle within the black movement, as Angela Davis and radical black lawyer Flo Kennedy have been able to do more recently. At the time of her initial successes the women's movement was almost nonexistent, anyway. Now with black radicalism more diffuse Aretha Franklin seems to be evolving only as a sex symbol, appearing naked (except for a mink stole draped over her shoulders) on the cover of her 1974 album. The power that she projected musically reinforced the black struggle, but her own politics were never clearly radical. For her to contribute musically to the women's movement at this point she would have to become more consciously political.

Opening the Gates: *The Singer-Songwriters*

Although individual singers who wrote and performed their own material like Dylan, Arlo Guthrie, and Janis Ian had been around in the last half of the sixties, it was not until 1970 or so that the "singer-songwriter" was singled out as a trend by the music industry. In 1970-71 three singer-songwriters had tremendous commercial impact: James Taylor, Cat Stevens, and Carole King. There seemed to be room now among the hard rock and soul of the time for a softer, more individual sound. Conditions were ready for a return of women singers for the first time since the pre-Beatles girl groups.

Carole King was the most popular of the breed. She was hardly a newcomer to the music industry, however. She had co-written "The Locomotion" for Little Eva, who was her parents' maid, back in 1962. She was a songwriter in the Donny Kirshner stable for several years, and wrote dozens of songs with Jerry Goffin, whom she married, for acts like the Shirelles, Aretha Franklin, and the Drifters, all before she recorded her own songs. "Tapestry," her second LP, is now the biggest selling album of all time. While she discusses relationships with a certain amount of frankness and has prepared the way commercially for other women singer-songwriters Carole King treats women in her lyrics (mostly written by men) in the most hopelessly standardized manner of any woman rock singer. Women in most of her songs are passive, submissive, willing to wait forever for their men. With few exceptions ("It's Too Late," "You Go Your Way, I'll Go Mine," "My My, She Cries") Carole King usually has no more advice for herself or other women than to stay in love and keep to the kitchen. Her style as a performer and musician is no less passive. Sessions are set up by her manager Lou Adler, who also consciously isolates her from the press. She rarely tours or puts together bands.

Joni Mitchell's artistry, like Carole King's, is consummate. Her roots are not in r&b and pop rock songwriting, however, but in folk music. Her first break came when Judy Collins recorded her "Both Sides Now" in 1968. She stayed acoustic through the hard rock of the early seventies, but on later albums she added a rock backup band. The move to rock has broadened her audience considerably. It gives her a power to be influential that is denied to acoustic folkies. When she appears live she is essentially a singer backed up by a band, but since she writes nearly all the songs that are played, she is in a more controlling position than other women singers fronting rock bands. It now seems she is doing her own producing on albums. Joni Mitchell's control of technique, compositon, and production are of course helpful for women in rock music, as a model. Her lyrics are also progressive, at least some of the time. They are much more sexually aggressive than the lyrics of most female rock singers.

At other times, though, as in "A Case of You," her songs display an almost masochistic vulnerability. They speak of such exquisite pain that her developing rock toughness is put in doubt. Will she cope with the grittiness of life in the United States or stay, sighing, in Laurel Canyon? For Joni Mitchell is an extremely isolated rock star. She rarely tours. She does virtually no interviews. Perhaps she is an inherently shy person, but her isolation is certainly encouraged by her manager, Eliot Roberts, who long ago stopped her interviews. To Roberts, Joni Mitchell (and some of the other musicians he handles), "looks to us for direction."

> They're not out there on the street . . . they don't know what's happening. They're not concerned with that. I mean they're really, truly . . . artists, they are. For the most part they're consumed with art. . . .They are all very—not closed necessarily, because they are all actually very open, but they are—they only see a certain spectrum and they expect us to fill them in on the rest of the spectrum. On the rest of what's happening. And we do.[9]

Joni Mitchell, as Roberts is quick to point out, is a wealthy woman. It is too easy for her to assume the role of the rich hippie.

Joni Mitchell is a woman who has made it on her own in a man's "profession." As a success, she may feel that any other woman could do the same. Like certain black people in high positions, many extremely talented women cannot see themselves as exceptions. They would rather believe that other women could have made it as they did, if they had worked hard. They do not see that only the most exceptionally gifted women and, in Joni Mitchell's case, the most beautiful in male eyes as well, have a real chance in a structurally sexist industry which automatically screens out women of less than exceptional talent.

So You Want to Be a Rock'n'Roll Star

"So you want to be a rock'n'roll star
Well, just pick up a guitar and learn to play"
—The Byrds

Women singer-songwriters have established a female perspective in rock music lyrics. Perhaps a greater obstacle to the equal participation of women at this point is the taboo against women instrumentalists. All of the female vocal groups of the early sixties used studio musicians for their instrumental backup. Women singers like Janis Joplin and Aretha Franklin still did not play their own instruments. It was an unwritten rule that only the men could deal with the hardware. Where women did play instruments, they played acoustic guitar or piano, never electric instruments and almost never brass. With few exceptions the situation remains unchanged.

Carole Kaye is a successful session musician who has played bass on a number of Motown hits including "Love Child," "Bernadette," "Get Ready," and "I Was Made to Love Her." There are a few other women session musicians like Hope Ruff, but they are never in the public eye. The horn players in Sly Stone's band are both women, but as the only interracial, intersexual group ever to make the pop charts, Sly and the Family Stone has been an exception for years. Ruth Underwood now plays with Frank Zappa; Maureen Tucker used to drum for the Velvet Underground. A few, regionally known, all women rock bands have been formed, but most have been short lived. Pressures have been great. The group Eyes broke up, as did the Enchanted Forest. Ace of Cups could not get a contract. Of those that remain, Fanny is the best known.

Within the women's movement, Fanny was something of an embarrassment. With album titles like Charity Ball and Fanny Hill, not to mention the name of the group itself, their women's consciousness was not hard to question. Within the music industry, Fanny was seen as a novelty group, and even when their concerts were well received, the prevailing attitude was "Not bad . . . for chicks." Although the band's own double entendre image made it more difficult for them to be received as serious musicians, and certainly served to objectify them as women, a male band with a similarly sexist name and album titles might still have been listened to for their music. Fanny had the same problem with their image that Grace Slick did. They both were based on male fantasies and depended largely on male adulation for their success.

Fanny must be put in the proper historical context. It is not surprising that the first successful women's rock band was composed of women who were not an active part of the women's liberation movement (although in part they owed their success to it). An all women rock group with a highly developed women's consciousness probably could not have existed in the late 1960s, much less have become famous. At that time women committed to feminism would have self-selected out of rock music for lack of support. Feminism of any kind was limited to small groups of intellectuals and radicals. That was the choice. The women who started Fanny chose to become rock stars, and by picking up electric instruments have helped neutralize one of the strongest taboos against women in the field. Like Joni Mitchell they have unfortunately left it to others to progress further.

The first real ray of hope was probably Joy of Cooking. The group had three men in it, but it was led by two women—Toni Brown and Terry Garthwaite. They played electric piano and electric guitar, respectively, and wrote most of the material. Their music came from a number of sources, but it was rock'n'roll. Joy's instrumentation, stage demeanor, and public image might just have been the beginnings of a nonsexist tradition in commercial popular music. But with three albums and some national exposure under their belt, Joy of Cooking broke up. There was no cataclysmic scene. The members of the group had simply evolved in different directions until Joy was no longer the best vehicle for their music. Toni and Terry went on to record a fourth album together called Cross Country. Terry is still performing, but primarily as a solo artist.

Beyond the development of women-centered bands, the last few years have seen the emergence of out-front homosexual musicians. However, the movement that was promised in the early David Bowie albums, especially Hunky Dory, toward a more honest treatment of male and female sexuality and homosexuality and toward a gentleness in emotional relations was soon betrayed by Bowie and numerous camp followers, who began to sell sexual ambiguity as commercial thrill, rather than moving to establish a strong homosexual perspective in rock music. Most performers who were gay, like Lou Reed, simply lied about their homosexuality, and worse, continued to write songs degrading to women. An exception is perhaps the out-of-the-closet Ray Davies of the Kinks. The tough green genie lyrics of superficially gay rock music, and the caricatured gay stage style of leers, minced steps, and stuffed crotches, has not yet given way in rock music, if it ever will, to principled and loving treatment of gayness. As for gay women rock performers, greater inhibition seems to rule. No economically successful gay women's bands have yet surfaced, despite a number of regionally operating women's bands.

Rock'n'Roll Women in the Seventies

At present the way is opening slightly for women to perform successfully in the rock idiom. A number of new rock'n'roll women such as Rita Coolidge, Linda Ronstadt, Maria Muldaur, Patti Smith, and Bonnie Raitt are rising on the rock circuit. They are all articulate and college educated (though most dropped out before graduating). The rock'n'roll women of the seventies have had other options than rock music, and compared to the desperate blues women of the thirties or the constricted vocal groups of the early sixties, their dues have been relatively light.

Although none of these women has shown any particular affinity for feminism as such, they owe their success in part to the influence of the women's movement and to the growing women's audience for rock music, and acknowledge that the women's movement has affected their lives. All of these women have at least some awareness of the conflicts affecting any woman trying to make it in rock.

In the first place women artists are subject to the same commercial formulas that the music industry imposes on male artists. Bonnie Raitt is a case in point. Starting out as a Cambridge folkie doing mostly blues material, she now plays some of the best bottleneck guitar in the business. Her image is a toned down Joplin blues mama, although she went to Radcliffe. Primarily a live performer, her straightforward stage act has brought a devoted cult following. She is not a studio artist. Until recently, Raitt has enjoyed complete control over her production—"I pick the studio, the producer, the musicians, and the material." On her first three LPs she used nonsession musicians and a production style geared to capture the electricity of her live performances. However, in the career plan of her label, Warner-Reprise, a first album is expected to sell around 50,000 copies, the second 150,000, and the third enough to go Gold. She did alright with the first two but when her third, Takin' My Time, showed no increase, Warners insisted that she use a "track record" producer and studio musicians on Streetlights, her fourth album. The result was Jerry Ragavoy, the Hit Factory in Manhattan, and plenty of strings and horns in the background. It is most definitely a studio album. It is even a good studio album, but it is not Bonnie Raitt. The songs lack the vitality of live material. Warner hoped that with its slick production Streetlights would boost Bonnie Raitt to that next plateau. The price she paid was a partial loss of control over her own image, and less input in the production process.

Only a handful of female acts compete with men in terms of record sales. Of all the records to be certified Gold between 1972 and 1974, less than 12 percent were by women. Of the women in the pop/rock category, the music is of two basic types: the soft rock sound of Carole King, Carly Simon, or Joni Mitchell, and the interpretative stage acts like Bette Midler or the Pointer Sisters. Helen Reddy would be somewhere in the middle. At this time there are no hard rockers among the women who sell Gold, although there are a few heavy duty women rockers who have reached middle-level popularity, most notably Patti Smith.

On the Road

For male stars whose records are in the Gold Record class, like the Allman Brothers or CSN&Y, there exists a coliseum, raceway circuit of concerts which pays as much as $100,000 per night. More importantly, since this market caters to huge numbers of young people, it is the place where culture heroes are made. Unfortunately, the few women who reach this level of sales seem to pull out of the grueling youth circuit once they begin to sell records. They become simply recording stars or songwriters. As Carole King's Tapestry album has brought her millions in royalties, she has become, as Katherine Orloff puts it, "a housewife who writes songs." Carly Simon no longer tours either, staying home instead, as she explained to an interviewer, trying to get husband James Taylor to help her change Sarah's diapers. But then as an heiress to the Simon and Schuster publishing fortune, she does not need the money in the first place.

Life on the road is alienating for almost anyone, but for women musicians it is also an exercise in schizophrenia. A touring solo woman is likely to have a male manager, male roadies, and male sidemen. There may be some "old ladies" and occasional groupies, but she will most likely be the only woman on the tour with a substantive role. On stage she will be encouraged to be sexy yet if she hangs out after the show she will be regarded as "one of the guys." Conflict is built into the position, and it is difficult to straddle both roles. America is no more able to accept women in primary roles than it is to accept men in secondary positions. Furthermore, "it's very threatening," as Maria Muldaur quickly learned, "for a lot of guys to see a woman with her own scene together. She isn't going to just want to pack up her sleeping bag and wander off with him."[10]

Helen Reddy is something of a special case. She arrived in New York from Australia in 1966, struggled along with a three-year-old daughter, no husband and no money, got a few breaks, and came out with "I Am Woman," a number one single. "I Am Woman" was explicitly feminist and sold far beyond the older FM audience to hundreds of thousands of teenage women. Reddy has been outspoken on women's issues (less so on other social issues) and might have become an extremely strong model for women listening to or playing rock music.

Her yen for the good life and tendency toward schlock have compromised her now. In 1973 Ellen Willis wrote that Helen Reddy "at her best"

> has the ability to merge two forms, straddle the straight-pop and soft-rock audiences, and help (along with Bette Midler) to revive and refine interpretive singing. But if she does not maintain a delicate balance—and I think it has to be consciously and deliberately sought—she will end up just a very good pop singer, hipper than most but irrelevant to young people and to what has become the mainstream of popular culture.[11]

288

Since that article Helen Reddy has played the Carol Burnett Show, the Flip Wilson Show, the Johnny Carson Show, the Merv Griffin Show, the Mike Douglas Show, and done her own TV show and a number of specials. She and her husband/manager Jeff Wald now own his and hers Mercedes Benzes. She is faced with the same problem confronting certain male stars like John Lennon, who have a fair amount of political principle. That problem is, how to maintain any roots outside the music business when they are being showered with millions of dollars. Helen Reddy seems to have made her choices.

Are women such as these to be blamed for copping out on other women? To an extent, yes, of course. But the real blame lies with the music industry which diverts women from positions of influence in mainstream youth culture.

The Industry: *Men at the Top*

Although certain women artists seem to be making some progress moving into rock music—changing lyrics, playing instruments, and so forth—the advances have been slow. By gradually removing the taboos on women playing instruments a base is being formed for more participation by women in rock music, but in terms of women on the year-end charts, not a lot has changed. The album percentage may have recovered a bit from the onslaught of progressive male rock in the sixties, but has shown a decline from 18 percent in 1971 to 12 percent in 1974. The singles percentage is also lower than it was in 1971, still lower than in the 1962-64 period, and much lower than the 1952-55 period. A major reason for the situation is discrimination against women behind the scenes, in the music industry itself.

The music industry forms the invisible structure which enables a few performers to become visible and make it, and it selects what attitudes toward women will be projected. While there have been some notable exceptions through the years, few women have held high- or middle-level executive positions. Almost no women have ever been producers, the key creative position. The image of women used by the industry to sell its high energy sexual product has always of commercial necessity objectified women, treating them more as bodies than people. And the two vehicles for popularizing music, radio and the hip press, have been dominated by men. If women were to occupy these positions in significant numbers more women singers and musicians would be signed, produced, and heard, and women's music would be free to develop in a way that it is not now permitted. The danger of cooptation, something along the Helen Reddy model in which women become no different than rich male stars, isolated from most women (and men) in the audience and simply part of money-making American industry would of course always be there; and ultimately the only guarantee against that cooptation is a strong women's movement outside the business.

The few high level women in the music industry come to mind quickly: Florence Greenberg, the founder and head of Sceptor/Wand, Miriam Bienstock, former comptroller at Atlantic, Barbara Skydell, vice president of Premier Talent, Eileen Briscoe, head of Bang Records, Betty Benneman, national music director at RKO Broadcasting, Suzanne de Passe, vice president and head of creative services at Motown, and different heads of classical divisions at one or two major labels over the years. But these women are exceptions. There are virtually no others in high executive positions in record companies, radio chains, and agencies, let alone management and concert promotion companies and clubs, where there are only a small handful of important women.

A rough estimate of the situation can be gleaned from an analysis of *Billboard's* weekly column "Executive Turntable," which lists names, titles, and brief job descriptions of people being promoted throughout the industry. The turntable is naturally not systematic, but it gives a reasonable overview. A complete sifting of all the columns from fall 1973 to fall 1974 shows that of some 1,400 promotions reviewed, less than 100 or only 7 percent went to women. Of these 10 percent were euphemisms for secretary, or perhaps glorified secretary: "assistant to" the national sales director, "assistant to" the vice president in charge of sales, "assistant to" the promo director. "Assistant to" titles are often used to comply with affirmative action regulations, and do not reflect genuine administrative positions. A number of middle-level positions such as publicity director and assistant art director were legitimate.

The record and music industry is a liberal industry. It is reasonable to assume that more and more women will be added to middle-level management positions as corporate, nonradical "feminism" continues to grow among professional and upper-class women, and as, on the other hand, the audience for women's music expands. For now, however, the music industry is far less liberal on hiring women than the image it projects suggests, and the lack of women means, for record companies, that fewer women will be signed.

Easily the most important creative position from which women are absent is producer. There are no successful producers, independent or staff, who are women. (In the sixties at Motown, Valerie Simpson produced some of Marvin Gaye's records with Nick Ashford. Simpson and Ashford are now a singing duo at Warner Brothers.) As shown in earlier chapters, the producer is the pivotal person in determining the style of recording a record company does. In many cases the producer determines who gets a contract. Except with successful autonomous acts, the producer functions as a film director and movie producer rolled into one.

With commercial success the primary goal of most producers, women performers usually are put into an image mold that male producers think will sell records. Sammi Jo, for instance, a country singer who made the pop hit "Tell Me a Lie," was brought to producer Sonny Limbo of Fame Studios by her manager Tony Caterine, who had bragged of turning her into "your basic city fox." Limbo told her:

> Do everything I tell you and I'll make you a star. She did. I did. And We did. That kind of attitude, an outasight voice and a motherfucker song—to break a chick that's what it takes. Then if she looks good and has big tits—she just might make it.[12]

Toni Brown and Terry Garthwaite, both probably more concerned than Sammi Jo, ran into similar problems with David Rubinson, now the manager of the Pointer Sisters:

> He told Terry and me, when he was thinking of producing us, that we'd better wear low-cut gowns, and why don't we get out there and try to turn people on . . . that and other things made it impossible to work with him.[13]

Rubinson, however, went on to produce Garthwaite's first solo album.

Male producers and managers clearly feel that women must project sexuality to keep (sexist) male audiences clapping and buying. Maria Muldaur posed the question, "What if I went to the Troubador in L.A. wearing my hiking boots and a baggy pair of pants and a sweatshirt? Would they like me for my music?" Although far more general, the situation confronting women is analogous to the one that confronted Jimi Hendrix. Industry forces exerted pressure to keep his highly saleable "psychedelic oversexed black man image," and they enforce similar restrictions to stop women from developing images that do not appeal directly to sexist male audiences.

Standard treatment of women in music business advertising reinforces sexist images. Women have been exploited sexually for years to sell male cockrock, of course. Examples are legion, from the most boring cheesecake shots of bikinied women on beaches (on The Sandpipers' album covers and countless others) to the elaborate grossness of the campaign for Humble Pie's *Eat It* album, which included dozens of women wearing sandwich boards emblazoned with "Eat It" parading in traffic centers of major cities, to the imaginative sexism of Alice Cooper including paper panties in the *Schooldays* album. Some ads show a more direct perversity that reflect the cruelly rapist fantasies forming the underbelly of American sexism, such as an ad for a set of Warner-Reprise albums and tapes with the caption "Bound to Please—Now Released for

Your Pleasure," under a picture of a woman bound over a rotating spiked wheel which was aimed upward toward her thighs.

The series of ads Warner did for Joni Mitchell which angered her and in part caused her to leave the label are fairly typical of the industry ads for women performers, although perhaps a bit more sophisticated than the average. As described in the section on Warner Brothers, the series included titles like "Joni Mitchell Is 90 Percent Virgin," referring to the fact that she had only sold a tenth as many albums as Judy Collins, "Joni Mitchell Takes Forever," complaining about the long wait between her albums, and "Joni Mitchell Finally Comes Across," trumpeting the arrival of her third album. The double entendres contained in the captions are obvious.

Airplay is the main way that artists are heard and popularized, yet there are few disc jockeys who are women. RKO-General, probably the most important AM radio chain in terms of rock music, has a national music director who is a woman but almost no women djs at its stations. AM stations prefer aggressive fast talking djs and feel women would be out of place. "I've heard some women jocks," says RKO-General president Bruce Johnson, "but I haven't heard a really good one. I understand there are a couple, but I haven't heard them yet myself. I don't know. We have no restrictions against it, we just haven't found one we like yet."[14] RKO is an anomaly to have a woman in such an important decision-making position as national music director.

FM stations usually have no more than a single woman dj, if that, and often the women chosen by male administrators are specialists in heavy metal male groups or british rock. Rachel Donahue, formerly at KSAN-FM in San Francisco, now at KMET-FM in L.A., and Maxanne Sartori at WBCN-FM in Boston are examples. Boston is representative of the situation in one major market. Except for Sartori at BCN there are no full-time women djs at the city's major stations. One woman has a once a week show in the Saturday night graveyard slot at WBZ-AM, and tiny WCAS-AM in Cambridge has a woman dj. The lack of women at FM stations is especially important in this discussion because, theoretically at least, a woman FM dj could program significant numbers of women artists, as well as less sexist male groups that might be current such as John Lennon and Country Joe McDonald. At AM stations, even if the situation were changed to permit women djs on the air, they would have no power to play women artists or less sexist material.

Hip newspapers and undergrounds are not as important as radio in popularizing artists, but the situation in relation to women is similar. Major papers like *Rolling Stone* have a woman or two that review some albums, not necessarily women's albums, but often as not the music departments at sea-level and underground papers are all-male. In addition record reviewers are usually limited to comments on lyrics and style and rarely have the space or inclination to talk about institutionalized sexism in the overall music industry. *Rolling Stone* covers women in rock outside the record review pages, but only to titillate its largely male audience with hot flashes about Buffy St. Marie exposing a nipple on her latest album cover, or Suzi Quatro "flexing her leather," or showing snapshots of a naked groupie hugging an embarrassed Jerry Garcia and a woman dancing bare-breasted on stage next to Leslie West.*

Solutions

In the production of rock music women face a constellation of problems. In any full solution women would have to learn to play all instruments while continuing to write songs. It would be necessary for them to master the technology, learning how to operate mixing boards, recording studios, and sound equipment, to become producers, engineers, and technicians in addition to being musicians. Those women that come to see themselves as feminists and radicals should have control to fashion their own public image. More women would have to become djs and effective critics. In our opinion the solution must also be a mass one involving the main pop audience not just coteries of isolated women playing in outmoded (usually nonelectric) styles. Finally, and probably most difficult of all, given the sophistication of the music industry, the women in rock, like the men, would have to avoid being coopted. As their music develops it will have to keep its critical content.

An obvious but limited and eventually unsatisfactory vehicle for the solution of some of these problems would be "female capitalism," the creation of an all-women record company run for the profit of the women founders. Presumably such a company would indeed develop women engineers and producers, record women singers, bands, and songwriters, and with more difficulty, fashion nonsexist advertising campaigns to promote its women artists. But even if the company avoided the rapacious gouging of its artists that occurred at Motown, it would, as a capitalist institution whose primary function was to turn a profit, be subject to pressure from the old style business oriented industry and media outside it. And of course, the fact that the company would be run by women executives rather than men does not change at all its basic character, which fundamentally involves exploiting people's labor.

The tendency would be for such a company to become integrated into the sexist and profit-making industries it would be part of, and work

---

*It is too early to know whether the recent addition of former *Ms.* and *New Yorker* writer Ellen Willis will cause any ripples at the *Stone*.

with, every day. If profit were the driving force of the company, as it is for every other business, compromises with sexist club owners, concert promoters, agents, and program directors would eventually be made. Each record and artist would come to be seen as a commodity, profitable if sold, disposable if not; and the women who sang the songs and played on the records would be viewed as commodities as well, and in the same way, as their product. The company would also become an oppressive institution within the context of American corporate society, even if it held to feminist values, because it would be just another hip capitalist prop to a total class system which requires that the majority of the population produce profits for a small minority.

The question is posed whether feminism pushed to its limits could be reached within capitalist society. Since nearly half the workforce of this country are women, and no equality can be reached between owners and workers under capitalism, this is a doomed strategy. Yet an elite of privileged women, well-paid and relatively unalienated, existing in institutions like this capitalist record company, *is* conceivable. A model for this elitist nonsolution already exists: *Ms.* magazine. The magazine started with some of the goals that a feminist record company would have but quickly deteriorated into a flashy, well-written organ for professional and upper-class women, integrating them into the top levels of corporate America, which can tolerate women managers, much as it can black managers, as long as they support capitalism.* It is too early to tell whether the recently-formed Olivia Records, a company owned and operated by and for women, will eventually fit into this model or not.

A second institutional way out would be the formation of nonprofit, alternative record companies as well as similar concert/agency organizations. Small groups have been extremely successful in the feminist movement so far. Discussion groups, self-help groups, women's groups of all kinds have spread feminism across the country with, obviously, no commercial promotion at all. Could a similar pattern work to popularize women singers and musicians? To a certain extent, yes. Women's centers and dances can support women singers like the New Haven and Chicago Women's Liberation Rock Bands. Noncommercial distribution can get records like those by Holly Near and the Red Star Singers or Elaine Brown into feminist and radical bookstores. But no mass listenership can be gotten for women artists outside of large scale broadcasting, concert promotion, and record production. Small scale activities do not have the capital to set up and operate record

*One quarter of *Ms.* is now owned by Warner Communications. The magazine was originally bankrolled, in part, by Katherine Graham, the millionaire businesswoman and publisher of the *Washington Post*.

studios and radio stations. Small, usually low paying concerts and club dates cannot support equipment and road costs for modern rock groups. While a feminist base is absolutely necessary for the emotional support and political aid of women musicians, it cannot serve as the principal network, at least at this point, for bringing women's music to a mass audience. The base must exist but women must also move into certain key positions within the record industry as well.

The money and adulation showered on rock stars, the tendency for the music industry to become their daily life and sole reality, and the basic fact that they are producing products, including themselves, which are packaged, bought, and sold, is really enough to isolate any musician, woman or man, who has had poor or working class roots, or who has developed any radical political tendencies. The music business is a sophisticated, complete, cooptive institution. It is deceptive since jobs within it, when compared to jobs in most of the rest of American society, are exciting, well-paying, and sexually less restrictive.

However, for a woman's music to develop it is absolutely necessary for more women to become producers and radio djs. There is no way that women can take over positions in most other music industry fields like sales, promotion, advertising, and general high level administration without completely compromising themselves and their feminism by supporting a sexist industry, and without becoming part of the capitalist corporate structure, however "pleasant" a job. In short these other positions are inherently cooptive.

Of course it is easy for women or men to lose any progressive identity they may have by becoming producers, djs, and program directors too. Successful producers make hundreds of thousands of dollars a year. Successful djs make $300-$700 a week at top FM stations, about $30,000-$70,000 a year at AM stations. Yet woman's music cannot be made without women producers, and it will never really be aired without feminist djs. Even a few women producers would make the development of women's music much easier. A greater number of women djs than producers would be necessary to build any feminist momentum.*

Women's rock music is just beginning to develop. Women are beginning to write about themselves as *women* and not just as lovers of men. They are picking up electric guitars and they are being heard by a

---

*A dual approach such as this could also work in the wider music scene to develop more politically left music. Some producer and disc jockey positions would have to be secured to insure a mass audience. At the same time an alternate network of small clubs, benefit concerts, and the like which would be avowedly politically radical would be necessary. The two methods would support and reinforce each other so that fewer people both inside the industry and out would become isolated.

growing audience of women whose lives are being changed by the women's liberation movement. Women have been only the subjects for rock music for so long, and have been excluded from positions of power and creativity within the music industry to such a complete degree that it will take some time for women musicians and a women's rock music to establish itself. The movement will have many defeats, and many women performers, like men, will be coopted, but if a productive tension can be preserved between the women in the small autonomous less-cooptive organizations that make up feminist musical and political alternatives and the women in necessary positions in the larger music industry, a strong, nonsexist women's rock music can be established.

Key to its success will be the fate and growth of the wider women's movement outside of the music, and, in turn, its level of struggle, and work with other radical liberation movements.

BILLION DOLLAR BABY: THE COOPTATION OF ROCK

Rock and the System

Since the fifties a good deal of rock'n'roll and rock music has expressed attitudes and postures against the American economic/political system.

Rock'n'roll in the fifties attacked, often indirectly, many of the institutions that helped to control young people of all classes during the otherwise Silent Years of the Eisenhower regime—1952-60. The authoritarian attitudes of the time were used to whip up the anticommunist hysteria necessary to enlist the American people's support for the massive economic and CIA "aid" which preserved most of Europe for corporate capitalism. An unwavering consensus was also needed to gear up the economy for the huge peace-time defense production necessary to keep the economy out of the recessionary slide experienced after the Korean War. The authoritarian attitudes helpful in maintaining public agreement in support of these programs essential for the growth and consolidation of the American business establishment were to a great degree a product of and reinforced by the traditional family structure and by a concomitant sexual organization of rigidity and repression.[1]

With their suggestive stage manner, guttural vocals, double entendre lyrics, and so on, Presley and the rest of the visceral rockers were seen by the establishment critics of the 1950s as attackers of sexual decency and the stable family. Rock'n'roll fostered a separation of youth from parental control. This separation was encouraged even under the less overtly sexual schlock rock of the Philadelphia sound. The creation of a teen culture was clearly not a revolutionary development, but it did distance young people to a certain degree from home and church, and provided a wedge from which inchoate rebellion could be expressed, if not yet directed *at* the establishment.

Most of the rockers of this era were from poor and working-class backgrounds, in the beginning from poor regions in the South and the border states (Presley, Lewis, Perkins, Little Richard). They assaulted the standards of decency, the straight-laced morality, and to a certain extent the upper middle-class concept of the fifties Good Life put out by previously dominant, prerock pop singers like Perry Como and Doris Day. The new rock'n'rollers also broadened the mass audience for records beyond the adult middle and upper class. Obviously not politically radical, the new music was still socially progressive.

The same class base was the stage for the revival of rock in Great Britain in the 1960-64 period—with some major differences, of course. Members of the early British groups were mostly from the British working class or were proletarianized students (Jagger for instance), but were not from a rural hinterland. None existed. Early rock music in Britain was a national urban phenomenon and not, as it was in the United States, a regional rural development. Rock'n'roll in the United States has been the amalgamation of several regional root music genres—country and western and rhythm and blues. But in Britain, too, the music was an attack on established values, the values of the traditional institutions of the conservative trade union culture of the working class as well as the values of the British ruling class. The Rolling Stones, the Animals, the Kinks, and even the more whimsical Beatles all rebuked the British family structure, general standards of "decency," and the elitism of the upper class.

With the rise of progressive rock in the United States, encouraged in part by some of the British groups, a more formulated and directed rebellion developed in rock music. Throughout the fifties the American capitalist economy had become increasingly consumer oriented. Production of heavy industrial goods, especially those needed in the burgeoning defense sector, continued unabated, but consumer commodities were becoming a central part of the American economy. This consumer production was made possible by a new affluence among a majority of the population. The affluence itself was predicated on the new dominance of the world capitalist system by the United States after World War II, which had bankrupted Great Britain and temporarily eliminated the rival capitalist nations of Japan and Germany. The growth of the American economy led to the need for more sophisticated middle-level managers, for numerous new technicians, scientists, and engineers to oversee its technical advances. The need for these trained managers and technicians necessitated the vast expansion of the American university system. The relation of the university boom of the late fifties and early sixties to the new needs of corporate capitalism was consciously recognized by university planners.[2] The percentage of young people attending college reached unprecedented proportions; more than half of all young people between the ages of seventeen and twenty-seven in the Western states had spent some time in college, for instance. The expansion of the government and the bureaucratization of other sectors of American life during this time are accepted and commonplace observations.

The point of all this is that this new bureaucratic consumer capitalism gave rise to—and there is not enough room to detail the process— widespread protest by the children of the affluent middle class, and to a lesser degree by the children of the upper class as well. There was a history of early moral protest of varying degrees of sophistication stretching from ban-the-bomb marches through the beatnik phenomenon to the civil rights demonstrations. But although some political and cultural leaders for the later movements came from these earlier struggles, the mass middle-class base was formed as a result of the changes in the needs of the capitalist system and in reaction to the Vietnam War of the sixties, with its compulsory draft system.

This movement was first developed in the most middle-class, comfortable, consumer-oriented, suburbanized areas of the country: California and the suburbs of New York. It was centered in the bureaucratic institutions that now involved large numbers of American young people—the universities and their attendant drop-out communities.

The protest against American consumer capitalism in the sixties was reflected to varying degrees in the new progressive rock music by numerous, mostly middle-class groups like the Mothers of Invention, Grateful Dead, Jefferson Airplane, Country Joe and the Fish, the Fugs, the Doors, and Bob Dylan. The new bands appealed to the newly expanded student and drop-out audience. (A large student audience was not a major factor in the support of newer rock music in Britain, since the British economy was nowhere near as automated as the U.S. economy—70 percent of the workers were involved in manual labor— and consequently had less need of a large university educated work force.) The war in Vietnam and the earlier civil rights protests were specific issues that politicized much of the audience for the music as well as a few of the musicians, as much as did the generally alienating conditions of society.

299

At this time, then, rock music shared many of the antiestablishment attitudes of the nascent youth culture and the older radicals. Fundamentally, it was against materialist consumerism and puritanical sexual organization. In many cases it was specifically against the Vietnam War and in favor of black liberation.

Over the next few years, however, the critical effect of rock music was lost.

The position of the music as an increasingly important cultural commodity within a consumer economy weakened any of the explicit antimaterialist content of the music. The sexually liberating aspects of the music remained, but sexual liberation itself was integrated into the system as an important selling tool for the "liberated" economy. The sexually liberated personality, instead of increasingly opposing the system, became the psychological type most appropriate to a consumer society. And finally, the music became separated from the political ferment that had provided it with its critical edge (as well as themes and images) in the earlier sixties. Musicians and the creative personnel within the music industry were integrated into an entertainment business now firmly part of the American corporate structure. How was this possible?

Culture as Commodity

As the music industry had grown and the consumer economy had expanded, the potential for cooptation of rock music had always been present. Although first perceived as a threat to the system culturally, economically rock music has never posed a problem for the capitalist organization of the economy. Whether in the form of a record, a tape, a concert ticket, or a booking agency fee, rock music was a packaged commodity that was bought and sold like any other consumer commodity, be it films or shoes. The handling of the music commodity was completely carried out within the capitalist structure, first by innovative entrepreneurs and small companies, later by stratified conglomerates and monopoly corporations.

Furthermore, the American capitalist system has had a tendency from the beginning of this consumerist period, and continues to this day, to integrate forms of leisure and the aspects of everyday life into the consumer commodity system. The tendency increases as the society becomes more affluent, as production is automated, and the overall capacity of the economic system to turn out goods and services is increased. The basic needs of a still industrializing country are no longer sufficient to create demand* for its immense productive capacity when it

---

*Demand in this economic sense means the desire or need by any sector of the economy, industrial or consumer, for goods and services necessary to continue production or to satisfy wants.

becomes an advanced capitalist system. An overproduction or surplus of goods, investment capital, manpower, and knowledge "requires"— under threat of stagnation—further outlets through stimulated consumer and government demand. The demand created by heavy industry, and also by the "infrastructural" additions, such as communications systems, road and transportation networks, and educational institutions, all of which are necessary to reach full industrial capacity, is no longer enough to keep the economy moving, because the economy is already industrialized in this basic manner.†

In recent years the surplus has been taken care of (never adequately, as periodic recessions like the current one demonstrate) by the creation of demand in three areas: overseas expansion, government expenditure, and increasing consumerism. Foreign sales and profits have become more and more important to American corporations, including record companies, as shown earlier, and have steadily increased in proportion to domestic sales and profits. Government demand is, due to the distribution of political power in this country, to the greatest degree confined to defense and defense related applied research and aerospace construction sectors. Government demand for the services of private corporations can be seen as a form of *subsidy* to those big businesses.

Consumerism, the third sector of this expanded economy, has increasingly commoditized leisure activity, home life, and all aspects of everyday living to a far greater extent than was possible before the Second World War. For example, through consumerism leisure activities are broken down into units and things that can be packaged and sold: vacation tours, sports equipment, movies, and records. Leisure activities are turned into commodities or products with price tags, turning a profit for some corporation.

Although completely different to the consumer, these newer commodities are no different to profit-making corporations than more standard products or commodities like wheat, cars, or refrigerators. By and large, a person in the United States has to pay money to private corporations to satisfy needs for leisure, while in a society not organized around the principles of private property and profit, such needs along with more basic ones like health care and food are provided for as a matter of course by the society as a whole. No private corporation, in this second sort of economic system, makes a profit from their satisfaction.

Leisure and entertainment industries such as the music industry, film

†Note: For a good part of the following discussion to hold true, the American economy must continue in relative strength. That is the economy must not be plunged into a depression as bad as the one of the thirties because the base of "average" consumers would then be eroded. Likewise if the present (1974-76) recession continues for the rest of the decade, a consumerist strategy will become increasingly obsolete because to maintain the system government and business will have to encourage

(continued on page 302)

industry, and vacation industry have now become integral parts of the capitalist system. As far as the satisfaction of economic demand is concerned, leisure and entertainment businesses are as important as primary heavy industry.[3] Part of the growth of these industries can be attributed to the increased leisure time and extra money enjoyed by the relatively large and affluent "middle" and upper classes in this country, and by that portion of the working class that is highly paid and usually highly skilled, whose own wealth is partly dependent on United States imperialism and corporate activity abroad that exploits workers in other countries.

Much of the growth is predicated on another dynamic, however, and that is that the conditions of work and urban life in the United States create a *need* for leisure, relaxation, and escape. Most work is boring and alienating. People at work have no control over the goods they produce, over the conditions in the factories and offices where they work, or over the spending of the profits their labor has earned for the corporations that employ them. Furthermore, under present conditions, many jobs are physically unsafe and extremely tiring. Most people therefore need relaxation in the form of drugs, liquor, TV, movies, and music when they get home.

The deteriorating quality of life outside of work also creates a host of secondary needs. The threat of crime and psychotic attack creates the need for security—for guarded apartments and homes, insurance policies and self-defense training. Air and noise pollution furthers the need to "get away," to leave the cities for the country (if only for weekends or short vacations), to hole up in one's room with records, TV, and books. General tension also creates a need for escape—for relaxing drugs like alcohol, for sports, and so on.

The incredible irony of the situation is that the capitalist economy that has created the intolerable conditions on and off the job profits from all the attempts by people to recuperate, relax, and escape from these same conditions. The consumer goods and services necessary for leisure are sold back to people by private corporations. Private land developers

(continued from page 301)

investment and production in more basic sectors of the economy in order to satisfy less frivolous needs and to provide higher employment. For us it is too early for predictions. Outside factors may easily affect the position of the American economy. Much depends on the success of liberation movements that deny sectors of the "free and capitalist" world to American corporations, the progress of socialist movements in developed countries such as Portugal, France, and Italy, and finally the growth of real competition to U.S. corporate hegemony from rival capitalist powers like West Germany and Japan.

For what it's worth, the music industry sector of the American consumer economy experienced record profits in 1975 at a time when many other industries were feeling the pinch of the recession.

control the sale of quiet and secure homes, apartments, and resort land. Hotel and tourist corporations own resorts, campgrounds, amusement parks like Disneyland, and so forth. Private corporations market sporting goods, film, TVs, liquor, and records.

As a cultural commodity worth billions in the aggregate, rock music fits well into the needs of the American consumer economy. Its form as a product like any other weakens any critical thrust that the content of the music might from time to time convey. But before describing how the content of the music was specifically coopted, it is helpful to show how the sexuality of rock also lost its critical force.

When a capitalist country is industrializing it is necessary for it to maintain the discipline of the work force. And since the bulk of profits need to be plowed back into further expansion of heavy industry and equipment, of basic industrial capacity, a personality type that emphasizes frugality, thrift, asceticism, and hard work is most effective in the first stages of the growth of the system. The sexual mode usually linked psychologically to a disciplined and frugal personality is one of rigidity. In the sense used here this rigidity refers both to a retentive "anal"* personality structure and to a person generally "uptight" about sexual relations, nudity, and the like. Sexual rigidity, especially in the latter aspect, has historically been formed in the tight, patriarchal, religious family. Advocacy of sexual promiscuity, through frank images, song lyrics, suggestive dancing, and so on, is therefore an assault on the character structure most conducive to the period when a capitalist country is industrializing (accumulating).

Such cultural assaults are perceived as harmful to the authority structure and to institutions that form personality and preserve order, like schools, colleges, and the army. Likewise, emphasis on what has come to be called "instant gratification" assaults the necessary concepts of frugality (the deferment of pleasure) and hard work. When the society is sufficiently industrialized, however, the need arises for a personality more open to free consumer spending.

Such a personality is open to instant gratification, rather than to the delayed gratification of the accumulation period. A "good" consumer has an adolescent or even childlike attitude toward acquiring possessions—he/she reacts positively to the manipulation of planned obsolescence and style changes. A good consumer, for example, prefers the latest car model to the one previous, or a musician's latest album rather than an earlier one, without regard to quality.

Such a "sexually liberated personality" (that is, to repeat, a personality that prefers instant gratification in the consumer objects it wants, and that has looser attitudes toward sexual relations, obscenity, and nudity—a limited and manipulatable "liberation") still poses problems for the

*A better term using less psychological jargon would be "tight-assed."

303

institutions of the society like the school, army, and factory that still require the older authoritarian type, but it is quite appropriate to the consumer economy.

A tension is thus present. Split behavior in which a person behaves one way at work and another way during leisure hours would be ideal for the maintenance of the system, but it does not seem to have developed as yet. In certain sophisticated sectors of the economy where old-style working conditions produce employee sabotage and absenteeism, efforts are being made to change work conditions to more closely resemble leisure conditions, to make work more "fun." (In Sweden this motivation has led to the breaking up of the old-style assembly line, as at Volvo car manufacturing plants.)

In the form of antiauthority attitudes and spontaneity the sexual liberation espoused in rock music can carry over to the work place and assembly lines resulting in actions that attack the system, but in the consumer sphere the "liberated" personality is simply more effectively integrated into consumerism.

Sexuality has also increasingly been harnessed to the job of selling goods. The association of naked bodies (so far almost always women) with milk, air travel, cameras, or any number of other products that are essentially neutral sexually is an obvious and effective advertising technique that was not possible in the sexually repressed culture of the prewar period. The sexuality espoused by rock music has helped, along with other creative media, to create the climate in which sexuality has been made a permissible selling aid. This is not to imply that sexual liberation is always a prop to the system, but rather to say that the system is able to make use of a freer sexual climate to serve the purpose of selling consumer goods. Sexuality thus loses much of its critical force.

Of course this consumer sexuality is not truly liberating. It is in reality unfree and alienating. Since sexuality is broken into images used to sell products, men and women tend to see their own sexuality in terms of the abbreviated and manipulated images used in ads. Furthermore, "sexual freedom" in the United States too often means only that more men are more free to fuck more women more freely without worrying about old taboos against premarital and extramarital sex.

In this limited, male-oriented sexual "liberation," women are still bound to old concepts of passivity, to the supine position. Men are limited in their roles as aggressors and dominators. Both men and women are limited to heterosexual relations. The women's movement has been the cutting edge of criticism to this objectifying and limiting of sexuality. Unfortunately rock music has been almost without exception a reinforcement of standard images of sexuality, especially of women. In a context where sexual liberation itself serves the purposes of the commodity system, uncritical support for it through rock music only bolsters the system.

What Happened?

The structure of the music industry sets up the specific processes of cooptation. During the entire period of rock'n'roll and during the first few years of the progressive rock period in the United States music was generated from people in cultures different from the one people in the music industry lived in. Performers then would turn over their songs and be managed by industry personnel whose lifestyles, especially in the 1954-64 period, were different from those of the performers—poor whites, ghetto blacks, drug-using hippies from the new youth communities. The music was created by outgroups but produced by straight executives and entrepreneurs. "I don't make culture," said Dick Clark, "I sell it."

As the industry grew in size and sales volume, the differences between the creators and the producer/merchandisers were reduced. On the industry side, executives and technicians became hip: grew their hair long, began to smoke dope, adopted "relaxed" lifestyles, and changed their clothing. Jac Holzman, then head of Elektra, the label for the Doors, Tim Buckley, and Judy Collins, gave his formula at an industry conference: "To comprehend the music of tomorrow, expand your musical vistas, sensitize yourself because the vibrations of contemporary existence cannot be had secondhand."

Top executives tended to change their lifestyles and "sensitivity" less, which made sense, since they had to operate at the purely financial as well as musical level and carry out transactions with the parent, nonmusic companies that owned the major labels. Producers began to live and look like the artists they recorded. And promotion men switched from the old style "booze and broads" technique of the fifties, and began to smoke the dope they were handing out, dress like the new FM djs they were visiting, and even, it is rumored, listen to the records they were promoting. Advertising people "got down" with their audience. Even sales personnel at retail stores and the managers of some chains like Tower adopted the cultural lifestyle of their customers.

From the performing side, artists developed a professionalism that naturally led them to behave like the actual paid professionals in the production departments of record companies. The industry became the world in which artists and songwriters existed. Artists associated much more easily with record company personnel than they had in the past. It was also possible to leave performing and become an independent or staff producer; there was a crossover between the creator and producer of product.

The process of selling records inherently coopted both music and musicians by commoditizing them. An artist or his music is essentially reduced to an image consisting of several "selling points." The abbreviated image is then put out through advertising, radio spots, print ads, and the like. If the image-making is done carefully, the artist's selling image is consistent in cover pictures, merchandising displays and devices, and the choice of the group the act tours with. The act is packaged. A good example of a consistent and abbreviated image is the various Alice Cooper campaigns. And who knows more about Alice Cooper or individual band members than can be stated in a sentence or two, or summed up in as many visual images? (Alice's image, of course, is the Billion Dollar Baby.) The broader personalities of musicians are no more known by the public than the personalities of politicians. The selling of both is now roughly the same in the United States.

The biggest rock stars are commoditized to an even greater degree. Their image is transferred to everyday items of clothing, toiletries, and toys, and sold piecemeal to an adulating public. Elvis, the Beatles, the Monkees, and the Osmonds are the most prominent examples. The business in Beatle mementos at one time amounted to over $100 million, by conservative estimate. Rock artists also play the role of trend-setters much as movie stars did decades ago. The general trends often are initiated in the youth and ghetto cultures the musicians come from, but the broader public does not know that. To them the fashions come from the rock stars who popularize them.

The standard contract requirement to produce two albums a year so that the record company can keep the artist's image before the public and recoup its investment often has a tendency to weaken the music itself. If an act cannot write good material for two albums, then it puts out admittedly bad songs along with the better ones.

The amount of artistic control given to acts does not change this process of commoditization. Even when the record company relinquishes certain aspects of image-making, such as album covers, to the act, the records still have to be marketed and sold and are sold in the standard manner. Really all that happens is that the artist has been integrated into the selling process in a more complete way.

The fact that rock acts in the sixties received large advances and lucrative contracts in comparison to acts of a few years before did not change the industry in any fundamental way. Arguing that new power for rock groups *did* change things Ralph Gleason wrote in *Rolling Stone* in 1968: "Change the way the money changers change money, and you change the society. Rock is doing that."

In fact entertainers have always had a certain primary power in the entertainment industries under capitalism, since they are the only ones that can do the creating. Record companies are perfectly happy, or at least resigned, to letting their most consistently high selling and stable acts have a bigger slice of the pie if they will agree to stay with the company. One of the central problems of an entertainment industry is how to provide a steady flow of artistic material. Corporations are willing to give artistic freedom and to pay large sums of money in order to preserve this flow. Companies that have not been willing to do this, like MGM, have suffered for it. In the record industry, as shown earlier, the problem has been structurally solved to a large degree by the institution of the independent producer and the label deal which gives the lucrative stable artist creative autonomy while securely tying him to the record company in a financial way. Historically the record industry seems to have avoided any real moves by rock groups to separate themselves completely from larger companies. The one possible exception is the Grateful Dead, who set up their own record company in 1974. (They have since given up and are distributed by—ironically—United Artists.)

The film industry suffered a far more important defection in its history when the three most successful actors of the time—Mary Pickford, Charlie Chaplin, and Douglas Fairbanks—along with one of the most important directors, D.W. Griffith, set up the original United Artists company in order to keep all the profits. They gave themselves *total* creative and promotional autonomy, too. Needless to say, United Artists did not change either the money-changers or the society.

The growth in listenership and ad revenues led to the cooptation of FM radio—although to a large degree FM stations coopted themselves during this process. Originally FM had been tied to youth and ghetto communities. The stations supported community issues in a far more participatory way than AM stations, which were only worried about the number of "public service" programs they could tote up for the FCC license review board. The ads on many early FM stations reflected, as well as could be done while still depending on private advertising, an antimaterialist base. Many stations made a concerted effort to solicit advertising from small businesses in the youth and ghetto communities. Judgments were made as to the "morality" of the advertiser. KPPC in Los Angeles, sister station to KSAN in San Francisco, limited or refused national advertising from companies like Pepsi Cola.

These restrictions were gradually ended. As FM stations won huge listenerships, in some cases audiences larger than most AM stations had in the same city, the ad rates for air time naturally went up. They went up astronomically in comparison to what they had been in the first couple of years of FM rock radio. The high rates eventually led to the inclusion of national companies, and naturally to the exclusion of small shops and community businesses. They also allowed disc jockey salaries to rise.

When national advertisers first realized the power that FM had in the youth market, they simply sent over the same ads they used on AM stations, even those created for nonrock MOR stations. The ads did not sound good in the hip rock format, and FM stations objected to them on aesthetic grounds. As noted earlier, at KSAN and later at other major FM rock stations, station personnel set about rewriting and reproducing the ads to make them jive with rock music and laid-back dj patter. The new ads were liked by disc jockeys because they sounded better, and eventually by the national advertisers because they sold their products better. The big national advertisers were now effectively reaching the youth market and the "revolutionary rock" FM stations were effectively integrated into the big-time consumer commodity economy. Tom Donahue, the station manager at KSAN, once said he did not know how FM radio had really been coopted. He should not have had to look far for part of the answer: they coopted themselves.

The success and popularity of rock music was one of the major reasons it was coopted. It was so effective in reaching large numbers of young people that large sums of money were spent at every level to produce it. Record companies were quite willing to pay good salaries to creative services, promotional, and advertising personnel, and to artists: the music was worth it to them financially. It was a gold rush dynamic.

The use of rock in general advertising was another factor that integrated the music into the consumer system. Again the effectiveness of rock in reaching the youth market made it attractive to advertisers of other youth-oriented products. Rock music used in jingles and endorsements by rock stars was explicitly used to sell goods. Coca-Cola spent millions of dollars in the 1960s sponsoring rock ads for its soft drink. The endorsement of a hip rock group seemingly transformed the advertised product, no matter how mundane it really was, into a flashy youth product, in the same way that associating a naked woman with a particular model camera gives it sexuality. When the Jefferson Airplane made avant-garde commercials for Levi Strauss jeans they undercut their revolutionary stance. They were functioning as just as much a part of the capitalist system as Fred MacMurray does when he endorses Greyhound bus travel. The Airplane were also helping break a strike at the Levi Strauss factory by encouraging young fans to buy pants produced by scab labor.

The loss of much of the revolutionary feeling and explicitly critical content contained in many rock songs was brought about by a number of factors. On the objective level, the war in Vietnam was perceived as winding down as American ground troops were withdrawn; many people in youth ghettos grew older and took jobs; the youth culture in dilute form spread to the majority of American youth, and older people; the use of stronger psychedelics like LSD and mescaline decreased; the Nixon administration in particular set up or framed leaders within radical political movements. These developments removed some of the political thrust coming from the environment many artists lived in. These changes did not affect the black community in the same way. Since the black community remained what it always had been, an economically oppressed ghetto, the music of political black musicians retained its criticism of the *status quo.*

The role of record companies in relation to antiestablishment music has *not* been, at least since the fifties, one of heavy handed repression or censorship. Far from it. Music with Left-leaning lyrics would most likely be recorded by most (not all) record companies if it was judged to have commercial potential. Folk music, the genre of a great deal of American music with political content, is certainly not commercial any longer. A decision not to record political folk music is therefore economically motivated, not politically motivated. Music advocating black equality and later black liberation was kept off the air much longer than white music with political content, but in the white field a turning point of sorts was reached with Barry McGuire's immortal "Eve of Destruction." Lou Adler, the song's producer, had wanted to cash in on folk-rock, but he thought the song would be too rhetorical and too controversial to be played. Jay Lasker, who, significantly enough was Adler's business partner, predicted the song would make it. It did. It was the number one single in September 1965.

Some of the more conservative radio chains refused to play political songs after "Eve," but most stations began to open up. AM chains, such as RKO, will not play songs judged controversial because they are, they say, afraid of losing listeners. The area of concern and censorship by radio stations has by and large not been political content but references to drugs. This is because the FCC, backed by the courts upon review, waged a campaign in 1970 against songs containing drug lyrics and threatened stations with loss of their licenses if they continued to play such songs.

The more successful record companies have in the past affected a solidarity with the youth culture and with revolutionary sentiments. The solidarity has been hypocritical, of course. It has been manufactured in order to try to fool young people into buying records. CBS was best known for its youth identification campaigns. It introduced one new batch of releases as "The Revolutionaires" and headlined another ad, "The Man can't bust our music." It is impossible to charge CBS with coopting anyone with this series of ads. It's highly doubtful that anybody in the "target audience" was unable to see through the appeals. You never can tell what kind of dope was floating around out there in 1971, though. Warner Brothers was less hypocritical in its projected identification with the youth scene, as shown earlier. The company talked about its true financial motivations with a clever candor that was accepted by a large number of record buyers.

The record company practice of advertising in underground papers had an effect on weakening that institution within youth communities. Unlike some of the trade papers, the undergrounds did not exchange favorable reviews and coverage for advertising money, but they did come to rely on record companies as a major source of advertising, and consequently as a major supporter of the papers. When record companies decided to limit their advertising in the more community centered undergrounds, and the undergrounds simultaneously refused sex ads the papers were often forced to fold. They had not solicited alternate sources of advertising. (Some editors have charged that the Nixon administration asked the major record companies to stop their support of radical underground papers by cutting their advertising. There may well have been some political motivation behind the record company action, although in hindsight at least it seems clear that FM radio was the emerging record promoting medium, and that *Rolling Stone* and FM were better advertiser buys than the unstable, political, community-based papers.)

The record company ads also tended to weaken the antimaterialist thrust of the editorial copy. Few undergrounds were able to keep a clear line between their antimaterialist objectives and the capitalist intentions of the record companies who were placing ads like Columbia's "The Man can't bust our music."

The main reason why songs with political lyrics are seldom heard lies not with the record companies or radio stations (at least FM ones) but with musicians and groups themselves.

Rock'n'Roll Suicide: *The Cooptation/Alienation of the Musician*

At this point in the United States, the middle seventies, it is possible for an established artist or act to write and record pretty much what it wants to, always operating within the bounds of commercial success. If an artist puts out several albums in a row that do not sell, his power with record companies, concert promoters, and the rest of the industry is lost. But no censorship is exerted to limit what an artist wants to say politically.

Certain exceptions should be dealt with directly, before proceeding. New artists with no proven ability to repeat their first successes are under more pressure to conform; songs with unusually explicit or perverted sexual lyrics, or songs that talk about drugs too frankly will be censored by radio stations, although not by many record companies. A complete political breakdown in the United States would certainly result in censorship of a mass medium like records, but such a breakdown would cause other media, educational institutions, political organs, and so on, to be censored even earlier. Some forms of music like folk music are "censored" more because they do not sell than because they are radical, as explained earlier. Finally, black acts operate under somewhat differ-ent and tighter ground rules.

Most political "censorship" of record artists is self-censorship. Artists could be roughly, although artificially, placed into two groups: those who want to make it more than anything else, and those who care more about their music than they do for money and adulation. Artists in the first group are more likely to do what their manager, who is motivated by either long-term or short-term profit, tells them. They will adapt the length of their songs to fit AM radio, eliminate offensive words from songs, play ball with agents and concert promoters. In short they pose no problem for the argument: if an act wants to make money most of all, they have *already been* coopted. Or put another way, they were never critical in the first place. They always held one of the more destructive American goals, to get rich. "I have American ideals," says Alice Cooper. "I love money."[4]

But a large number of musicians obviously care a great deal about their music and what they are trying to say through it. Most of them, too, are unable to develop a radical music. To some degree many of these musicians are also too willing to make compromises, especially in the beginning of their careers. Those that are insecure then become afraid to change their styles for fear of losing the audience that supports them psychologically. More common, musicians that do care about their music simply become isolated.

Ironically, the high quality of their music makes it easier for them to lose touch because high quality music sells well and supplies a musician with a truly incredible amount of money. It has been estimated that at least fifty superstars make more than a million dollars each year. The money puts the musician in a qualitatively different position than most of his audience.* A musician who makes even $50,000 or $100,000 each year, and several hundred do, has a different lifestyle than the twenty-five-year-old bricklayer, secretary, or factory worker who buys his record. And even though the orientation toward sex and drugs is similar

---

*Some of the highest paid musicians become sophisticated corporate investors. Bob Dylan owns oil stock, for instance, and Neil Young owns a string of shopping centers. His ventures are managed by Segal, Rubenstein & Gordon, Los Angeles financial counselors.

between a rock star and a young kid on the street who is not working, the level of enjoyment is so much higher that there is really no comparison in their personal experiences.

It does not take long for a musician with a poor or working class background to lose his roots under these conditions. His life is so different from what he is used to, that he usually finds it hard to relate to his old friends. He begins to hang out with other successful musicians and with producers and other music industry personnel who share the same lifestyle. Top stars, the Rolling Stones being a particularly spectacular example, have become part of the standard bourgeois jet set. Their violence is not frightening to heiresses and movie stars. It's titillating.

Different musicians have developed different ways of handling the pressures of stardom besides becoming jetsetters or integrating themselves into the music industry. The two most common alternate nonsolutions are no less alienating, however. Some stars like Santana or Mahavishnu have gone the utterly ridiculous, old-time religion route, fooling themselves and a few followers. Others like Joni Mitchell have used their wealth to isolate themselves completely.

Many musicians can find no solution at all to the problem of instant wealth. They just destroy themselves. The early rockabilly singer Carl Perkins is still archetypical. "When you're a country boy just a month from the plow," he said, "and suddenly you're a star with money in your pocket, cars, women, big cities, crowds, the change is just too fast. . . . You can't take the strain without a crutch."[5] Perkins first turned to the bottle, then after some years, hooked up with the Johnny Cash tour. Country music provided security for the first wave of burned out rockers, but it does not exist for younger musicians from the cities. Those that cannot take it now turn to junk and fade away.

A few established musicians have managed to come to grips with the situation, see beyond the music industry, and develop some principles. Gil Scott-Heron, Country Joe McDonald, the Persuasions, and at times, John Lennon, are all examples. But the pressures of recording in a corporate system tend to isolate them, too. To stay sane they have to make special efforts to keep in contact with people who are not in the music industry and who are not just fans. This task is easier whenever there is a large, radical, cultural, and political movement around them. In fact for political music to develop at all a large radical movement outside the music industry is probably necessary. (The breakup of the radical movement of the sixties and the absence of support from the profit-oriented industry for a political songwriter who was having a hard time writing were two of the main pressures which led to the suicide of Phil Ochs in April 1976.)

The situation with black music and black artists is somewhat different. Black music has, except for the Motown phase, been generally more political than white music. Most black music is not political, of course, but only standard pop fare. It lags behind the politics of the black community as a whole, where radical politics, despite the lulls, defeats, and constant police harassment, is a steadily growing force. Still, black music and musicians are more political, taken as a whole, than white music.

This essential difference again goes back to the relative positions of the two communities in the United States. Unlike whites, the position of blacks in the United States has been a constant one. They are now and always have been an oppressed minority confined to ghettos whose economic function has been to form a pool of unskilled labor at the fringe of the economy which serves to keep wages down. They do the worst jobs for the lowest pay. Last to be hired and housed, blacks are first to be sent to fight to defend United States interests abroad.

Coming out of this day-to-day reality black acts have understandably often been more political. Years before modern black jazz and r&b, blues singer Bill Broonzy popularized the old employment hall refrain, "If you're white all right, if you're brown stick around, but if you're black get back." In the forties the bebop musicians were framed and put in prison. The Korean War angered Charles Brown and later, the Vietnam War prompted Marvin Gaye, the Persuasions, John Lee Hooker, and others to condemn white corporate America (in less specific terms!).

Forever Is a Long Time: *The Potential Resurgence of Rock*

At this point it should be evident that the vast majority of rock music does little to challenge either the basis of American society—production for private profit, or its current organization—consumerism (and general waste/defense production), or even the sophisticated institutions and attitudes that hold it together—cooptative corporations,* hip media, pleasureful consumption, sexuality in the service of the system.

The situation is not entirely one-dimensional. There is a constant tension between rock music and youth culture on the one hand and the American system on the other. The tension gives even current apolitical rock music a progressive effect in two major institutions that unlike the consumer sector cannot easily absorb sexually liberating attitudes or attitudes that undermine discipline: the army and (so far) the workplace.

---

*Country Joe and the Fish once found themselves on the same jet with Colonel Sanders, the fried chicken king who dresses in the white linen of a plantation owner: "Do you like Hippies, Colonel?" asked Dewey, one of the Fish. "Well, dey eats chicken, don't dey?" he answered with a smile.

Rock music, drugs, antiauthoritarianism, and sexual liberation have done much to destroy the morale of the American armed forces. The music and the culture coupled with explicit political formulations of the imperialist role of the United States in Vietnam forced a virtual showdown in the American invasion/occupation forces in Southeast Asia.[6] The music/dope/liberation/politics configuration was probably the major impetus to the many pseudoreforms introduced into the Armed Forces and to the creation of an all-volunteer army. The best example of this configuration putting a stop to trade unionism as usual was the Lordstown General Motors strike in Ohio which was against working conditions and work-place alienation as much as for the standard wage increase. The strike threw a monkey wrench into General Motors' plans for semiautomated, sped up assembly lines and new management techniques for control of its work force.

The tension between the need for control over workers and the partial liberation of their sexual impulses necessary to continued consumption in a commodity culture will probably not be resolved in a sort of Brave New World organization of production and private life (no longer private, of course) in which an omniscient state presides along with monopoly corporations over a stable, policed social order that uses sexuality and pleasure as props. On the other hand if U.S. imperialism continues to be defeated abroad, the loss of foreign markets, and control of the foreign work force, and resulting recession, unemployment, and inflation at home will curtail the sensuality of the Brave New World solution. The system will not be able to handle its many inherent problems or provide decent lives for its people, or even the illusion of decent lives.

This historical development will not lead inevitably to breakdown; opposition movements within the United States calling for fundamental changes in the current system of production and life must be generated. Opposition movements from which revolutionary activity will develop will themselves have a base in youth, as they always have, and any new movement toward radicalism will influence young musicians as well. If the movement is a broad one culturally, the musicians coming out of it, even those that express themselves via traditional capitalist media, will be able to withstand cooptation from the music industry for at least as long a period as did the musicians in the formative years of the progressive rock period.

But to keep waves of political rock music from being only cyclical, the radical culture itself must become stable. It is not stable at this time although a radical culture among young working people, in traditional blue collar and manual labor industries as well as in newer automated and technical industries, seems to be developing. If it spreads then the music can cease to be escapist and can take the cultural offensive against the conditions that have forced a mental retreat among most musicians. The formation of a radical cultural critique that continually links rock music to the conditions of youth in American society would have some influence on some musicians (the Crosbys and the Lennons), but the mass vehicle for putting out such a critique does not exist at the present. The magazine with the position but not the critique, *Rolling Stone,* is unlikely to change unless its readership moves to the Left first. FM radio has ceased to produce musical innovation and has moved away from the communities that supported it when it was beginning. None of the institutions of youth culture will become political, or useful to a radical movement, until that movement is broad and powerful enough to take control of existing institutions. Nor will youth culture itself be the foundation of revolutionary activity. It can win no victories that have any meaning unless it is linked inextricably to the only real and continuing revolutionary goal: the abolition of class society.

Perhaps the greatest potential for change in rock music lies in the way that it is made. Unlike film or even video, music and rock are inherently a grass-roots medium. Anyone can pick up a guitar, play bass, drums, or organ—millions do. In this respect rock is a people's music.

In fact, rock music has the potential if our social system were changed radically, to become one basis of a revolutionary mass culture. In the two most important socialist societies, the Soviet Union and China, musical forms from the nineteenth century and before have been defined and encouraged as people's art: the ballet, the symphony, and the opera. But these institutions were essentially the creations of presocialist, feudal, and business elites. In the United States and Western Europe, for the first time, electronic technology and advanced communications have universalized a folk music—*rock music*—to a generation of young working people.

For now, of course, rock'n'roll is here to pay. It is a packaged commodity which enriches a few monopoly corporations. But just as surely, rock'n'roll is here to stay. Beneath the year-end profit charts and the $10 million recording contracts, despite the rip-off of the Arthur Crudups and the Fred Parriss, the denial of women's music, and the rock'n'roll suicides—the music plays on. Its potential as a true people's music is still there.

How long it will take to realize this potential remains to be seen.

AFTERWORD

In the middle sixties Traffic wrote a famous song about a man in a suit who profited from a musician's dream. Bob Dylan called that music man "Dear Landlord."

The landlords in their suits—the Albert Grossmans and the Clive Davises of the music scene—could write a better book about the rock'n'-roll industry than we have. Their books would tell you more about the power struggles have gone down, would lay out more industry gossip, would present the inside story.

Neither of us managed Janis Joplin or signed up Blood, Sweat, and Tears. But we don't think anyone at the top of the industry is going to write a history that shows any but the corporate perspective. Or if you will, the hip corporate perspective. That's why we wrote this book.

Rock'n'Roll Is Here to Pay was a hard book to do right by. We won't know for a few years whether we succeeded.

We wrote it in as popular a style as possible given our own abilities as writers, our differing opinions on what was interesting and what was funny, the complexity of the subject matter, and the arguments and distinctions we wanted to make.

There may be criticism, particularly from the Left, of our writing about the treatment of women and blacks in the industry. But we felt that such a discussion was crucial to understanding the business as a whole, and that our general understanding of the overall industry gave us insight enough to begin, so we plunged ahead. With the exception of jazz, which of course is distinguishable from rock, the political character of pop music has not been taken up extensively by black or feminist writers. Hopefully more voices centered in the black and feminist experience will soon be heard.

317

We would like frankly to acknowledge a problem common to independent writers, time and money. This book was written by two people working on separate phases of research and writing, and together on editing and typing. It was prepared over the course of a two-year period ending in 1975 and often involved full-time research. Hopefully the manuscript has suffered less than our personal lives.

NOTES

Chapter 1   The Early Years

1. "The 50-Year Story of RCA Victor Records," mimeographed (New York: RCA Co., 1953), p. 8.

2. Gleason L. Archer, *History of Radio to 1926* (New York: American Historical Co., 1938), p. 178.

3. Charlie Gillett, *The Sound of the City: The Rise of Rock and Roll* (New York: Outerbridge and Dienstfrey, 1970; Dell, 1972), p. 11.

4. Edward Zwick, "An Interview with the Father of Hi-Fi: Dr. Peter Goldmark," *Rolling Stone*, Sept. 27, 1973, pp. 44-45.

Chapter 2   Rock'n'Roll Is Here to Stay

1. "World of Soul," (special) *Billboard*, June 23, 1967, p. 26.

2. *Billboard*, June 23, 1967, pp. 16-17.

3. Armed Forces Network, Sept. 1962, quoted in Gillett, *The Sound of the City: The Rise of Rock and Roll* (New York: Outerbridge and Dienstfrey, 1970; Dell, 1972), p. 34.

4. *New Musical Express*, Sept. 21, 1956, quoted in Gillett, pp. 328-329.

5. Peter Guralnick, *Feel Like Going Home: Portraits in Blues and Rock 'n' Roll* (New York: Outerbridge and Dienstfrey, 1971), pp. 188-189.

6. *Rolling Stone,* Oct. 11, 1973, p. 16.

7. Michael Lydon, *Rock Folk: Portraits from the Rock 'n' Roll Pantheon* (New York: Dell, 1968), p. 10.

8. *Hit Parade* (Britain), January, 1957, quoted in Gillett, p. 39.

9. Lydon, pp. 9-10.

10. *Hit Parade* (Britain), January, 1957, quoted in Guralnick, p. 142.

11. Arnold Passman, *The Deejays* (New York: Macmillan, 1971), p. 90.

12. *New Musical Express,* Sept. 23, 1956.

13. The accounts of this landmark concert make an interesting statement on the accuracy of rock history. Arnold Passman, author of *The Deejays,* says there were 18,000 tickets sold for the 10,000 seating hall, and that the overselling created the excess crowd. Charlie Gillett, usually accurate, placed the crowd at 30,000 in *Sound of the City,* presumably quoting a *Billboard* story that used the 30,000 figure. Ian Whitcomb in a brilliantly witty book, *After the Ball,* which contains more than its share of literary exaggerations, put the figure at 80,000, most likely misreading his notes. If a crowd of 80,000 black and white teenagers turned out for a rock'n'roll concert in Cleveland, Ohio, in 1952, with the police, Kent State would have occurred two decades earlier than it did.

14. Siepmann, *Radio's Second Chance,* pp. 186-7 as cited in Erik Barnouw, *History of Broadcasting in the United States Vol. II* (New York: Oxford University Press, 1966), 221.

15. Roger Karshner, *The Music Machine* (Los Angeles: Nash Publishing, 1971), p. 102.

Chapter **3** **Music for Music's Sake Means More Money:** *The Sixties*

1. Michael Lydon, *Rock Folk: Portraits from the Rock 'n' Roll Pantheon* (New York: Dell, 1968), p. 117.

2. Steve Chapple, Interview with Joe Smith, 1973.

3. Gilbert B. Friesen (A&M Records), "New Techniques to Update the Standard American Promotional Package," in Paul Ackerman and Lee Zhito, eds., *The Complete Report of the First International Music Industry Conference* (New York: Billboard Publishing, 1969), pp. 18-19.

4. *Billboard,* Nov. 7, 1970, p. 1.

5.   Steve Chapple, Interview with Lou Adler, 1973.

6.   Ibid.

7.   *Billboard*, Aug. 31, 1968, p. 8.

8.   Arthur Mogull (Tetragrammaton Records), "The Independent Artist/
Composer/Producer as a Self-Contained Organization," in Ackerman and Zhito
(op. cit.), p. 82.

9.   *Billboard*, Sept. 16, 1967, p. 6.

10.   Ibid., Dec. 28, 1968, p. 3.

11.   Robert Greenfield, "Keith Richard: Got to Keep It Growing," in Ben Fong-
Torres, ed., *The Rolling Stone Interviews: Vol. 2* (New York: Warner Paperback,
1973), pp. 291-292.

12.   Stanley H. Brown, "The Motown Sound of Money," *Fortune*, Sept. 1, 1967,
p. 104.

13.   *Billboard*, Nov. 19, 1955.

14.   Ibid., Jan. 26, 1974.

15.   Willard F. Mueller, "The Measurement of Industrial Concentration," in
*Hearings before the Subcommittee on Antitrust and Monopoly of the Commit-
tee on the Judiciary, United States Senate, 88th Congress, Second Session,
Pursuant to Resolution 262,* July 1, 2 and Sept. 9, 10, 11, 1964, pp. 115-120.

16.   Irwin Tarr (RCA Records), "Current Impact [of Tape Systems] in the
United States—and Prospects," in Ackerman and Zhito (op. cit.), pp. 247-248.

17.   *Billboard*, July 12, 1968.

18.   Ibid., Jan. 22, 1972, p. 10.

19.   Clive J. Davis, "Creativity within the Corporation," in *The Music Industry: Markets and Methods for the Seventies* (New York: Billboard Publishing,
1970), p. 288.

20.   *Billboard*, Nov. 18, 1972, p. 76.

21.   Jann Wenner, "Joe Smith, Record Company Executive," in Fong-Torres,
ed. (op. cit.), p. 338.

22.   Arnold Passman, *The Deejays* (New York: Macmillan, 1971), p. 288.

23. Steve Chapple, Interview with Bruce Johnson, 1973.

24. Ibid.

25. Steve Chapple, Interview with Tom Donahue, 1973.

26. Ibid.

27. Ibid.

28. *Rolling Stone*, April 2, 1970.

29. Ibid.

30. Donahue interview.

31. *Rolling Stone*, April 6, 1968.

32. Donahue interview.

33. *Rolling Stone*, April 2, 1970.

34. Ibid., April 16, 1970.

35. Ibid., April 2, 1970.

36. David Beal, Interview with Scott Muni, 1974.

37. Donahue interview.

38. Ibid.

39. Muni interview.

40. *Rolling Stone*, April 2, 1970.

Chapter **4**   **The Expanded Industry**

1. David Beal, Interview with Frank Barsalona, 1974.

2. Ibid.

3. Ibid.

4. David Beal, Interview with Don Law, 1974.

5. Barsalona Interview.

6. Law interview.

7. David Beal, Interview with Herb Spar, 1974.

8. David Beal, Interview with Ralph Mann, 1974.

9. Spar interview.

10. Peter McCabe and Robert Schonfield, *Apple to the Core: The Unmaking of the Beatles* (New York: Pocket Books, 1972), p. 31.

11. Ibid., p. 50.

12. Steve Chapple, Interview with Eliot Roberts, 1973.

13. Ibid.

14. Ibid.

15. *Billboard*, May 6, 1967, p. 104.

16. Spar interview.

17. Ibid.

18. Law interview.

19. *Rolling Stone*, July 1967.

20. Ibid.

21. Ibid.

22. Ibid., Dec., 1969.

23. *Talent and Booking*, Sept., 1972.

24. Steve Chapple, Interview with Shelly Finkel, 1974.

25. Ibid.

26. Joel Rogers, personal conversation, 1973.

27. Finkel interview.

28. *Zoo World,* Aug. 29, 1974.

29. Spar interview.

30. *Village Voice,* Nov. 21, 1974.

31. Ibid.

32. Roger Karshner, *The Music Machine* (Los Angeles: Nash Publishing, 1971).

33. Joel Rogers, Interview with Jim Miller, 1974.

34. Joel Rogers, Interview with Jon Landau, 1974.

35. *The Bulletin of the American Society of Newspaper Editors,* Sept. 1971 (reprint available from *Rolling Stone*).

36. *Rolling Stone,* Jan. 20, 1972.

37. *Fusion,* Aug. 1972.

38. *Rolling Stone,* Nov. 9, 1967.

39. Joel Rogers, Interview with Langdon Winner, 1974.

40. *Rolling Stone,* April 5, 1969.

41. *Fusion,* Aug. 1972.

42. Winner interview.

43. *Billboard,* ad run at several different points in fall 1974.

44. "Rolling Stone Advertiser Kit," as cited in *Fusion,* Aug. 1970.

45. *Los Angeles Times,* Aug. 25, 1974.

46. *Time,* April 25, 1969.

47. *Rolling Stone,* Nov. 11, 1971.

48. Ibid.

49. *Billboard.*

50. Landau interview.

51. Robert Christgau, *Any Old Way You Choose It: Rock and Other Pop Music, 1967-1973* (Baltimore: Penguin Books, 1973), p. 87.

52. *New York*, 1974.

Chapter **5**   **Solid Gold:** *The Record Business Today*

1. CBS, *Annual Report* 1973, p. 8 (as based on data from McCann Erickson, Inc., and CBS/Broadcast Group Economics and Research).

2. Central Sources: Consumer Electronics, *1973 Annual Review;* CBS, *Annual Report* 1973; Music U.S.A., *1973 Review of the Music Industry and Amateur Music Participation.* The concert figure is an estimate based on interviews with agency executives and concert promoters. Hardware figures include imports and do not exclude U.S. production intended for export. TV sales are for all sets, color and black and white.

3. R. Serge Denisoff, "The Vinyl Crap Game," *Journal of Jazz Studies,* June 1974.

4. Steve Chapple, Interview with Joe Smith, 1973.

5. Ibid.

6. Steve Chapple, Interview with Ahmet Ertegun, 1974.

7. Ibid.

8. Gerald W. Purcell (producer, manager, president of GWP Records and Gerald W. Purcell Associates), "Teamwork: The Agent, Publisher, and Record Company" in Paul Ackerman and Lee Zhito, eds., *The Complete Report of the First International Music Industry Conference* (New York: Billboard Publishing, 1969), p. 25.

9. Neil Bogart, "Multimedia Promotion," in *The Music Industry: Markets and Methods for the Seventies* (New York: Billboard Publishing, 1970), p. 20.

10. Steve Chapple, Interview with Stan Cornyn, 1973.

11. Smith interview.

12. *Billboard International Music Industry Directory* (New York; 1973-74), p. 9.

13. *New York Times*, Oct. 12, 1973, p. 31.

14. Paul Mills, "Capitol Records: Number Three and Counting," *Fusion*, Aug. 1973, p. 57.

15. Steve Chapple, Interview with Mike Maitland, 1973.

16. Ibid.

17. "$2 Billion Worth of Noise," *Forbes*, July 15, 1968, pp. 22-23.

18. Jann Wenner, "Joe Smith, Record Company Executive," in Ben Fong-Torres, ed., *The Rolling Stone Interviews: Vol. 2* (New York: Warner Paperback, 1973), p. 350.

19. Ibid.

20. Smith interview.

21. Cornyn interview.

Chapter **6**   **Who Owns Rock:** *The Politics of the Music Industry*

1. Steve Chapple, Interview with Joe Smith, 1973.

2. Ibid.

3. *Billboard.*

4. CBS-TV, "The Trouble with Rock," Aug. 11, 1974.

5. Ibid.

6. Ibid.

Chapter **7**   **Black Roots, White Fruits:** *Racism in the Music Industry*

1. Reebee Garofalo, Interview with Johnny Otis, 1974.

2. Ibid.

3. Ortiz M. Walton, *Music: Black White and Blue* (New York: William Morrow, 1972), p. 98.

4. *Billboard,* Jan. 3, 1953.

5. Steve Chapple, Interview with Ahmet Ertegun, 1974.

6. *Billboard,* Aug. 22, 1970.

7.   Lee Eliot Berk, *Legal Protection for the Creative Musician* (Boston: Berklee Press, 1970), p. 177.

8.   Reebee Garofalo, Interview with Fred Parris, 1974.

9.   Peter Guralnick, *Feel Like Going Home: Portraits in Blues and Rock 'n' Roll* (New York: Outerbridge and Dienstfrey, 1971), pp. 25-26.

10.   *Rolling Stone,* Jan. 18, 1973.

11.   Guralnick, pp. 150-151.

12.   Michael Lydon, *Rock Folk: Portraits from the Rock 'n' Roll Pantheon* (New York: Dell, 1968), p. 32.

13.   Otis interview.

14.   *Rolling Stone,* Jan. 18, 1973.

15.   Charlie Gillett, *The Sound of the City: The Rise of Rock and Roll* (New York: Outerbridge and Dienstfrey, 1970; Dell, 1972), p. 21.

16.   *Rolling Stone,* Jan. 20, 1968.

17.   Ibid., May 11, 1968.

18.   Ibid., May 25, 1968.

19.   Ibid., Jan. 18, 1973.

20.   Margo Jefferson, "Ripping Off Black Music," *Harper's Magazine,* Jan. 1973. 1973.

21.   *Rolling Stone,* Oct. 2, 1968.

22.   Reebee Garofalo, Interview with Dick Waterman, 1974.

23.   Ibid.

24.   *Billboard,* Mar. 29, 1969.

25.   *Rolling Stone,* May 3, 1969.

26.   Ibid., Apr. 30, 1970.

27. Ibid., May 11, 1968.

28. Ibid., May 23, 1974.

29. Ibid., May 13, 1971.

30. Ibid., May 23, 1974.

31. Ben Fong-Torres, "Marvin Gaye: Honor Thy Brother-in-Law," in Ben Fong-Torres, ed., *The Rolling Stone Interviews: Vol. 2* (New York: Warner Paperback, 1973), p. 368.

32. *Billboard,* Apr. 4, 1970.

33. Ibid., Nov. 20, 1971.

34. Ibid.

35. Ibid., May 6, 1972.

36. Ibid., Aug. 23, 1969.

37. Ibid., Aug. 8, 1973.

38. *Rolling Stone,* Jan. 11, 1970.

39. Ibid., July 19, 1973.

Chapter **8** **Long Hard Climb:** *Women in Rock*

1. Katherine Orloff, *Rock 'n' Roll Woman* (Los Angeles: Nash Publishing, 1974), p. 24.

2. *Rolling Stone,* May 11, 1968.

3. Ortiz M. Walton, *Music: Black White and Blue* (New York: William Morrow, 1972), p. 35.

4. Carl Belz, *The Story of Rock* (New York: Oxford University Press, 1969; 2nd ed., Harper and Row, 1972), pp. 181-182.

5. *Rolling Stone,* Feb. 15, 1969.

6. *Billboard,* Oct. 19, 1968.

7. Steve Chapple, Interview with Tom Donahue, 1973.

8. Hettie Jones, *Big Star Fallin' Mama* (New York: Viking, 1974).

9. Steve Chapple, Interview with Eliot Roberts, 1973.

10. Orloff, p. 101.

11. Ellen Willis, "Rock etc.," *New Yorker,* Mar. 3, 1973.

12. *Rolling Stone,* Aug. 15, 1974.

13. Orloff, p. 35.

14. Steve Chapple, Interview with Bruce Johnson, 1973.

Chapter **9**   **Billion Dollar Baby:** *The Cooptation of Rock*

1.   For an explanation of the psychological basis of this organization and its importance to the preconsumerist economy see (among others) Theodore Adorno, *The Authoritarian Personality* (New York; 1969); Theodore Adorno and Max Horkheimer, *The Dialectic of Enlightenment* (New York; 1972), particularly Chap. 3; Herbert Marcuse, *Eros and Civilization* (Boston; 1955); Wilhelm Reich, *The Sexual Revolution* (New York; 1972); Idem, *The Mass Psychology of Fascism* (New York; 1970); and Reimut Reiche, *Sexuality and Class Struggle* (New York; 1970).

2.   See the writings of Clark Kerr, former Chancellor of the University of California, especially *Uses of the University* (Cambridge, Mass: Harvard University Press, 1963).

3.   This is not to say that leisure and entertainment businesses are as important as primary industries to maintaining a stable economy. An economy that places too much emphasis on nonindustrial sectors, such as leisure and service industries, can become lopsided, since less capital in proportion to labor is used than with production in basic industries (steel, mining, etc.). With a larger percentage of the economy devoted to services it becomes more difficult to maintain the previous growth of productivity and hence of wages. Unfortunately, this is a complex point which cannot be developed adequately in a book on rock'n'roll.

4.   "The Rockers Are Rolling in It," *Forbes* Apr. 15, 1973, p. 29

5.   Michael Lydon, *Rock Folk: Portraits from the Rock 'n' Roll Pantheon* (New York: Dell, 1968), p. 41.

6.   Spontaneity, antiauthority attitudes, and behavior that breaks down discipline have a positive, progressive affect when aimed against the U.S. corporate

and military order. But within Left movements being built in opposition to this order, such an orientation is usually not seen as positive. Within the Left organization itself discipline, hard work, and a long-range perspective are often considered necessary. Some radicals disagree with such discipline and lack of spontaneity, arguing that they undermine the very development and purpose of the radical organization. The debate is of immediate tactical importance in developing an opposition order. Whatever its immediate resolution, true sexual liberation does not clash with the needs of a socialist movement.

BIBLIOGRAPHY

Ackerman, Paul and Zhito, Lee, eds. *The Complete Report of the First International Music Industry Conference.* New York: Billboard Publishing, 1969.

Adorno, Theodore. *The Authoritarian Personality.* New York: Harper, 1950; Norton, 1969.

Andreano, Ralph L., ed. *Superconcentration/Supercorporation: A Collage of Opinion on the Concentration of Economic Power.* Andover, Mass.: Warner Modular Publications, 1973.

Archer, Gleason L. *History of Radio to 1926.* New York: The American Historical Company, 1938.

Articles on the American Economy in *Monthly Review.* Eds. Paul M. Sweezy and Harry Magdoff.

Baran, Paul A. and Sweezy, Paul M. *Monopoly Capital: An Essay on the American Economic and Social Order.* New York: Monthly Review Press, 1966; Modern Reader, 1968.

Barnouw, Eric. *History of Broadcasting in the United States.* New York: Oxford University Press, 1966.

Belz, Carl. *The Story of Rock.* New York: Oxford University Press, 1969; 2nd ed., Harper and Row, 1972.

Berk, Lee Eliot. *Legal Protection for the Creative Musician.* Boston: Berklee Press, 1970.

Cockburn, Alexander and Blackburn, Robin, eds. *Student Power: Problems, Diagnosis, Action.* Baltimore: Penguin Books (in association with New Left Review), 1969.

Cohn, Nik. *Rock from the Beginning.* New York: Stein and Day, 1969; Pocket Books, 1970.

Christgau, Robert. *Any Old Way You Choose It: Rock and Other Pop Music, 1967-1973.* Baltimore: Penguin Books, 1973.

Debord, Guy. *Society of the Spectacle.* Detroit: Black and Red, 1970. (No copyright. No rights reserved.)

331

Denisoff, R. Serge. *Great Day Coming: Folk Music and the American Left.* Chicago: University of Illinois Press, 1971; Baltimore: Penguin Books, 1973.

Denisoff, R. Serge. *Songs of Protest, War, and Peace: A Bibliography and Discography.* Santa Barbara: American Bibliographical Center—Clio Press, 1973.

Domhoff, G. William. *Fat Cats and Democrats.* Englewood Cliffs, N.J.: Prentice-Hall, 1972.

Dowd, Douglas. *Twisted Dream: Capitalist Development in the United States since 1776.* Cambridge, Mass.: Winthrop, 1974.

The Editors of *Rolling Stone. The Rolling Stone Interviews: Vol 1.* New York: Warner Paperback, 1971.

Fong-Torres, Ben, ed. *The Rolling Stone Interviews: Vol. 2* New York: Warner Paperback, 1973.

Friendly, Fred. *Due to Circumstances Beyond Our Control.* New York: Random House, 1967.

Gage, Nicholas, ed. *Mafia U.S.A.* New York: Dell, 1972

Garcia, Jerry, Reich, Charles, and Wenner, Jann. *Garcia: A Signpost to New Space.* San Francisco: Straight Arrow Books, 1972.

Gillett, Charlie. *The Sound of the City: The Rise of Rock and Roll.* New York: Outerbridge and Dienstfrey, 1970; Dell, 1972.

Gorz, Andre. *Socialism and Revolution.* New York: Anchor Press, 1973.

Green, Mark J., ed. *The Monopoly Makers: Ralph Nader's Study Group Report on Regulation and Competition.* New York: Grossman, 1971.

Guralnick, Peter. *Feel Like Going Home: Portraits in Blues and Rock 'n' Roll.* New York: Outerbridge and Dienstfrey, 1971.

Guthrie, Woody. *Bound for Glory.* New York: E.P. Dutton, 1943; New American Library, 1970.

Hampton, Benjamin B. *History of the American Film Industry.* New York: Covici, Friede, 1931 (under the title: *A History of the Movies*); Dover, 1970.

Head, Sydney. *Broadcasting in America.* Boston: Houghton-Mifflin, 1956.

Heckman, Don. "Five Decades of Rhythm and Blues" in *BMI: The Many Worlds of Music.* New York: Broadcast Music, Inc., 1969.

Horkheimer, Max and Adorno, Theodore. *Dialectic of Enlightenment.* New York: Seabury, 1972,

Hurst, Walter E. *The Music Industry Book: How to Make Money in the Music Industry.* Hollywood, Ca.: Seven Arts Press, 1963.

Jones, LeRoi (Baraka, Imamu). *Blues People.* New York: William Morrow, 1963.

Karshner, Roger. *The Music Machine.* Los Angeles: Nash Publishing, 1971.

Keil, Charles. *Urban Blues.* Chicago: University Press, 1966.

Kerr, Clark. *Uses of the University.* Cambridge, Mass.: Harvard University Press, 1963.

Kofsky, Frank. *Black Nationalism and the Revolution in Music.* New York: Pathfinder Press, 1970.

Laing, Dave. *Buddy Holly.* London: November Books, 1971. New York: Macmillan.

Lydon, Michael. *Rock Folk: Portraits from the Rock 'n' Roll Pantheon.* New York: Dell, 1968.

Mabey, Richard. *The Pop Process.* London: Lawrence and Wishart, 1967; Panther Arts, 1969.

Magdoff, Harry. *The Age of Imperialism: The Economics of U.S. Foreign Policy.* New York: Monthly Review Press, 1969.

Marcus, Greil. *Rock Will Stand.* New York: Beacon, 1970.

Marcuse, Herbert. *One Dimensional Man.* Boston: Beacon Press, 1964.

McCabe, Peter, and Schonfeld, Robert D. *Apple to the Core: The Unmaking of the Beatles.* New York: Pocket Books, 1972.

Menshikov, S. *Millionaires and Managers.* Moscow: Progress Publishers, 1969.

Morse, David. *Motown and the Arrival of Black Music.* London: November Books, 1971; New York: Macmillan, 1972.

The Music Industry: Markets and Methods for the Seventies. New York: Billboard Publishing, 1970.

NACLA Research Methodology Guide. New York: North American Congress on Latin America, 1970.

Orloff, Katherine. *Rock 'n' Roll Woman.* Los Angeles: Nash Publishing, 1974.

Passman, Arnold. *The Deejays.* New York: Macmillan, 1971.

Reich, Wilhelm. *The Mass Psychology of Fascism.* New York: Farrar, Straus, and Giroux, 1970.

The Sexual Revolution. New York: Octagon, 1972.

Reiche, Reimut. *Sexuality and Class Struggle.* New York: Praeger, 1970.

Roberts, John Storm. *Black Music of Two Worlds.* New York: Praeger, 1972; Morrow Paperback Editions, 1974.

Roxon, Lillian. *Rock Encyclopedia.* New York: Grosset and Dunlap, 1969.

Rucker, Bryce. *The First Freedom.* Carbondale, Ill.: Southern Illinois University Press, 1968.

Sanjek, Russ. "The War on Rock," mimeographed.

Sarlin, Bob. *Turn It Up! I Can't Hear the Words.* New York: Simon and Schuster, 1973.

Scaduto, Anthony. *Bob Dylan.* New York: Grosset and Dunlap, 1971; New American Library, 1973.

Schiller, Herbert. *Mass Communications and American Empire.* Boston: Beacon Press, 1971.

Schwartz, Bernard. *The Professor and the Commissions.* New York: Knopf, 1959.

Shemel, Sidney and Krasilovsky, M. William. *This Business of Music.* New York: Billboard Publishing, 1971.

Sidran, Ben. *Black Talk.* New York: Holt Paperback, 1971.

Sweezy, Paul M. and Magdoff, Harry. *The Dynamics of U.S. Capitalism.* New York: Monthly Review Press, 1965.

Taylor, Derek. *As Time Goes By.* San Francisco: Straight Arrow Books, 1973.

Walton, Ortiz M. *Music: Black White and Blue.* New York: William Morrow, 1972.

Whitburn, Joel. *Top Pop Records: 1955-1972*. Menomonee Falls, Wis.: Record Research, 1973.

Whitcomb, Ian. *After the Ball: Pop Music from Rag to Rock*. New York: Simon and Schuster, 1972.

Williams, Richard. *Out of His Head: The Sound of Phil Spector*. New York: Outerbridge and Lazard, 1972.

INDEX

Perkins, Carl, 28, 39, 40, 41, 42, 52;
    quoted, 245, 312
Perkins, Gary, 149, 150
Perlman, Sandy, 157
Persuasions, the, 312, 313
Peter, Paul, and Mary, 50, 74, 132, 133,
    202, 276
Petty, Norman, 78
Philadelphia Enquirer, 63
"Philadelphia schlock" rock music,
    50-52, 246-48, 297
Philles Records, 78-79
Phillips, Dewey, 30
Phillips, John, 73, 143
Phillips, Sam, 48, 245; and the
    discovery of Elvis Presley, 40-43
Phillips Corporation, 95, 194
Phonograph Record, 166, 167
Phonographs, sales of, 23
Piano Red, 34
Pickwick International, 91, 92
"Piece of My Heart," 250
Pigg, Tony, 112
Piracy of recordings via tape, 97-98
"Planet Waves," 205
Platters, the, 50
"Please, Mr. Postman," 88
"Please Please Me," 70
Plough Top 40 chain, 104
Pointer Sisters, 287, 291
Politics, impact of the music
    industry on, 225-26
Polygram Records, 194-95
Poole, Brian, and the Tremaloes, 70
Pop market, growth of the, 44-45
Porter, Cole, 65
Powder Ridge(Conn.) rock festival,
    227
Powell, Ron, 142
Powell, Teddy, 262
Pratt, Andy, 136
Premier Talent agency, 125, 127,
    128, 130
Presley, Elvis, xii, xiii, 16, 28, 37, 55,
    78, 131, 186, 215, 234, 235, 238,
    245-46, 247, 297; discovery of,
    40-43; post-army career, 49;
    quoted, 41; record sales of, 209-11

Price, Lloyd, 31
Pride, Charlie, 39, 215, 237
Prism, 210
Procul Harum, 87, 125
*Professor and the Commission,
    The*(Schwartz), 62
"Professor Bop," 55
Promo Records, 230
Promotion, of records acts, 179-85;
    of rock music by agents and
    managers, 123-37
Prysock, Red, 56, 57
Puente, Tito, 80
Pulse Survey, 103
"Pusher Man, The," 115
Pyne, Joe, 114

Quatro, Suzi, 293
Quicksilver Messenger Service, 72,
    73, 74, 140

Race and racism in the record
    industry, 41, 231-67
Rachmil, Milt, 16
"Rack-jobbing," 89-92
Radio, Am billings, 105-7; black
    artists on, 263-65; decline of, 12;
    effect of, on the record industry,
    1; importance of exposure on,
    182-83; in the 1950s, 57-61; and
    rhythm and blues, 30-31; and
    rock music, 12-13; 54-64
Radio Free Europe, 221
Ragavoy, Jerry, 287
Rainbow People Ann Arbor Blues
    Festival, 146
Raitt, Bonnie, 257, 286, 287
Randall, Bill, 19, 55-56
Random House publishers, 213
Ray, Dave "Snaker," 253
Ray, Johnny, 13, 15, 36, 47, 55
RCA (Radio Corporation of
    America), 5, 15, 22-24, 81, 86,
    219, 220, 223; early rivalry with
    CBS, 5-6; and FM radio, 9, 12;
    origin of, 3-4; pioneering of car
    tape systems by, 94, 95, 96;
    purchase of Victor Records by, 2